SILENT VOICES

Recent Titles in
Contributions in Women's Studies

African American Women and Social Action: The Clubwomen and Volunteerism from Jim Crow to the New Deal, 1896–1936
Floris Barnett Cash

The Dress of Women: A Critical Introduction to the Symbolism and Sociology of Clothing
Charlotte Perkins Gilman, Michael R. Hill, and Mary Jo Deegan

Frances Trollope and the Novel of Social Change
Brenda Ayres, editor

Women Among the Inklings: Gender, C.S. Lewis, J.R.R. Tolkien, and Charles Williams
Candice Fredrick and Sam McBride

The Female Body: Perspectives of Latin American Artists
Raysa E. Amador Gómez-Quintero and Mireya Pérez Bustillo

Women of Color: Defining the Issues, Hearing the Voices
Diane Long Hoeveler and Janet K. Boles, editors

The Poverty of Life-Affirming Work: Motherwork, Education, and Social Change
Mechthild U. Hart

The Bleeding of America: Menstruation as Symbolic Economy in Pynchon, Faulkner, and Morrison
Dana Medoro

Negotiating Identities in Women's Lives: English Postcolonial and Contemporary British Novels
Christine Wick Sizemore

Women in Iran: Gender Politics in the Islamic Republic
Hammed Shahidian

Women in Iran: Emerging Voices in the Women's Movement
Hammed Shahidian

Rebecca West: Heroism, Rebellion, and the Female Epic
Bernard Schweizer

SILENT VOICES

Forgotten Novels by Victorian Women Writers

Edited by Brenda Ayres

Contributions in Women's Studies, Number 200

Westport, Connecticut
London

Library of Congress Cataloging-in-Publication Data

Silent voices : forgotten novels by Victorian women writers / edited by Brenda Ayres.
    p. cm. — (Contributions in women's studies, ISSN 0147–104X ; no. 200)
    Includes bibliographical references and index.
    ISBN 0–313–32462–X (alk. paper)
    1. English fiction—19th century—History and criticism. 2. Women and literature—
Great Britain—History—19th century. 3. English fiction—Women authors—History
and criticism. I. Series.
    PR878.W6 S55   2003   #NJG: 50
    823'.8099287—dc21   2002072824

British Library Cataloguing in Publication Data is available.

Library of Congress Catalog Card Number: 2002072824
ISBN: 0–313–32462–X
ISSN: 0147–104X

First published in 2003

Praeger Publishers, 88 Post Road West, Westport, CT 06881
An imprint of Greenwood Publishing Group, Inc.
www.praeger.com

Printed in the United States of America

The paper used in this book complies with the
Permanent Paper Standard issued by the National
Information Standards Organization (Z39.48–1984).

10 9 8 7 6 5 4 3 2 1

Copyright Acknowledgment

The author and publisher gratefully acknowledge permission for the use of the following material:

Excerpt adapted by the author from *Preaching Pit: Dickens, Gaskell, and Sentimentalism in Victorian Culture* by Mary Lenard, copyright © 1999 by Mary Lenard. Used
with permission of Peter Lang Publishing, Inc.

Dedicated to aunts,
in particular to the editor's aunts:

Aunt Izzie
Aunt Medie
Aunt Beulah
Aunt Ruth
Aunt Mary
Aunt Margaretta
Aunt Gladys
Aunt Dorcas
Aunt Ned
Aunt June
Aunt Honey
Aunt Shorty
Aunt Joanne
Aunt Paula
Aunt Norma
Aunt Joy

Contents

Preface

I dedicate this book to aunts, which I think is quite fitting, considering the topic. Aunts are like the women writers of the nineteenth century who are under query in this collection. Not George Eliot or Charlotte Brönte or Elizabeth Gaskell or even Harriet Martineau, the recognized "mothers" in the "Victorian canon," but the ones who often do not get as much as a footnote in literary history anymore, let alone serious consideration—women such as Grace Aguilar, Catherine Crowe, Charlotte Elizabeth Tonna, Annie E. Holdsworth, Ella Hepworth Dixon, Flora Annie Steel, Anne Thackeray, Mary Elizabeth Braddon, Sarah Grand, Dinah Mulock Craik, Ouida, Marie Corelli, Ellen Wood, Elizabeth Sewell, Isabella Beeton, Julia Buckley, Rosina Bulwer Lytton, Eliza Cheap, Irene Clifton, Rosa Nouchette Carey, Anna Maria Hall, E.P. Hamilton, Barbara Hofland, Margaret Hunt, Violet Hunt, Anna Jameson, Rachel M'Crindell, Emma Marshall, Mary Maurice, Dora Ross, Mary Martha Sherwood, Florence Warden, Charlotte Yonge, and so many more talented women, now forgotten. You can find their books only if you know first that at some point they existed. And then you have to work hard at getting your hands on copies buried in special collections here and there. If you're lucky, you might come across some of them through diligent searches or accidental discoveries at flea markets and used book sales. And then you need to turn their delicate pages with care or they will crumble and tear between your fingertips, because most of them have not been reprinted since the nineteenth century. These were written by women who at one time spoke with oft-heard voice that forged the attitudes, behavior, and perspectives of our old aunts and grandmothers and great-grandmothers, who, in turn, imprinted Victorian values in us. Maybe the books have been mostly lost to boxes in our attics and basements, and their sentiments equally as lost to our current understanding and accessibility to Victorian culture, but they are as important as aunts are to our legacy from the nineteenth century.

The aunts listed in my dedication were brought up in a Victorian environment. The aunts on my father's side are Isabel Ayres McCleary (deceased 1984), Almeda Ayres Royston, Beulah Ayres Walker, Mary Ayres, and Margaretta Bosley Ayres. Their first names alone are Victorian, many of them right out of the Bible. Their father was a severe patriarch who ruled the household with an iron fist. Aunt Medie tells of times when her father beat her for reading books. She was starved for knowledge and wanted more out of life than what domesticity could offer. Aunt Beulah, also an avid reader, is the one who inspired me to become a writer, having penned several novels herself that she never published. As for Aunt Izzie, I spent many days on her farm learning how to make mayonnaise, ketchup, root beer, and other useful items that she would never have thought to buy at any store. She cooked on a coal-burning stove even when *Sputnik* was making its way to the moon. Mary was the wife of Uncle Roy and often came to visit us on Sundays, especially the Sundays we had ham, considered unclean by the Seventh-day Adventists. With his sole mission being to save our family, Uncle Roy's evangelistic zeal came right out of the pages of Frances Trollope's *Vicar of Wrexhill.* Aunt Mary was the adjuster; she often subdued him and showed us through her smile and demeanor the love of God that Uncle Roy could only talk about. Aunt Margaretta was the wife of Uncle Levy, who died in a fire before I was born. The only thing I knew about her was her flamboyant nineteenth-style cursive signature on Christmas cards.

My mother had a large family. Like my father's father, hers was a tyrannical patriarch who reveled in being head of a large household without showing anything that his children would later call love. I never got to know my grandmother because she died a hideous death at age 46—after giving birth to fourteen children and suffering several miscarriages besides. She went to bed, her teeth having already turned black. She could not stop menstruating, and with spreading weeping eczema, she soon looked like a leper. At the ripe old age of eleven, my mother became mother to her four younger siblings. Ruth Irene Hildebrand Shearer died in 1943 of multiple complications, but of any one diagnosis, like the Victorians, no one would ever know for sure.

Aunt Gladys, who died Christmas 2001, was the nearest thing to a grandmother I had. She told of the time my grandfather, known throughout the county for his religious devotion as demonstrated in his regular Sunday school teaching at a Dunker church, beat his wife even when she was pregnant. Aunt Gladys, herself married and with children and although it was during the depression, took in her battered mother. However, a justice of the peace strongly advised Mrs. Shearer to return home; she had no other recourse but to remain married, in all ways, to my grandfather.

I could write an entire book about all of my aunts. Out of this home life, they became who they became, and passed on their attitudes to me. They were strong women who would not put up with patriarchal constrictions and were experts at dispensing their matriarchal responsibilities. I am a baby boomer, but when I was very young, I grew up in a Victorian house next to Aunt Ned and

Uncle Jimmy's nineteenth-century farmhouse in Glen Rock, Pennsylvania—where people still tell stories of how Glen Rock's caves, being so close to the Mason-Dixon line, were used to hide runaway slaves. Aunt Ned named me; I was the little girl she never had. I followed her everywhere, watching her take the ax to her chickens and plucking their feathers, all the while singing "Rock of Ages" in her resonant soprano voice. I learned how to finagle eggs from mean chickens before the sun came up, talk to cows, bake her applesauce cake that weighs ten pounds, make rag rugs, and crochet those complicated doilies that you used to find throughout American Victorian homes.

From Aunt Dorc (Dorcas, a wonderful biblical name) I learned how to cook and bake in the old ways of the Victorians, or more specifically, the Pennsylvania Dutch. People today pay good money to buy such culinary delights that can be found usually only in specialty stores. I could go on and on about my heritage, but that is another book. Instead, *Silent Voices* emerged from a similar heritage, one passed on through literature. I put out a call for papers on the Victoria listserv, asking for abstracts on novels by Victorian authoresses little known today. The response was overwhelming, with enough material to fill volumes. From that point on, I noticed how often members of the listserv discussed writings that have not been canonized. Apparently, now is the time that scholars appreciate the call to reassess the value of our aunts, of how their works have formed the identity of not only our developing literature, but cultures as well. Thus, this book is dedicated to our aunts whose voices at one time contributed much to the formation of what we call Victorian. It is the intention of this collection of criticism to allow their voices—silenced and excluded from the Victorian canon—to be heard again for readers to gain a fuller understanding of Victorian culture that continues to define many of our current ideals.

Introduction

Brenda Ayres

There was a time when Victorian houses went out of fashion. They fell into disrepair and were converted into apartment houses and then razed to make room for parking lots and post–World War II housing. I remember a Victorian mansion that perched at the top of a hill in the small town of my childhood. It was the proverbial haunted house. No one had lived in it for years; nevertheless, every Halloween night we kids dared each other to knock on its front door. To do so took incredible courage because we fully believed the house was residence to a host of malevolent spirits, and there was no telling which knock would be answered by what. Costumed as spooks, evil people, and monsters, we would take turns rapping three times and then racing down the hill, screaming at the top of our lungs.

Today the house has been restored to surely what was once its former glory. Its beauty—its eclectic and aesthetic detail—is not just a testimony of a bygone era; the house is a thing of art.

So are hundreds of thousands like it across the America. A walk through the Haight in San Francisco; or the Quapaw in Little Rock; or Cape May, New Jersey; or Madison, Georgia, bedazzles with their row after row of restored Victorian homes. They are not just structures of houses; they are the fickle expression of the human spirit in all of its rainbow colors and fanatical contours. That, then, is their true haunting, and a very pleasant haunting indeed.

Unfortunately, many novels, especially those by women writers, have fallen into the same neglect as these magnificent houses once did. Someone needs to knock on their doors and find out what is inside. Their value has yet to be recognized, their texts restored, and contemporary readers invited to tour or even to take up residence in them.

The mission of this volume, then, is to reassess the novels by British Victorian women writers whose work, although many of them once best-sellingly successful, failed to survive into the twentieth century. Even if some of them have been reprinted or preserved in film, most have not received the serious scholarship and readership they deserve. The collection's articles will argue the value of these works and beg for their restoration to the Victorian canon, or failing that, their retrieval for scholars of Victorian culture. The contributors believe that invaluable perspectives have been lost because of the exclusion of these works from Victorian studies. Once retrieved, they both positively complicate and clarify notions of nineteenth-century life.

This collection of never-before-published criticism covers a wide variety of British novels that were published in the nineteenth century. Each chapter focuses on different social issues, although most of them, naturally, are also interested in gender politics. Burstein is interested in a Jewish novelist's navigation through Protestant spirituality. Lecaros explores noncanonical governess novels; Sussex, noncanonical crime writers; and Richardson, New Woman adventure novels. The others investigate how their women writers worked for social reform and how some subverted patriarchically defined religious issues with approaches and insights singular to the Victorian novel. The chapters investigate different authors: Grace Aguilar, authors of noncanonical governess novels, Catherine Crowe, Charlotte Elizabeth Tonna, Annie E. Holdsworth, Ella Hepworth Dixon, Flora Annie Steel, Anne Thackeray, Sarah Grand, Dinah Mulock Craik, and Marie Corelli. Most of them address numerous works by each writer. Contributors wrote their articles specifically for this collection, with the purpose of reclaiming lost voices that have something to say to contemporary readers.

This project does not mean to classify these books as a genre unto themselves, as one might think of other genre tags conveniently classifying domestic, sentimental, and sensation or further division into the industry novels, or conditions-of-England novels, or novels of social reform. Instead, the books under study ought to be reassessed and dispersed throughout the Victorian canon, included under already existing genres and subgenres. This study does not propose that these titles be kept separate from, within, or without the Victorian canon, but that they be absorbed into the canon, period. Such signifiers as "domestic, sentimental, and sensational" persist with implication that these novels have value but little literary virtue; they might become canonized and yet remained stigmatized as those silly novels by silly women novelists. Academe, always politically correct if not the provocateur for political correctness, must treat them otherwise. Toward that end, we do not submit our proposed appendage to the canon for serious Victorian scholarship as a genre or subgenre within itself. Simply, these titles are works that over the past few decades have not been appreciated for the value and virtue they can offer the contemporary scholar of Victorian culture. The writers of this project would like to rectify this oversight. Our intent is to identify what these now obscure, silenced novelists have to say that is unique and what has been lost that is not available otherwise through the existing canon. Our goal is reclamation.

Appropriately, the first chapter emphasizes the uniqueness of silent voices. Miriam Elizabeth Burstein questions the availability of works by Victorian Anglo-Jewish writers today. In "'Not the Superiority of Belief, But Superiority of True Devotion': Grace Aguilar's Histories of the Spirit," Burstein is fascinated with the novels by Grace Aguilar, in particular *The Days of Bruce* (1852), along with Aguilar's historical novel on the Inquisition, *The Vale of Cedars* (1880). Aguilar was explicitly Jewish in an age when nearly every British novel written by Gentiles had something negative and stereotypical to say about Jews. It is a wonder that Aguilar could even get published in the nineteenth century, much less become an internationally popular best-seller of domestic and historical novels. Those hallmarks alone should evoke curiosity for her books. Against the tide of anti-Semitism, Aguilar's works negotiate Judaic spiritualism through a sea of Anglophonic Protestantism. What is most fascinating to Burstein is that Aguilar attempts "to detach Judaism from the charge of legalism and rationalism—the charge that linked it to the Roman Catholic Church—and to reconnect it with Protestantism's personal spirituality." Chapter 1 argues the novelist's importance in working out alternative modern moral "spaces" that could be cohabited by both Jews and Christians.

The next chapter focuses not on a single writer but provides a comprehensive overview of nineteenth-century governess novels. Cecilia Lecaros' "The Victorian Heroine Goes A-Governessing" examines the marginalization of the governess heroine, especially in relation to women around her. This intermediate position functions as a means of bringing the governess' plight into focus, while supplying the writer with a framework for examining female development. Additionally, Lecaros discusses the structure and chronology found in most governess novels. Her purpose is not only to show how similarly the novels are structured, but also to convey a picture of governess life as it is delineated in the genre. Such a project reveals much about the attitudes toward female employment, and it makes important observations on revealing aspects of Victorian middle-class ideology.

Lucy Sussex is interested in the female detective novel. She claims "The Detective Maidservant: Catherine Crowe's *Susan Hopley*" to be the most substantial work of early crime writing by a woman. Although Sussex does discuss crime fiction by other women as well as additional works by Crowe, she attends more to what makes *Susan Hopley* (1841) unique. Particularly singular is Crowe's use of primarily female detectives. Sussex also sees Crowe as a precursor to Collins and Poe who probably influenced their writing. However, Crowe's intricately plotted novel created a rigorously organized narrative structure that is more characteristic of the modern crime story. Crowe's contributions to the development of the genre, coupled with her uncommon portray-als of women and their capabilities, place a substantial value on Crowe's novel for readers of crime fiction as well as those interested in Victorian gender stud-ies.

Not surprisingly, most of the women writers whose works have been sub-merged, address social ills from the viewpoint of women who felt oppressed themselves. Novel writing became somewhat acceptable as legitimate female activity, as long as critics did not take their work seriously. The outcome was that women used the novels as a channel through which to raise social aware-ness and promote change and reform. Most of them had powerful things to say about the restrictions imposed upon women. Even if what was said was subtle or encoded and not vocalized from a podium, subversive notions of gender ide-ology were implied through character, plot, and dramatic tension.

One such social provocateur was Charlotte Elizabeth Tonna. She wrote, among other things, an antislavery novel, *The System* (1827); a novel about the factory system, *Helen Fleetwood* (1839–40); an exposure of the abuses of women and children laborers in *The Wrongs of Woman* (1844); an anonymous, nonfictional work condemning the factory system, *Perils of the Nation* (1843); and an autobiography, *Personal Recollections* (1841). Her works played a crucial part in forming a cultural discourse of social reform that perfectly fulfilled the cultural needs created by the material and historical conditions of early-nineteenth-century England, and continued to dominate Victorian literature for decades to come. Mary Lenard's "Deathbeds and Didacticism: Charlotte Eliza-beth Tonna and Victorian Social Reform Literature" values Tonna as an impor-tant literary figure because she, as well as other "sentimentalist social reform" writers, performed the crucial cultural work that taught nineteenth-century au-diences how to "read" and respond to social problems. Tonna was one of the originators of this cultural discourse—a woman who carved out a niche for her-self as a social activist and author through her skilled and impassioned use of conventional Victorian understandings of religion, morality, and womanhood.

Equally impassioned by what Victorian women writers had to say about so-cial ills, SueAnn Schatz has written about Annie E. Holdsworth's *The Years That the Locust Hath Eaten* (1895) and Ella Hepworth Dixon's *The Story of a Modern Woman* (1894). Schatz finds that these novelists share an affinity with the lower class in that their novels reveal patriarchal strictures oppressive to women of all classes. They also depict the added burdens middle-class status confers upon women. Both novels additionally disclose their authors' entangle-ment in middle-class ideology, including the late-Victorian assumption that women should not possess sexuality. These domestic-professional novels often unconsciously perpetuate the patriarchal bourgeois structure they had in-tended to transform. Thus they suggest that the system must be changed for an equitable society to be established.

Another woman novelist who formed a nexus between the middle-class woman and an oppressed caste was Flora Annie Steel. No other writer—not even Mr. Kipling—can tell as much about the intersection of colonial and gen-der discourses, the conflicted role of white women in the imperial mission, or the various genres competing for attention in the fin de siècle literary market. The 1880s and 1890s gave rise to two new and explosively popular genres that competed for the ideological sympathies of their readers: the colonial adventure novel of Kipling, Haggard, and Henty, and the New Woman novel of Sarah Grand, Mona Caird, and George Egerton. Steel combines the two genres in a way that sharpens one's understanding of what a "feminist imperialism" might be. She creates a genre LeeAnne Richardson calls the New Woman adventure novel, which aims to realize the ideal of social understanding and reveal the shortcomings of sexual and political imperialism.

Women writers did not need to transverse the Empire to find oppression and to create heroines that subverted gender politics evident in novels that ought to be read, if for no other reason, than for this. A critic who believes this to be true is Helen Debenham with her chapter "Re-reading the Domestic Novel: Anne Thackeray's *The Story of Elizabeth.*" Superficially *Elizabeth* (1862–63) is a gently orthodox tale that insists from the outset on the conventional necessity of disciplining feminine excess into dutiful submission before allowing the her-oine her happy marriage. The text everywhere balances an awareness of the contingency of narrative in ordinary life, and hence the contingency of the ide-ology that the reform plot inscribes, with an examination of the power of ideo-logical narratives to control women's behavior. Thackeray exposes and redefines the decorums of "proper" femininity; she plays with the limitations of "feminine" discourse, with the convention that a woman loves once only, and with the idea of the hero as "reward" for the heroine's reform. She transgresses generic boundaries by representing the heroine's mother as her rival and enemy in love. Above all, she equivocates about closure, not least through her partly ironic deployment of her female narrator.

Proper social behavior, especially gender mores, was more often dictated and mandated from the pulpit. However, many women novelists challenged the hegemonic interpretations promoted by religion. Like her American counter-parts working on *The Woman's Bible,* Sarah Grand critiques the androcentrism of institutional Christianity. In *The Heavenly Twins* (1893), Grand distin-guishes between the practices of Christian churches and the egalitarian roots of pre-Pauline Christianity. She explores how Church authorities manipulate bib-lical texts to maintain women's submission to husbands and fathers. Grand si-multaneously points to biblical heroines who demonstrate women's power, physical prowess, strength, leadership, and independence. Like Marie Corelli, her contemporary and the subject of the last chapter of *Silent Voices,* Grand refers to God as both male and female. Jennifer Stolpa, in her "'I Am Not Es-ther': Biblical Heroines and Sarah Grand's Challenge to Institutional Chris-tianity in *The Heavenly Twins,*" confers upon Grand the distinction of being a proto-Christian feminist whose novel aims to restore to Christianity the power to liberate men and women from gender-restricted roles.

Robyn Chandler looks at another novelist who seems to promote separate spheres and undermine its exclusivity at the same time. "Dinah Mulock Craik: Sacrifice and the Fairy-Order" is an examination of *Olive* (1850) and *A Life for a Life* (1859). Although the "male doubter saved by the influence of a good woman" plot was adopted enthusiastically by women novelists and thus came to characterize the novel of doubt, *Olive* was one of its first expositions. *Olive* investigates the representation of Christianity and its relationship to knowledge and to institute the female angel/artist as the midcentury inheritor of "religious capital" who achieves the redemption of patriarchy. Building upon this concept, Craik's *A Life for a Life* suggests an ideal social order based on a liberal version of Christianity that emphasizes equality for all. Craik argues that for Christianity to survive in the modern world, it must be brought within the domestic. Conversely, the redemption of patriarchy is reliant on female emancipation. This novel's gendered dual narration is at once an expression of "separate spheres" and an undermining of its exclusivity. Craik has developed innovative poetics to address contemporary hermeneutical and representational crises. She explores the notion of "sacrifice" of "a life for a life" as it relates to midcentury gender ideology and theology, and as it has played out in topical debates on capital punishment, the Crimean War, atonement theology, "fallen women," and women's work.

The final chapter in this collection deals, appropriately, with a writer who very much represented the fin de siècle, with all of its conflicts between religion and science, and pressing issues about imperialism and the New Woman's movement. Leading with her social criticism as well as correctives, Marie Corelli was deemed by many of her readers a voice of one anointed to speak to a generation torn within themselves as whether to dismantle Victorian morality and to reassert it at that same time. Corelli authored thirty novels and was the most popular best-selling novelist of the entire Victorian period, breaking every sales record that had preceded her. Yet she came under formidable attack by critics and continued to receive a biased treatment of her life and work by most biographers and critics, including those of recent years.

Corelli's story, as indicated in its chapter's subtitle (which is also the subtitle of Corelli's second novel, *Vendetta*) "The Story of One Forgotten," is not much different from the stories of all of the women writers who were featured in this collection. And her story is not much different than that of many others that have yet to be reconsidered and reassessed for what they can contribute to Victorian currency. Without them, lost are invaluable perspectives that sometimes mirrored, sometimes deflected social and religious ideas. Either way, their voices have much to say to the scholar of Victorian studies who values full recovery of ken. It is the sincere hope of the contributors of this collection that these voices be silent no longer.

"Not the Superiority of Belief, but Superiority of True Devotion"

Grace Aguilar's Histories of the Spirit

Miriam Elizabeth Burstein

According to *New York* magazine, Jewish spirituality is now "in." Although cynics might (rightly) doubt just how sincere this fashionable devotion to Judaism actually is, we should be interested in this attraction to Judaism as a *spiritual* religion. In the nineteenth century, Judaism was commonly defined not by its spirituality but by its antispirituality, its elevation of apparently meaningless ritual over true religious content. According to the Rev. Hugh M'Neile, despite "all the varieties" of Jew available for Christian contemplation, one aspect of Jewish practice always stood out: a "marked and remarkable uniformity of religious, or rather superstitious, usage," listing phylacteries, fringes, and mezzuzim as examples (417). Interpreted through the lens of Christian typology, Judaism was the type or "shadow" fulfilled and transcended by Christianity, its antitype and "substance." Christ's Incarnation once and for all evacuated Judaism's moral relevance from both secular and spiritual history.

Even though the Victorians may have been convinced that Judaism no longer spoke to modern Anglophone culture, this did not stop some Jews from trying to make their voices heard outside their immediate communities. Nineteenth-century Britain and America saw the emergence of a new Jewish print culture that tried to speak both for and to "modern" Jews. English-, Hebrew-, and Yiddish-language newspapers circulated within the Jewish community; new religious and secular schools were established, creating Jewish readers familiar with both their own culture and that of their national residence; and Jewish novelists and moralists found a niche for themselves that crossed religious barriers (e.g., Ashton, *Rebecca*; Cesarani; Galchinsky; Zatlin). Nevertheless, few self-identified Jewish writers achieved wide renown, with the rare exception of the author Israel Zangwill near the end of the century.

One Jewish author, however, managed to achieve a significant transreligious following in both England and America: the Sephardic novelist and popular theologian Grace Aguilar (1816–47). Although Aguilar's life remains murky—there is little information about her outside of a very brief memoir by her mother and editor, Sarah—during her short existence she wrote key works of English-language theology: a midrash on biblical women that became an international best-seller, and several extremely popular domestic and historical novels. Perhaps one of the best-known Jewish figures in her own day, Aguilar achieved (wrongly, one must note) canonical status among both Christian and Jewish readers as a hitherto unknown type: the Jewish woman writer (Galchinsky 151–56). Her work found favor with both Orthodox and Reform Jews, and her *Women of the Bible* became a Sunday school mainstay.

For twenty-first century readers new to her work, Aguilar's popularity seems anomalous: How could a Jewish writer find moral favor in a densely Christian, often evangelical atmosphere? Aguilar's wide-flung theological appeal has caused a different kind of concern for scholars of Jewish studies. The ease with which Aguilar can be appropriated as (a) orthodox (Ashton, "Grace Aguilar" 81; Weinberger); (b) a nominally orthodox neo-Karaite (Singer 53–58); or (c) moderately reformed (Galchinsky 240 n.21; Harris 163–64 n.5) points to the idiosyncratic nature of her religious thought in both her fiction and her theology. At least part of the confusion derives from historical context, for Victorian Anglo-Jewish culture was anomalous compared with its European and American counterparts. Without intense anti-Jewish sentiment spurring it on, the Reform movement never became the religious revolution that it did in Germany and the United States. Only one Reform congregation existed in all of England during Aguilar's lifetime. Moreover, what Anglo-Jewish Reform sentiments existed were often "Orthodoxy lite," with innovations confined to issues such as English-language preaching, the introduction of organ music, and increased decorum—some of which were also incorporated into Orthodox practice. But Reformers sidestepped the more radical alterations of their German or American peers, such as eliminating the prayer for restoration to Zion. Although some of these reforms might be described as "Protestantizing," the Anglo-Jewish community never went so far as its American cousin in emulating Protestant educational, governmental, and missionary structures.[1]

At the same time, Anglo-Jewry's sense of itself within a Christian and British culture differed markedly from that of the Christians. As Todd Endelman points out, the Anglo-Jewish community's primary concern was not conversion but assimilation. Anxieties about apostasy moved to the forefront only in the early twentieth century ("Social" 86). Aguilar herself warned readers against abandoning kosher laws and other distinctive rituals, even as she insisted that Jews and Christians shared identical spiritual goals. Nevertheless, Aguilar's own Sephardic community was also the "high-risk" group for conversion—but not by Christian missionaries, who usually had access only to the far more impoverished Ashkenazic population. By contrast, Sephardic Jews usually converted with social advancement rather than theological conviction in mind (Smith). Indeed, two of Aguilar's own brothers eventually converted (Abrahams 148). Also, a small but vocal body of Jews opposed the burgeoning emancipation movement on the grounds that it would promote religious "indifferentism." More loudly, emancipationists carefully played up the Englishness of Anglo-Jewry to their Christian auditors while taking care to maintain traditional religious institutions among themselves. Aguilar assured her readers that leaving aside the basic ritual observances, "it would be difficult to distinguish a Jewish from a native household" ("History" 276).[2]

For Aguilar's readers, the most problematic aspect of her project has been what Beth-Zion Lask Abrahams somewhat infamously called "Jewish Protestantism": the sense that Aguilar's bibliocentrism derives from Christian influence instead of the Jewish Reform movement (142; cf. Weinberger 84–86). Daniel A. Harris, for example, has recently attempted to reclaim her for the Reform movement by allying her work with that of German scholars such as Leopold Zunz (164 n.5).[3] For others, Aguilar's neo-Protestantism is a concession to Christian anxieties during an age of emancipation, domesticating or taming any sense of Judaism's potential political threat (Galchinsky 150; Valman 69). This resistance to thinking about the rhetorical productivity of Aguilar's relation to Christianity further manifests itself in a notable unwillingness to spend much time on her "Christian" fictions, such as the successful historical romance *The Days of Bruce* (published posthumously in 1852). But such debates ignore the key issues. Harris notes that the "Protestantizing" claim distorts Jewish thought, but Aguilar herself willingly participates in that distortion by trying to validate Jewish spirituality by equating it with Protestant spirituality.

Instead of trying to define Aguilar's affiliations, then, I want to focus on the rhetoric of her religious discourse as manifested in her fiction and nonfiction alike. In particular, I will concentrate on the problematic meaning of "Protestant" in Aguilar's work, particularly as it is juxtaposed against "Roman Catholicism." Aguilar's Protestant contemporaries figured Judaism as both the object of Catholic depredation (thus suitable for rescue) and the equivalent to Catholic superstition (thus necessarily anachronistic); their conversion narratives understand the shift from Catholic to Protestant and Jew to Christian as a change from letter to spirit, body to soul. In her theology, however, Aguilar appropriates conversionist rhetoric not to Protestantize but, rather, to insist on Christianity's mere reduplication of Jewish spirituality; yet as novels such as *The Days of Bruce* and *The Vale of Cedars* demonstrate, Aguilar herself can sing the praises of Jewish spirituality only by canonizing evangelical anti-Catholicism.

I

In 1809, the convert Joseph Frey founded the London Society for the Promotion of Christianity Among the Jews, which ultimately sponsored lectures, publishing enterprises, and workers' training for impoverished converts. Although it attracted much support from Christians, it had little effect on Jews. Between 1831 and 1880, the society managed 1,300 baptisms—an average, in other words, of fewer than thirty per year—at a rate, as Mel Scult points out, of about £500 per convert. Moreover, despite some spin-doctoring on the society's part, the new "Christians" were often lower class and, not surprisingly, were sometimes motivated more by the society's promises of material help than they were by spiritual considerations (97; Endelman 150).

What is of particular interest, however, is the society's philosemitism. Philosemitic discourse invoked the righteousness of the Christian cause while warning that Christians themselves were the major stumbling block to conversion. Jewish conversion was as much a call for internal Christian reform as it was a missionary enterprise, for nominal Christians had to be held partly responsible for any Jewish aversion. The heroine of *Leila Ada, The Jewish Convert* (1853) tries to avert her father's displeasure by arguing that "you must not suppose that the spirit of persecution and oppression which has been so often manifested towards the Jews, is at all sympathized with by the real Christian" (Heighway 109). Sympathy with the Jews is thus a sign of authentic Christian spirituality: "Real Christians" convert Jews, not oppress them. But such sympathy is a modern and specifically Protestant product. As the Rev. Alexander McCaul, one of the leaders of the conversionist movement, explained in 1878, the "Romish Church" bore much of the blame for any anti-Christian feeling: "who can wonder that the Jews should spurn at and resist the religion of those who treated them with the most unrelenting cruelty, or that they should even hate the name of the cross, when they had seen it lifted up as the harbinger of their destruction" (28). Any resistance to conversion on the Jews' part results from the lingering aftereffects of Roman Catholic brutality, therefore making any Jewish anti-Christian sentiment "reasonable" while providing further fuel for evangelical anti-Catholicism. Once it has been explicated as a product of environment rather than natural religious tendency, Christians can take the appropriate steps to counteract lingering distrust by merely changing their self-presentation. But detecting such "reasonability" also requires Christians to identify with the Jewish position, however temporarily, and in so doing forces them to acknowledge their spiritual kinship.

But kinship with what? Most Christian writers insist that insofar as Jews blind themselves to their own religious anachronism, they are incapable of developing the fully formed subjectivity reserved to Protestant Christians alone. Richard Whately put it bluntly: "Their religion, and theirs only, could be, and has been, thus abolished in spite of their firm attachment to it, on account of its being dependent on a particular place" (68). Contemporary Judaism was literally founded on an absence; it was a superstructure with no base and, by extension, a law without spirit. How could Jews practice their religion when the very locale that made the religion possible had vanished? Indeed, "modern" and "Judaism" was necessarily a contradiction in terms. As Amanda Anderson nicely surmises, "being modern meant having a self-active or reflective relation to one's cultural heritage; Jewish culture, by contrast, was construed as a form of legalism (extrinsic law) that one followed unblinkingly" (42). In 1874 Henry Hart Milman equated the Talmud with "mediæval legend" and argued that once Jews became more "enlightened" they would realize "that the faith which embraces the whole human race within the sphere of its benevolence, is alone adapted to a more advanced and civilized age" (3: 431). If from Whately's perspective Judaism was simply impossible, from Milman's, Jews were trapped in a psychological time warp: Relying on the epistemological foundations of a credulous era, Jews failed to recognize the changing historical conditions that made Christianity the only acceptably modern religious faith. Indeed, for Augustus and Julius Hare, Judaism was a childlike condition: "Something like Judaism or Platonism, I should think, must always precede Christianity; except in those who have really received Christianity as a living power in their childhood" (344). For the Hares, Judaism metaphorically represented an immature moment in each individual's spiritual development, en route to an authentic Christian self.

As writers would argue throughout the nineteenth century, Christianity introduced a new concept of selfhood based on the separation of the individual from the state. True individuality was possible only when human beings subordinated themselves to God instead of to mundane laws.[4] In 1841 W. Cooke Taylor claimed that Christianity made man "something more than a citizen, he became Himself,—a moral being, called upon by the Almighty to fulfil his duties, and receive his reward according to his works"; at the same time, "he received a new being in his moral sensibilities, which were no longer confined to a single state, but extended over the whole wide fellowship of humanity" (2: 166). By detaching the individual from the state, Christianity reorients the self toward God and grants a new priority to consciousness; at the same time, it also demands that human sentiments expand to incorporate all of "humanity," and not just a geographically limited nation-state. Moreover, under Christianity human aspiration itself is displaced from the temporal state and reassigned to the spiritual, the true source of "reward."

Yet Protestants acknowledged that there had been a roadblock in the way of the Christian self's emergence: the Roman Catholic Church. If the Reformation established that "theological claims based on human reason or on Church tradition were not an adequate basis for faith" because "Scripture alone ... could provide clarity and certainty," then Roman Catholicism collapses into neo-Paganism by elevating Church tradition—i.e., human reason—above the Word of God (Abraham 162). By symbolic transference, moreover, the supposed Roman Catholic fixation on tradition became a fixation on the human body itself: Just as the Church fatally substituted man's letter for God's spirit, it also substituted the ascetic discipline of the body for the authentic discipline of the soul. Thus, in Charles Kingsley's early verse drama *The Saint's Tragedy*, St. Elizabeth's spiritual guide, Conrad, martyrs her through his belief in the spiritual efficacy of extreme asceticism. In fact, this belief actually betrays an idolatrous fixation on the body, as in Conrad's evocation of Mary Magdalen: "Then go—/ Entangled in the Magdalen's tresses lie; / Dream hours before her picture, till thy lips / Dare to approach her feet, and thou shalt start / To find the canvas warm with life and matter / A moment transubstantiate to heaven." If for Kingsley's clerics asceticism manifests sublimated desire, for his women it manifests sheer narcissism; his St. Elizabeth must learn that although Christianity's true lesson is that "all spend themselves for others," her own spiritual quest is mere self-glorification, "vain conceits / Of self-contented sainthood" (21, 109). Kingsley's Roman Catholicism is a this-worldly religion, in which the mind feeds on its own sanctity instead of acknowledging man's dependence on Christ for salvation. Ultimately, Protestants thought that Roman Catholicism denied individuals their right of access to the Bible; improperly focused their attention on the body rather than on the spirit; and made reality infinitely malleable, subject to the Church's dictates.[5]

Even as philosemitic discourse represented the Roman Catholic Church as quintessentially anti-Semitic, however, it also equated Rabbinical Judaism *with* the Church. As the Rev. James Whyte explained, Rabbinical Judaism "holds that tradition is equally authoritative with the Bible, and it agrees with Popery in arriving at the meaning of tradition through the existing organ of the church" (201). Critics presumed that orthodox Jews considered the Talmud to be just as divinely inspired as the Scriptures, or even more so. One anti-Catholic propagandist had argued that to secure access to "truth" it was necessary to oppose "the establishment of a system which, sealing up the Scriptures, makes the judgment of all depend upon the opinion of the few (the Roman Catholic priesthood), and that few liable to have their judgment warped by selfish considerations from their very position" (*Anti-Maynooth* 155). Similarly, for the evangelical novelist Charlotte Elizabeth, Jewish tradition suppressed reasoned thought by denying laymen the ability to interpret Scripture on their own; she warns one of her Jewish characters, "we cannot rightly interpret these books without the help of our learned Rabbis, who devoted their lives to the discovery of hidden meanings, not discernible to such as we" (183). Like the Catholics, in other words, the Jews have enslaved themselves by elevating man's word over God's. Moreover, in denying themselves the right of interpretation, they deny themselves both faith (which allowed the humble to interpret the Bible properly) and right reason (which allowed the faithful to assess biblical evidences on their own merits). By contrast, tradition and Talmud create "deep" meanings to mystify mankind, thereby enslaving men to the projections of their own mind rather than enlightening them to the wealth of inspired Scripture.

Similarly, Jews repeat the Roman Catholic error of asceticism in a different register. Parents in conversion novels often attempt to wean their converted daughters back to the fold by disciplining their bodies in a misguided effort to reclaim their minds. Amelia Bristow's *Emma de Lissau* (1829) features a young convert packed off by her own mother to a mock "prison cell" and placed lower than even the servants in the family hierarchy. But "doubts and fears, and distrustful inferences, drawn from human reasoning, so common, yet so Christ-dishonoring, had no power to annoy and bewilder a mind kept simply trusting to what is revealed in the written word, and resting with child-like affiance on the sure accomplishment of all it contained" (1: 161). Elevating human reason above God's word "naturally" blinds the Jews to the distinction between spiritual and bodily strength; even the weakest convert is capable of surviving such "deprogramming" techniques on the strength of faith alone. Worse still: The Jews have willingly blinded themselves to the fact of the Incarnation—that is, to the central fact of Christian history itself. The implications for Judaism are clear. Jews are local, national, deindividuated, their psyches enthralled by legalistic and worldly rituals. And the Jew's refusal to convert is a refusal to enter modernity—to acknowledge that Judaism is no longer a viable spiritual and ethical system, but merely a "dead" object of knowledge.

This "death" manifests itself in both theology and literature as the phenomenon in which Jews become the sublime subjects of historical or spiritual reflection, without being allowed to reflect upon themselves. As Michael Ragussis has pointed out in respect to *Judah's Lion*, Jewish characters may be "virtually allegorize[d] . . . out of existence" (47). But this allegorizing process is also historicizing. To contemplate the Jews is to contemplate sacred history at work, but it is also to contemplate an embodied history: For Christians, the Jews carry the past into modernity, only to forever disappear as individuals under the weight of "Judaism" made flesh. The title character of Charles Maturin's *Melmoth the Wanderer*, for example, encounters the learned Jew Adonijah, only to feel "as if I beheld an embodied representation of the old law in all its stern simplicity—the unbending grandeur, and primeval antiquity" (267). Conversionists insist that modern Judaism erects its rituals as a last-ditch defense against what the Jews really suspect, namely, that the religion has lost its spiritual center. This claim is at work in Charlotte Anley's *Miriam; or, the Power of Truth* (1836), which features a fairly representative "Jewish" argument in favor of ritual. When challenged on the matter of Jewish sacrifices—the type fulfilled by Christ's sacrifice—Miriam admits that without the Temple, modern practices can never be the same as the ancient ones; still, "they are substitutes of those ceremonial sacrifices which are not in our power to offer. All we can do." Warns her interlocutor, "but this is the very thing we maintain; that God, in proof that the ritual law is abolished, has rendered the observance of it, in all its *essential* requirements, *impossible*" (137). Miriam's position contextualizes sacrifice, presuming that it is acceptable to approximate in one's obedience to divine commands. But this requires her to admit that modern Judaism is now inauthentic; it is necessarily a this-worldly religion whose practices depend on mutable circumstances. Hence the response, which points to the hollowness revealed at the very core of Miriam's defense.

Anley's novel suggests that when a Jew speaks of Judaism, he or she always inadvertently confesses to its historical emptiness. A Jew who awoke to authentic historical knowledge would necessarily also have to convert. It was therefore not surprising that in 1839 Anthony Ashley Cooper argued that "the fearful state of apathy and indifference, superstition and exclusiveness, is in some degree giving place to active inquiry, and thence proceeding, and so doubly hopeful, to earnest and spiritual piety" (185). Cooper celebrates a breakthrough in the European Jewish consciousness: Long oppressed by religious formalism, the Jewish community has awoken to the need for spiritual reflection. Devotion to ritual is becoming a thing of the past, for now the Jews are entering into a new phase of deep, internalized faith marked by "inquiry"—a reasoned, open-minded analysis of the biblical evidence. Yet, speaking of Jewish women, Grace Aguilar claimed that "they are free now, not only to believe and obey, but to study and speak of their glorious faith; to look themselves within their Bibles, and read there the foundation for all which we have sought humbly, yet most heartfully, to bring before them" (*Women* 566). Where Cooper sees bibliocentrism as a proof of increasing Jewish "rationality," not to mention imminent conversion, Aguilar finds in it instead a return to authentic Jewish spirituality, one freed from the accretions of postbiblical tradition. Aguilar's echo of Cooper leads us to the key problem facing anyone who studies her work: How can she possibly reconcile Christian, conversionist discourse with Jewish thought?

II

Aguilar's popular theology does not excite interest either for its originality or for its profundity. Rather, its fascination lies in Aguilar's attempt to detach Judaism from the charge of legalism and rationalism—the charge that linked it to the Roman Catholic Church—and to reconnect it with Protestantism's personal spirituality. Her books and essays are expressly *reactive:* They begin from the assumption that Jews (particularly Jewish women) are alienated from Jewish knowledge and culture, and that (worse still) what they do know is garnered from Christian sources. "How," Aguilar asks, "is she to reject prejudice, and to separate the true from the false, if all her information concerning the history of her people be derived from Gentile writers?" (*Women* 377–78). Yet Jews must maintain their status as a distinct people while becoming one with the nation of their residence. As she repeatedly insists, the Jews "are distinct in feature and religion, but in nothing else" ("History" 276). Inherently, such a claim insists on the illusionary nature of Christian modernity: Far from succeeding Judaism as its typological fulfillment, Christianity in its essence repeats Judaism. In fact, for Aguilar the entire ancient-modern debate is wholly irrelevant in the arena of Jewish faith—"there is no such thing as ancient and modern Judaism." Rather, there "is a distinction between ancient and modern *Jews*" (*Spirit* 50, 52). Modernity can be discussed only in terms of the Jewish people's immediate access to God or lack thereof (in the form of his appearances on earth, his direct communication with the chosen, and the like); but the faith itself is eternal, unchanging, and indeed unchangeable.

Aguilar's assimilating mode works not so much by collapsing "Jewish" and "English" as it does by denying the historical uniqueness of Christianity. Despite Aguilar's repeated claims that Judaism and Christianity are reconcilable with just a little work—"the points of difference ... are yet few ... while the points of agreement are many" (*Spirit* 23)—she in fact undermines this position by translating Christianity into a mere repetition of Judaism. She simultaneously agrees and disagrees with the conversionist attack on Jewish "formalism" while calling for a return to Scripture: a Jewish Reformation, of sorts. Aguilar argues that conversionists have misunderstood the role of sacrifices and other rituals in Jewish theology. The sacrifices, Aguilar explains, "were of *very secondary* importance, compared with the *spirit* which was to pervade the offering"; a "worship of the heart and mind came before that of hand and form" (*Jewish* 203, 208). The worth of the sacrifice, that is, depended on the worshipper's spiritual orientation, his submission to the divine will; but the sacrifice in and of itself meant nothing. Therefore, even though the Temple's destruction makes it impossible to offer sacrifices, it in fact does nothing to abolish the primary spiritual obligations: "if we give Him that sacrifice, which we can still give, if we obey every statute, which in our present captive and wandering state we *can* obey: our worship is as acceptable in His sight as it was in Jerusalem; for it needed the same mercy to purify and perfect it then as it does now" (*Spirit* 235). The worshipper's humility and submission before God trumps mere form as the authentic expression of Jewish belief. Aguilar's argument here recalls that of Anley's Miriam, but whereas Miriam rests on the efficacy of the rites themselves, and therefore presumes that "all we can do" means "compromise," Aguilar rests her case on the spirituality that informs the rites, and therefore presumes that "all we can do" means "all the rites we are now allowed to perform." Christian typological interpretations of the sacrifices are therefore invalid because they improperly situate them at the center of Jewish theology: Instead of a transition from Jewish law to Christian spirit, Aguilar substitutes a repetition of Jewish spirit in Christian spirit.

If one is going to ally Aguilar with her continental contemporaries, it may well be here. Nineteenth-century German-Jewish theologians increasingly deployed the language of "spirit" (usually Hegelian) and "spirituality" in their work, transforming Jewish "piety" from "obedience to the Divine Law as the precondition for the soul's closeness to God" to an autonomous state "drawing its nourishment from the autonomy of moral Reason, the subjectivity of feeling, and the objectivity of the Idea to which the spirit was able to elevate itself" (Altmann 115–16; cf. Eisen). This transformation was clearly influenced by similar movements in German Protestant theology. Aguilar herself tries to define "spirituality" several times. In what is perhaps her clearest attempt, she explains that because "we are composed of two natures," one of the earth and one of God's "essence," "we must give the spirit greater ascendency than the earthly; and to do this is the intention of all Revelation; the seeking it is to be SPIRITUAL, and the peculiar frame of heart and mind which it produces is SPIRITUALITY" (*Jew-*

ish 61). We are spiritual beings insofar as in submission to God we elevate our soul over our bodies, and "spirituality" describes the kind of subjectivity that results from such an elevation.

Now, although she grants the difference of "creeds," "ordinances," and even "modes of thought," "spirituality is common to every creed and to every nation who earnestly seeks to know and love the Lord, according the dictates of the Laws that each believes that He has given, and so observes" (*Jewish* 15). Forms, although important, are nevertheless subordinate to the universal faith and feeling that inspires all nations motivated by "love" for the divine. Aguilar inveighs against "the trammels of tradition" (*Spirit* 100) and "the trammels of rabbinism" ("History" 293) and attacks those rabbis responsible for making the original sages' "words ... take the place of the word of God"; the sorry result has been that tradition has been "made the means of superstition creeping in amongst us, of bigotry raising her dark and lowering standard, till together they had well nigh expelled the pure spirit originally pervading the religion of Moses" (*Spirit* 229). Aguilar here agrees with those Christians who interpret Judaism in legalistic terms and, from there, link it to Roman Catholicism. But she reads this legalism as a contingent instead of essential corruption of Jewish religious expression. Later, she still agrees that "inward spirituality did in some degree give place to outward form" (*Women* 530)—only, once more, the fault lies not in Jewish faith itself but rather in the medieval "persecution of the Gentile, and the darkening misery thence ensuing" (529). Again, Aguilar appropriates conversionist rhetoric while twisting it: The Roman Catholic Church is indeed responsible for the current state of Jewish religion, but the Church's persecution re-created Judaism in its ironic mirror image. The conversionist *analogy* becomes historical *causality*.

She therefore recovers the Reformation as part of Jewish history, for the moment that "freed England from the galling fetters of ignorance and superstition which must ever attend the general suppression of the word of Truth" ("History" 264) also largely freed the Jews from persecution. Protestant culture, as Aguilar would again agree with the conversionists, is indeed philosemitic, precisely because it returns to the Bible; for Christians it is "morally impossible for them to read the one [the New Testament] without connecting it with the other" (*Sabbath* 2). But even though Protestant culture liberates the Jews, in liberating them to the Old Testament, the culture actually reinforces Judaism rather than undermining it. And, in an ultimate twist on conversionist discourse, Aguilar slyly explains the difference between real and nominal Christians: Not only do real Christians not oppress Jews, "calm enlightened Protestants" do not try to convert them, either (*Jewish* 35).

In *The Spirit of Judaism*, Aguilar further conjoins Jewish and Protestant "feeling" by appropriating the gendered Protestant narrative of "feminine" religion. She confesses that her work "may be deemed too heartspringing, too feminine, too clinging" (x–xi) and styles Judaism as "the *religion* of the heart" (156). As Dianne Ashton has pointed out, Aguilar's theological writings are rhetorically identical to "Christian mentor literature" aimed at a female public: She invokes the language of "woman's mission," argues that mothers bear the primary responsibility for the child's religious education, and makes domesticity the primary factor in woman's happiness ("Grace Aguilar" 82). This rhetorical translation rebukes the conversionist rhetoric (discussed in greater detail by Ragussis) that insistently figures Judaism as "masculine" and the innocent convert as "feminine"—usually in a father-daughter relationship—and thus makes the transition between the two religions a transition from male power to female influence, force to love, law to spirit. Mrs. J. B. Webb-Peploe's *Naomi; or, the Last Days of Jerusalem*, for example, shows how the youthful convert Naomi discovers the "sinfulness" of her actions (120), whereas (until his conversion at the very end of the novel) her brother Javan is possessed by "the spirit of fanaticism which took possession of his soul, and rendered his religion a motive to fierce and arrogant conduct" (8). The feminine and feminized convert relinquishes all sense of self-worth, acknowledging that only in humbling oneself before Christ can one receive pardon for sin, whereas the masculine and masculinized self remains this-worldly, presuming that human action and reason are all-sufficient. By contrast, Aguilar's rhetorical tactic insists on the "belatedness" of Christianity's gendered history: The feminine qualities that Christianity ascribes to itself are always already there in Judaism.

Furthermore, Aguilar's gendering of Judaism also plays with an additional feminizing move in Christianity's popular history: its progress toward Protestant subjectivism, the emphasis on the individual's personal relationship with God instead of "mere" hardened dogmas and doctrines. A case in point is Wilkie Collins' *Antonina; or, the Fall of Rome*, which counterpoints the reforming zeal of Numerian with the gentleness of his daughter, Antonina, and sets both against the neo-Paganism of a priest-controlled church. Numerian's absolute subjugation of his daughter—"Can you imagine that a Christian virgin has any feelings disobedient to her father's wishes?"—repeats the fatal error of elevating human reason above God's will. When he believes that she has carried on an affair with a Roman senator, he rejects her as absolutely as he once controlled her, only to be immediately forgiven; by the end of the novel, she embodies the true reform of Christianity through living "humbly and gratefully" instead of executing visible, radical reforms (99, 103, 644). Again, Aguilar's texts suggest that this progress toward authentic spirituality is now and has been already under way within Judaism itself, negating the male-female binary put in place by conversionist or apologetic narratives. Thus, *The Women of Israel* represents Judaism as a religion of "love" particularly suited for women, one that grants them "the blessed conviction that His love, His tenderness, are hers, far beyond the feeble conception of earth" (15). Similarly, men may "be happy without religion," but women are subject to "trials peculiar to her heart," for which she needs "Him whose love surpasseth the dearest, most precious, upon earth!" (*Spirit* 172). Aguilar's critique of Jewish legalism reinstates divine "love" instead of "justice" at the heart of Jewish theology, indirectly critiquing the feminizing mode in Protestant thought that denies *comfort* to the Jewish believer. "True" Judaism is eminently womanly instead of manly: Christianity's gendered history merely repeats imperatives at the heart of Jewish spirituality.

Although Aguilar may insist that Christianity repeats Judaism in the domain of spirituality, one can see the real problems inherent in this argument once Aguilar tries to give *content* to spiritual practice. Aguilar has to make spiritual practice exceptionally vague to paper over the differences involved in the transition from theory to execution. The link lies in "the mutual belief of immortality, and that heaven is infinitely preferable to earth ... our mutually binding laws: 'Thou shalt love the Lord thy God, with all thy soul, and all thy might; and thou shalt love thy neighbour as thyself' ... [our] both being commanded to practise charity, modesty, humility, brotherly love, forgiveness of injuries, unquestioning faith, and childlike obedience" (*Women* 560). Aguilar's bibliocentrism might ring sympathetic chords with devout evangelicals: Her proposed conversational "space" relies on both sides' ability to value subjective, emotional, and deinstitutionalized relations between man and God. But the "belatedness" of Christianity in her account effectively denudes it of its own originality or content. Jesus and Trinitarian doctrine thus seem like an inexplicable anomaly instead of an important part of a specific faith: "The belief of trinity in unity, is the only part of the Christian code which I cannot comprehend; and the only part I shrink from with horror" (*Sabbath* 13). In her fiction, however, Aguilar tries another tack: re-reading both Christian and Jewish history through the lens of Jewish ethics.

III

According to Jewish theology, postlapsarian man naturally tends toward evil, but he does not bear an inherited burden of original sin. The "disobedience of our parents," Aguilar explains, "so far altered our nature as to give the *body* more powerful dominion than the *soul*," thus "exposing us to temptation of every kind" and "rendering it a difficult and often desponding task to give the *spiritual* dominion over the *corporeal*" (*Women* 33). Thus, although bodies are "naturally" sinful, man's soul is not—in contradistinction to the Christian theology that testifies to man's total and innate depravity. As Aguilar maintains, each individual soul returns to God "untouched by any sin but those of the body in whom it was breathed" (33). By critiquing the concept of original sin she strips the logic from the concept of "vicarious atonement." If a man's sins are the result of his own freely willed choice, then he and he alone can atone for them through repentance and suffering; each man "has the power within himself to subdue the evil, sufficiently to attract toward him God's grace and aid to give the good sufficient ascendency" (*Jewish* 189). For Christ to mediate between God and man is therefore not only unnecessary, but more importantly a denial of both God's mercy and man's free choice: The sins of one man can never be assumed by another. Moreover, righteousness is not a matter of Calvinist election but, again, man's exercise of free will in choosing good over his natural propensity for evil (*Jewish* 154).

Aguilar's interest in sin and free will pervades both her theology and her fiction, but it is developed at greatest length in, of all places, a novel about Robert the Bruce. At first reading, *The Days of Bruce* is a conventional enough historical romance. Its central narrative follows Robert the Bruce's emancipation of Scotland from English rule. Punctuating and echoing this political narrative are the love stories of Alan and Agnes, the children of the treasonous Earl of Buchan and the patriotic Lady Isabella. (The two children are invented; the real Isabella was only nineteen at the time of the Bruce's coronation.) Agnes becomes insane after witnessing the execution of her husband, Nigel Bruce; Alan, thought to be either dead (murdered by his father) or treasonous, returns to Scotland as "Amiot" in what turns out to be a misguided effort to detach himself from his father's sin. The novel's conclusion figures Scotland's emancipation in two registers: freedom not only from English tyranny but also from mental tyranny, the burden of improperly borne paternal guilt.

The novel defines historical process not so much through events, however, as through sin and atonement: the need for historical actors to repent, and do it well, in pursuit of the larger good. The Bruce must repent for his murder of the treacherous Sir John Comyn; the Earl of Buchan for the evil done to his wife and children; and even Lady Isabella for her inability to wholeheartedly accept everything entailed by her marriage vow. Alan/Amiot suffers improperly for his father's criminality; the Bruce's wife, Queen Margaret, is incapable of suffering; and Edward I allows his physical and mental suffering to destroy his chivalric character. But the importance of repentance and suffering in Aguilar's text carries with it another aspect of her theology: her insistence that Old Testament characters in their very imperfection are the ideal spiritual models, precisely because their life stories figure the necessary connection of sin-repentance-pardon. What is at stake here is not an allegory of Jewish emancipation. Instead, Aguilar's novel manifests the vitality of Jewish ethics by reinterpreting a "canonical" British historical moment in the light of Judaic spiritual values. By suggesting the compatibility of the Anglo-Scottish historical record with a Jewish interpretation, then, Aguilar performs the Judeo-Christian reconciliation for which her theology had striven.

By insisting on the necessary imperfection of the hero, Aguilar's novel revises Jane Porter's 1808 best-seller, *The Scottish Chiefs*, which foregrounded William Wallace as Scotland's savior. In Porter's novel, the perfectly virtuous William Wallace is an obvious Christ figure who unifies Scotland under the Christian moral banner, feminizing the masculine realm through "maidenly mercy" (166). Although Wallace himself does not live to see the "new" Scotland, he does produce the ethical and spiritual conditions under which an antiviolent Scottish nationalism can flourish. Robert the Bruce, meanwhile, spends an inordinate amount of time flat on his back, as he has a habit of falling into ravines at inopportune moments. Porter's version of the Bruce comes into his own only at the very end of the novel, once Wallace has been imprisoned and executed; as the novel concludes, one finds the Bruce and his wife, Isabella—both definitely lesser versions of Wallace and his beloved Helen Mar—presiding over "a lasting tranquillity" that "spread prosperity and happiness throughout the land" (671). In other words, the Bruce is Wallace's beneficiary, rather than the prime mover of Scottish independence; he inherits a Christianized Scottish nationalism that forever banishes the older military model.

In contrast, Aguilar makes the central figure a sinner instead of a Christ figure. For the Bruce, his murder of Sir John Comyn at the altar becomes the central event in both his personal and his political history, one that affects not only him but his entire country. Insofar as the murder lies behind his quest for both kingship and Scotland's freedom, it places the entire nation under the aegis of his sin. According to John Barbour's medieval epic *The Bruce*, "He mysdyd thar gretly but wer / That gave na gyrth to the awter, / Tharfor as hard myscheiff him fell / That Ik herd never in romanys tell/Off man sa hard frayit as wes he / That efterwart com to sic bounté [He acted wrongly there, without doubt (for he did) not respect sanctuary at the altar. Because of it such great misfortu[n]e befel him that I have never heard tell in a romance of a man so hard beset as he was, who came afterwards to such good fortune]" (2: 43–48). Or, as Aguilar revises Barbour's observation while admiring the Bruce's "self-government of temper, passion, spirit," although he is "destined in the end to be the savior of his country" still it seemed "as if that same Almighty power which so destined him, who turned even his one evil deed to good, had manifested His judgment and his power to him, as to His servants of olden time" (Aguilar, *Days* 349–50). Situating the Bruce in God's divine plan, Aguilar insists on the pivotal nature of his sin. Earlier, his "whole soul revolted from the bitter remembrance of that fatal act of passion which had stained his first rising" (157); the murder that embodies the potentially fatal flaw in the Bruce's personality, his "passion," is singled out as the event that leads to his repentance through "self-government." Such repentance leads to divine pardon and, moreover, to the recuperation of the deed itself as part of the method for reclaiming Scotland's freedom. In the process, the Bruce is brought to a direct and personal experience of God's "judgment" in action, one that again allies him with the moral exemplars of the Old Testament.

Moreover, Aguilar tells us, the sufferings of not only Bruce but, even more painfully, his followers, figures forth the inexorable nature of God's punishment. Although his personal "sufferings ... would have been in themselves sufficient evidence of an all-seeing Judge," it is through "the death, the cruel death of too many of his noble friends, men whose fidelity and worth had twined them round his very heart-strings, whose loss was fraught with infinitely deeper anguish than his own individual woes, [that] we may trace still clearer the hand of vengeance, tempered still with long-suffering, yet unending mercy" (350). God's justice leads the truly penitent self beyond the existential fact of suffering to a

true awareness of providence; personal pride is obliterated in the new consciousness of God's will. But this new awareness is not merely individual, but
national, for Scotland's own sufferings derive from the Bruce's murder of Sir
John Comyn. If the Bruce's free choice of sin lies at the beginning of the nation's
quest for self-governance, then the long battle for freedom is incorporated into
the process of atonement. At the same time, the Bruce's similarly free choice of
repentance and humility earns God's mercy and, ultimately, forgiveness—as
manifested in the nation's ultimate freedom and righteousness. And the very
greatness of the sin and its punishment reveals the real workings of sacred history, God's dual adjudication of mercy and retribution.

Thus, the Bruce's heroism is translated into atonement: "Yet will I now atone
for the neglected past. . . . My country hath a claim, a double claim upon me; she
calls upon me, trumpet-tongued, to arise, avenge her, and redeem my misspent
youth" (28). He understands his sin as double: both Sir John Comyn's murder
and his own neglect of his duty to the nation's cause. His devotion to Scotland
thus works out his reliance on God's love. At the same time, it must also work
to reform his Scottish allies, who cannot see the murder as anything but justified: "And can it be thou art such craven, Robert, as to repent a Comyn's death—
a Comyn, and a traitor—e'en though his dastard blood be on thy hand?" (29).
Pride and self-justification here confront the Bruce's humility, in figuring a willing submission to God's justice as mere cowardice. For Jacob Neusner, this opposition is a key conflict in Rabbinic ethics: "The only choice is whether to cast
one's fate into the hands of cruel, deceitful men or to trust in the living God of
mercy and love"; the "arrogance" of the former position "alienates" God, the
latter leads to salvation (150). Moreover, the speaker errs by hypostatizing the
Comyns as an innately worthless group, for whom treachery seems a both natural and inevitable conjunction. But for now, the Bruce's sin and redemption
represents the victory of the repentant over the arrogant man; it makes authentic
heroism the product of repentance itself, instead of an original perfection.

If the Bruce's personal transformation cannot be separated from his nation's,
then neither can Edward I's. Atonement fuels the Bruce's nationalism, meaning
that Scotland's quest for freedom is not merely a this-worldly revolution, but
instead a willing *submission* to God's divine ordinances. By contrast, Edward I's
yen for Scotland is driven by the conflict between "ambition" and his increasing weakness: "Ambition, indeed, yet burned within, strong, undying, mighty;
ay, perhaps, mightier than ever, as the power of satisfying that ambition glided
from his grasp" (Aguilar, *Days* 57). Whereas the Bruce aims to glorify God, Edward I aims to glorify himself. But his continued quest for self-glorification is,
in fact, a refusal to learn the lesson of his illness. If his military might "again
and again prostrated the hopes and energies of Scotland into the dust," now he
"lay prostrate," showing "how in the sight of that King of kings, from whom
both might and weakness come, the prince and peasant are alike—the monarch
and the slave!" (57) God's might manifests the ultimate significance of "mere"
military endeavor, but Edward I resists rather than embraces this shift in per-

spective. His interpretation of events is resolutely secular; Comyn's murder, for example, is an "insult alike to our authority, our realm," to be "avenged" by his own power rather than God's (63).

More to the point, ambition "paganizes" the self by turning it away from God and toward its own strength. In briefly describing Edward I's dying commands, Aguilar invokes "ambition" three times and observes that his instructions to his son "partak[e] ... infinitely less of a civilized and enlightened monarch (for such was Edward, ere ambition crept into his soul) than of the barbarous customs of a savage chief" (351). In its relentless focus on the glorification and gratification of the self, ambition presumes that the world can be satisfactorily ordered, conquered, and governed through a wholly adequate human power; moreover, it makes happiness solely consequent on the gratification of that power. The ambitious soul thus greets God's judgment as an inexplicable event or personal affront, rather than as a call to submission. By contrast, Aguilar argues, the Bruce's patriotism can "scarcely" be termed "ambition" because he "sought but the delivery of Scotland from chains, but the regaining an ancient heritage, and sought no more" (157): The Bruce's campaigns submerge the self in the nation's higher good.

Aguilar thus transforms the clash between Scotland and England into a moral battle defined by "good suffering"—the ability to repent, do penance, and be saved. True historical awareness requires not conversion from one religion to another, but instead a consciousness of the self's personal relationship to God. Yet she also critiques those who improperly ascribe or assume sins: Improper suffering is just as dangerous to repentance as the unwillingness to suffer at all. The Comyns are popularly regarded as the very embodiment of treachery. Alan early on confesses anxiously to the "dark blood of Comyn in my veins" while swearing fealty to the Bruce (5); similarly, Agnes worries "that the dark stain of traitor, of disloyalty is withering on our line, and wider and wider grows the barrier between us and the Bruce" (13). Both the Earl of Buchan's children and the Scottish aristocracy more generally presume that the sins of the father naturally descend upon the children, and that such sins can never be erased. Kidnapped by his father, who believes him dead, Alan returns to Scotland as "Sir Amiot de la Branche" and refuses to identify himself until he has completed his quest to free his mother from imprisonment. But this produces difficulties when he falls in love with the beautiful Lady Isoline: Given that he is part of a "traitor race," he doubts that "even my mother's merits, her truth, her loyalty, her worth" would count much in his favor (395).[6] Alan's morbid obsession with his bloodline on both his father's and his mother's sides deliberately obliterates his own personhood. He is misguided in three senses: first, in collapsing sinful body and divine soul into an integral unit; second, in daring to presume that sin is permanent (thus denying the possibility of divine pardon); and third, in not realizing that, after all, the sole responsibility for sin falls upon the sinner. Alan is punished for his mistake when it appears that his beloved Lady Isoline will marry a rival instead of himself; by concealing that his real quest is for his mother, he accidentally deceives Isoline into believing that he is already in love with another. His suffering, in other words, is in large part self-induced.

Yet the novel's most important (and, indeed, ultimate) lesson lies with the earl of Buchan, whose ultimate reclamation demonstrates God's all-merciful nature. Faced with the son he had believed dead, the earl experiences a spiritual cataclysm, "love," which transforms him utterly—"bowed to the very dust, his whole being changed, every dark thought for the moment crushed beneath the mighty power of one emotion ... breathing of that divine origin which the veriest sinner cannot utterly cast aside" (471). If Edward I is the Bruce's mirror opposite, a chivalric knight destroyed by ambition, then the earl of Buchan is the negative to the Bruce's positive, an absolutely sinful knight. But the earl is given an opportunity for redemption that Edward I conspicuously misses. Here is the "spiritual" in action: the sinning man coming to simultaneous consciousness of the good within himself—that spirit of love that is, in fact, the sign of a higher being—and the absoluteness of his sin. Asked for a blessing from his son, he can only stutter, "Boy, boy, I cannot bless; I know no prayer, no word meet for that dreadful Judge I never thought of until now. I will learn prayers to bless thee, and then—oh God, my son, my son!" (472). In this sudden coming-to-consciousness of his absolute separation from God lies the key to the earl's possible repentance and ultimate pardon, a literal enlightenment—"there seems a black veil withdrawn from my heart and eyes" (472). And the novel ends not with the Bruce's triumph, but with news of the earl's death and transformation: "Lady, he whom you seek, the injurer and the penitent, thy noble, thy generous kindness can no longer avail; he hath gone where man may not reach him— where earth may not bless. John Comyn, earl of Buchan, sinning but repentant, cruel but atoning, lies with the dead" (577). In these, the novel's closing lines, we find the earl resolving the binary of Edward I and the Bruce, balanced between "injurer," "sinning," "cruel" and "penitent," "repentant," "atoning." The reader, seesawing between the two sets of terms, uncertain which one describes the earl's final spiritual state most accurately, is warned (like the other characters) away from casting his own judgment; we, like the earl, must put our faith in God.

What is conspicuously missing from this novel, however, is a real institutional context for such religious experience. All of the characters experience religion in highly personal and subjective terms, with little assistance from the clergy (aside from some advice from a pious abbot) and, noticeably, no intervention from a mediating Christ. Instead, the Roman Catholic faith is as "closeted" as Judaism will be in Aguilar's fictions about the Inquisition. Catholicism's practices "clothed" religion in "a veil of solemn mystery," and "its ceremonies, its shrines, its fictions" inspire what Aguilar's contemporaries would consider "mere visionary madness"—although in accordance with Jewish belief, Aguilar reminds her readers that "according to the light bestowed, so is devotion demanded and accepted by the God of all" (86). That important rider aside, Aguilar repeats conventional Protestant readings of Catholicism as ritualistic, sensuous, and fantastic. Insofar as it "clothes" religion, too, it forces man (unwittingly enough) to reflect upon his own creations rather than God's. In this system, authentic spirituality is the possession of a precious few, one that retroactively sanctifies Catholic ritual: "Revelation in its doctrines belonged to the priests alone; faith and obedience demanded by the voice of man alone, were all permitted to the laity, and spirits like Nigel's consequently formed a natural religion, in which they lived and breathed, hallowing the rites which they practiced, giving scope and glory to their faith" (309). This "natural religion" grants substance to the mere symbol of Church ritual; it provides an avenue for a personal relationship to God denied by the Church itself. To the extent that institutional religion exists, then, it exists as a momentarily acceptable but historically contingent form of devotion, but one that even in its own time is insufficient to the needs of those with the emotional capacity to *feel* the divine presence.

Aguilar's historical project here also points to the second and more polemical goal of her fictional and theological writings: undermining the conversionist exchange between Judaism and "Popery." Even as she demonstrates just how viable a Jewish rereading of British history can be, she also manifests the outer limits of her tolerance. Aguilar's Jewish historical fictions reread Catholic history again through the problem of suffering, making the Inquisition embody Roman Catholicism's ethical perversion.

IV

Aguilar's now best-known historical novel, *The Vale of Cedars; or, the Martyr*, is one of her many stories about Spanish crypto-Jews persecuted by the Inquisition. Marie, the protagonist, falls in love with an Englishman, Arthur Stanley; recognizing her sin, she warns Stanley that as a Jew she can never marry him and instead agrees to marry her cousin, Ferdinand, another crypto-Jew who has achieved high favor at Ferdinand and Isabella's court. Some time later, after her marriage has proven happy instead of the torture she had once anticipated, she encounters Stanley again—he, unaware of Ferdinand's religion, furious at what he thinks is her deception; she, no longer caring for him as anything more than a very dear friend. Another courtier, Garcia, tries to destroy her marriage to Ferdinand by telling him of an angry Stanley's visit to Marie; instead, Stanley swears vengeance on Ferdinand, only to be framed for murdering him. Marie is called to testify in Stanley's behalf and admits that she is Jewish—an admission that leads to her torture and eventual death.

Whereas *The Days of Bruce* links historical process to authentic repentance and suffering, *The Vale of Cedars; or, the Martyr* maps Spain's national decline onto its substitution of Roman Catholic and Inquisitorial "suffering" for authentic penance: "Superstition had not then gained the ascendency which in after years so tarnished the glory of Spain, and opened the wide gates to the ruin and debasement under which she labors now" (29). Aguilar positions the novel on the brink of Spain's "fall" into neo-Pagan hubris. The *Vale of Cedars* in fact proposes a new etiology for the Inquisition's emergence as an official arm of the Church by making the catalyst none other than the "martyrdom" of its protagonist, Marie. Torquemada[7] argues that "the fact of a zealous Catholic … wedding and cherishing one of the accursed race, and conniving at her secret adherence to her religion, [was] a further and very strong incentive for the public establishment of the Inquisition, whose zealous care would effectually guard the sons of Spain from such unholy alliances in future" (214). His justification for the Inquisition would ring danger bells for any Victorian familiar with anti-Catholic propaganda, which insisted that Catholicism interfered with the domestic sphere; here, Torquemada effectively displaces the loving mother with the "zealous" power of the Inquisition in maintaining spiritual alliances. Marie's consistent refusal to convert, first under loving intervention and then under torture, effectively maddens her Catholic tormenters: The turn to the Inquisition symbolizes not simply the inadequacies of Catholicism, but in fact the inadequacies of the entire conversionist project.

As in *The Days of Bruce,* the protagonist sins early on and must repent: Marie falls in love with a Christian. Although Aguilar sympathizes with her character's plight, she has no praise for intermarriage either here or in her other work. In her novella *The Perez Family,* one character's intermarriage results from religious self-hatred—"a union with a Christian would put a barrier between me and the race I had taught myself to hate"—and ends with him painfully aware instead of the religious bar between his beliefs and his wife's (66). Marie "had sought to banish every dream of Arthur, every thought but that in loving him she had sinned against her God" (*Vale* 37); as part of her penance, after confessing to her father, she vows "that his will should be hers, even did it demand the annihilation of every former treasured thought!" (40–41). Marie's anxiety arises first and foremost from internal conviction, not external persuasion; it is thus internalized morality that is at issue here, not the extrinsic laws stereotypically associated with Judaism. Conscious of her struggle, she accedes to her father's request that she marry another crypto-Jew, Ferdinand, despite her agonies about the rightness of marrying him without confessing the state of her sentiments and fearing that "if suffering indeed atone for sin, terribly will it be redeemed" (41). Marie's pain and submission seems, at first, to repeat contemporary attacks on the excessively patriarchal nature of the Jewish family, in which the father demands unquestioning obedience from the children to an ultimately destructive extent—particularly when interfaith marriages were at issue. "I loved my child with the strongest affection of a heart, rocked by all the tides of passion," exclaims Salathiel, the Wandering Jew, "but I could bear to look upon the pale beauty of her face—nay, in the wrath of the hour, could have seen her borne to the grave—rather than permit the command to be disputed by which she was to wed in our tribe" (Croly 131). Yet, in fact, her father's advice proves a help instead of a hindrance: By humbling herself before him in admitting her sin, she also humbles herself before God.

It is not coincidental that the novel confines its most intense critique of Roman Catholic practices to the second half of the book, for the Inquisition parodies Jewish spirituality in its insistence on confession, penance, and punishment. Marie's voyage through the Inquisition's "subterranean" (*Vale* 29) chambers grotesquely echoes the closeted nature of crypto-Jewish observances, and her torture again manifests the Church's deadly confusion of bodily with spiritual disciplines. True suffering, as Marie explains on her deathbed, is permitted "to try our spirit's strength and faith, and so prepare us for that higher state of being, in which the spirit will move and act, when the earthly shell is shivered, and earthly infirmities are forever stilled"; although "we cannot think thus" at the actual moment of pain, in retrospect she can "bless God for every suffering which has prepared me thus early for his home" (246–47). For Marie, suffering reminds the penitent of the body's fragility, so that even Inquisitorial torture can be translated into part of providence. Yet—and here is where the Inquisition goes awry—the sufferer can understand the divine significance of pain only in retrospect (recollected in tranquility, so to speak). The shape of God's plan is indiscernible at the moment of action or pain; true wisdom is always after the fact. An immediate interpretation of events for their spiritual value, in other words, is likely to be misguided—an act of misapprehension instead of inspired understanding.

Queen Isabella, Marie's patron and would-be protector, becomes her parodic opposite, the self who misapprehends the meaning of suffering: "Once impressed that it was a religious duty, she would do violence to her most cherished wishes, sacrifice her dearest desires, her best affections, resign her most eagerly perused plans—not without suffering, but, according to the mistaken tenets of her religion, the greater personal suffering, the more meritorious was the deed believed to be" (173). Whereas Marie, personally recognizing her sin in loving a Christian, renounced him and willingly accepted the emotional suffering that had to follow as atonement, Isabella must be convinced that her attempt to protect Marie goes against her duty—thereby signaling that the Church operates through external pressure instead of private awareness. Marie, too, has a sense of duty; as she warns Stanley, "There is a love, a duty stronger than that I bear to thee. I would resign all else, but not my father's God" (21). But her duty is spiritual, a devotion to God's will instead of man's. By contrast, Isabella's "duty" is to assert the righteousness of her faith over and above the righteousness of divine love. Also, Roman Catholics here are made to sound like inverted Gradgrinds, substituting a calculus of pain for a calculus of pleasure as a measure of moral worth. In this ultimately sadistic equation of pain and goodness, the *higher* meaning of suffering—the body's sinfulness as opposed to the soul's—vanishes in favor of a purely this-world belief in the value of pain itself. Furthermore, the Catholic calculus of pain presumes that God's plan can be immediately known by the sufferer, while locating righteousness in a specific act (good acts are painful) instead of within the self (pain tests the soul)—returning us, in other words, to the debate over works versus faith.

If, as I suggested earlier, Aguilar's "Christianity" wrongly understands itself as Judaism's successor instead of merely its echo, then her "Roman Catholicism" is degraded one step further: not an echo, but an empty parody wholly detached from God's will. In Aguilar's reading, the Inquisition sins by, above all, taking suffering out of God's hands and into its own. Says Garcia, the grand inquisitor, "I tell thee, pain of itself has never yet had power to kill; and we have learned the measure of endurance in the human form so well, that we have never yet been checked by death, ere our ends were gained" (179): The fatal slip lies in his reference to "our ends" rather than God's; equally damning, the Inquisition has made a science out of torture, transformed pain into a rational operation. Marie's rejoinder that "my soul thou canst not touch" represents the divide between the two theories of suffering: The inquisitor works upon bodies to achieve human ends, whereas Marie understands that the soul cannot be touched by physical pain unless her own will falters. Like the much put-upon characters of conversion novels such as *Emma de Lissau*, Marie withstands physical suffering through faith.

The novel's only ray of historical hope lies, ultimately, in the experience of shared sorrow. After Stanley and Marie's relative Julien kneel together in prayer after her death, "the young Christian turned, and was folded to the heart of the Jew. The blessing of the Hebrew was breathed in the ear of the Englishman, and Stanley disappeared" (251). For all of its apparent mutuality, this scene suggests instead transference: It is the Jew who comforts the Englishman, the Jew who blesses him. The Jew's blessing is returned not personally but nationally, in the form of Stanley's future care for the Jews after the edict of expulsion: "He did all in his power to lessen their misfortune, if such it may be called, by relieving every unbeliever that crossed his path" (255). Aguilar's conclusion disqualifies romantic love between Jews and Christians as a means of reconciling the two religions; rather, her text insists on a universalized charity for the suffering of all nations. Jews and Christians can meet only by maintaining their separation. Stanley's return to England at the end of the novel, complete with a devoutly Catholic wife, heralds the translation of true "Christianity" onto English soil; he comes bearing a Catholicism that disdains doctrinal rigidity in favor of mutual spirituality. The Inquisition, however, which insists that neither romantic nor spiritual love can exist among Christian and Jew, destroys Spain's own spiritual viability along with its supposed heretics.

V

When Grace Aguilar appropriates conversionist discourse, then, she does so to speak to a double constituency: the Protestant audience with whom she seeks common ground, and the Jewish audience whose religiosity she seeks to revive. Aguilar transforms apparently Christian and conversionist rhetoric into claims for Jewish superiority: Far from transcending and superseding its Jewish predecessor, Christianity unwittingly mimics its spiritual and moral practices. Such, perhaps, is the hidden joke of *The Days of Bruce,* whose purportedly Christian characters think of sin and repentance in purely Jewish terms. At the same time, by insisting that true Judaism is bibliocentric rather than Rabbinic, Aguilar performs the kind of attack on religious nominalism familiar to those who have studied the late-eighteenth-century evangelical revival. But, less positively, Aguilar's emphasis on "spirituality" leads her to endorse and enshrine evangelical anti-Catholicism; her rhetorical project requires her to support Protestantism's self-interpretation as "progress," the better to detach Judaism from its own negative associations with the Roman Catholic Church. Aguilar's own discourse, however, was itself increasingly anachronistic in the Victorian period. As Jews became not just a religion, but a biologically distinct "race," attempts to convert them met "scientific" opposition. Toward the end of the century, the novelist Benjamin Farjeon argued in *Aaron the Jew* (1894) that Jews and Christians were racially predisposed to their respective religious beliefs; for a Jew, Christianity was literally unthinkable. One suspects that Aguilar would have been dismayed by such an argument, for her own beliefs, good or ill, rested on the conviction that spiritually, all men were or could be as one.

WORKS CITED

Abraham, William J. *Canon and Criterion in Christian Theology from the Fathers to Feminism.* Oxford: Clarendon P, 1998.

Abrahams, Beth-Zion Lask. "Grace Aguilar: A Centenary Tribute." *Jewish Historical Society of England* 16 (1952): 137–48.

Aguilar, Grace. *The Days of Bruce: A Story from Scottish History.* New York: Burt, 1852.

———. "History of the Jews in England." *Essays and Miscellanies. Choice Cullings from the Manuscripts of Grace Aguilar.* Ed. Sarah Aguilar. Philadelphia, 1853. History of Women, reel 237, no. 1157.

———. *The Jewish Faith: Its Spiritual Consolations, Moral Guidance, and Immortal Hope . . . .* Philadelphia: Sherman, 1853.

———. *The Perez Family. Home Scenes and Heart Studies.* London: Routledge, 1891. 1–94.

———. *Sabbath Thoughts and Sacred Communings.* London: Wertheimer, 1853.

———. *The Spirit of Judaism.* Ed. Isaac Leeser. Philadelphia: No. 1 Monroe Place, 1842.

———. *The Vale of Cedars; or, the Martyr.* New York: Appleton, 1880.

———. *Woman's Friendship: A Story of Domestic Life.* London: Groomridge and Sons, 1850.

———. *The Women of Israel; or, Characters and Sketches from the Holy Scriptures and Jewish History Illustrative of the Past History, Present Duties, and Future Destiny of the Hebrew Females, as Based on the Word of God.* London: Routledge, 1889.

Alderman, Geoffrey. *Modern British Jewry.* Oxford: Clarendon, 1992.

Altmann, Alexander. "The New Style of Preaching in Nineteenth-Century German Jewry." *Studies in Nineteenth-Century Jewish Intellectual History.* Ed. Alexander Altmann. Cambridge, MA: Harvard UP, 1964.

Anderson, Amanda. "George Eliot and the Jewish Question." *Yale Journal of Criticism* 10 (1997): 39–61.

Anley, Charlotte. *Miriam; or, the Power of Truth. A Jewish Tale.* 5th ed. London: J. Hatchford, 1836.

The Anti-Maynooth Petition. A Tract for the Times by a Delegate to the Anti-Maynooth Conference. Anti-Catholicism in Victorian Britain. Ed. E. R. Norman. New York: Barnes, 1968.

Arnstein, Walter. *Protestant Versus Catholic in Mid-Victorian England: Mr. Newdegate and the Nuns.* Columbia: U of Missouri P, 1982.

Ashton, Dianne. "Grace Aguilar and the Matriarchal Theme in Jewish Women's Spirituality." *Active Voices: Women in Jewish Culture.* Ed. Maurie Sacks. Urbana: U of Illinois P, 1995. 79–93.

———. *Rebecca Gratz: Women and Judaism in Antebellum America.* Detroit: Wayne State UP, 1997.

Barbour, John. *The Bruce.* Ed. A.A.M. Duncan. Edinburgh: Canongate, 1997.

Bristow, Amelia. *Emma de Lissau; A Narrative of Striking Vicissitudes and Peculiar Trials; With Notes Illustrative of the Manners and Customs of the Jews.* 2nd ed. London: Gardiner, 1829. 2 vols.

Cesarani, David. *The Jewish Chronicle and Anglo-Jewry, 1841–1991.* Cambridge: Cambridge UP, 1994.

Collins, Wilkie. *Antonina; or, the Fall of Rome.* New York: Peter Fenelon Collier, n.d.

Cooper, Anthony Ashley. "State and Prospects of the Jews." *Quarterly Review* 63 (1839): 166–92.

Croly, George. *Salathiel the Wandering Jew; A Story of the Past, the Present, and the Future.* New York: Funk, n.d.

Eisen, Arnold M. "Secularization, 'Spirit,' and the Strategies of Modern Jewish Faith." *Jewish Spirituality: From the Sixteenth Century Revival to the Present.* Ed. Arthur Green. *World Spirituality: An Encyclopedic History of the Religious Quest,* Vol. 4. New York: Crossroad, 1987.

Elizabeth, Charlotte. *Judah's Lion.* London: Seeley, 1870.

Ellens, J. P. "Which Freedom for Early Victorian Britain?" *Freedom and Religion in the Nineteenth Century.* Ed. Richard Helmstadter. Stanford, CA: Stanford UP, 1997. 87–119.

Endelman, Todd M. *Radical Assimilation in English Jewish History 1656–1945.* Bloomington: Indiana UP, 1990.

———. "The Social and Political Context of Conversion in Germany and England, 1870–1914." *Jewish Apostasy in the Modern World.* Ed. Todd M. Endelman. New York: Holmes, 1987. 83–107.

Farjeon, Benjamin L. *Aaron the Jew. A Novel.* 3rd ed. London: Hutchinson, 1896.

Finestein, Israel. "Jewish Emancipationists in Victorian England: Self-Imposed Limits to Assimilation." *Anglo-Jewry in Changing Times: Studies in Diversity 1840–1914.* London: Valentine Mitchell, 1999. 82–101.

———. "Anglo-Jewish Opinion During the Struggle for Emancipation, 1828–58." *Jewish Society in Victorian England: Collected Essays.* London: Valentine Mitchell, 1998. 1–53.

Galchinsky, Michael. *The Origin of the Modern Jewish Woman Writer: Romance and Reform in Victorian England.* Detroit: Wayne State UP, 1996.

Glatzer, Nahum N. "The Beginnings of Modern Jewish Studies." *Studies in Nineteenth-Century Jewish Intellectual History.* Ed. Alexander Altmann. Cambridge, MA: Harvard UP, 1964. 27–45.

Hare, Augustus, and Julius Hare. *Guesses at Truth: By Two Brothers.* From the 5th London ed. Boston: Ticknor, 1861.

Harris, Daniel A. "Hagar in Christian Britain: Grace Aguilar's 'The Wanderers.'" *Victorian Literature and Culture* (1999): 143–69.

Heighway, Osborn W. Trenery. *Leila Ada, The Jewish Convert. An Authentic Memoir.* Philadelphia: Presbyterian Board of Publication, 1853.

Kingsley, Charles. *The Saint's Tragedy. The Poems of Charles Kingsley.* London: J. M. Dent & Sons Ltd. and New York: Dutton, 1927. 7–134.

Maturin, Charles. *Melmoth the Wanderer.* 1820. Ed. Douglas Grant. Oxford: Oxford UP, 1989.

McCaul, the Rev. Alexander. *Equality of Jew and Gentile in the New Testament Dispersion. A Sermon Preached at the Parish Church of St. Clement Danes, Strand, on Thursday Evening, May 2, 1833 ... .* 6th ed. London: London Society's House, 1878.

Meyer, Michael A. *Response to Modernity: A History of the Reform Movement in Judaism.* New York: Oxford UP, 1998.

———. *The Origins of the Modern Jew: Jewish Identity and European Culture in Germany, 1749–1824.* Detroit: Wayne State UP, 1967.

Milman, Henry Hart. *The History of the Jews, From the Earliest Period Down to Modern Times.* From the newly rev. and corr. London ed. 3 vols. New York: Widdleton, 1874.

M'Neile, the Rev. Hugh. "The Jews and Judaism. A Lecture ... Delivered Before the Young Men's Christian Association, in Exeter Hall, February 14, 1854." *Lectures Delivered Before the Young Men's Christian Association ... .* London: Nisbet, 1854. 411–46.

Neusner, Jacob. *Rabbinic Judaism: Structure and System.* Minneapolis: Fortress, 1995.

Norman, E. R. *Anti-Catholicism in Victorian Britain.* New York: Barnes, 1968.

Paz, D. G. *Popular Anti-Catholicism in Mid-Victorian England.* Stanford, CA: Stanford UP, 1992.

Porter, Jane. *The Scottish Chiefs.* 1808. Chicago: Rand, McNally, n.d.

Ragussis, Michael. *Figures of Conversion: "The Jewish Question" & English National Identity.* Durham, NC: Duke UP, 1995.

Scult, Mel. *Millennial Expectations and Jewish Liberties.* Leiden: Brill, 1978.

Silverstein, Alan. *Alternatives to Assimilation: The Response of Reform Judaism to American Culture 1840–1930.* Hanover and London: Brandeis UP, 1994.

Singer, Steven. "Orthodox Judaism in Early Victorian Britain 1840–1858." Diss., Yeshiva U, 1981.

Smith, Robert Michael. "The London Jews' Society and Patterns of Jewish Conversion in England, 1801–1859." *Jewish Social Studies* 43 (1981): 275–90.

Taylor, W. Cooke. *The Natural History of Society in the Barbarous and Civilized State: An Essay Towards Discovering the Origin and Course of Human Improvement.* New York: Appleton, 1841. 2 vols.

Valman, Nadia. "Muscular Jews: Young England, Gender and Jewishness in Disraeli's 'Political Trilogy.'" *Jewish History* 10 (1996): 57–88.

Webb-Peploe, Mrs. J. B. *Naomi; or, the Last Days of Jerusalem.* 1860. 17th ed. London: Routledge, n.d.

Weinberger, Philip M. "The Social and Religious Thought of Grace Aguilar (1816–1847)." Diss., New York U, 1971.

Whately, Richard. *A General View of the Rise, Progress, and Corruptions of Christianity*. New York: Gowans, 1860.

Whyte, the Rev. James. "Lecture VI. Present State and Character of the Jews—Intellectual, Moral, and Religious.—What Has Been Attempted towards their Conversion by Christians." *A Course of Lectures on the Jews*. New York: Arno P, 1977. 191–259.

Williams, Bill. *The Making of Manchester Jewry 1740–1875*. Manchester: Manchester UP, 1976.

Wolffe, John. *The Protestant Crusade in Great Britain 1829–1860*. Oxford: Clarendon, 1991.

Zatlin, Linda. *The Nineteenth-Century Anglo-Jewish Novel*. Boston: Twayne, 1981.

NOTES

1. The best history of the Reform movement is Meyer, *Response*; for the English situation, see 171–80. On the marginality of the Reform movement in England, see Endelman, *Radical*; Singer; and, for a local instance, Williams. Contrast with the American case as described by Silverstein.

2. For this ideological back-and-forth within the emancipation movement, see Alderman, ch. 2; Finestein, "Anglo-Jewish" and "Jewish."

3. But in any case Aguilar's theology has little to do with the primary concerns of scholars such as Zunz, Geiger, Jost, or Graetz; their "Science of Judaism" was a Hegelian historical project that put theology very firmly in its place. See, for example, Glatzer; Meyer, *Origins*.

4. On the shifting political importance of this idea in the Victorian period, see Ellens.

5. My understanding of Victorian anti-Catholicism has been much helped by Arnstein, Norman, Paz, and Wolffe.

6. Aguilar plays with this theme in other novels, such as *Woman's Friendship*: the protagonist's parents conceal the fact that she has been adopted from both her and everyone else, because they fear that she was born out of wedlock; they and the rest of society thus err in ascribing the mother's (possible) sin to the daughter's account.

7. Torquemada is a character in *Vale of Cedars* based on the actual Torquemada (1420–98), the First Grand Inquisitor of the Spanish Inquisition.

2

The Victorian Heroine Goes A-Governessing[1]

Cecilia Wadsö Lecaros

The governess held a peculiar position in nineteenth-century England, because she was a wage-earning, middle-class woman in a society in which middle-class femininity was defined by domesticity and nonparticipation in the public labor market. The number of governesses substantially increased toward the middle of the nineteenth century, coinciding with a period of economic insecurity. The economic turmoil that brought wealth to many families also brought disaster to those who had invested all their money in businesses and banks that failed, with the result that many parents had to send their daughters out to work. Employment as a teacher and governess was considered suitable, because the work so strongly resembled the traditionally feminine tasks of the middle-class wife and mother. Additionally, resident governesses to some extent could maintain their status as members of a middle-class household, although they had entered employment. Although governess work was deemed appropriate, contemporary records give a clear picture—no woman seems to have taken up governessing unless she was forced to do so for financial reasons. In *The Relative Position of Mothers and Governesses* (1846), Anna Jameson said that "the occupation of governess is sought merely through necessity, as the *only* means by which a woman not born in the servile classes *can* earn the means of subsistence" (6).

Census figures show that there were approximately 25,000 governesses in 1851, whereas the number of female domestic servants was as high as 750,000 (Peterson 4). Despite their relatively small number, governesses attracted much more attention in the contemporary debate than did other groups of wage-earning women, such as domestic servants and women in the industry. One explanation for this may be that the unequivocal and fixed class distinction, which served to define both master and servant, was not applicable to the relation between employer and governess. Because of her position as a middle-class woman, who was also a domestic hireling, the Victorian governess was trapped in an intermediate and undefined position. As for class, she ranked above the servants, but she was as dependent as they were. In 1848, Elizabeth Rigby explained that the governess "is a being who is our equal in birth, manners, and education, but our inferior in worldly wealth" (176). The governess was supposedly her employers' equal; nonetheless she was paid to work for them. Furthermore, she was remunerated for performing the tasks that, according to the prevalent middle-class ideal, were supposed to be the natural mission of her mistress. A master-servant relationship between people so outwardly similar yet so differently positioned posed an obvious dilemma. Added to the governess' problem was that employers who themselves sought social advancement saw her as a status booster. In Victorian England the employment of servants was an essential class marker, especially for newly rich families. As Bruce Robbins puts it, "the safest way of distinguishing oneself from the laborers was to employ labor oneself" (15).

The socially intermediate position of governesses generated a debate, which was especially active from the 1840s until the end of the century. This debate can be said to have consisted of articles in the press, a large number of manuals and advice books published for the specific purpose of improving the conditions for governesses, and reports from charitable endeavors such as the Governesses' Benevolent Institution (GBI). This philanthropic institution was founded in 1843 for the specific purpose of ameliorating the situation of governesses. Money was raised to create funds that would distribute grants to aged and unemployed governesses in temporary need of money. Homes for unemployed and old governesses were established, and different schemes for employment and savings were created. In 1848, the activities of the Governesses' Benevolent Institution were expanded, and the first college of education for women in England— Queen's College in London—was set up.

Whereas nonfictional material such as articles, advertisements, and autobiographical journals no doubt spelled out the conditions of governess life as they were perceived by the writer, manuals and guidebooks offered advice on how to cope with difficulties connected with the occupation. Such books show how governesses, and sometimes their employers, were advised to behave. However, it must be remembered that advice books usually presented ideal circumstances that may have been impossible to achieve. Still, the sheer number of governess manuals that were published during the nineteenth century indicates that there was a considerable market for them.

Furthermore, the large number of novels focusing on the governess question also formed an important part of this discussion. Many writers chose the governess character as a central figure explicitly because they wished to improve the situation of a vulnerable group of women. By bringing up issues that were repeatedly put forward in the contemporary debate concerning governesses' working conditions and social position, novelists took an active part in this debate. Although the governess was a common figure in nineteenth-century fiction, a large group of novels deal with governesses in ways that are so similar in plot lines, characterizations, and scenes, as well as in aim and intention, that they can be referred to as belonging to a specific genre. In the genre of governess novels, key themes such as loss of social status, intermediate social position, and moral worth are treated in ways that show great resemblance.

Although a small number of governess novels, such as Anne Brontë's *Agnes Grey* (1847) and Charlotte Brontë's *Jane Eyre* (1847), are still read today, most of the novels in the genre have not received any critical attention in our time. On the contrary, they belong to the mass of forgotten Victorian so-called minor fiction. A probable reason why most governess novels have fallen into obscurity, although they were widely read in their own day, is their highly specialized topic. Nonetheless, as this essay hopes to show, they deserve to be acknowledged as part of an important debate concerning female employment, and they also make important observations on several aspects of Victorian middle-class ideology.

A few governess novels were written by men, but the genre predominantly consists of works by women writers. A majority of the authors seem to have turned to writing from financial necessity. Although this was the case for many nineteenth-century women writers, it is worth observing that, like their heroines, authors of governess novels were middle-class women who were forced to earn their own living. Some of the novelists had themselves worked as teachers or governesses, and it may be assumed that they, at least to some extent, expressed their own experience in their literary works. Anne and Charlotte Brontë, for instance, had both faced the difficulties of governess life; Barbara Hofland, whose *Ellen, the Teacher* (1814) portrays a very young but competent governess; and Rachel M'Crindell, who wrote the highly religious *The English Governess: A Tale of Real Life* (1844), had both run schools, as had Elizabeth Sewell, who, besides the governess novel *Amy Herbert* (1844), wrote advice books on female education. Some writers of governess novels, such as Lady Blessington and Mrs. Henry Wood, were prominent in other genres. Writers of silver-fork[2] and sensational novels, as well as publishers of social criticism in fictional form, are found among the writers in the genre.

Previous scholars have been hesitant to talk about a governess-novel genre. Susan Nash, for instance, claims that "the simultaneous, paradoxical centrality and marginality of governesses and governess fiction has made their sustained importance to female writers and readers evident, but hard to define ... attempts to define a governess *genre* ... often dissolve into a bewildering variety of Victorian narrative modes" (28). However, I would claim that a substantial number of governess novels share what Alistair Fowler has called "family resemblance." Discussing the concept of genre, he says that "representatives of a genre may ... be regarded as making up a family whose septs and individual members are related in various ways, without necessarily having any single feature shared in common by all" (41).

It is my intention to show both the multiplicity of the genre and the consistency in the characterization of the governess heroine throughout the nineteenth century. The genre of governess novels, therefore, incorporates works that could also be read as children's stories, silver-fork novels, domestic novels, social problem novels, novels of development, or social or religious tracts. Although some of the novels are more or less straightforward accounts of governess life—some, indeed, read like catalogs of all the privations a governess could encounter—many writers chose to borrow traits from other fictional genres. Incorporating features from other genres was to some extent a way of reaching specific groups of readers. For instance, governess novels could reach a broad middle-class audience by fitting into the pattern of domestic realism. Many governess novels reproduce middle-class fears and feelings concerning loss of class and social mobility, and the stories are often enacted in a kind of setting that would be familiar to the reader.

The main difference from mainstream domestic fiction is the aim and intention of alleviating the precarious situation of a particular group in society. It could be argued that new literary forms and genres arise when groups in society try to "create themselves as subjects" (Mitchell 289). Juliet Mitchell, who discusses the emergence of women's writing, says that by writing about their own domestic experience, women could establish themselves as a group. A major task of feminist literary criticism, therefore, has been to study why women "write the novel, the story of their own domesticity, the story of their own seclusion within the home and the possibilities and impossibilities provided by that" (289). In this context the governess novel is an interesting phenomenon since it indeed outlines the "possibilities and impossibilities" of a specific group.

The fictional characterization of governesses can be traced back to the eighteenth century. Books for children—school stories, for instance—contain characteristics that are also found in the Victorian governess novel, such as didacticism and female development. Although school stories, such as Sarah Fielding's *The Governess; or, Little Female Academy* (1749) were published in the eighteenth century, novels featuring resident governesses and their relation to employers and pupils did not appear until the turn of the century. Early examples include H. S.'s *Anecdotes of Mary; or, the Good Governess* (1795) and Maria Edgeworth's novella "The Good French Governess" (1801). The governess characters in these stories differ from the genre prototype that developed from the 1830s. The main differences concern the changing attitude to paid work, the heroine's position in her employer's household, and her relation to the lady of the house.

Although most early literary portrayals of governesses have a clearly didactic purpose and present highly appreciated teachers, a noticeable shift in attitude seems to have taken place in the 1830s. From then on, the governess heroine was usually depicted as a victim of circumstances at the mercy of inhospitable or even hostile employers. The economic and social changes in the mid-1800s affected the position of governesses, and those shifts seem to have influenced and intensified the fictional delineation of governesses. Although different in some respects, novels such as Mary Martha Sherwood's *Caroline Mordaunt; or, The Governess* (1835), Julia Buckley's *Emily, the Governess* (1836), Miss Ross' *The Governess; or, Politics in Private Life* (1836), and Lady Blessington's *The Governess* (1839) all represent this new kind of governess novel, and it is with novels such as these that the genre started to take shape. In the 1830s, themes such as sudden impoverishment, paternal insufficiency, and conflicts with *nouveaux riches* employers were introduced into the plot. Although still didactic in intention, the plots of these novels revolve around the working conditions and social position of the governess heroine in a much more explicit way than those of earlier works.

Most governess novels show great concern with governesses' working conditions and social position. When the governess question increasingly became an issue in the social debate of the 1840s and 1850s, a more dogmatic approach to governess work was consequently seen in governess novels. Dinah Mulock Craik's *Bread upon the Waters: A Governess's Life* (1852) was published explicitly for the benefit of the Governesses' Benevolent Institution, as was Anna Maria Hall's *Stories of the Governess* (1852), which includes two short stories, the short novel *The Governess,* and a "Working Memoranda" for the GBI. Hall, who was active in various charitable schemes, wrote several works on the wretched situation of governesses.

The governess novel was further developed during the second half of the nineteenth century with the introduction of the sensational novel and the detective novel. New groups of writers came to make use of the characteristics of the governess-novel genre, which was well established by this time. One aspect that probably attracted these authors was the fact that a governess could easily be portrayed as a woman of whom little, or even nothing, was known. The eponymous protagonist of Mary Elizabeth Braddon's *Lady Audley's Secret* (1862) is thus a woman who goes out as a governess under disguise, as is Lady Isabel Vane in Ellen Wood's best-seller *East Lynne* (1861). Wood's novel has, in fact, much more in common with the genre of governess novels than previous criticism has recognized. By playing with the double identity of governess/mother, Wood explored the complex position of the resident governess. Another aspect that made the governess an attractive character for new groups of writers was the fact that her introduction into a household could instigate the disclosure of secrets about her employer. This is the case in quite a few novels where the presence of the governess clearly triggers the revelations of family secrets. After some time in her new situation, the protagonist of Florence Warden's *The House on the Marsh* (1883) realizes that her employer is a criminal man who confines his terror-stricken wife in the house.

Although new genres appeared and made use of governess-novel traits, traditional governess novels were published all through the nineteenth century. Henry Courtney Selous' *The Young Governess: A Tale for Girls* (1871), and Irene Clifton's *The Little Governess* (1900), for instance, show little difference in the handling of the governess theme from governess novels of the 1830s and 1840s. After the turn of the century, 1900, when the extent of governess employment decreased in real life, interest in the governess as a literary character seems to have diminished accordingly. Additional occupational spheres opened for women, and literary representations of other kinds of working women broke the governess' near-monopoly as a professional heroine. However, the literary influence of the governess has not entirely vanished. Writers of modern romances, such as Barbara Cartland and Victoria Holt, have incorporated characteristics of the Victorian governess novel in their work.

Most Victorian governess novels depict some kind of progress toward maturity or improvement on the part of the heroine, and because of the heroine's specific situation the genre corresponds well to the *Bildungsroman*. The journey out into the world of the traditionally male protagonist is paralleled in the one undertaken by the governess. The governess heroine usually goes through a personal development similar in terms of plot and themes to that experienced by the male protagonist of the *Bildungsroman*. There is usually some kind of initial loss, which forces the young protagonist to leave her home. During the course of the novel, she encounters a number of trials, which ultimately develop her mind and character into adulthood and maturity. Along the way, the protagonist meets various kinds of characters. In the *Bildungsroman*, the hero often encounters two women who represent, respectively, vice and virtue. Although not always as pronounced, a similar characterization can also be found in the genre of governess novels. Many heroines have to face unwelcome attention from men before they meet their future husband. Other parallels between governess novels and novels of development include the protagonist's progress, which is often coupled with some kind of religious or spiritual crisis, and the fact that although the process toward maturity is often long and arduous, there is a final reward, consisting of the protagonist's rehabilitation into her/his legitimate place in society.

A fundamental aspect of the fictional characterization of the governess is her relation to the other female members of the household. Her position as a wage-earning, middle-class woman is always at the center of attention in the novels, and this clearly sets her apart from other female characters in nineteenth-century fiction. M. Jeanne Peterson discusses the social incongruence of the Victorian governess, meaning the "conflicting notions about the propriety of paid employment for a 'lady'" (11). She discusses ways in which the Victorians—governesses and employers alike—tried to bridge these conflicts. For instance, she claims that the fact of employment was toned down, as was the governess' womanliness (14). I would argue that the opposite is the case in the novels. Since writers of governess novels wished to put the situation of the governess under debate, conflicts concerning the heroine's position in the household are of fundamental importance. The governess heroine's position in relation to her employer and to the servants of the house is crucial in the genre. It is not only, or perhaps predominantly, determined by a middle-class patriarchal culture, but also by other dominated, but to the governess dominant, groups of women.[3] The main opposition faced by the heroine actually comes from women.

The position of the governess in the employers' household could be illustrated by three partly overlapping circles, in the following manner:

Figure 2.1
The Intermediate Position of the Governess Heroine

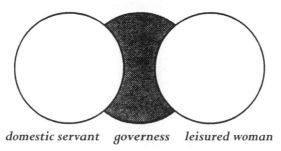

domestic servant   governess   leisured woman

Although the governess heroine is the central figure of the novels, she is socially marginalized in her employers' household. In her dependent and wage-earning position, the governess is similar to the domestic servant, but she also resembles the mistress of the house because of her middle-class background. In Figure 2.1, the zone between these two opposites of Victorian women symbolizes the marginalization of the governess.

This central area of the figure represents the zone that is occupied exclusively by the governess. It symbolizes her position, at once intermediate and isolated, which in most novels is clearly manifested in social life. The overlapping areas of the figure represent areas of conflict between the governess and the other categories. Such aspects in the novels as the governess' accommodation and remuneration belong in the overlapping areas. To affirm her own social position, it seems to be necessary for the mistress of the house to exclude the governess from her own sphere. Therefore, both the accommodation of the governess and the salary she receives indicate that her employers view her as a servant, rather than as their middle-class equal. The heroine is often opposed to her mistress in a way that underlines her superior moral principles and sometimes her more exalted social origin, too. The intermediate position of the governess heroine within her employers' household made her a convenient tool for social observation. By contrasting governess and employer, the writer could comment on the behavior of newly rich employers and their urge for upward social mobility.

The characteristics outlined thus far are presented to the reader in a number of genre-typical scenes and characteristics. By and large, the function of these appears to consist in marking the heroine's position in relation to her employers. For instance, after an initial catastrophe that forces the heroine to take up

work, she faces problems in procuring a situation, and the journey then undertaken to reach the place of employment is often described as long and weary.
When the heroine has entered her employers' house, her first glimpse of her accommodation tells her whether she is regarded as a lady or a menial. After such
introductory scenes, discussions concerning terms of employment, salary, hol-
iday, and so forth are introduced, and then the governess faces the difficulties of
the schoolroom.

In governess novels, the heroine's background is of importance both for the
plot and for the development of the governess character. The personal humility
and Christian values of the clergyman's daughter is a topic of interest to several
authors. It is often used as a way of emphasizing a morally wicked atmosphere
in the employers' house, demonstrating the governess' superior moral qualities
compared with those around her. Both manuals and many novels point at the
value of religious instruction, and in fiction this duty is assigned to the governess, although it was often claimed at the time that the responsibility for religious instruction should rest on the mother. Another type of background is the
impoverished aristocratic or upper-class governess who can reveal the upstart
qualities of newly rich employers, as her own gentility is made to contrast with
their manners. In other words, the background of the governess, whether predominantly pious or genteel, can be used by the author as a means of creating
a distinction between the governess and her employers. It seems as if many writers explicitly wished to emphasize the difference between governess and employer in order to lay open the perceived injustice toward the former.

Historical records indicate some variety in the social background of governesses in nineteenth-century England. In *Private Education; or, a Practical
Plan for the Studies of Young Ladies* (1815), Elizabeth Appleton listed the fathers of governesses as "naval and military officers, clergymen, barristers, physi-
cians, and merchants" (6), and similar family background is mentioned by later
commentators, too. In the novels the fathers of governesses are also commonly
solidly middle-class men. One possible reason for this may be that the author
wished to invest the heroine with a genteel status in the eyes of the reader. It
seems that however socially and economically degraded the heroine becomes,
she always manages to keep up a ladylike appearance. The more ladylike she is,
the greater will her difficulties be in adjusting to her new situation, and the more
she will suffer from her mortification. Authors use the governess heroine both
to satirize the social behavior of others and to air the plight of governesses as a
group.

References to social degradation were often stressed in advice books. Mary
Maurice, for instance, discussed the difficult transition from being a daughter of
one house to becoming the governess in another in *Governess Life: Its Trials,
Duties and Encouragements* (1849). She brought up the painful "contrast of the
former and present condition" that would be evident to every governess who
felt confined in her dependent position (55). Jeanne M. Peterson and Mary
Poovey both connect the difficulties of the Victorian governess with the eco-

nomic and political turbulence of mid-nineteenth-century England. Novelists caught on to the fictional potentialities of the governess figure, which grew out of this social instability. Here we find a clear correspondence with the fictional genre, where the theme of reversed fortunes and sudden impoverishment is indeed prominent. Sudden reversal is often linked to financial instability and the unexpected death of the father. In the nineteenth century, voices were raised against the danger of financial speculation instigated by social ambition. For instance, it was claimed that if parents would look to their children's interests instead of their own, their daughters would not have to go out as governesses.

Adversities quickly brought on owing to a father's financial speculation are legion in governess novels. Disaster hits a family in Eliza Cheap's *The Nursery Governess* (1845) when the protagonist's father, who is a businessman, dies "just at the moment when his speculations in business were likely to be realized to advantage" (15). The military father in the anonymous *Margaret Stourton; or, a Year of Governess Life* (1863) is similarly ruined when the mercantile house where he has invested his fortune fails unexpectedly; "undreamed-of liabilities started up on all sides; and the happy and prosperous family at Witham were in one moment brought to the very verge of ruin" (2). An author often uses rapid change, despair following on hope, to start off the plot. Indisputably, the initial loss has a catalytic function in governess novels, but there might be an inherent criticism of society in this device, too. In a society of rapid changes, many people were unprepared for adversity, and their aspirations for riches or social advancement made them neglect taking precautions that would have saved their family. The catastrophe that befalls a fictional family might be seen as a metaphor for what might happen in and to society. The fear of failing is of course a common feature in nineteenth-century British fiction, and by no means unique to the governess novel. Nonetheless, this genre effectively highlights the problem, as it generally portrays a young woman who has to face the consequences of financial misfortune for which her father is—at least to some extent—responsible.

The consequences of his ruin, however, will have to be borne by his daughter, who thus has to atone for the father's misdeeds. Several contemporary critics commented on paternal insufficiency; in *Principles of Education* (1865) Elizabeth Sewell attacked "fathers who neglect to provide for their daughters, when it is in their power," saying that "the sins of the fathers are, by the working of natural laws, visited on the children" (247–48). It is important to note that although paternal insufficiency may be the primary reason why a young woman has to go out as a governess, the lack of maternal support is also significant in many novels. When the mother of the governess heroine is alive, she seldom manages to be of help, herself being weakened by the degradation they both suffer.

Characteristically, the daughter, orphaned or not, must carry the yoke of her father's mistakes unaided. Although the Victorian era saw large families, governess heroines seldom have brothers or sisters to help them. In many novels they stand completely alone, as there are usually not many friends outside the family to trust either. Excluding the protagonist from social connections is to some extent a fictional convention serving to enhance her vulnerability. On the other hand, it is known, for example from letters and diaries, that many real-life governesses also suffered from such loneliness and social isolation.

A few governess heroines come from affluent backgrounds. In Julia Buckley's *Emily, the Governess*, the protagonist's forced separation from her background is instigated by the selling of her home. Emily Seymor's widowed and ailing mother tells her,

You have hitherto lived but in the sunshine of the world; you must not expect your future years to pass like the latter. You are now to embark upon a fresh and dangerous voyage, where you will often find the winds contrary, or beset by trials and temptations, which nothing but an Almighty arm can support you to go through. (5)

Here, the bitter truth that Emily will have to face difficulties hitherto unheard of is conveyed by means of seafaring imagery, as if to emphasize the perils of what lies ahead. The lack of "domestic freedom under which life flows on in a full and easy stream," as Harriet Martineau called the privations of governesses some twenty-five years later (270), will be hard for Emily Seymor. To her, the imminent transition from the state of wealth to that of dependence is indeed one "beset by trials and temptations," and like many other fictional governesses, she has been poorly prepared. An additional and consequential aspect of Emily's new position is her now dead father's way of driving his family to despair. After happy early years, he "plunged headlong and deeply into the vortex of dissipation—one pleasure led to another—one vice introduced another still more heinous" until he had gambled away fortune, house, and everything else (43). Emily thus faces not only poverty, but also the humiliation brought on her by her father's actions.

Not all governess protagonists have entered the profession because of their fathers' failure, however. Especially in novels from the second half of the century, a number of fictional governesses have become governesses as a way of escape, often under disguise. The governess of Dora Russell's *The Vicar's Governess* (1874) and the heroine in Rosa Nouchette Carey's *Only the Governess* (1888) both escape unhappy marriages and become governesses as a way of concealing themselves. Some novels, such as Wood's *East Lynne* and the anonymous *Charlotte's Governess* (1902) feature protagonists who turn out to be long-missing people who come back to the family residence for personal reasons.

The fact that the heroine in most novels comes from a fairly stable middle- or upper-class background is vital in connection to the aspect of social criticism. By belonging to the same social stratum as her employers, the governess is in a unique narrative position to interpret the treatment she receives. As pointed out, real-life anxieties, such as economic instability and aspects of class mobility, are echoed in the genre. Whether the protagonist is a gentle heroinelike character, or a woman using governessing as a disguise, her taking up work becomes linked to aspects such as economic instability, class mobility, and discussions about womanhood.

The same is true when it comes to the educational background of the governess heroine. In an era that paid such an interest in edification, the schooling and learning of the protagonist becomes important in the genre, because of the elements of contradiction that it entails. Peterson claims that because the Victorian governess had herself received the kind of education she was hired to bestow on her pupils, "her employment became a prostitution of her education, of the values underlying it, and of her family's intentions in providing it" (11). This paradox is significant within the governess-novel genre, too, where the educational background of the heroine is used as a way to position her vis-à-vis the employers. Generally depicted as less educated than the governess, they buy from her the kind of education they deem essential for their daughters' advancement.

In Blessington's *The Governess*, the Williamson children inform Clara Mordaunt that their mother has told them that "governesses were *never* ladies, but were merely useful to teach young people how to behave as ladies" (31). For newly rich people like the Williamsons, the main use of a governess is not to impart knowledge to their daughters, but to initiate them into the society of which the family aspires to be a part. Clara's upper-class background has equipped her with qualities to which the Williamsons need access in order to climb the social ladder. However, although they realize that she is suitable because of her background, they are not prepared to give her any credit for it, since that would endanger their own social status. The lack of education among employers is often used to satirize middle-class pretentiousness. In Anna Maria Hall's *The Governess*, for instance, a woman is determined to find a governess who can teach all languages to her children, but she is herself at loss when formulating the advertisement; "G-r-, there are two 'ees' in Greek?" she asks her friend (4).

Concerning the educational background of the governess, there is a noted difference between fact and fiction. Nonfictional sources repeatedly pointed out that a great number of governesses were in fact poorly prepared for the occupation. The discrepancy may be explained by the fact that many novels were written as sympathetic pleas concerning the bad working situation of governesses. Thus, authors might have wished to portray the governess as an innocent victim of circumstances, rather than supporting the—probably justified—contemporary claim that governesses would have to be better educated to gain more respect.

When governesses in novels are said to be insufficiently educated, this does not function to criticize them, but rather to illustrate the employers' lack of concern over their children's education and welfare, or as a device used to move readers to compassion for the governess. The former is clearly the case in Miss Ross' *The Governess; or, Politics in Private Life*, in which three aristocratic sis-

ters are contrasted through their respective governesses. The cold-hearted Lady
Oakley leaves her two daughters in the total care of

Miss Mason [who] was the ignorant tyrant of her real domain, the school-room;—her
pupils were looked upon as the ills necessary to her situation in life, as spies on her conduct, and that of her only associate, the waitingwoman: she was recommended [by Lady
Oakley's mother and her own old governess] as "accommodating, low-born, and cheap."
(83)

The reader feels no pity for this woman, who seems to be as devoid of any interest in pedagogical matters, and indeed of maternal feelings, as her employer.
The governess heroine of this novel, on the other hand, comes across as well educated and even able to teach her employer how to become a better mother.

When the decision to go out as a governess has been made, the heroine often
finds it difficult to obtain a suitable situation. When a post has been procured,
the young woman's passage from the state of being the daughter of one house
to becoming the governess among strangers in another becomes the next touch-
stone. This important transition is of consequence in the governess novel genre;
symbolic or dramatic language is frequently used to mark the heroine's passing
from the one social station to the other. The intended effect seems to be to bring
out the element of alteration of the heroine's status. In governess novels, the
rite-of-passage-like qualities of the heroine's introduction into the house of her
employers is relevant in the sense that the mortification she suffers is something she will have to cope with to develop and ultimately be relieved of the
governess yoke. Novels within the genre are structured around a series of esca-
lating and more or less humiliating episodes and circumstances, which serve to
reflect the heroine's moral superiority over her employers.

When the heroine arrives at her employers' house, she first encounters their
servants. Odious footmen feature in several governess novels, and because they
would regularly be the ones to answer the door, the governess often encounters
them first. Accompanied by her aunt, Blessington's Clara Mordaunt in *The Governess* enters the house of her first situation. The coachman has to knock several
times on the door before someone opens it, and he is then severely rebuked by
the footman for not ringing the bell instead: "a *single* knock, or a ring at the bell,
would have been more *properer* for sich [*sic*] like folk" (10). This servant then
refuses to carry Clara's box up the stairs until her aunt has bribed him. A number of governess heroines face difficulties in knowing how to approach the door
of their employers. The bell, which would be heard in the kitchen area of the
house, announced deliveries or servants, whereas knocking seems to have been
the privilege of gentlefolk. The question of how the governess should enter thus
became a matter connected to her status. When this surfaces in the novels, the
heroine's position is questioned not only by her employers, but—more significantly—by the domestics of the house. The question is whether the governess is
a lady who should be admitted as a guest, or whether she is to enter as a servant.

When the governess heroine has arrived at her employers' house, most novels pay some attention to her reception. Although she is promptly admitted in some novels, others depict her having to wait to be received by those who have hired her. When Agnes Grey arrives at Horton Lodge, the home of the Murrays, for instance, she does not see her mistress "till eleven o'clock on the morning after my arrival, when she honoured me with a visit, just as my mother might step into the kitchen to see a new servant girl—yet not so, either, for my mother would have seen her immediately after her arrival, and not waited till the next day" (119).

By thus contrasting the mistress to Agnes' own mother, whom the reader knows to be a high-principled woman, Anne Brontë manages to introduce Mrs. Murray as a strikingly incompetent employer. The governess' family background here functions as a kind of resonance box for what happens in the novel. The reference to how Mrs. Grey would have acted on the employment of a new servant girl further underlines the difference between the Greys and the Murrays.

Presumably, the contemporary reader would also immediately have recognized this late welcome as a premonition of Mrs. Murray's insufficiencies. Manuals of the age stressed the virtue of early rising; in Isabella Beeton's *Beeton's Book of Household Management* (1861) it is even called "one of the most essential qualities which enter into good household management" (2). The reader's suspicions would have been strengthened by the fact that Mrs. Murray apparently delays telling the new governess what is expected of her for several days. This defies another of Beeton's rules. She points out "an error—and a great one it is—into which some mistresses fall. They do not, when engaging a servant, expressly tell her all the duties which she will be expected to perform" (7). The early editions of this manual admittedly do not talk about governesses but about domestic servants; still, a comparison is warranted, as many fictional employers do treat their governesses as servants. Comparing herself with "a new servant girl," Agnes also indicates the degradation she experiences by not being introduced to her employer upon her arrival.

The duties of the Victorian governess varied, depending on the grandeur of the household. In real life, the question of whether the governess should only teach, or whether her duties would include other chores, seems to have been dependent on the financial situation of the employers. In governess novels, on the other hand, prosperity does not appear to be the decisive factor. Rather, it is the employers' attitude and degree of benevolence that determine the governess' terms of employment and her remuneration. In spite of the large number of governess manuals published in the nineteenth century, it is difficult to define the tasks and position of a governess exactly. Was she exclusively a teacher, or was it her duty to manage the children from morning to night? Was she a lady living in the house, or should she be regarded as a kind of superior servant? These questions are important in the novels in the sense that the governess, to some extent, becomes a surrogate mother to her pupils.

Although manual writers criticized the delegation of maternal responsibilities, many fictional mistresses refuse to see the governess as a teacher only. Because governessing was an undefined area of work, the issue of assignments becomes a field of conflict between governess and employer. Owing to her weak position, the heroine is seldom in a position to fight openly for her right to be treated as a lady. Such a conflict is referred to in Miss Ross' *The Governess; or, Politics in Private Life* when a woman tells her friends how she recently dismissed a governess who had refused to carry her pupil's bonnet. She claims that "a governess may surely be a lady, and yet not refuse to perform an office of kindness for her pupils. She is well paid for all she does" (166). A gentleman present reacts against this way of reasoning. He asserts that

It is the miserable fact that she is paid, which ought to induce her firmly, but respectfully, to withstand any attempt on the part of her employers to enforce on her any office not absolutely connected with those superior acquirements for which they engaged her; and that same fact will ever operate on a liberal mind in producing the most delicate consideration. (166)

In thus criticizing the exploitation of the governess by using her for non-teaching tasks, his views find support in several manuals. Anna Jameson, for instance, said that a good employer would feel "that it is a great mistake,—if it be not a grievous sin,—to regard the human being who dwells under [her] roof, and in the shadow of [her] protection, merely as an instrument to be used for [her] own purposes" (25).

The principal points in the Victorian governess debate were the workload and the socially intermediate position of the governess. The novels also often assign a symbolic significance to the actual residential quarters of the governess, with a bearing on the question of the position of the governess within the household. If she were seen as a lady, the governess was given the right to a private sphere. If, on the contrary, she were regarded as one of the domestics, there was no reason to treat her differently from the maid. The governess' room, whether it is her private sphere, or she shares it with her pupils, is part of the setting in most governess novels. Often, but not always, the room can be seen as a reflection of the status that the employers accord the governess in their house, as well as an indication of the nature of her employment. In many cases the accommodation of the governess bears a greater resemblance to that of servants than to the room to which she has been accustomed before leaving her home.

Although restricted space was often a reason for lodging the governess with the children in Victorian England, this is not the case in the novels. In fiction, the explanation is rather that she is expected to take total responsibility for her charges. Difficulties experienced by real-life governesses owing to practical circumstances—such as small houses—thus take on symbolic implications when addressed by fictional writers. The physical marginalization of the governess heroine has to be connected to her social status within the household.

Several characteristics recur in descriptions of governess accommodation. Situated on one of the top floors of the house, the heroine's room seldom has the advantage of a view of the surrounding park or landscape. Rather, the location of the chamber emphasizes her feeling of being confined within a house where she does not belong. The room is generally scantily furnished and sometimes without a fire. Such lack of comfort serves to underline the precarious situation of the heroine, especially if it is contrasted to her life before going out as a governess. When she is left in total charge of her pupils, the heroine's isolation becomes even more painful than if she is given a room of her own, as the constant company of the children effectively distances the governess heroine from any adult company.

In Henry Courtney Selous' *The Young Governess: A Tale for Girls*, Martha Smyth is shown to a cold attic room with a fire "plainly not intended to be used" (6) when she arrives at her employers' house. Because of a fall in childhood, she has a back problem, which makes the "steep flight of corkscrew stairs" (6) an additional burden in her predicament. There is no doubt that the turret room in which Martha is accommodated is on the top floor at the back of the house. The spiral stairs indicate that her room is part of the servants' quarters; large Victorian houses had back stairs for servants. Furthermore, Martha's room is very poorly furnished. When she arrives, there are neither curtains nor a carpet, but a good-natured maidservant does her best to supply the room with these articles to lend it some domestic comfort. When the lady's maid hears about this, she resolutely strips the chamber of all snugness again. Martha's room expresses the level of comfort she is granted by her employers. It also becomes a battleground for the struggle for power between the maidservant and the lady's maid. In this context, it should be pointed out that in Victorian households, the governess' room was normally the maid's domain, and the lady's maid presided over the mistress' chamber.

In the governess-novel genre, unpleasant accommodation seems to have been such a stock ingredient that the opposite functions as a warning to the governess—and to the reader—that appearances are deceptive in households that grant the governess a pleasant room. Indeed, in such families it is not the governess, but a family member, who is marginalized. Several governess novels incorporate features characteristic of the gothic novel, which saw a revival during the second half of the nineteenth century. Discussing *Jane Eyre*, Jerome Beaty mentions possible gothic sources of inspiration for Brontë (*Misreading* 65–76). It seems that *Jane Eyre* likewise inspired later novelists to combine the motif of the "deserted wing," housing an imprisoned spouse, with an account of the fortunes of a governess. This is the case in Margaret Oliphant's *Janet* (1891), in which the protagonist finds herself surprisingly well received and well accommodated. Janet's pleasure at the warm welcome she receives from her mistress soon changes into alarm when she finds out that her pupils' father is imprisoned by his wife. It is not only the name of the protagonist that makes Oliphant's novel resemble *Jane Eyre*. Gothic-like mysteries, including an enigmatic servant carrying food to an unknown person wailing at night somewhere in the house also brings Charlotte Brontë's novel to mind.

Jane Eyre is pleasantly surprised when she sees her room at Thornfield. She describes it as "a bright little place ... as the sun shone in between the gay blue chintz window curtains, showing papered walls and a carpeted floor" (113). Not only is the room light, but it also has the aspect of being well furnished. In many novels, the house itself is described as elegant, although the governess' room is poor. In *Jane Eyre* we rather meet the opposite, as her room at Thornfield appears to be much brighter than the rest of this house. Because her experience as a governess differs greatly from that of most other fictional governesses, the description of Jane's chamber might be seen as a prelude to later developments at Thornfield. It is noticeable, too, that Jane sees her room as her "safe haven," (113) although it proves not to be so later in the novel.

Another aspect of governess work that is often discussed in the novels is remuneration. Governess salaries were notoriously low in Victorian England. In an increasingly competitive labor market, many governesses were not in a position to set the financial terms of their employment. By calling the governess "a needy *lady,* whose services are of far too precious a kind to have any stated market value," Elizabeth Rigby identified an important reason for the poor salaries (179). Rosina Bulwer Lytton also commented on the disadvantageous position of governesses when depicting her governess heroine in *Very Successful* (1856) thus: "thanks to that anti-commercial argil, of which all real ladies and gentlemen are, unfortunately, composed; wherever driving a bargain was concerned, she invariably underrated her own pretensions" (10). Such low self-esteem and the lack of a stated market value served only the employers. The overcrowding of the profession led to uneven quality, and consequently to an increase in the difference between wages.

The question of payment must also be seen in relation to the contemporary ideas of woman's mission. Discussing the ideologies of motherhood in Victorian England, Sally Shuttleworth claims that "few ideological constructs seem[ed] to arouse such uniform responses" as that of woman's mission (31). Not even the rise of the women's movement in the early 1860s created an urge to challenge the ideals of motherhood. One reason for this might have been an urge to justify the only obvious option for women. In other words, it seems as if the emphasis on motherhood to some extent served both conservative and radical aims.

The underlying conflict in the role of the Victorian middle-class woman—on the one hand, she was regarded as an unproductive unit in respect to work and on the other she was idealized as a reproductive unit within the home sphere—must not be underestimated. Shuttleworth says that the idea of motherhood was "a field of potent conflicts in itself," mainly owing to the competing roles that motherhood implied (31). This is an important statement in relation to governess novels as well. The stress on woman's mission, and the contemporary fear of women encroaching on male privileges within the middle-class domain of paid work, are most significant in a discussion concerning the fictional characterization of governesses. The employment of a governess to some extent indicated that the lady of the house for some reason chose not to fulfill her traditional maternal duties. This aspect must not be overlooked in relation to the low level of salaries. Since the governess was brought into the household to perform work that the mother would otherwise have done unpaid, it was difficult to assess the value of her work.

In fiction, employers' unwillingness to pay for their children's education is often seen in relation to the readiness with which they spend money on things more immediately beneficial to themselves. Thus, in the anonymous *Gogmagog-Hall; or, The Philosophical Lord and the Governess* (1819), a governess-employing lady is angry with other people who, besides a deplorable lack of interest in their children's upbringing, "will haggle, too, about an odd fifty pounds a-year in such a case, and pay one hundred and fifty guineas for a set of teeth, or two hundred guineas for an opera-box!" (3: 28). In Miss Ross' *The Governess; or, Politics in Private Life*, the governess' champion Dr. Jameson is indignant about the low salaries of governesses, saying that it is common "for a man to object to a high salary for the lady who is to take on herself the charge of his three children's temporal and eternal welfare, and to give three hundred a-year to his cook, or a similar sum for a hunter" (168).

In 1848 Sarah Lewis, who had been a governess herself, made a statement similar to that of Dr. Jameson when she compared the employment of the governess with that of a seamstress:

Is it not monstrous, that while a lady will not give her dress to be made to any one but the first-rate dress-maker, she will give her children to be educated by a second or third-rate governess? That she will commit their training for this world and the next to a woman whose only qualification is, that she has had a twelvemonth's apprenticeship in an inferior boarding-school, or—that her father failed last week? (413)

As the number of governesses increased, their quality varied, and Lewis was far from alone in seeing a danger in this. Several articles in *Punch* commented on the problem, and Dinah Mulock Craik criticized people's "lavishing expense on their house, dress, and entertainments—everything but the education of their children; sending their boys to cheap boarding-schools, and engaging for their daughters governesses at 20£/a year, or daily tuition at sixpence an hour" (*Woman's* 45–46).

Whereas practical circumstances, such as restricted space or difficulties in recruiting certain kinds of domestic servants, may have been the reason for real-life governesses' having felt slighted, their fictional counterparts are frequently depicted as suffering from their employers' animosity. Predicaments that surface in real-life records are accented in fictional treatment to create a particular effect on the reader. The age of the governess novel coincided with an immense public interest in education and self-improvement. Although the novels seldom refer to any specific pedagogical approaches, they clearly draw on the general didactic ideas that were in vogue at the time. Even if she is young and inexperienced, the heroine usually proves to be a far better implementer of the pedagogical ideas embraced by the author than the children's mother, who, on the contrary, is portrayed as a warning example of the kind of education that is criticized.

Although there are occasional references to actual lessons in most governess novels, schoolroom activities generally do not take up much space compared with what goes on outside school hours. This is worth noticing, as real-life governesses spent long hours in the schoolroom, the school week usually being five-and-a-half days long. One plausible reason for the discrepancy between fact and fiction in this respect is the objective of the writers of governess novels, which was not primarily to depict the governess as a teacher, but to put her life outside the schoolroom before the readers. Her social position therefore becomes more interesting than her educational skills, and education is generally related to social issues. Schoolroom scenes address matters such as employers' expectations of the governess, and their attitude to children's education, rather than indicating the author's interest in pedagogy. This is all the more significant because several of the writers within the genre in fact had firsthand experience of the profession.

From the point of view of marketability, social issues would probably be of greater interest to a novel-reader than an explication of how the heroine tackles teaching geometry or French. Another explanation of the relative scarcity of schoolroom scenes in the novels is the fact that the intended readers were sometimes employers of governesses. Miss Ross, for example, specifically expressed her hope that the rich would read her novel and afterward treat their governesses better (Preface). Thus the role of the employers needs to be central to the plot, which is more easily achieved outside the schoolroom and outside school hours. The contemporary debate also devoted more interest to the nonteaching aspects of the governess question, concentrating on general working conditions and conflicts linked to the governess' intermediate position. Furthermore, since novelists may have realized that governesses would need to be better prepared for their work to gain more respect from their employers, concentration on matters not directly connected with the actual work of the governess may thus have been an authorial way of avoiding what was a recognized problem.

When it comes to contemporary educational ideals, governess novels do not vary much from the ones that prevailed in real life among the middle classes. Many nineteenth-century parents wished their daughters to display signs of an appropriate class identity. The tendency to concentrate on and favor so-called accomplishments before more intellectual attainments, or indeed topics that would be more useful for girls in their future roles as wives and mothers, is relevant in connection with the governess novel. In the educational debate, critical voices were repeatedly raised against the craze for accomplishments. Similarly, writers of governess novels often paint crude portraits of parvenu bourgeois employers who prefer to see their daughters excel at the piano to having them adequately prepared for adult life.

The Victorian emphasis in female education on so-called accomplishments, which consisted of French and other foreign languages, drawing, music, dancing, and fine needlework, was striking. As Anne Brontë's Agnes Grey says, it seems as if many parents wanted their daughters "as superficially attractive and showily accomplished as they could possibly be made" (120). The main reason why accomplishments were regarded as more important than intellectual training was their high social value. The education of middle-class girls must therefore be seen in connection to the development of nineteenth-century society. One way for middle-class men to verify their position and to distinguish themselves from the lower classes was to show that they could afford to keep their wives and daughters at leisure. Many critics saw this leisure as pernicious, however, and equated it with a female decline in utility.

The idea that middle-class women were seen as "declining in usefulness" because of their faulty education was brought up throughout the nineteenth century. In 1844, for instance, an anonymous writer in *Fraser's Magazine* criticized the superficial nature of girls' education by deploring how "every miss must grind a waltz, daub a piece of paper, and chatter bad French" ("Hints" 582). The disastrous effect of such social pretensions is visible in cases such as that of Rosalie Murray in *Agnes Grey*, whose only aim in life is to catch the attention of a local aristocratic bachelor. Although Agnes endeavors to make her see the drawbacks of a life of mere material splendor, Rosalie marries the good-for-nothing Sir Thomas Ashby and is consequently doomed to an existence dominated by boredom and dissatisfaction.

Because one of the governess' main tasks was to form the character of her pupils, it was deemed that through her class background she would be more suitable for this than the nurse. The stock characterization of servants as being irrational and ignorant in comparison with the governess seems to be based on a wish to emphasize the latter's superior position by birth. The idea of the ignorant working classes served the purpose of elevating the status of the class-conscious middle classes. Besides doing the kind of work that their employers wished to be relieved of, servants—as well as governesses—thus also functioned as status boosters. A few novels feature children imitating the servants' idiom; in H. S.'s *Anecdotes of Mary; or, the Good Governess*, for instance, the eight-year-old Mary uses unladylike expressions such as "I'll be hanged" prior to the arrival of her governess. One of the prospective employers in Anna Maria Hall's *The Governess* states the necessity of having a ladylike governess, because "children so easily imbibe vulgar habits" (6). Nothing is said about what the mother herself could possibly do to hinder her children from adopting such undesirable habits.

In governess novels, the transition from nurse to governess often marks a shift from ignorance to reason, and nurses are consequently described as ignorant or even detrimental to children's development. In the introduction to *The Nursery Governess*, Eliza Cheap claimed that the mind by nature is prone to evil, and that a nursery governess, by "cultivating and opening [the] intellect from its first dawning," may be able to lead children into the right path from an early age (xiii). Cheap made clear that a nursery maid would not be suitable for such a task; "her duties and training [belong to] an *inferior*, though a materially necessary department, chiefly confined to bodily cares; and whatever good influences *might* be hoped for, are merely accidental, and always limited" (xii). Although governess work was considered appropriate for women because it involved tasks similar to those of the mother, this analogy also posed a threat to middle-class stability. Since it was assumed that the married woman's principal duty in life was to raise her children, she could be seen as neglecting her natural task by employing a governess. The ambiguity concerning the mother's responsibility is indeed a prominent feature in most novels, and the relation between mistress and governess often harbors an intense conflict. Typically, the governess heroine finds herself employed to perform the mother's tasks, but not supposed to expect anything except her wages in return. Charlotte Brontë's personal experience may serve as an example of the difficulties governesses could face in this respect. When one of her pupils had behaved rudely to her, Brontë chose not to punish him or tell his parents about it. Later that day, the grateful boy took her by the hand and told her that he loved her, upon which her employer reportedly exclaimed, "Love the *governess*, my dear!" (Barker 312).

There are several novels that focus on employers' displeasure with their children's affection for the governess. In Hall's *The Governess*, Mrs. Hylier enters the schoolroom just as one of her daughters has flung her arms around the neck of her governess Emily Dawson and told her that she will "certainly do her best to improve" in the future. On seeing this sign of affection toward the governess, the mother exclaims, "Caroline, take your hand out of Miss Dawson's; I hate to see that sort of familiarity" (32). Like the experience of Charlotte Brontë, this fictional example indicates the annoyance some mothers feel at their children's attachment to the governess. Since the roles of mother and governess are not truly separated, the presence of the latter reveals the flaws of the mother.

In the novels, such incidents become all the more obvious as the governess never tries to challenge her mistress, nor in any way acts so as to supersede her in the children's affection. The bad conscience of the mother is awakened by the perfectly normal behavior of the governess. This kind of emotional trap is common in the novels, the most striking example occurring in *East Lynne*. Here, the dilemma of the governess is focused through her remarkable relationship to her pupils. The only way for Lady Isabel to make amends after having left her husband for another man is to return disguised as an unsightly French governess, Mme Vine. She thus suffers the humiliation of being the governess in her former home. Although the new Mrs. Carlyle does not appear to be a jealous woman—nor is she in fact the children's mother—she still reacts against the overwhelming goodness of the governess.

Several handbooks stressing the importance of the mother's work appeared, and the general opinion seems to agree with the anonymous mother behind *Hints on Early Education: Addressed to Mothers* (1852), who said that "the most important and responsible business that any one can be engaged in, is that of education" (3). According to her, this responsibility should be undertaken by the parents, after having brought the children into this world, and "transmitted to them their own evil disposition and tempers" (4). Not surprisingly, in governess novels, this attitude is not generally held by employers. They would much rather part with any responsibility for their children than relate those children's conduct or disposition to themselves. Parents readily hand over the responsibility for their children to the governess. Many heroines encounter charges that are minor versions of their parents, but after some time they have influenced the children into docility and obedience. In the novels it thus seems as if the maternal influence of the governess is stronger than that of the real mother, which may account for the rivalry between the two.

Historically, through her work, the governess challenged the mother's role, as she was being paid to do what the latter ought to do for free. The power exposed in a class frame was ambiguous in relation to the governess, as there was no appreciable class difference between her and the mistress. In the mistress's desire to demonstrate social superiority over the governess lies one explanation of arising conflicts. The tensions between mistresses and governesses in the novels involve both the actual tasks of the governess and her presence in the household as a woman. Some novels focus on one of these two features, but often the one influences the other.

Mary Poovey's discussion of the Victorian governess concerns her relation to the assumption of a specific maternal instinct. An important part of the Victorian "ideological equation," as Poovey calls it, was to uphold the belief in the importance of the mother's role for "morality and class stability" (143). According to this middle-class ideology, "maternal instinct is paradoxically both what distinguishes the mother from the governess and what naturally qualifies the former to perform the services the latter must be trained to provide" (143). This is a crucial question. Mary Maurice claimed that a mother who employed a governess for her children must realize that "she has a helper, but she cannot have a substitute" (105), which implied that the mother was in fact irreplaceable. Most governess novels in contrast present the mother as a hindrance to the happiness of her children. By portraying governesses as the more motherly characters, novelists not only created heroines that fitted the contemporary female ideal, but also found a profitable way of criticizing the lack of maternal feeling and competence that was thought to exist in many middle- and upper-class mothers. The fact that the governess was not a mother herself only enhanced this paradox.

Miss Ross' *The Governess; or, Politics in Private Life* opens with the narrator saying that "it has always been a favorite opinion of mine, and one which extensive intercourse with society has not induced me to forego, that the world was made up of 'men, women, and governesses'" (1). By placing the governess outside the common classification of people as either men or women, the author touched on a fundamental element in the nineteenth-century governess debate.

The notion of governesses as a category of their own keeps recurring in the governess novels, as well as in the nonfictional material. Not only unkind employers seem to have resorted to such marginalization of the governess; to some extent, even advocates of the governess cause viewed them as separated from society. As I suggested above, the marginalization of the governess was more complex because of her professional status. The point is that governesses were contrasted not only with men, but also with other women.

Words such as "class," "race," or "caste" were frequently used in the nineteenth century to accentuate the separateness of governesses. "Hints on the Modern Governess System" discussed the situation of "the newly risen race of governesses" (572), and the statutes of the Governesses' Benevolent Institution stated as one of its aims "to raise the character of Governesses as a class" (Governesses' Benevolent Institution 1848). One writer even described governesses as "a race apart, pariahs" ("The Governess Question," 1859, 169).

Novelists, too, often stressed the separateness of governess life by using such terms. In a letter to her niece, Marguerite Blessington explained that her intention in writing *The Governess* (1839) had been to rouse the "attention and excite sympathy toward a class from which more is expected and to whom less is accorded, than to any other" (qtd. in Thomson 43). Such discourse is also used in various ways in the novels. In Ross' *The Governess; or, Politics in Private Life*, the aristocratic Herbert Lyster tells his sister Mrs. Elphinstone how a friend of his, Annesley, has "married, of course a poor woman; and to my horror I heard it, his sister's governess." Although Mrs. Elphinstone tries to assure him that a governess "may be a delightful woman," Lyster retorts that he "must see a great many Mrs. Annesleys before I can tolerate them as a race" (40–41). It is worth noticing, however, that Herbert Lyster in the end actually marries the governess of his sister's children.

The physical isolation of the governess heroine in relation to her accommodation was discussed above. It was shown how the actual location of the heroine's room signals her position in the household. Another sign of her lowered social status is her lack of protection. Blessington's Clara Mordaunt unwittingly vexes her first mistress when she receives attention from the master of the house. Mr. Williamson's benevolence is of such a nature that it could have been granted to any lady; it is clearly the fact that the governess is his object of attention that upsets his wife. Interestingly, however, she does not object to the unsubtle advances of the visiting West Indian Hercules Marsden. To Clara's horror, he openly flirts with her and before long he has talked his mother into buying her, as he says he wishes to have a governess. Marsden's attitude, together with the fact that the Williamsons do not make the least pretense of shielding Clara from the assault she is subjected to, puts the governess' precarious position in focus. Although residency with a family was seen as part of the respectability of the governess' work, she was obviously in a dangerous position if she could not trust her employers to protect her.

It is perhaps not surprising that many governesses think of themselves as aligned with other exposed groups. For instance, in the anonymous *Chance and Choice; or, the Education of Circumstances: The Young Governess* (1850), the heroine compares herself to the serfs of Russia. Similarly, Emily Seymor in Julia Buckley's *Emily, the Governess* sees herself as related to the invalid daughter of her employers, and a number of heroines face difficulties that make them feel kinship with the poor and weak whom they visit in charity.

Yet another way for the writer to emphasize the social isolation of the governess heroine was to contrast her with the employer. In many novels the portrayal of the employer's family seems to be a conscious attempt to criticize contemporary social issues, such as the urge for social advancement. The danger of striving for outward success, thereby losing private happiness, is reflected in the family situations of several employers. Whereas the governess heroine's own parents have clearly married for love—although this may entail loss of position and inheritance—her employers, on the contrary, enter into matrimony for status reasons and consequently become miserable in their marriages. The heroine, who arrives as an outsider in a household, becomes an unwilling witness to marital disputes or parents' difficulties with, or lack of interest in, their children. Since most writers within the genre seem to have regarded the deplorable situation of governesses as their prime concern, criticizing the employer became an effective way of showing the heroine's distress. There are of course many unhappy marriages in Victorian fiction, and governess novels are not unusual in this respect. However, the narratological position of the governess character furnishes the author with an exceptional tool for observation.

Owing to the intermediate position of the Victorian governess, it was not clear whether she was to be seen as a family member and join her employers in their social activities, or reduced to remaining in the schoolroom even after lessons were over for the day. It is important to remember that the governess' absence from the drawing room was not necessarily linked to small-mindedness on the part of the employers. New middle-class social patterns, in which the head of the family left home for work and returned only in the evening, evolved during the nineteenth century. A new importance was therefore placed on privacy among the upper and middle classes. These social changes are reflected both in the governess debate and in the novels.

Mary Maurice acknowledged that "the lonely evening" was a common lament among governesses, but asked whether it would not be worse to feel oneself in the way than to spend the evening in solitude (36). This matter was brought up repeatedly in the nineteenth-century governess debate. It was claimed that "one cannot conceive a greater anomaly than that which makes a woman responsible for children, and their exemplar in all things, whose mother treats her as if she were unfit to associate with herself and her guests" ("Hints" 573). It was further argued that children who see that their governess is herself excluded from the social life she is supposed to prepare them for "must draw the inference that their governess is a mere machine of teaching. To their eyes, she appears wholly cut off from the links in their chain of sympathies" (573).

The inconsistency between employers' expectations and their own behavior is often made into an issue in the novels, as it so pointedly marks the intermediate position of the governess. Some novels put great emphasis on the issue of governess participation in the employers' social life, devoting lengthy discussions to the advantageous effects of making her a member of the family circle. The sensible Dr. Jameson in *The Governess; or, Politics in Private Life,* for instance, urges families to welcome the governess into their social life. His main argument is that it would keep "up in her that elegance of manner so necessary in one who is to be the principal instrument in forming the minds and manners of her pupils" (167). This particular novel actually put a finger on several of the issues brought up repeatedly later in the century. The three governess-employing sisters of the story exemplify different opinions regarding the social status of their children's teachers. The coldhearted Lady Oakley opposes Mrs. Elphinstone's admitting her governess Gertrude Walcot to the dinner table, for instance: "Nothing . . . can be so absurd, so ill-judged, and I am persuaded so repugnant, to the proper feelings of those people of rank and fashion who visit here" (85). The reader, who knows of the Elphinstones' radical improvement since Gertrude's arrival, cannot fail to see that Lady Oakley's comment only reveals her own snobbery. Ross was apparently aware of the criticism that her novel might evoke among her intended upper-class readers. Therefore, she expressed her special concern about readers' reaction to her desire of "placing the 'Governess', on an equality with the mistress of the Family" (309). By discussing this topic, Ross believed that she could provoke comments on who should take care of the children in the evenings if the governess was to amuse herself in the drawing room. Her own reply was that it would not be a problem, since pupils were either old enough to join their governess in the drawing room, or young enough to be in bed at the late hour when fashionable parties would start.

A well-known scene that raises and illustrates the topic of the governess' participating in drawing-room activities is Jane Eyre's experience at the big house party at Thornfield Hall. Despite their knowing that Jane is present in the room, the discussion among the lady guests concerns their experiences of governesses. When one of the ladies realizes that the governess hears every word of what is said and informs her neighbor about this, the latter answers, "I noticed her; I am a judge of physiognomy, and in hers I see all the faults of her class" (210). Blessington had depicted a similar humiliating situation in *The Governess.* When Clara Mordaunt is walking in Hyde Park with her second employer Lady Axminster, they meet some friends of the Axminsters, who comment on Clara's good looks. There will always be problems with beautiful governesses, they say, even giving examples from their social circle of governesses who enticed husbands or caused embarrassment in other ways. Blessington makes a point of the "peculiarly awkward" position Clara finds herself in here, by stressing that the ladies were "perfectly reckless as to their remarks being overheard by [Clara], that they spoke as loud as if she were not near them" (185).

Such manners could be seen in relation to the way in which middle- and upper-class employers habitually talked openly in front of domestic servants, assuming that they had neither ears nor eyes (Robbins 108). Peterson also explains that "drawing room conversations about the governess served to bring her into public 'view' ... Even complaining about a governess was a way of 'showing her off'"(5). Thus, employers could choose to display their governess "as a symbol of [their own] economic power, breeding, and station" (5). In the novels, such behavior emphasizes the governess heroine's position in a markedly negative way, as the employers are portrayed as unfeeling and snobbish.

One of the imperative assets for the nineteenth-century governess was to be an accomplished piano player. This was important not only in her capacity as a teacher, but also for the benefit of her employers. In the novels, piano playing not uncommonly assumes a central role in the heroine's social life with her employers. Barbara Wynne in the Hunts' *The Governess* (1912)—a late governess novel—is one of many fictional governesses expected to come downstairs to play the piano after dinner, because her employers say they are most interested in music. To Barbara's sorrow, however, they usually fall asleep during the performance. Another piano player is Eleanor Somers in Emma Marshall's *The Governess; or, Pleading Voices* (1876). The fact that the governess is asked to entertain her employers and their guests every evening is one of the factors contributing to her mental and physical breakdown, thus forcing her to give up work.

Although the governess' musical accomplishments were desired, they were sometimes used against her. In several novels, the heroine's command of music gives rise to envy among other women. Interestingly enough, the governess' musical skills, rather than any beauty she may possess, is a chief cause of jealousy. There are a number of governesses who play a little too well according to the lady of the house. Mr. Byfield in Hall's *The Governess*, who all through the story comments on employers' manners toward their governesses, lends expression to the jealousy felt by many female characters. He rebukes one lady for expecting her governess to teach all the accomplishments, but still not letting her "play anything in society except quadrilles." The simple but important reason for this restriction was that the governess "played so well that she might eclipse the young ladies who, not being governesses, play for husbands, while she only plays for bread" (22).

Among the governess novels included in my study, a large majority close with the governess exchanging the position of governess for that of wife. One of the characteristics of the governess novel, according to Beaty, is that the governess, if she is a heroine, "marries a gentleman or clergyman" ("Genre" 640). This does not seem to be the whole truth, however. First, governess heroines are more catholic in their choice of husbands, and second, the marriage theme is generally complicated by conflicting views concerning the idea of marriage to a governess. In several cases, unworthy but high-ranking men, whose families reject the idea of marrying a governess, assail the heroine. In *Chance and Choice; or, the Education of Circumstances: The Young Governess*, the uncle of Lucy Clifford's Russian pupils falls in love with her. Although he has no intent "beyond beguiling his idle time at Tœplitz" (71), Lucy's employer is

> overcome with anger and indignation, that her brother-in-law, Prince Ivan Drascovitz, should stoop to pay attentions to a poor governess. "And what," thought she, "if, with his perverse and wilful disposition, he should be weak enough to marry her? Knowing it to be the very thing to displease all his family,—what a horrible idea!"(71)

For a large part of the novel, the Russian prince pursues Lucy, never respecting her lack of consent. Rather, he regards Lucy as conquerable by tact or force. Prince Ivan's antithesis in the novel is another military man, the gentlemanly Colonel Falconer. Having been posted to India, he has been unaware of his fiancée's difficulties. Back in England, he sets out across Europe in search of her as soon as he learns about her having gone out as a governess. A similar pair of contrasted male characters is found in another governess novel set abroad—E. P. Hamilton's *The English Governess in Russia* (1861), in which a man who has neither wife nor children employs the unsuspecting Adelaide. As soon as her fiancé learns about her precarious situation, he embarks on a voyage to rescue her. However, both Lucy and Adelaide manage to escape from their Russian villains unaided, and later marry their fiancés.

As a contrast to the unwanted attention, the heroine is respectfully wooed by the man she later marries. Even if the contrast is not always as clear-cut, many novels delineate an opposition between two men who are attracted to the governess. It may be noted, too, that several of the male characters who imperil the honor of the heroine are decidedly non-English; in addition to the Russians referred to above, the West Indian Hercules Marsden in Blessington's *The Governess* is the total opposite of Clara's fiancé. Although the reader never doubts the heroines' virtue, the encounter with dangerous men who try to seduce them can be seen as a kind of test that the governess character has to master on her developmental journey.

What kinds of men do governess characters marry, then? To a certain extent, there is conformity between the profession of the heroine's father and that of her future husband. Thus, clergymen's daughters, such as Sherwood's Caroline Mordaunt and Anne Brontë's Agnes Grey, marry men of the Church; gentlemen's daughters such as Lady Blessington's Clara Mordaunt marry titled men, and Lucy Clifford in *Chance and Choice; or, the Education of Circumstances: The Young Governess*, who is an officer's daughter, marries a military man. When governess heroines marry, their educational journey comes to a close. After having been thrown upon the world and encountered difficulties, they are eventually reestablished in society by marriage.

In some respects, the genre of governess novels follows the formula of romance novels. Thus, most heroines go through an important change in the opening of the novel; they encounter difficult and even threatening situations and people, but they are usually restored to happiness in the end. What makes the genre differ from the romantic formula is the presence of a debate. Through scenes, characteristics, rhetoric, and more or less overt references to the key issues in the contemporary debate about the situation of governesses, the novels provide a vital part of that debate. As Miss Ross put it in *The Governess; or, Politics in Private Life:*

In presenting my little work to the Public, I am fully aware of the criticism and the censure to which I expose myself; if, however, I succeed in bringing the subject on which I have principally written, into discussion, I shall be satisfied. My labour will not have been in vain; for I am persuaded, it is one which, if freely and impartially canvassed, must be amended. (309)

Miss Ross was one of many writers who chose the governess character as a central figure not only for the reason that she could be made into a romantic heroine, but explicitly because they wished to improve the situation of a marginalized group in society.

The genre of Victorian governess novels is of interest to modern readers and scholars for several reasons. The large number of governess novels published during the nineteenth century, the highly specialized topic of the genre, and its consistent argument concerning governess employment indicate how important the governess problem was perceived to be, by writers and readers alike. Like no other literary genre, the Victorian governess novel focuses on the difficulties encountered by women who enter paid employment. Often written by women who had personal experience of teaching, and perhaps even of governessing, these works also take an active stand in the educational debate of the time, clearly refuting the traditional emphasis on accomplishments in female education, for instance. Like much minor fiction, governess novels focus more strongly on the topic they aim to discuss than on the artistic representation of it. Thus, we find detailed argument on subject matters such as reversed fortunes, female employment, and education presented in a highly formalized framework. Whereas contemporary articles give one side of the governess debate, the novels often supply a complementary view of a problem that was perceived as highly relevant at the time.

Despite the specialized topic of the genre, the catalytic propensities of the governess character enable the novels to explore more general issues such as middle-class stability and gender roles. To what extent, for instance, does the governess heroine bring the Victorian striving for progress and social mobility into focus? Furthermore, how does the governess heroine subvert the notions of the Victorian female ideal? Although carefully portrayed as endowed with feminine qualities, like no other Victorian female character, the governess heroine leaves the boundaries of the domestic sphere and ventures out into the world unprotected.

Although the highly specialized topic of the governess novel is what makes it interesting, this is also the reason for it having fallen into obscurity. Still not totally vanished, the governess novel nonetheless expired as a genre when new areas for female employment appeared and the position of the governess no longer was on the social agenda. Although the twentieth century saw many novels with professional heroines, no genre like the governess novel can be seen as a clear descendant—probably because no line of employment has entailed the intermediate position of the governess. However, modern society may harbor similar female opportunities of employment. Although au-pair girls of today, for instance, go out for completely different reasons, many of them experience the marginalized position and intermediate station described in Victorian governess novels. Who knows? Before long we may see the rise of a new genre—the au-pair novel.

WORKS CITED

Adburgham, Alison. *Silver Fork Society: Fashionable Life and Literature from 181 to 1840*. London: Constable, 1983.

Appleton, Elizabeth. *Private Education; or, a Practical Plan for the Studies of Young Ladies With an Address to Parents, Private Governesses, and Young Ladies*. 1815. London: Colburn, 1816.

Ardener, Edwin. "The 'Problem' Revisited." *Perceiving Women*. Ed. Shirley Ardener. London: Malaby P, 1975.

Barker, Juliet. *The Brontës*. London: Phoenix, 1995.

Beaty, Jerome. "*Jane Eyre* and Genre." *Genre* Winter 1977: 619–54.

———. *Misreading* Jane Eyre. *A Postformalist Paradigm*. Columbus: Ohio State UP, 1996.

Beeton, Isabella. *Beeton's Book of Household Management*. 1861. London: Chancellor, 1994.

Blessington (Gardiner), Marguerite, Countess of. *The Governess*. 1839. Paris: Baudry, 1840.

Braddon, Mary Elizabeth. *Lady Audley's Secret*. 1862. Oxford: Oxford UP: 1987.

Brontë, Anne. *Agnes Grey*. 1847. London: Penguin, 1988.

Brontë, Charlotte. *Jane Eyre*. 1847. London: Oxford World's Classics, 1985.

Buckley, Julia. *Emily, the Governess: A Tale*. London: n.p., 1836.

Bulwer Lytton, Rosina. *Very Successful*. London: Whittaker, 1856.

Carey, Rosa Nouchette. *Only the Governess*. 1888. London: Macmillan, 1920.

Chance and Choice; or, the Education of Circumstances. Tale I. The Young Governess. London: Parker, 1850.

Charlotte's Governess. London: Stevens, 1902.

Cheap, Eliza. *The Nursery Governess*. London: Seeley, 1845.

Clifton, Irene. *The Little Governess*. London: Partridge, 1900.

Craik, Dinah Mulock. *Bread upon the Waters: A Governess's Life*. 1852. Leipzig: Tauchnitz, 1865.

———. *A Woman's Thoughts About Women*. 1858. London: Hurst, n.d.

Edgeworth, Maria. "The Good French Governess." *The Bracelets and The Good French Governess*. London: Houlston, 1868.

Fielding, Sarah. *The Governess; or, the Little Female Academy*. 1749. London: Oxford UP, 1968.

Fowler, Alistair. *Kinds of Literature: An Introduction to the Theory of Genres and Modes.* Oxford: Clarendon, 1982.

Gogmagog-Hall; or, the Philosophical Lord and the Governess. London: Whittaker, 1819. 3 vols.

"The Governess Question." *English Woman's Journal* Nov. 1859: 163–70.

Governesses' Benevolent Institution. *Reports of the Board of Management, 1843–1853.* London: Brewster, 1844–54.

Hall, Anna Maria (Mrs. S. C. Hall). *The Governess. A Tale. Stories of the Governess.* London: Governesses' Benevolent Institution, 1852.

Hamilton, E. P. *The English Governess in Russia.* London: Nelson, 1861.

Hints on Early Education Addressed to Mothers: By a Mother. London: Masters, 1852.

"Hints on the Modern Governess System." *Fraser's Magazine for Town and Country* Nov. 1844: 571–83.

Hofland, Barbara. *Ellen the Teacher.* 1814. London: Griffith, 1879.

Hunt, Margaret (Mrs. Alfred Hunt), and Violet Hunt. *The Governess.* London: Chatto, 1912.

Jameson, Anna. *The Relative Position of Mothers and Governesses.* 1846. London: Spottiswoode, 1862.

Lecaros, Cecilia Wadsö. *The Victorian Governess Novel.* Lund, Swed.: Lund UP, 2001.

Lewis, Sarah. "On the Social Position of Governesses." *Fraser's Magazine for Town and Country* April 1848: 411–14.

Margaret Stourton; or, a Year of Governess Life. London: Rivingtons, 1863.

Marshall, Emma. *The Governess; or, Pleading Voices.* 1876. Norwich: Jarrold, n.d.

Martineau, Harriet. "The Governess: Her Health." *Once a Week* 1 Sept. 1860: 267–72.

Maurice, Mary. *Governess Life: Its Trials, Duties and Encouragements.* London: Parker, 1849.

M'Crindell, Rachel. *The English Governess: A Tale of Real Life.* London: Dalton, 1844.

Mitchell, Juliet. *Women: The Longest Revolution, Essays in Feminism, Literature and Psychoanalysis.* London: Virago, 1994.

Nash, Susan A. "'Wanting a Situation': Governesses and Victorian Novels." Diss. U of New Jersey, 1980.

Oliphant, Margaret. *Janet.* London: Hurst, 1891.

Peterson, M. Jeanne. "The Victorian Governess: Status Incongruence in Family and Society." *Suffer and Be Still: Women in the Victorian Age.* Ed. Martha Vicinus. Bloomington: Indiana UP, 1973. 3–19.

Poovey, Mary. *Uneven Developments. The Ideological Work of Gender in Mid-Victorian England.* Chicago: U of Chicago P, 1988.

Rigby, Elizabeth (Lady Eastlake). Rev. of *Vanity Fair* and *Jane Eyre. Quarterly Review* 84 Dec. 1848: 153–85.185.

Robbins, Bruce. *The Servant's Hand: English Fiction from Below.* 1986. Durham: Duke UP, 1993.

Ross, Miss. *The Governess; or, Politics in Private Life.* London: Smith, 1836.

Russell, Dora. *The Vicar's Governess. A Novel.* London: n.p., 1874.

S., H. *Anecdotes of Mary; or, the Good Governess.* London: Newbury, 1795.

Selous, Henry Courtney. *The Young Governess: A Tale for Girls.* 1871. London: Griffin, 1872.

Sewell, Elizabeth. *Amy Herbert.* 1844. London: Longman, 1858.

———. *Principles of Education, Drawn from Nature and Revelation, and Applied to Female Education in the Upper Classes.* London: Longman, 1865.

Sherwood, Mary Martha. *Caroline Mordaunt; or, The Governess.* 1835. London: Darton, n.d.

Showalter, Elaine. "Feminist Criticism in the Wilderness." *Critical Inquiry* Winter 1981: 179–205.

Shuttleworth, Sally. "Demonic Mothers: Ideologies of Bourgeois Motherhood in the Mid-Victorian Era." *Rewriting the Victorians: Theory, History, and the Politics of Gender.* Ed. Linda M. Shires. New York: Routledge, 1992.

Thomson, Patricia. *The Victorian Heroine: A Changing Ideal 1837–1873.* London: Oxford UP, 1956.

Warden, Florence. *The House on the Marsh.* London: William Stevens, 1883.

Wood, Ellen (Mrs. Henry). *East Lynne.* 1861. London: Dent, 1994.

NOTES

1. This chapter is based on my study *The Victorian Governess Novel* (Lund UP, 2001), which defines the Victorian governess novel as a specific genre, and positions it in the contemporary debate of female middle-class work. The study is based on comprehensive material consisting of approximately eighty-five novels, forty-five manuals and advice books, thirty-five contemporary articles, and five diaries and collections of letters.

2. I am indebted to Edwin Ardener's research on the cultural spheres of men and women and Elaine Showalter's article "Feminist Criticism in the Wilderness," in which she comments on Ardener's model.

3. Often referred to as the fashionable novel, the silver-fork novel was a prolific literary genre from the 1820s to the 1840s (see, e.g., Adburgham). The best-known writers of these novels were Catherine Gore, Theodor Hook, and Marguerite Blessington. With an increasing middle-class fascination for high life and aristocracy and an increasing middle-class readership, these novels became very popular. Since the governess character could easily be made into an observer of her employer's life, it is not surprising that some governess novels share some traits with the silver-fork novels.

3

The Detective Maidservant

Catherine Crowe's Susan Hopley

Lucy Sussex

The year 1841 is when detective fiction is popularly regarded to have been "born," with Poe's first Chevalier Dupin story, "The Murders in the Rue Morgue," published in April of that year. This "conception" is, however, somewhat erroneous, as Poe had notable detective fiction precursors. Consider William Godwin, father of Mary Shelley and author of *Caleb Williams* (1794), the eponymous hero being regarded as the first detective in fiction; and the 1827 anonymous novel *Richmond; or, the Adventures of a Bow Street Runner*, which initiated the police detective as protagonist. These instances are well known to crime fiction historians, and there are many others. More obscure names worthy of greater attention include the German playwright Adolph Müllner, who wrote the 1828 "Der Kaliber" ("The Caliber") a forensic mystery dependent upon—as the title indicates—a murder weapon's caliber. Significant among this regiment of little-known crime writers are women authors, such as Frances Trollope, mother of Anthony and a formidable writer in many genres.

Those appreciative of that modern crime fiction trope the female detective should note that it has a long history (or herstory), effectively beginning with Ann Radcliffe's *The Mysteries of Udolpho* (1794). This work is generally classed as a novel in the female gothic mode, but its sustained mystery and suspense was influential upon the emergent crime fiction genre, and its heroine Emily can be read as a prototype female sleuth. Her structural role is certainly comparable to that of the detective, being a rational elucidator of the mysteries of the castle, which includes searching for traces of crime.

Emily was followed by other examples of female proto-sleuths, and it might be argued that this trope was rather more common in early Victorian fiction than her male counterpart. The antecedents of the woman detective appear, for instance, in writers as diverse as Jane Austen (*Northanger Abbey*, 1818), Hoffnung ("Mademoiselle de Scudéry," 1820), and James Hogg (*The Private Memoirs and Confessions of a Justified Sinner*, 1824). Indeed a novel containing no fewer than three female detectives, which is also arguably the most substantial work of early crime by a woman, appeared in the same year, 1841, as Poe's "seminal" "Morgue." Crime fiction historians have not noted that he was preceded, by only a few months, by an English novel called *Adventures of Susan Hopley; or, Circumstantial Evidence*. It was advertised as "now ready" in the *Athenaeum* of January 9 (38).

Subsequent editions of the novel had a different title: *Susan Hopley; or, the Adventures of a Maid-Servant*, which suggested a domestic fiction. However, as the original subtitle made clear, *Susan Hopley* is also a novel of mystery, crime, and detection, being constructed around a crime investigation, a murder, and disappearance occurring in the first few chapters and solved only at the novel's end. It fulfills John Cawelti's definition of a classical detective story, that is, it "begins with an unsolved crime, and moves toward the elucidation of its mystery" (80).

In 1841, however, the word "mystery" suggested not crime but the gothic, as in *Udolpho*, with its long drawn-out use of suspense; the following year the term was to become associated with the "Mysteries," a feuilleton novel form of which the most famous example was Eugene Sue's 1842–43 *Les Mystères de Paris*. Sue's novel and its many imitations comprised sprawling and near interminable tomes of what might be described as "urban melodrama." Though they included crime matter, they can be effectively regarded as a Neanderthal dead end on the detective fiction evolutionary tree; in terms of crime fiction history it is Poe's Dupin stories that can be regarded as the Cro-Magnon of the crime genre.

Susan Hopley is a novel that, although anticipating the multivolume and interconnected crime narratives of Sue, is far closer to modern crime fiction (and Poe) in its rigorously organized narrative structure. The novel is intricately plotted: My detailed synopsis covers pages of foolscap. An early reviewer, John Forster (later to be Dickens' biographer) noted that the contents of its three volumes were highly "interdependent and interwoven with each other" (132). Moreover, the book is most unusual—for the time—in that its story of crime and consequences is generally told through the experience of women.

The novel puzzled Forster—indeed it was an original, arguably so far ahead of its time as to defy the contemporary critical vocabulary: "We hardly know what to say of this book. It perplexes us extremely. It is powerful, beyond all question; but unsatisfactory ... . When we had read the first twenty pages, the book was not again laid down" (132). He almost struggles for the words to describe the author's careful accumulation of clues:

His incidents, at first minute and carelessly thrown in, grow up by degrees into matters of great importance and elaborate art. Precisely as in real life, facts and recollections of apparently the most trivial kind, which have got remotely away in some inaccessible corner of the memory, come gradually out into more and more prominence, until, some last link in a long chain of occurrences wanting, they suddenly and thoroughly supply it. The writer, in a word, has the art of *reality*. You are struck with the trifling minutenesses, yet find them not so trifling as you at first supposed. (132)

Susan Hopley was published anonymously, and Forster reviewed it as a man's work. Subsequently the novel was acknowledged as the creation of a woman: Catherine Crowe (1800–72). She was born Catherine Stevens in Kent, and after her marriage to Lieutenant Colonel John Crowe in 1822, moved to Edinburgh, then a center of writing activity, with magazines such as *Blackwood's* and *Chambers' Edinburgh Journal*. Here she moved in literary and intellectual circles, having wide interests, including the fashionable pseudoscience of phrenology, based on the interpretation of bumps in the skull. Alexander Ireland recalled her as a "very clever, eccentric person" with "the reputation of dabbling a little in science." She was even credited with writing the anonymously published *Vestiges of the Natural History of Creation* (1844), a cause célèbre for its subject matter—the book being an important if somewhat wrong-headed precursor of Darwin's *Origins of Species*. It was also attributed to individuals as diverse as Ada Lovelace and Prince Albert. Crowe was unique, however, in being accused of the authorship of "that naughty book" while at the dinner table of the actual (though unknown to almost everyone present) author, Robert Chambers. Her response was to laugh and say nothing.[1]

Some indication of her standing within the Edinburgh intelligentsia, as well as her "eccentricity," is given by the following anecdote. In 1847 Crowe was invited to a dinner for the famous children's fabulist Hans Christian Andersen. It was a memorable evening, the host being Dr. James Young Simpson, who would several months later discover chloroform. Simpson used himself as an experimental subject; and also on this night, his guests. Andersen recorded in his diary: "Dinner at Dr Simpson's, where Miss Crowe and yet another authoress drank ether; I had a feeling of being with two mad people, they laughed with open, dead, eyes. There is something uncanny about this; I find it wonderful for an operation, but not as a way of tempting God" (qtd. in Bredsdorff 194). Crowe was a writer of much versatility; and it is her working in various literary forms that makes her problematic for the literary critic, as she does not, to quote Foucault's critique of the canon, represent "a certain unity of writing," nor a single "source of expression" (111). She is generally (and wrongly) classed as a writer of domestic realism, although she also wrote for children, adapting *Uncle Tom's Cabin* for the younger reader in 1853. However, she is perhaps best known for her interest in the paranormal, having an early and profound involvement in the Spiritualist movement, in which mediums summoning table-rapping spirits became almost a form of Victorian parlor game. Her involvement in this area began with her translation (London, 1845) from the German of Andreas Justinus Kerner's *The Seeress of Prevorst*, an account of a noted clairvoyant. Three years later she followed with *The Night Side of Nature* (London, Newby, 1848), an original, pioneering, and clear-eyed investigation of psychic phenomena. In its introduction she declared her belief that the supernatural would eventually come "within the bounds of science" (17).

The Night Side was highly influential, being read avidly and widely. It was cited, for instance, in the celebrated ghost story "What Was It?" (1859) by the Irish-American writer Fitzjames O'Brien. In O'Brien's story, a reading group of Crowe fans are well primed by her text for the arrival of an actual apparition: "One of the boarders, who had purchased Mrs. Crowe's 'Night Side of Nature' for his own private delectation, was regarded as a public enemy for not having bought twenty copies. A system of espionage was established, of which he was the victim. If he incautiously laid the book down for an instant and left the room, it was immediately seized, and read aloud in secret places to a select few" (828). Yet the popularity of *The Night Side*, still regarded as an important text by Spiritualists, obscures Crowe's day side, and arguably her real significance—her work as a fiction writer. Moreover, her interest in the paranormal ultimately led to a mental crisis, from which she (and her literary reputation) never recovered.

Susan Hopley was her first novel, although she had previously published the forgotten and forgettable verse tragedy *Aristodemus*. The novel begins with two elderly people, Harry Leeson and Susan Hopley. He is the owner of a wealthy estate, and she is his companion-housekeeper (there is never any suggestion that the relationship extends beyond that). The book is an account of their early lives, Harry being the writer but also transcriber of Susan's speech: "whose own words we shall frequently take the liberty of using" (8).

As a child, Leeson is part heir to a fortune, the other heir being Fanny Wentworth, engaged to Mr. Walter Gaveston, who is resolved to inherit *all* the property. He first tries to drown Harry, but Andrew Hopley, Susan's brother, saves Harry's life. Subsequently Fanny's father, Mr. Wentworth, is found murdered and Andrew goes missing, along with another servant, Mabel Jones. Gaveston accuses Andrew of murdering Mr. Wentworth for his money and fleeing with Mabel, this story being generally believed. In addition the will benefiting Harry cannot be found.

Susan, who has had a foreboding dream, turns sleuth, as an *Atheneaum* reviewer notes: "Through all the intricacies of the story, she winds her way with preternatural ease—the Dea Vindix ['Avenging goddess,' in her Greek form known as Nemesis] who unties all its knots."[2] She becomes the principal detective of the text, the first in a series of amateur investigators found throughout the novel. "Her most earnest desire ... was to go over the house that had been the scene of the catastrophe, and inspect every part of it herself" (Crowe, *Susan* 34): Although Susan lacks the magnifying glass of Sherlock Holmes, she inspects the scene of the crime. Having "a notion that she might make some discovery by examining the ground under the window of Andrew's room" (37), she finds significant evidence. However, it is not evidence upon which this relatively powerless individual can act. Susan is only a servant, who could be suspected of "having the purpose of shifting odium from her own family to others" (42). The family having sacked her for being sister to the murder suspect, she goes to London in search of work. There, she finds more evidence of Gaveston's perfidy, including Julia Clerk, a fallen woman with a small child.

The narrative technique of *Susan Hopley* is to switch between viewpoints, from Harry to Susan and back again. Now an interlude, occupying chapters 16–22, tells the story of Julia's mother, Julie Le Moine. This character is an example of the thwarted female detective *par excellence:* "[B]orn with the spirit of a heroine, the passions of a Medea and the temper of a vixen" (167). Her lover Valentine (the passion being unrequited, for he loves another woman) is accused of attempted murder, and this spurs Julie into action, certain that her rival will "weep, but she'll do nothing" (137). In any case she had been spying on Valentine on the night in question, and saw some suspicious characters in the vicinity. With the help of her maid and confidante Madeleine, Julie cuts her hair, dresses as a page, and tracks the real villains to their den. She discovers important evidence—but is shut in a cellar with a corpse for her pains. At this point her strength of mind deserts her, as is typical with early Victorian female detectives of the heroine ilk (whose sleuthing success is usually followed by physical or mental breakdowns, from which they emerge suitably chastised for their "unwomanliness" and ready to marry the hero). Crowe comments: "Many's the time that love has conquered fear, even in the most timid breasts, as it had thus done in poor Julie's—she must be forgiven if fear for a short time gained the ascendant and the heroine sunk into the woman" (141). Madeleine summons the police, who track Julie and rescue her, but during the ordeal in the cellar the sleuth has gone mute, losing her voice permanently. She has proved Valentine innocent, but gained and lost from the discovery. He marries her, from pity and a sense of duty, and unsurprisingly, the marriage is unhappy.

Within the greater context of *Susan Hopley*, Julie's story represents a perfect encapsulated female detective narrative, told with a skill that would make it eminently suitable for inclusion in a historical anthology of the female detective. She reappears in the novel, as a mute but formidable figure of action, an innkeeper from hell, gaining a long delayed but highly satisfying revenge on the villains who imprisoned her. However, the narrative returns first to Harry's adventures, then back to its original female detective, Susan, who moves from employment to employment, generally using her detective skills efficiently.

A female employer of hers is accused of stealing lace from a shop—Susan proves her innocent. The next employer has three daughters, the eldest of whom marries a bogus Italian count, Susan accompanying the bride and her sisters on a continental honeymoon tour. There she meets the missing servant milkmaid Mabel, now called Amabel, who has become the common-law wife of a French duke. However, Mabel/Amabel knows nothing of Susan's missing brother. The two women join forces, both having been wronged by Gaveston, to uncover the mystery and find justice. Other detectives are in pursuit, too. A clerk from Wentworth's firm and the family lawyer all join in the chase, which culminates in a climactic court scene. Most of the villains in the book prove to be Gaveston and his cronies under different names. At the end, the murdered body of Andrew Hopley is found by the novel's detectives, and Susan is vindicated.

Susan Hopley is a triumph of complex plotting, a woven design of crime whose threads all come neatly together at the end. Forster notes: "there is no end to the circumstantial plots and counterplots, of which [Susan] is first the unconscious and unhappy centre, and at last the quiet and triumphant unraveller" (although in his opinion too many of its plot threads are broken for a final successful tapestry). It is significant as perhaps the first substantial novel of crime by a woman, even without its female detectives, the humble-born, efficient, and imperturbable servant Susan, Julie, and, to a lesser extent, Mabel/Amabel.

Yet recent critical attention given to the book has been scant, with the exception of Sally Mitchell's *The Fallen Angel* (1981), which noted its sympathetic treatment of fallen women. John Sutherland, in *The Longman Companion to Victorian Fiction*, calls the novel a "simply written romance" (615) and further indicates he had not read it by declaring Susan to be a colonel's daughter. That revelation does not occur in *Susan Hopley* but in Crowe's later novel *The Story of Lilly Dawson* (1847).

The novelist Adeline Sergeant, writing in 1897, was rather more perceptive, noting that the book "had all the ingredients of a sensational story" (which term, from the 1860s, it considerably predated) and that "Susan's energy" for detection is a key factor in exposing Gaveston (157). The richness of *Susan Hopley*'s tableaux and its ornate crime plotting deserve much more attention. And its influence cannot be underestimated. It is difficult to see how Poe could have been unaware of the work, either as a book or in its adaptation for the stage, which occurred within six months of the original publication, and toured internationally.

Sally Mitchell notes *Susan Hopley*'s use of "carefully controlled viewpoints to provide suspense," a "technical experiment" used and "polished" by "later detective writers, most notably Wilkie Collins ... until it became both a conventional form and a philosophical approach to the question of reality" (164). However, Collins took more than the viewpoint technique from *Susan Hopley*. "Anne Rodway" (1856), his first crime story, had as its protagonist a maid-detective. Furthermore a plot device from *Susan Hopley*—identifying a criminal by cutting, unobserved, a scrap of cloth from their clothing, then producing it, like a jigsaw piece, in evidence—reappears in his novel *No Name* (1862).

Susan Hopley was a best-seller among all classes of society, with its editions priced for the circulating library clientele (three-volume form), then as less expensive weekly and subsequently monthly numbers, and a "Cheap Genuine Edition." It also had interference run by the hack writer T. P. Prest,[3] who published in 1842 *Susan Hoply: or, the Trials and Vicissitudes of a Servant Girl*—a "violent romance," says Sadleir, which had nothing to do with Crowe's novel apart from the deliberate similarity of title. (1: 56) The novel also enjoyed a second lease on life, much as today's novels do via filming, being adapted as a crime melodrama by George Dibden Pitt. The play was first performed in London on 31 May, 1841, with great success: "Susan Hopley ... has been applauded in London for upwards of three hundred nights, and in the provinces for about as many more. She has travelled to America and to Sydney."[4]

The sensation fiction author Mary Braddon was very familiar with the theater version, indeed professionally so; she was a member of the Henry Nye Chart theatrical company, which toured with the play. Almost certainly she played one of its female roles, possibly even the lead of Susan Hopley herself (Carnell 1999). Such is suggested by an 1861 letter she wrote to the journalist George Augustus Sala, apropos of his renting a country house called Upton Court:

I am glad you are in Buckinghamshire, and not at Upton [the site of Pitt's melodrama] where Susan Hopley lived and everybody murdered each other. To a person of my theatrical experience there is always something rather awful in the sound of "Upton." I am sure you must have "my murdered brother, Andrew," walled up in your bedroom. Some day, when you are shaving or hanging up your coat, you will touch a secret spring in the wainscot, and he will come out with a back-fall, green and festering. (qtd. in Wolff 486)

The constraints of performance meant that the story of *Susan Hopley* was modified considerably in its progress from book to stage, not only in the change of scene to Upton. Pitt, in his need to reduce the narrative to three acts (a miniseries would have best suited the novel as a whole, had the form existed in the 1840s), simplified the text considerably. He removed most of the detection and also Julie, perhaps the most interesting figure in the book. Thus the play version was not as strikingly an anticipation of the modern detective story as the original novel. Crowe had no say in the production. Indeed the weakness of the existing copyright laws meant that she could not intervene legally to stop, modify, or even benefit from the performances. *Susan Hopley* was thus pirated and she did not receive a penny of the proceeds.

Crowe wrote more novels, of which the most generically crime was *Men and Women; or, Manorial Rights* (1843). She was producing novels at the same rate that Poe was producing his short detective stories, his "Facts in the Case of Marie Roget," being published in 1842–43. *Men and Women* again had a theme of circumstantial evidence, with a more rigorous structure: Sir John Eastlake is found shot dead, and three suspects are, one after the other, accused of the crime. As a reviewer in the *Examiner* noted:

The weight of circumstance bears heavily on all three; as one slowly emerges, it is only that the cloud may more darkly envelope the other ... . A great many persons are introduced, and all, with a wonderful constructive art, are made to serve some purpose in detection of the master-crime. Incidents with no visible connection, but of indefinable sympathy rise in almost every chapter: gradually the link is formed, the chain of evidence imperceptibly extends, and the murderer is enmeshed.[5]

It was Crowe's involvement in Spiritualism that led to a scandal in early 1854, which was reported gleefully and widely, in the newspapers, anti-Spiritualist magazines, and by sundry literary gossips. By her own account, after an illness in Edinburgh on 26 February, Crowe suffered a period of mental disturbance lasting five or six days. On the 7th of March, in London, Dickens wrote to a correspondent that

[Catherine Crowe] has gone stark mad—and stark naked—on the spirit-rapping imposition. She was found t'other day in the street, clothed only in her chastity, a pocket-handkerchief and a visiting-card. She had been informed, it appeared, by the spirits, that if she went in that trim she would be invisible. She is now in a madhouse, and, I fear, hopelessly insane. One of the curious manifestations of her disorder is that she can bear nothing black. (7: 285–86)

The source of the story is unknown, but it certainly spread at an alarming rate. Crowe wrote to the press and protested that she had done nothing of the sort, though allowing that she had experienced what would now be termed a breakdown. She had, she said, fallen for some days into "a state of unconsciousness [and] aberration" in which she "talked of the spirit-rapping, and fancied spirits were directing" her writing, quite appropriately, as her current topic *was* Spiritualism. She added that she was not "mad about spirits or anything else," although she admitted in a letter to one publication that she had briefly been sent to an asylum before recovering (Dickens 7: 286).

The story was persistent, false though it was, and especially unlikely, given late winter weather conditions in Edinburgh, when even a madwoman would hesitate to venture outside naked. It was rather too entertaining to be squashed, not least because of the absurd visual image created: of a respected middle-aged female author as Lady Godiva. Moreover, it was all too easily credited by those with prejudices against women and their writing, not to mention Spiritualism—against which there was an emergent backlash. Dickens' response was probably typical; he had earlier been intrigued by psychic phenomena, in 1848 knowledgeably if skeptically reviewing *The Night Side* in the *Examiner*. His review began with these words: "The authoress of 'Susan Hopley' and 'Lilly Dawson' has established her title to a hearing whenever she chooses to claim one. She can never be read without pleasure and profit, and can never write otherwise than sensibly and well."[6]

Now he dismissed Crowe as a "medium and an Ass," although she had never claimed to have any supernatural powers. Dickens knew Crowe, for he had published her in his magazine *Household Words*, and had invited her to dinner (the other guests including the Carlyles and Elizabeth Gaskell)—yet he dismissed her illness callously. However, in the same paragraph, he allowed that *Susan Hopley* was "rather a clever story" (Dickens 7: 288).

It seems likely that Crowe's breakdown was precipitated by the strain of defending her Spiritualist beliefs, with the unpleasant irony that it was then used as ammunition by the anti-Spiritualists. Clearly her reputation suffered from the calumny. It is said that "she wrote little" subsequently, although her writing continued to appear, if sporadically and mainly in reprint form (R.G., 237). Her last book was a short nonfiction treatise, *Spiritualism and the Age We Live In*, which Diana Basham calls "obviously troubled"—not surprisingly if it was what she was writing at the time of her illness (154). After that date, like her heroine Julie, she was effectively silenced. Gaskell records her in 1865 as regularly staying in a hotel in Dieppe, most probably to save money, and she died in 1872 (778–79).

At present, given her more than 150 years of neglect, it is hardly surprising that none of Crowe's works is in print; indeed she lacks scholarly editions and even a biography. Yet she was a writer of considerable range and interest and has more than historical significance as an early woman crime author.

WORKS CITED

Basham, Diana. *The Trial of Woman: Feminism and the Occult Sciences in Victorian Literature and Society.* London: Macmillan, 1992.

Bredsdorff, Elias. *Hans Christian Andersen: The Story of His Life and Work, 1805–75.* New York: Scribner, 1975.

Carnell, Jennifer. E-mail to Lucy Sussex. 14 Dec. 1999.

Cawelti, John. *Adventure, Mystery and Romance: Formula Stories As Art and Popular Culture.* Chicago: U of Chicago P, 1976.

Crowe, Catherine. *Aristodemus.* Edinburgh: Tait, 1838.

———. *Men and Women; or, Manorial Rights.* London, 1843.

———. *The Night Side of Nature.* London: Newby, 1848.

———, trans. *The Seerest of Prevorst; Being Revelations Concerning the Inner-life of Man, and the Inter-diffusion of a World of Spirits in the One We Inhabit.* By Justinus Andreas Christian Kerner. London: J. C. Moore, 1845.

———. *Spiritualism and the Age We Live In.* London: Newby, 1859.

———. *The Story of Lilly Dawson.* London: Colburn, 1847.

———. *Susan Hopley; or, The Adventures of a Maid-Servant.* 1841. London: Nicholson, n.d.

Cumberland's Minor Theatre. London, n.d.

Dickens, Charles. *The Letters of Charles Dickens.* Vols. 2, 3, 5–7. Clarendon, Oxford, 1974–93.

Forster, John. Rev. of *Susan Hopley; or, Circumstantial Evidence,* by Catherine Crowe. *Examiner* 28 Feb. 1841: 132.

Foucault, Michel. "What Is an Author?" *The Foucault Reader.* Ed. Paul Rabinow. Middlesex: Penguin, 1984.

Garnett, Richard. "Catherine Crowe." *Dictionary of National Biography.* Vol. 5: 237.

Gaskell, Elizabeth. *Letters.* Ed. J. A.V. Chapple and Arthur Pollard. Manchester: Manchester UP, 1966.

Ireland, Alexander. Introduction. *Vestiges of the Natural History of Creation.* 12th ed. By Robert Chambers. London: Chambers, 1884.

Mitchell, Sally. *The Fallen Angel: Chastity, Class and Women's Reading 1835–1880.* Bowling Green, OH: Bowling Green U Popular P, 1981.

O'Brien, Fitzjames. "What Was It?" *Australian Journal* 25 Aug. 1866: 827–30.

Prest, T. P. *Susan Hoply: or, The Trials and Vicissitudes of a Servant Girl.* London: Lloyd, 1842.

Richmond; or, the Adventures of a Bow Street Runner. London: Colburn, 1827.

Sadleir, Michael. *XIX Fiction, a Bibliographical Record Based on His Own Collection.* London: Constable, 1951. 2 vols.

Secord, James. E-mail to Lucy Sussex. 11 Oct. 1999.

———. *Victorian Sensations: The Extraordinary Publications, Reception, and Secret Authorsip of Vestiges of the Natural History of Creation.* Chicago: U of Chicago P, 2000.

Sergeant, Adeline. "Mrs. Crowe. Mrs. Archer Clive. Mrs Henry Wood." *Women Novelists of Queen Victoria's Reign: A Book of Appreciations.* 1897. London: Norwood, 1977.

Sutherland, John. *The Longman Companion to Victorian Fiction.* Harlow: Longman, 1988.

Wolff, Robert Lee. *Sensational Victorian: The Life and Fiction of Mary Elizabeth Braddon.* New York: Garland, 1979.

NOTES

1. Ireland, xx. He does not name Crowe, but she is identified by James Secord in *Victorian Sensation.*

2. Jan. 1841: 94.

3. Prest also wrote *Sweeny Todd.*

4. Remarks. *Cumberland's Minor Theatre:* 8.

5. Dec. 1843: 788.

6. Feb. 1848: 131.

Deathbeds and Didacticism

Charlotte Elizabeth Tonna and Victorian Social Reform Literature

Mary Lenard

In her 1977 book, *Literary Women*, feminist critic Ellen Moers wrote: "Of all the minor women of the epic age, this lady ... Mrs. Tonna ... is the one about whom I most wish to satisfy my curiosity" (36). Moers' curiosity was certainly warranted, as Charlotte Elizabeth Tonna's long and distinguished career as an evangelist and social reformer merits more recognition than it has received. Editor of the influential *Christian Lady's Magazine* from 1834 to 1846 and *The Protestant Annual* from 1841 to 1846, and author of several significant fictional works, Tonna was certainly known to contemporaries as an important contributor to public debates on social issues. She wrote, among other things, an anti-slavery novel, *The System* (1827); a novel about the factory system, *Helen Fleetwood* (1839–40); an exposure of the abuses of women and children laborers in *The Wrongs of Woman* (1840–44); an anonymous, nonfictional work condemning the factory system, *The Perils of the Nation* (1843); and an autobiography, *Personal Recollections* (1841).

In the years since Ellen Moers' statement, Tonna's life and work have achieved some recognition from such critics as Joseph Kestner, Barbara Kanner and Ivanka Kovacevic, Catherine Gallagher, and Christine Krueger. All of these critics recognize Tonna's importance as part of the historical record: Joseph Kestner argued, for example, that Tonna's *The Wrongs of Woman* (1843–44) is "an important text of social industrial protest" ("Industrial Protest" 212). Although Kestner closes his article with the statement that "the nineteenth-century canon must be expanded to include such achievements" (212), he fails to explain or theorize why a text that he analyzes, in effect, as a historical document should even be considered as literature. This is a problem, unfortunately, that was inherited from other critical considerations of Tonna's work—for instance, Barbara Kanner and Ivanka Kovacevic, who, when they put up a spirited defense of Tonna's historical importance in 1970, said flatly that "the literary value of her [Tonna's] writing is too mediocre to call for defense" (158).

Such assessments, however, depend on a modernist definition of literature that is outdated, narrow, and nonhistorical. Charlotte Elizabeth Tonna played a crucial part in forming a cultural discourse of social reform that perfectly fulfilled the cultural needs created by the material and historical conditions of early-nineteenth-century England, and continued to dominate Victorian literature for decades to come. This sentimentalist discourse relied on such literary conventions as the emotional depiction of illness, pain, and death; an impassioned, "preachy" direct address to readers; and typological characterization.[1] Because of its reliance on these much-maligned conventions, sentimentalism has been pointedly ignored by the literary academy. Accordingly, many critics who have attempted to recover Tonna in the past have done so by denying or ignoring her sentimentalism. Most recently, for example, Christine Krueger insisted in *The Reader's Repentance* (1992) that "Tonna tried in her fiction to eschew conventions of the lending-library romances and present as much as possible, a realistic, unsentimental picture of her subject matter" (126). This claim is inaccurate because it fails to recognize Tonna's sentimentalist innovations from the evangelical tradition that she inherited, innovations that I will demonstrate later in this essay by contrasting Tonna and her predecessor Hannah More.

Tonna is an important literary figure because she, as well as other sentimentalist social reform writers, performed the crucial cultural work that taught nineteenth-century audiences how to "read" and respond to social problems. Many scholars, both historians and literary critics, have recognized that crucial shifts in cultural attitudes toward social issues such as poverty occurred in the first few decades of the nineteenth century. A cursory glance at the literature of the period reveals such shifts; pitiable victims of social problems in nineteenth-century novels such as Dickens' *Bleak House* or Gaskell's *North and South* clearly do not belong in the abstract and comfortably ordered world of earlier social polemicists such as Hannah More.[2] The later works both follow in a more openly "feminine" tradition of sentimentalist discourse evident in writers such as Charlotte Elizabeth Tonna; they are more emotionally engaging and morally strident because they reflect important changes in nineteenth-century structures of feeling.

Cultural critic Raymond Williams uses the term "structure of feeling" to describe social attitudes and assumptions that go beyond formal ideology, encompassing cultural values as they are manifested, almost unconsciously, in popular culture and everyday life: "It is not only that we must go beyond formally held and systematic beliefs, though of course we have always to include them. It is that we are concerned with meanings and values as they are actively lived and felt ... characteristic elements of impulse, restraint, and tone; specifically affective elements of consciousness and relationships" (*Marxism* 132). Williams' term "affective" is particularly appropriate to this topic, which has everything to do with feeling. Sentimentalist novels tried to effect change by influencing the hearts and the feelings of their readers, exploiting the "feminine" cultural value of feeling for political purposes. This belief that feeling and emotion were the logical starting mechanisms for political change is exemplified by Tonna, in whose factory novel, *Helen Fleetwood,* one of the Lord Ashley-esque factory reformers says, "I hope it may please God, before long, to rouse the *feelings* of our fellow countrymen on behalf of the poor children in these mills. If that was done, we should soon see a change for the better" (326; emphasis added).[3] The rampant emotionalism of Tonna's novels, in which frequent deathbed scenes and portrayals of physical and emotional distress are presented for political ends, the very qualities that often doom them to critical obscurity, are, in short, an integral part of their cultural work, work that was essential to the shifts in nineteenth-century structures of feeling that made emotion and feeling politically meaningful.

Tonna also made skilled and impassioned use of commonly held nineteenth-century religious beliefs, beliefs that were, as I will show later, the special province of women. These religious beliefs account for almost all of her fiction's most pertinent characteristics: from the urgently didactic "preacher" rhetoric that Christine Krueger has so usefully analyzed, to the flat characterizations that draw on the traditions of biblical typology, to, again, the ubiquitous deathbed scenes. When characters such as Tonna's Helen Fleetwood, Dickens' little Dick, and Gaskell's Bessie Higgins die, they testify to "the reality of the life to come" and to all that this reality entails (Tompkins 129). To further that end, Tonna continually reminds her readers in her fiction and nonfiction that the world they know is subject to a higher power: "Oh, it is an awful thought that so many believing, confiding prayers of the poor destitute are recorded in the book of HIS remembrance, whose piercing eye is never for one moment averted from the hidden plannings of the mercenary deceiver's heart! Very terrible will be the day of public inquisition and divine retribution" (Tonna, *Fleetwood* 42–43). According to the system of eschatological Christian beliefs that guides the sentimentalist vision, the earthly world is subject to the cosmic order of a higher power, an order beginning with the Creation and ending with the Last Judgment. The purpose of sentimentalist discourse is to influence the reader not only through pathos but through the whole "feminine" system of moral and religious values that the pathos epitomizes, a value system exemplified by both the urgent preaching of a narrator and emotional enactments of Christian eschatology.

The cultural prominence of Tonna's fiction signals, therefore, important shifts in social attitudes and literary conventions—shifts that resulted in a new structure of feeling, a new cultural discourse. This sentimentalist discourse came from two major factors. The first factor is that material conditions in the first half of the nineteenth century created the need for a new, affective morality in social reform discourse. Even in the eighteenth century, social and economic changes such as enclosure, the disenfranchisement of the small farmer, the growing poverty of laborers, and population shifts from rural areas to urban areas signaled the slow death of what historian E. P. Thompson has termed the "moral economy," a traditional, paternalist social system based on complex social relationships of trust, deference, and obligation. In a historical study of the eighteenth-century grain market, Thompson argues that eighteenth-century food riots were expressions of "a popular consensus ... of the proper economic functions of several parties within the community, which ... can be said to constitute the moral economy of the poor" ("Moral Economy" 78–79). He demonstrates that an older paternalist system existing in "an eroded body of Statute law, as well as common law and custom" enforced an economy of provision in which the primary responsibility of the food producers was to meet the needs of their immediate community, even to the detriment of their own profits (83). This moral economy assumed the existence of a tightly woven community, in which all members, both producers and consumers, were responsible for each other; the local farmers, millers, and bakers, under this system, were under obligation to meet the needs of their neighbors, to "provision," in other words, at a price the local consumers could pay. Thompson maintains that in the eighteenth century, a new, more impersonal, money-based, market economy, "disinfested [sic] of intrusive moral imperatives" (90), gradually replaced this older moral economy, and that the food riots expressed popular indignation over the change.

The death of the moral economy did not result just from the victory of one economic theory over another, however, but from a complex network of social and economic changes, by which England evolved from a rural nation of small, tightly knit communities to an industrial and urban nation. Historian Francis Sheppard says that at the beginning of the nineteenth century, three-quarters of the population of England and Wales still lived in the country, or in towns with a population less than 20,000, whereas by 1871, this proportion had fallen to less than half. Raymond Williams also gives a thumbnail sketch of this process of change in *The Country and the City*, linking a rising number of displaced people in the countryside caused by the practice of enclosure to a corresponding growth of population in the cities as the new industrial system of production demanded workers. Finally, Williams contends, "the crisis of poverty, which was so marked in towns and villages alike in the late eighteenth and early nineteenth centuries, was a result of this social and economic process as a whole" (98).[4]

Although Williams refuses to characterize these social changes as "the substitution of one [social] order for another" (98), it is clear that contemporary writers, observing the growing separation of social classes, perceived the gradual disappearance of a traditional system, namely the paternalist moral economy, as a contributing cause to the crisis of poverty. Many observers lamented the moral breakdown caused by class separation and the disappearance of community in the late eighteenth and early nineteenth centuries, and these accounts increased in the 1830s and '40s, when the migration of people from the countryside to London and to the factory towns seemed to bring the situation to a state of crisis.[5] Most nineteenth-century scholars are familiar with Friedrich Engels' famous observation of this phenomenon in Manchester in *The Condition of the Working Class in England* (1844):

Owing to the curious lay-out of the town it is quite possible for someone to live for years in Manchester and to travel daily to and from his work without ever seeing a working class quarter or coming into contact with an artisan. He who visits Manchester simply on business or for pleasure need never see the slums, mainly because the working-class districts and the middle class districts are quite distinct. (54)

In London itself, the construction of railways at midcentury facilitated the middle- and upper-class move to the suburbs that intensified "the social differentiation of the various parts of London" (Sheppard 8), but it is clear that this process of class separation was already well under way even before that, provoked by the rapid expansion that led William Cobbett to call London an "infernal Wen" in 1822 (qtd. in Sheppard 83–84).[6] James Grant asserted in 1842 that "the great mass of the metropolitan community are as ignorant of the destitution and distress which prevail in large districts of London ... as if the wretched creatures were living in the very centre of Africa" (qtd. in Dyos 135).[7] This phenomenon closely resembles Engels' descriptions of Manchester, and the similarity suggests that all of Britain's cities were probably characterized by this same physical separation of classes. This conclusion is also supported by urban historian H. J. Dyos, who notes that "the bulk of the annals of the slums between the 1840s and the beginning of the 1880s are basically of this type, social reportage that was meant to supply unpleasant facts to those unlikely to obtain them for themselves" (134).

For the purposes of this study of Tonna, I am interested in the *perception* of the moral economy's breakdown, particularly as it affects the cultural discourses of the 1830s and '40s. This perception exists not only in historical observers such as Engels, but also in literary discourse, and the two became, in some ways, inseparable. One example of this phenomenon is the critical reception of Dickens' *Oliver Twist* (1837–39), in which the rookeries inhabited by Fagin's gang and Bill Sikes, quite literally are portrayed as "hideouts" where middle-class values and institutions can penetrate only with difficulty. Dickens imports a virtual army of policemen and a mob suffused with righteous indignation to bring the criminals, Bill Sikes and Fagin, to justice. Sikes is finally hunted down in Jacob's Island, a slum that Dickens calls "the filthiest, the strangest, the most extraordinary of the many localities that are hidden in London, wholly unknown, even by name, to the great mass of its inhabitants" (442).

The influence of this literary portrayal on the public imagination was illustrated in 1850, when at a meeting of the Metropolitan Sanitary Association both the bishop of London and Dickens himself made speeches in which they called attention to the problem of sanitary conditions in poor districts by referring to Jacob's Island. According to K. J. Fielding's edition of Dickens' speeches, a week later, when the Marylebone Vestry was debating whether to use tax money to educate poor children, Dickens' enemy Sir Peter Laurie[8] took the opportunity not only to oppose this measure, but to attack reformers in general, reading the passage about Jacob's Island from the bishop's speech at the Sanitary Association meeting, and saying, "The Bishop of London, poor soul ... in his simplicity, thought there really was such a place ... whereas it turned out that it only existed in a work of fiction, written by Mr. Charles Dickens ten years ago" (108–09).[9]

The real significance of the Dickens/Laurie anecdote is that it highlights the additional function(s) that cultural discourse, and particularly fiction such as the novels of Tonna, and later, of Dickens, came to fulfill in this new social environment. Laurie was able to argue that Jacob's Island didn't exist because, clearly, no one in his audience had ever been there, and had experienced the slum only through the medium of Dickens' fiction. Engels and other observers commented on the disastrous moral effects of class separation, which made it easier for the wealthier strata of society to ignore the appalling living and working conditions of the poor. As W. Cooke Taylor lamented in 1842, "We have improved on the proverb, 'One half of the world does not know how the other half lives,' changing it into 'One half of the world does not care how the other half lives'" (qtd. in Thompson *Making* 322). Since middle-class Victorian readers were increasingly isolated from the suffering caused by social problems, often the only contact they themselves had with this suffering was through the medium of written discourse, usually through fiction. Fiction, then, became the principal medium by which affective bonds were constructed between different social groups. With the devaluation of eighteenth-century sentimentalism that occurred after the French Revolution, this function in the nineteenth century was primarily identified with and performed by women authors such as Tonna, who fought their audience's indifference and desensitization to suffering with the culturally sanctioned emotionalism of their writing.[10]

The second major factor behind the new structure of feeling represented by Tonna is, therefore, the domestic ideology that gave women "natural" dominance over both morality and affect. By the 1840s, the idea that the rich and the poor were two opposing camps, isolated from each other, dominated cultural discourse.[11] The perceived need to construct affective bonds between these two groups created a new function for many women authors, who, because of their culturally sanctioned roles as guardians of "sympathy" and "mutual understanding" ("Lady Novelists" 24), figured prominently in the arena of social reform literature. The nineteenth-century reading public came to accept, even to expect, that literary works, particularly novels, would address issues such as slavery, poverty, working and housing conditions, prostitution, and so on, and equally to expect women to be the authors of these novels. It also became a widely accepted cultural truism that novels by women had an important influence over the reading public, to the great concern of conservative literary critics such as *The National Review*'s W. R. Greg, who lamented "The False Morality of Lady Novelists" in 1859. Greg's review operated within a well-established nineteenth-century critical trope that defined novels as "light literature," and therefore feminine, and characterized novel reading as "addictive, sensational, and irresponsible" (qtd. in Ferris 18). As the title of Greg's review suggests, its main purpose is to lament the moral influence that novels had on their readers, and to condemn the "fantastic and flatulent morality" of "sentimental" women novelists (158).

A few years later, in 1864, a *Westminster Review* critic commented that novelists were also politically influential, because of their ability to reach a wide audience:

The novelist is now our most influential writer. . . . The influence of the novelist is beginning, too, to be publicly acknowledged of late more frankly than was once the fashion. For a long time his power over society, except as a mere teller of stories and provider of easy pastime, was ignored or disputed. It was, indeed, something like the power of women in politics; an influence almost all-pervading, almost irresistible, but silent, secret, and not to be openly acknowledged. ("Novels" 27–28)

Both Greg and the anonymous *Westminster Review* critic expressed anxiety about the influence of novels, and one source of this anxiety revealed itself both in the title of Greg's review and in the last sentence of the anonymous review, which compared the influence of the novel to the "power of women in politics." Even a cursory glance at the history of nineteenth-century British social reform literature shows that novels by women were an important political presence, one not to be underestimated.[12]

Tonna was clearly one such politically influential woman. Her prestige as an editor and author inspired the Christian Influence Society to ask her in 1842 to write a study of the condition of Britain, which resulted in her *Perils of the Nation*. Tonna's husband recalled after her death that "the book ... had a marked and decided influence, not only on the tone of public feeling, but directly on the Legislature, admits of no doubt. It was quoted on platforms and discussed in private circles" (qtd. in Krueger 151). Although *Perils* itself was published anonymously,[13] Tonna would not have been asked to write it if her fiction had not already given her a degree of political influence, and it is this female political influence, introduced insidiously through the medium of fiction into "private circles," that disturbed critics such as Greg and the *Westminster Review*. The conclusion that Tonna's work did have influence is supported by the fact that Samuel Kydd's *History of the Factory Movement* (1857) commended Tonna's *Helen Fleetwood* as important among those works that helped the cause of factory reform (qtd. in Cazamian 235).

In spite of the prominence of women novelists in the arena of social reform, though, most of the literary criticism on the subject of novelist as social polemicist has focused on male novelists, particularly the most popular and influential of nineteenth-century novelists, Charles Dickens. This intense focus on Dickens does not give an accurate picture of nineteenth-century cultural discourse because it exaggerates Dickens' originality. Dickens—dubbed "Mr. Popular Sentiment" by his fellow novelist Anthony Trollope—was a writer whose greatest skill lay in his ability to meet his readers' expectations. As his most recent biographer Peter Ackroyd puts it, "there never was a writer more adept at judging his readership than Charles Dickens. He knew precisely what effect to achieve, and precisely the means with which to do it" (856). In fact, much of Dickens's effectiveness as a popular novelist and social reformer was dependent on sentimentalist conventions, and by extension on his audience's comprehension and acceptance of these conventions. The pathos and preachiness of works such as *A Christmas Carol* were effective *only* because its audience already, because of authors such as Tonna, knew how to "read" Tiny Tim and the other scenes of suffering that the three Spirits use to convert Scrooge.

Like Tonna, Dickens used fiction to advocate the creation of moral consciousness; he played the role of the "good spirit who would take the house-tops off ... and show a Christian people ... pale phantoms rising from the scenes of our too-long neglect" (*Dombey and Son* 738). Tonna's brand of sentimentalist social reform discourse, with its use of Christian preaching and pathetic scenes of physical and emotional suffering, was clearly one of the most effective methods that he used to fulfill that design, because that is what his audience had come to expect. As Dean Arthur Stanley put it in his funeral sermon for Dickens, the "exaggerated forms" of Dickens' characters—the crossing-sweeper Jo in *Bleak House*, Betty Higden in *Our Mutual Friend*—enabled his readers to see and feel the urban poor (qtd. in Collins 524). Dickens' goal and the means by which he achieved it had both already been established by Tonna and other female sentimentalist writers.

If the success of Dickens, and of other important midcentury literary figures such as Elizabeth Gaskell and Elizabeth Barrett Browning, was dependent on what seem to be accepted cultural conventions, then this success indicates the existence of a now largely unknown sentimentalist cultural discourse that would account for such conventions. In fact, this discourse did exist, but its dominant figures, women writers such as Charlotte Elizabeth Tonna, have been almost entirely forgotten. They are, in the words of the anonymous *Westminster Review* critic, the "influence almost all-pervading, almost irresistible, but silent, secret, and not to be openly acknowledged" ("Novels" 28). Although, as I have argued elsewhere, Dickens' use of sentimentalism did injure his critical reputation, his juggernautlike popularity, fueled by his use of the nineteenth-century version of PR (such as his public reading tours), enabled him to weather the decline of sentimentality with greater success than his female contemporaries. The critical reputations, even of well-known women writers such as Elizabeth Barrett Browning and Elizabeth Gaskell, suffered because of their association with sentimentalism. And meanwhile, the earlier women social reform writers such as Tonna, who had originated all the conventions of sentimentalist social reform writing, disappeared almost entirely from literary history.[14]

This exclusion was largely caused by a high-culture backlash against sentimentalism, in which, as Suzanne Clark has argued, "[Modernist] critics used their aesthetic anti-sentimentality to make distinctions, to establish a position of authority against mass culture," a mass culture that included a tradition of politically active women writers (5). Even in the nineteenth century, many critics generally associated moral didacticism with women writers, and therefore with unseemly sentimentality: for example, G. H. Lewes theorized in 1852 that in women novelists, "Sentiment without Observation [leads] to rhetoric and long-drawn lachrymosity" (137). Fifty years later, Louis Cazamian, whose 1903 study, *The Social Novel in England: 1830–1870*, was for many years the authoritative work on nineteenth-century British social reform fiction, disparaged the emotionalism of Tonna's fiction—"her inner passion was a matter of sentiment, rather than will or intellect"—although he also commended its "deeply sincere and weighty seriousness" (237). The distinctions in literary criticism between "good" aesthetically pleasing literature and "bad" sentimental social polemic became increasingly evident in the nineteenth century, and they grew more extreme with the new formalism of modernist New Criticism, when, in the work of critics such as I. A. Richards, the word "sentimental" became an overt "expression of contempt" (241). Such simplistic distinctions ignored the fact that sentiment is an integral part of any writing intended to change the minds and hearts of nineteenth-century readers. Such writing had to show suffering to create empathy and enact social change, and, as Jane Tompkins pointed out in her analysis of sentimentalism in Harriet Beecher Stowe's antislavery novel *Uncle Tom's Cabin* (1851–52), it had to change the hearts of its readers by enacting the religious discourses of conversion, redemption, and salvation:

If the language of tears seems maudlin . . . it is because both the tears and the redemption that they signify belong to a conception of the world that is now generally regarded as naive and unrealistic. . . . Because most modern readers regard such political and economic facts as final, it is difficult for them to take seriously a novel that insists on religious conversion as the necessary precondition for sweeping social change. But in Stowe's understanding of what such change requires, it is the *modern* view that is naive. The political and economic measures that constitute effective action for us, she regards as superficial, mere extensions of the worldly policies that produced the slave system in the first place. Therefore, when Stowe asks the question that is in every reader's mind at the end of the novel—namely, "what can any individual do"?—she recommends not specific alterations in the current political and economic arrangements, but rather a change of heart. (132)

Tompkins' analysis of Stowe applies equally well to Tonna, because Stowe, whose *Uncle Tom's Cabin* bears more than a passing resemblance to Tonna's earlier antislavery novel *The System*, had read Tonna and written an introduction to an 1844 American edition of the older writer's works.

The distinctions imposed by later literary critics also failed to take into account the cultural imperatives that informed Tonna's "sentiment." As feminist Ann Cvetkovich claims, "the assumptions that affective expression forms the basis for political action and itself constitutes a political act derive from a nineteenth-century discourse that made affect meaningful." This discourse, Cvetkovich argues, results from "the gendered division between the private and public spheres and the assignment of women to the affective tasks of the household" (6). This analysis derives in part from feminist critic Nancy Armstrong's explanation of the eighteenth- and nineteenth-century domestic ideology: "according to the middle-class ideal of love ... the female relinquishe[d] political control to the male in order to acquire exclusive authority over domestic life, emotions, taste, and morality," creating a "sexual contract" that gave women control over morals and affect (41).

Armstrong quotes Frederick Rowton's introduction to his 1848 anthology of women poets to elaborate on this gendered "division of labor" (93) as it applies to literature: "Man has to bear outward, tangible rule; and his faculties are necessarily of an authoritative, evident, external commanding order. Woman has to bear invisible sway over the hidden mechanism of the heart; and her endowments are of a meek, persuasive, quiet, and subjective kind. Man rules the mind of the world; woman its heart" (40).[15] The gendered separation of powers does give women influence, but only over emotional matters, "the heart," and morality, as is shown when Rowton writes later in his preface that the poems in his anthology do not "accelerate man's political advancement; whilst every page will display some effort to stimulate his moral progress" (41). Rowton's preface also indicates—through the use of phrases like "Man has to" and "Woman has to"—the extent to which this domestic ideology was naturalized in nineteenth-century culture, to the point that it was not a choice but an imperative of nature.

This domestic ideology made it possible—indeed, almost necessary—for women writers, coming from their "naturally" more emotional and spiritual perspective, to construct a cultural discourse of social reform based on these feminine qualities, and to become identified with it. Women writers were perceived to be the "natural" authors of a discourse that would create affective bonds between the "two nations" divided by the disappearance of the moral economy. In an 1853 issue of *The Gentleman's Magazine,* a reviewer trying to assess the achievement of "The Lady Novelists of Great Britain" explicitly designated this affective task as one especially suited to women novelists:

Let no one neglect or throw contempt on the impulse which leads the higher classes— high whether in the social or the moral scale—to communicate freely with the lower ... our literature and our morals require more and more for their basis a sound increasing knowledge and sympathy between all orders of men. Mutual comprehension—mutual understanding of each other, how inestimable a privilege it is! This is what women can especially forward. (24)

This identification of women with "sympathy" and "sentiment" does create a political function for women, although theoretically, it keeps them contained within the domestic sphere.[16] The reviewer in *The Gentleman's Magazine* even sanctions this political role when he commends the French novelist George Sand and Harriet Beecher Stowe for their novels on political issues:

With the means of high religious and moral cultivation within her reach ... why should not a woman write fiction admirably well? Bear witness to a woman's power, most wonderful Consuelo! Stand forward, earnest, inspired, duteous, magnanimous 'Uncle Tom,' and say what there is, what long-standing system of wickedness, that may not be shaken to its centre by the touch of a woman's hand! ("Lady Novelists" 19)

The domestic ideology, then, gave women writers a political voice, and a great deal of political power to arouse reader sympathies for oppressed groups, but this power was inextricably linked to "sentiment," and the "high religious and moral cultivation" that literary critics would come to reject.

The contrasts between Tonna's work and that of her friend and mentor, the eighteenth-century evangelist and social commentator Hannah More, show how Tonna's innovations responded to both the new material circumstances of the industrial era, and the domestic ideology that gave women a specific political and social function to enact within those material circumstances. Tonna herself considered her relationship with More to have been one of the greatest influences on her public career—and the two writers certainly have a great deal in common. Both women were politically conservative, intensely pious, and extremely skillful at manipulating the ideology and rhetoric of evangelism to shape social discourse. There are significant differences in the ways that the two deal with social issues, however, as literary critic Catherine Gallagher acknowledges in *The Industrial Reformation of English Fiction* (1985) when she says that Tonna's characters in *Helen Fleetwood* "are not characters who could have been imagined by Hannah More" (50–51). These differences, in my opinion, represent significant innovations from More's evangelical tradition, innovations that make Tonna a more important literary figure, at least for Victorian studies, than More.

Tonna particularly admired More's *Cheap Repository Tracts* (1795–98), a collection of short political and religious pamphlets, as "an enterprise worthy of especial note" because of its "effective championship of the good cause [the Anglican church], by means most admirably suited to its furtherance" (*Personal Recollections* 210).[17] One of More's tracts, "The Lancashire Collier Girl," tells the story of the devastation experienced by one family caught up in the beginning phases of the Industrial Revolution. The heroine, Mary, loses her father to an industrial accident, her mother and brothers to overwork and malnutrition, and nearly dies herself before she is "rescued" by the local gentry. More addresses her audience simply and directly, often stopping in her narrative to prescribe meanings to be inferred from the events she relates. After Mary's father is killed, for instance, More tells her readers, "I will here remark that the most grievous afflictions are often appointed by Providence to be the means, in one way or other, of calling some extraordinary virtue into exercise" (5: 144).[18] This directly stated religious didacticism, or "preachiness," is one element that early evangelical writers such as More contributed to sentimentalist discourse whose "stated purpose," as Tompkins explains, "is to influence history, and which therefore employ[s] a language ... common and accessible to everyone" (125).

More's didacticism, however, lacks the more urgent religious imperatives that give Tonna her force. Driven by the cultural conditions created by the death of the moral economy, she drives her message of charity home by vehement references to the Bible like this one from the fourth part of *The Wrongs of Woman:*

He, the LORD, who changes not, looks down from the height of his glory on the very humblest of his handmaidens toiling below, no less benignantly than in the days of his flesh, he beheld the sorrows, heard the plaint, and answered the prayer of those who appealed to him. How, then, dwelleth the love of Christ in us, if we connive at the cruel oppression exercised over the helpless young females of our land? (107)[19]

In *The Perils of the Nation*, Tonna used the same attitude of religious judgment to argue that England, as a Christian nation, should conform to the laws of God:

God looks down from heaven upon the children of men, whose frame he well knows, and whom he never willingly afflicts or grieves; each one of whom in nakedness and helplessness must stand before him at the great day [of judgment]; and what a spectacle does he behold! Not among savage and barbarous nations, who never heard of the great Creator and his laws, of the blessed Redeemer and his love ... but in a country where the knowledge of his will in all things is attainable by every human being who enquires concerning it, does this [factory] system exist. (20)

Clearly, Tonna recognized little or no distinction between spiritual and civil law, and as far as she was concerned, those in power needed to behave as representatives not only of civil, elected authority, but also of divine authority. Later in the same text, she addressed the members of Parliament: "We would not willingly believe concerning any man that he held the future judgment of God so light a thing as to be braved for a little present gain" (242).

The passages from *The Wrongs of Woman* and *Perils of the Nation* contain two themes in common: first, the eschatological certainty that present actions will be subject to future divine judgment, and second, that divine (biblical) pronouncements are innately superior to earthly laws and conventional codes of behavior. Unlike More's, Tonna's Christianity urges her readers to share in its eschatological expectations and its moral judgments—it portrays contemporary events as parts of the transcendental history revealed in the Bible, and as therefore subject to the same divine laws. To further this portrayal, her fiction also uses a kind of typological characterization in which characters not only refer to the Bible in their dialogue, but actually are portrayed as biblical characters. The most obvious example of this is the title character in *Helen Fleetwood*, who suffers from physical abuse and humiliation in a way that strongly resembles the descriptions of Christ's sufferings leading up to the Crucifixion. Even as the description of Jesus' sufferings in the New Testament is intended to refer to the prophecy of Isaiah in the Old Testament"—"He was oppressed and afflicted, yet he opened not his mouth" (Isa. 53.7)—so is Tonna's characterization of Helen in *Helen Fleetwood* intended to refer to Jesus. She bears her sufferings "patiently" while "continual sorrow oppressed her heart," and is "resigned to endure for any length of time the trial of her own precious faith" (381–82, 384).

Tonna's use of the Bible—in both direct preaching from the narrator and typological characterization—also implies that God will punish those readers who fail to pity the "helpless young females," a message that is never present in More's tracts. More's "The Lancashire Collier Girl" does appeal somewhat to the Christian values of its audience in that it argues that the rich should take some responsibility for showing charity and fairness to the poor, but her moral and philosophical framework seems to assume that upper-class readers are already aware of this responsibility. The primary message of "The Lancashire Collier Girl," and of More's other celebrated tracts such as "The Shepherd of Salisbury Plain," is to lower-class readers, who are told to practice the virtues of self-help, to be patient and submissive, and to "do their duty in that state of life, into which it hath pleased God to call them" (5: 155). Upper-class readers, on the other hand, are not instructed in their responsibilities until the very end of "The Lancashire Collier Girl," when they are told "not to turn the poor from their doors, merely on account of first appearances, but rather first to examine into their character, expecting sometimes to find peculiar modesty and merit, even in the most exposed situations" (5: 154).

Tonna's most important innovation from More is the way that she describes the physical and emotional suffering of her subjects in detail. Like More, Tonna distanced herself from eighteenth-century sentimental morality in *Perils of the Nation*, when she claimed that "Tenderness for the poor is not among the spontaneous impulses of man's evil heart; if that were so, we should find line upon line … enjoining it in the word of God" (186). Nevertheless, her works contain so many heart-wrenching scenes of suffering, clearly meant to influence her audience's emotions, that the actual content of her works belies that claim. Her factory novel, *Helen Fleetwood*, is intended to call attention to the plight of the factory workers, and to denounce the factory system and the way that the Utilitarian-sponsored New Poor Law forced destitute people into the factories as laborers. The novel tells the story of Widow Green and her orphaned grandchildren, who are driven from their country home by the pressures of the New Poor Law and forced to work in one of the textile mills in the town of M (Manchester). Mrs. Green's other married daughter, Mrs. Wright, already lives with her family in M, and has four children who have worked in the factories since early childhood. Long passages in the novel describe how factory labor has warped these children physically, mentally, and emotionally, but the most injured is the oldest daughter Sarah:

The girl who occupied a low chair near the chimney-corner appeared to be naturally much taller than Phoebe [her younger sister], but was so twisted and crooked that she scarcely reached her height. Every feature betokened consumption far advanced; and her large glassy grey eyes seemed to rove about in quest of some object to interest them; while an expression of melancholy discontent shewed how vain was the search. A large shawl pinned close round the throat fell over her shoulders and body; and she evidently was as helpless as an infant. (71)

This passage not only gives a detailed physical description of Sarah, but also invites the reader to put him or herself in Sarah's place, to feel her physical helplessness and the mental and spiritual destruction caused by her condition. Later passages in the novel portray the psychological and spiritual dynamics of Sarah's unhappy family situation, and further the reader's identification with her. Similar passages in *Helen Fleetwood* and Tonna's other novels give detailed physical and emotional accounts of consumptive seamstresses, malnourished factory workers, deformed child laborers, and so forth. One of the most affecting of these is in the third part of *The Wrongs of Woman:*

Stunted in their growth, bony, pallid, and most wretchedly unhealthy in their looks; filthy beyond expression in their persons, with scarcely rags enough to hold decently together, these miserable little beings appear conscious of but two objects capable of attracting their notice beyond the work about which their poor dirty little hands are incessantly moving. One of these is the very small fire-place, where an exceedingly scanty portion of fuel is just emitting smoke enough to prove that fire smoulders beneath. Toward this, many a longing look is cast, while the blue lips quiver, and the teeth chatter, and the fingers are well-nigh disabled from moving by the benumbing influence of cold. One might suppose that the crowding of so many living creatures within that confined space, would ensure heat enough; but oppressive as the air feels, it evidently brings no warmth to them. Empty stomachs, and curdling blood, never set in motion by exercise or play, will produce a chill not to be overcome by these damp exhalations. (18)[20]

Such passages are obviously meant to dramatize suffering, and represent "social problems as affective dilemmas" (Cvetkovich 2)—in other words, as matters of the heart. At the beginning of this section, entitled "The Little Pin-Headers," Tonna comments ironically on the how the "tenderer sensibilities" of her female readers can be moved by "some fanciful painting" depicting the "touching" and "beautiful" scene from the New Testament of Jesus calling the children to him (5–6). She then claims that she will show her female readers another, very different scene: "Ah, lady, take from any part of your apparel that very trivial though indispensable appendage, a common pin: look well upon it, and I will show you another picture" (7). Such sentences seem to argue for a very unsentimental realism. Yet Tonna also clearly dramatizes details, such as the "poor dirty little hands," to arouse the sympathies of her readers, because "if these humble but truthful pages may help to warm one heart … it will be a crown of rejoicing to her who has penned them" (140).

This move, of course, puts social problems squarely within the realm of the feminine and makes use of that ideology that gives women control over morality and emotion. Tonna specifically appeals to that ideology countless times in her writings, even as early as the beginning of her editorship of *The Christian*

Lady's Magazine in 1834, when she justified her monthly political editorials with the following:

Can we write for CHRISTIAN LADIES, and be guiltless, if we neglect to enforce upon them their high responsibility, in the use of that mighty talent, female influence? ... It is when his [man's] home becomes the abode of gentle sympathy and intellectual companionship, and spiritual communion, that man begins to feel that he has somewhat worth fencing around with more and enduring bulwarks than shield and spear. And thus ... does the talent of female influence form the basis of even all commercial intercourse among the nations of the earth. ("Politics" 249–50)

In this passage, Tonna carefully restrains this "talent of female influence" to the home, in accordance with the domestic ideology, but she constructs this domestic role in a way that includes, even demands, the "high responsibility" of moral activism. Tonna also refers to female influence in *Helen Fleetwood* in a specifically political fashion, as an impetus toward legislative factory reform:

Now suppose a lady ... looking upon her own children and thinking what she should feel if they were situated like the wretched little ones in the factories ... don't you think these ladies would use their influence over their own husbands, fathers, brothers, and friends, to make it a point with the candidate they vote for that he should support our cause in Parliament? (326)

This passage is particularly significant because it shows how important sympathy, or affect, was in causing the changes of heart that would, in turn, result in the women's influence over their men. Even in *The Perils of the Nation*, which was anonymous and therefore comparatively genderless, there is this direct appeal to women's influence. The last section of *Perils* consists of a series of appeals for action on social reform, directed toward the various segments of society (Parliament, the Ministers of the Crown, the Church of England bishops and clergy, magistrates, the legal and medical professions, etc.), and it is probably no accident that the very last of these appeals is to female influence, "mighty for good or ill" (345). It is clear that Tonna considers this affective morality to be feminine, and equally clear that it is crucial to her concept of her own efficacy as a writer and reformer.

Hannah More, on the other hand, seems determined to deflect the pity and emotion of the audience in "The Lancashire Collier Girl," rather than to arouse it. The text of the tract glosses over the deaths of Mary's father, mother, and brothers, and the narrator describes the heroine Mary's own illness with an absolute minimum of detail, saying only that "she began to be bowed down in some measure by the afflictions which she had endured" (148). The narrator immediately goes on to observe "how lamentable a thing is it, that while so many people are seen who are apt to complain too soon, there should be any who do not tell their distresses to those who can help them" (149). More's constant, calmly, and matter-of-factly phrased interjections actually have a distancing effect on the readers' emotions toward Mary, and the rhetorical effect of the text is rational, rather than affective.

Beth Tobin has argued that nineteenth-century writers such as Elizabeth Gaskell and Anne Brontë "sought to destabilize traditional moral authority and to erect in its place a new, feminine version of moral authority" based on "feminine traits such as sympathy and kindness" (105), an argument that is obviously related to my own. She maintains that this feminine moral authority is the direct result of Hannah More's "professing a 'religion of the heart' ... better suited to women and their newly constructed feminine graces of sympathy and kindness than to men" (Tobin 111). There is undoubted truth to Tobin's reasoning, but I think that Hannah More's eighteenth-century narratives still differ significantly from nineteenth-century sentimentalist texts because they do not dramatize suffering but instead rely on logical argument in that the stories "prove" the truth of the lessons the author prescribes. More does not wish to overarouse the emotions of her audience because that overarousal would lead to what she describes in her tracts as the "wrong" kind of charity.

Another pamphlet from the *Cheap Repository Tracts,* "The Cottage Cook," presents the most evident example of More's aversion to excessive emotion. The opening of this text characterizes its heroine Mrs. Jones by her excessive feelings and her capacity to be easily moved. After the village rector preaches a moving sermon on charity one Sunday, he calls on Mrs. Jones and finds her "in tears" because, as she tells him, she has "been much *moved* by his discourse, and she wept because she had so little to give to the plate, for though she *felt* very keenly for the poor in these dear times, yet she could not assist them" (4: 6; emphasis added).

This capacity to be moved by others' misfortunes seems to set Mrs. Jones up as a potentially good heroine for a sentimentalist social reform novel, in which her emotional responses would lead her not only to feel, but to do good things for those around her. More, however, presents emotion as an undesirable impediment, and interjects disapprovingly that "she [Mrs. Jones] was not aware how wrong it was to weep away that time which might have been better spent in drying the tears of others" (6). After inaugurating a new life of practical charity, Mrs. Jones never weeps again in "The Cottage Cook" or in the two sequel tracts that follow it. More also attacks generosity based on emotion in her tract "Estimate of the Religion of the Fashionable World" because for her, acts of charity based only on feeling, and not on a disciplined faith in God, were morally suspect (Tobin 96).

More's attitude toward affect and pathos reflects the fact that when she was writing, the changes in structures of feeling that I described earlier in this essay had not yet taken place. This attitude is also demonstrated in "The Cottage Cook," because Mrs. Jones' new usefulness, resulting from the severity of the pastor, takes the form of her inducing various people to behave correctly, through logic and appeals to their self-interest. She persuades the two local gentlemen to donate money for building a large parish oven, and we are told that "Sir John subscribed to be rid of her importunity, and the squire because he thought every improvement in economy would reduce the poor-rate [tax used for poor relief]"

(19). More's moral vision, in other words, presumes the existence of a tightly knit rural community in which all citizens, both rich and poor, are interdependent, and therefore support each other because they have common interests.

The results of the shifts in social structure described earlier in this essay can be seen clearly in the transition from More's work to Tonna's. It is Tonna who uses her culturally sanctioned role to bring the suffering of the workers and urban poor to the attention of her audience. The happy confidence with which More assumes that the problems of the poor can be solved with judicious, personalized charity like that of Mrs. Jones has been replaced by Tonna's strident outcries against the indifference of the middle and upper classes. More assumes the existence of the communal affective bonds that allow individualized charity to take place; Tonna must construct these bonds artificially through her skilled use of the cultural assumptions embedded in the domestic ideology: "The abstract idea of a suffering family does not strongly affect the mind; but let the parties be known to us, let their names call up some familiar images to our view, and ... we are enabled much more feelingly to enter into their trial" (*Wrongs*, "The Forsaken Home" 120). It is to create these bonds of feeling that Tonna relies on the "feminine" language of sentiment and morality; changes in social and economic conditions have clearly resulted in a new, more strident and emotionally engaging, feminized discourse that would remind its audience of their responsibilities as Christians. It is in Charlotte Elizabeth Tonna, then, that the older, class-based moral economy with its reciprocal bonds of deference and charitable responsibility has been replaced in the Victorian period by new, feminized sentimental morality. That in itself makes her a worthy object of scholarly recognition, and it is ironic that it is not Tonna, but More, an eighteenth-century author, who gets referenced so often in the scholarly literature as a representation of Victorian evangelical attitudes.

In addition to her work's crucial contribution to Victorian culture, Tonna's work represents an important challenge for feminist criticism. This challenge was illustrated for me when I first began research on her work and had to obtain many of her works through interlibrary loan. When my long-awaited copy of *The Wrongs of Woman* finally arrived, the young woman at the desk started, guiltily, and then said, "Oh, I was hoping that you wouldn't come for another couple of days—I've been reading that one." Because, like most scholars, I am amazed when "normal" people from the outside world take an interest in what I'm researching, I was not quite prepared for her next question. She said, "I don't understand this writer. I started reading thinking that this was a feminist book because of the title, but I'm really confused because of all this stuff that says women are sinful and not equal to men. Was this writer a feminist or not?"

Her question points to the crux of the issue. Are writers such as Tonna, who constantly deny that they seek equality for women, valid subjects for feminist study? In her introduction to *The Wrongs of Woman*, Tonna says that "if we undertake to discuss the wrongs of women, we may be expected to set out by plainly defining what are the rights of women. This is soon done. We repudiate all pretensions to equality with man save on the ground specified by the Apostle [Paul], that 'In Christ Jesus, there is neither male nor female'" (3). Tonna also concedes Eve's responsibility for the Fall, but in contrast, she goes on to hint that female faults are caused by the "greater feebleness and dependency" of women, which, in turn, are caused by social oppression (10). The whole book, from that point, goes on to address the wrongs of women, progressing from the factory system that Tonna blames for the breakup of the family, to the great evil of child labor in "The Little Pin-Headers," and the hardship of seamstresses in "The Lace-Runners." In the sense that she responds to the social oppression of women, Tonna is a feminist in the tradition of Mary Wollstonecraft. And in that sense, it is no surprise that her book's title is the same as the subtitle of Mary Wollstonecraft's unfinished novel *Maria, or, the Wrongs of Woman.*

Tonna's refusal to embrace women's suffrage and her conformity to traditional social and religious conventions make her inconsistent, however, with twentieth-century feminist ideals. It is in response to these inconsistencies that some feminist scholars have failed to embrace sentimentalist authors as part of the feminist literary tradition. For example, Elaine Showalter's well-known critical survey *A Literature of Their Own*, which was published in 1977 at the height of the women's liberation movement, attempts to construct a history of women's fiction in England from Brontë to Lessing. This study represents, above all, a paradox. While attempting to remedy the "residual Great Traditionalism" that has "reduced and condensed the extraordinary range and diversity of English women novelists to a tiny band of the 'great'" (7), Showalter herself constructs an evolutionary history of women's literature that ends up excluding the very "minor writers" she wishes to recover. Even the table of contents suggests a progression forward from the "feminine" novelists of the nineteenth century to the "feminist" novelists and so on, and Showalter's introduction explicitly outlines this evolution:

First, there is a prolonged phase of imitation of prevailing modes of the dominant tradition, and internalization of its standards of art and its views on social roles. Second, there is a phase of protest against these standards and values. . . . Finally, there is a phase of self-discovery, a turning inward freed from some of the dependency of opposition, a search for identity. An appropriate terminology for women writers is to call these stages, *Feminine, Feminist,* and *Female.* (13)

This evolutionary model implies a rejection of the earlier "phases" of women's literary development, because it constructs the "feminine" novelists as the essentially weak and troubled precursors to a later, more admirable tradition. Showalter argues that these novelists struggled to define themselves by essentially male conceptions of femininity. Since women's work (as opposed to men's work) meant "work for others," the "feminine" novelists preached "submission and self-sacrifice, and by denouncing female self-assertiveness, they worked to atone for their will to write" (21–22). Showalter sees women's social-protest fiction both as an extension of this feminine ideal and as a kind of psychological projection that "translated the felt pain and oppression of women into the championship of mill-workers, child laborers, prostitutes, and slaves" (28).

Even though Showalter often shows a great deal of insight, especially in her discussion of the nineteenth-century critical double standard, her evolutionary model implicitly privileges those women writers in whose works the feminine ideal is questioned or problematized. She identifies sensation fiction, and then the activist feminist novels of the 1980s and '90s, as subversions of the "feminine" novels that had merely represented women's painful experience, or even worse, had displaced this experience on other oppressed groups and actively condoned patriarchal constructions of femininity. Charlotte Elizabeth Tonna, a writer who not only condoned, but also actively made use of these patriarchal constructions to further other political ends, such as the abolition of slavery and factory reform, with "the talent of female influence," would clearly fall into the "feminine" category in Showalter's evolutionary scale.

I believe that the tendency toward this blind spot in feminist criticism partly comes from the influence of formalist literary criticism, but part of it also comes from a liberal/rationalist feminist tradition that is inextricably linked to the myth of the "extraordinary" woman. This tradition rejects women writers who conformed with the social and religious values that are seen as patriarchal and instead celebrates those who are seen as rebelling against these values. Conversely, I am not saying that we should turn this formula inside out and celebrate "ordinary" women writers at the expense of "extraordinary" women writers. Instead, I do not believe that it is an either/or situation.

What we need to realize is that the seeming conservatism of writers such as Tonna may have actually contributed to, not limited, the eventual enfranchisement of women. For one thing, it offered a medium through which women could participate in the political arena, such as Tonna's "Politics" column in *The Christian Lady's Magazine,* and still conform to nineteenth-century definitions of femininity.[21] Second, women's increasing involvement in worldly affairs through their growing control of philanthropic institutions—a phenomenon clearly fostered by Tonna and other sentimentalist women writers—may quite possibly have led to women's involvement in explicitly political movements, such as women's suffrage. At least one historian, F. M. Prochaska, has pointed toward this conclusion by showing that "women trained in charitable societies were prominent among those who petitioned the House of Commons praying for the enfranchisement of their sex" in 1866 (226–27).

The enigmatic figure of Charlotte Elizabeth Tonna—described by Harriet Beecher Stowe as "a woman of strong mind, powerful feeling, and of no inconsiderable share of tact in influencing the popular mind" (1)—is revealed, therefore, as a crucial influence not only on the cultural history of the Victorian period, but also on the evolution of women's political consciousness. Both of these achievements are of great literary, historical, and political value.

WORKS CITED

Ackroyd, Peter. *Dickens*. New York: Harper, 1990.

Armstrong, Nancy. *Desire and Domestic Fiction*. New York: Oxford UP, 1987.

Booth, Charles. *The Life and Labour of the People of London*. 1902. 5 vols. New York: Angus M. Kelley, 1969.

Brissenden, R. F. *Virtue in Distress: Studies in the Novel of Sentiment from Richardson to Sade*. New York: Macmillan, 1974.

Cazamian, Louis. *The Social Novel in England: 1830–1870*. Trans. Martin Fido. Boston: Routledge and Kegan Paul, 1973.

Clark, Suzanne. *Sentimental Modernism*. Bloomington: Indiana UP, 1991.

Collins, Philip, ed. *Dickens: The Critical Heritage*. New York: Barnes and Noble, 1974.

Cvetkovich, Ann. *Mixed Feelings: Feminism, Mass Culture, and Victorian Sensationalism*. New Brunswick: Rutgers UP, 1992.

Dickens, Charles. *Bleak House*. London: Penguin, 1985.

———. *The Christmas Books*. Vol. 1. London: Penguin, 1987.

———. *Dombey and Son*. New York: Penguin, 1977.

———. *Oliver Twist*. New York: Penguin, 1986.

———. *Our Mutual Friend*. New York, Penguin, 1986.

———. *Speeches*. Ed. K. J. Fielding. Oxford: Clarendon, 1960.

Disraeli, Benjamin. *Sybil*. London: Longmans and Co., 1920.

Dyos, H. J. *Exploring the Urban Past*. Ed. David Cannadine and David Reeder. Cambridge: Cambridge UP, 1982.

Ellis, Markman. *The Politics of Sensibility: Race, Gender, and Commerce in the Sentimental Novel*. Cambridge: Cambridge UP, 1996.

Engels, Friedrich. *The Condition of the Working Class in England*. Trans. and ed. W. O. Henderson and W. H. Chaloner. Oxford: Basil Blackwell, 1958.

Ferris, Ina. "From Trope to Code: The Novel and the Rhetoric of Gender in Nineteenth-century Critical Discourse." *Rewriting the Victorians*. Ed. Linda Shires. New York: Routledge, 1992.

Gallagher, Catherine. *The Industrial Reformation of English Fiction*. Chicago: U of Chicago P, 1985.

Gaskell, Elizabeth. *North and South*. Ed. Angus Easson. New York: Oxford UP, 1992.

Greg, W. R. "The False Morality of Lady Novelists." *National Review* 8 (1859): 144–69.

Himmelfarb, Gertrude. *The Idea of Poverty: England in the Early Industrial Age*. New York: Knopf, 1984.

Johnson, Claudia. *Equivocal Beings: Politics, Gender, and Sentimentality in the 1790's*. Chicago: U of Chicago P, 1995.

Kanner, Barbara, and Ivanka Kovacevic. "Blue Book into Novel: The Forgotten Industrial Fiction of Charlotte Elizabeth Tonna." *Nineteenth Century Fiction* 25 (1970): 152–73.

Kestner, Joseph. "Charlotte Elizabeth Tonna's *The Wrongs of Woman:* Female Industrial Protest." *Tulsa Studies in Women's Literature* 2 (1983): 193–214.

———. *Protest and Reform: The British Social Narrative by Women*. Madison: Wisconsin UP, 1985.

Krueger, Christine. *The Reader's Repentance*. Chicago: U of Chicago P, 1992.

"The Lady Novelists of Great Britain." *Gentleman's Magazine* 40 (1853): 18–25.

Lenard, Mary. "'Mr. Popular Sentiment': Dickens and the Gender Politics of Sentimentalism and Social Reform Literature." *Dickens Studies Annual* 27 (1998): 45–68.

————. *Preaching Pity: Dickens, Gaskell, and Sentimentalism in Victorian Culture.* New York: Peter Lang, 1999.

Lewes, George Henry. "The Lady Novelists." *Westminster Review* 58 (1852): 129–41.

Moers, Ellen. *Literary Women.* New York: Doubleday, 1977.

More, Hannah. *Cheap Repository Tracts.* Vols. 1–8. New York: American Tract Society, n.d.

"Novels with a Purpose." *Westminster Review* 26 (1864): 24–49.

Prochaska, F. M. *Women and Philanthropy in Nineteenth-Century England.* Oxford: Clarendon, 1980.

Richards, I. A. *Practical Criticism: A Study of Literary Judgment.* New York: Harcourt, 1929.

Sheppard, Francis. *London 1808–1870: The Infernal Wen.* Berkeley: U of California P, 1971.

Showalter, Elaine. *A Literature of Their Own: British Women Novelists from Brontë to Lessing.* Princeton: Princeton UP, 1977.

Smith, Sheila. *The Other Nation.* Oxford: Clarendon, 1980.

Stowe, Harriet Beecher. Introduction. *The Works of Charlotte Elizabeth.* By Charlotte

————. *Uncle Tom's Cabin.* New York: Norton, 1994.

Thompson, E. P. *The Making of the English Working Class.* New York: Vintage, 1966.

————. "The Moral Economy of the English Crowd in the Eighteenth Century." *Past and Present* 50 (1971): 76–136.

Tobin, Beth. *Superintending the Poor.* New Haven: Yale UP, 1993.

Tompkins, Jane. *Sensational Designs.* New York: Oxford UP, 1985.

Tonna, Charlotte Elizabeth. *Helen Fleetwood.* 1839–40. London: Seeley, 1848.

————. *The Perils of the Nation.* London: Seeley, 1843.

————. *Personal Recollections.* London: Seeley, 1841.

————. "Politics." *Christian Lady's Magazine.* March 1834.

————. *The System: A Novel of the West Indies.* London: Westley, 1827.

————. *The Wrongs of Woman.* New York: Dodd, 1844.

Williams, Raymond. *The Country and the City.* New York: Oxford UP, 1973.

————. *Marxism and Literature.* Oxford: Oxford UP, 1977.

Wollstonecraft, Mary. *Maria, or, the Wrongs of Women.* 1798. London: Pickering & Chatto, 1991.

NOTES

1. By "typological characterization," I mean flat characters who are meant to be understood in terms of the biblical characters they resemble.

2. *Bleak House* was published serially in 1852–53, and *North and South* in 1854–55. The portrayals of characters such as Jo and Bessie Higgins differ significantly from characterizations of poverty in More (1745–1833).

3. Lord Ashley was a well-known Evangelical, and a tireless advocate in Parliament of humanitarian causes such as factory and sanitary reform.

4. Even conservative historian Gertrude Himmelfarb admits, "However one may qualify the idea of an agricultural or industrial 'revolution,' there can be no doubt of the enormity of the changes in the countryside and towns. There were fewer 'deserted villages' than the poets thought, but many depressed ones; fewer large cities by later stan-

dards, but many rapidly growing ones with all the problems they brought in their wake" (135). Himmelfarb qualifies this link between these social changes and increased poverty with her statement that other problems, such as poor harvests and the Napoleonic wars, created economic problems. I am, of course, more interested in the perception of a previous "moral economy," than in arguing about whether this social shift really existed or not, but the fact that a conservative historian such as Himmelfarb admits, however grudgingly, the existence of a previous social order, and even uses the term "moral economy" in her analysis, gives credence to the arguments of Marxist historians and critics such as E. P. Thompson and Raymond Williams.

5. Also see Beth Tobin's discussion of these eighteenth-century sources in *Superintending the Poor* (1993), 8–9.

6. The population of Cobbett's home parish of Kensington increased from 14,000 in 1821 to 120,000 in 1871 (Sheppard 83–84).

7. By the 1890s, when sociologist Charles Booth made his famous survey of *The Life and Labour of the People of London*, Booth's maps—in which districts were color-coded according to income level—reveal lower-income districts surrounded by a "camouflage" of commercial property, and separated distinctly from higher-income districts.

8. Dickens had satirized Laurie in his characterization of the hypocritical Alderman Cute in *The Chimes* (1845).

9. Sheila Smith's book on nineteenth-century literary portrayals of the poor, *The Other Nation* (1980), describes this episode at length.

10. I refer to "eighteenth-century sentimentalism" because the idea that social benevolence had to come from the heart rather than the head was, in many ways, a carryover from the eighteenth-century "cult of sensibility." However, the values of sensibility fell somewhat into disrepute after the Reign of Terror and the Napoleonic era, because of their association with the French Revolution. This devaluation is also characterized by an increasingly negative feminization of these values. See, for example, the 1798 concluding issue of a Tory satirical review, the *Anti-Jacobin*, which consists of a long poem by George Canning condemning Sensibility, the "Sweet child of sickly Fancy" and "her fair votaries." A large Gillray cartoon accompanies the poem, and the cartoon depicts a revolutionary mob worshipping the female figure of Sensibility, who weeps over a dead bird while her foot rests on the severed head of Louis XVI (Brissenden 62–64). R. F. Brissenden's *Virtue in Distress* and Claudia Johnson's *Equivocal Beings: Politics, Gender, and Sentimentality in the 1790's* contain descriptions of Canning's poem and Gillray's cartoon. Markman Ellis' *The Politics of Sensibility* also contains a detailed analysis, as well as a picture of the cartoon. I discuss the relationship between eighteenth-century sensibility and nineteenth-century sentimentality at length in my book *Preaching Pity: Dickens, Gaskell and Sentimentalism in Victorian Culture* (Peter Lang, 1999).

11. This attitude is evidenced most famously in Disraeli's novel *Sybil* (1842):

> "Two nations; between whom there is no intercourse and no sympathy; who are as ignorant of each other's habits, thoughts, and feelings, as if they were dwellers in different zones, or inhabitants of different planets; who are formed by a different breeding, are fed by a different food, are ordered by different manners, and are not governed by the same laws."

> "You speak of"–"said Egremont, hesitatingly.

> "THE RICH AND THE POOR."

12. Joseph Kestner's 1985 book *Protest and Reform* thoroughly catalogues the overwhelming presence of women writers in the history of nineteenth-century British social protest fiction. Although he does not go on to analyze the whys and wherefores of this phenomenon, Kestner successfully proves that women writers actually dominated this subgenre of literature, which gave them a great deal of political and cultural authority (213).

13. Tonna published the work under the name of her longtime publisher, Richard Seeley, who published *The Christian Lady's Magazine* and Tonna's own *Helen Fleetwood* and *Personal Recollections.* Even though I do not know for sure why Tonna published this work anonymously, I suspect that her longtime affiliation with Seeley, as well as her well-known involvement in factory reform, probably meant that her authorship of *Perils* was not as unknown to her contemporaries as it was to become to twentieth-century literary critics and historians. As recently as 1982, historian H. J. Dyos' *Exploring the Urban Past* attributed *Perils* to Seeley; it was not until feminist literary critic Joseph Kestner researched Tonna extensively for his book *Protest and Reform* (1985) that she was correctly identified as the author of *Perils.*

14. My article "'Mr. Popular Sentiment': Dickens and the Gender Politics of Sentimentalism and Social Reform Literature" thoroughly analyzes Dickens' sentimentalism and its effect on his critical reputation. In addition, my book *Preaching Pity* discusses Dickens and Gaskell, as well as Elizabeth Barrett Browning, in relation to this issue. Since I have dealt with these authors at greater length elsewhere, I will not do so here, except just to say that the critical reception histories of all three of these writers provide ample evidence for what I have said.

15. Rowton's generalization is representative of many nineteenth-century literary critics. George Henry Lewes, for example, says, in his 1852 *Westminster Review* article on "The Lady Novelists," that "the Masculine mind is characterized by a predominance of the intellect, and the Feminine by the predominance of the emotions" (131–32).

16. The review uses the words "sympathy" and "sentiment" several times.

17. Tonna obviously admired More's adaptation of fiction as a political and religious tool, and More's works overcame Tonna's prejudice against fiction. In general, Tonna disapproved of fiction (see *Personal Recollections*), but it became acceptable when used for a "good cause," such as More's advocacy of the Anglican church, or Tonna's own later use of fiction for causes such as factory reform and poor relief.

18. For the purposes of this study, I used an eight-volume edition of the *Cheap Repository Tracts,* distributed by the American Tract Society. No publication date is given, but the illustrations indicate that the edition is from the mid-nineteenth century.

19. *The Wrongs of Woman* is divided into four parts, each a separate story: "Milliners and Dressmakers," "The Forsaken Home," "The Little Pin-Headers," and "The Lace Runners." The American edition that I used (M. W. Dodd 1845) is in one volume, but the pages of each section are numbered independently.

20. In "The Little Pin-Headers," the orphaned children of the family in "The Forsaken Home" are employed in a pin factory, putting the heads on top of pins.

21. Christine Krueger has already made an argument along these lines in *The Reader's Repentance* (1992).

5

Class Counts

The Domestic-Professional Writer, the Working Poor, and Middle-Class Values in The Years That the Locust Hath Eaten *and* The Story of a Modern Woman[1]

SueAnn Schatz

We must rid ourselves of the idea that there are any *real* class distinctions. The only essential differences that there are between us, as human beings, are to be found amongst the individuals in every social class.
—Sylvia Pankhurst

The poor are wiser, more charitable, more kind, more sensitive than we are.
—Oscar Wilde

In this chapter, I examine class issues in two novels of the 1890s that I term "domestic-professional"; that is, fiction that features a central female character who is both a professional writer and maternal figure. Domestic-professional authors employ traditional formulaic characterizations of the ideal Victorian woman, "the angel in the house," at the same time their heroines transgress into the public arena of publishing. Having a career that allowed her to work in the house, this middle-class female figure offered women readers who wished to expand their influence outside of the domestic sphere prototypes for success. However, it also offered readers a model of a woman who, although a transgressor of boundaries, was not an aggressor: She appeared "safe" precisely because she was inside the home. But although it seems that the angel and the woman writer are contiguous, what is revealed is the angel's unsatisfying and unsatisfactory position in society. Hence, domestic-professional fiction suggests new models for women. It is concerned with immediate social issues, and through the co-optation and subversion of the angel ideal, the domestic-professional woman claims her right to confront these issues and offer solutions. Ultimately, the character is anything but "safe" as she attempts to change the status quo. However, because many domestic-professional authors were middle class and thus products of their culture, they often unconsciously ended up perpetuating the patriarchal bourgeois structure they hoped to transform.

Annie E. Holdsworth's *The Years That the Locust Hath Eaten* (1895) and Ella Hepworth Dixon's *The Story of a Modern Woman* (1894) compare the dilemmas of their middle-class writing protagonists with those of the lower classes, particularly of working-class women. They show how patriarchal strictures oppress women of all classes and reveal the added burdens middle-class status confers upon women. Both novels additionally disclose their authors' entanglement in middle-class ideology, including the late-Victorian assumption that women should not possess sexuality. Yet, that these domestic-professional novels expose their authors' inability to escape this snare offers readers the realization that the system must be changed for an equitable society to be established.

Recent feminist criticism has noted that the late-nineteenth-century British women's movement was class-biased; that is, the majority of the women calling for suffrage, equal education, and other rights were strictly middle class in their thinking and attitudes, and maintained their middle-class privileges by excluding women of lower orders, a problem with which contemporary feminists are still grappling. Can a middle-class white woman speak for all women? Even with the best intentions, can any woman speak outside of her race and class? Or, as Ann Rosalind Jones muses, "I wonder again whether one libidinal voice, however unphallocentrically defined, can speak to the economic and cultural problems of all women" (258). However, not all late-Victorian feminists were concerned solely with middle-class women's issues. Many socialist feminists, such as Beatrice Webb, Sylvia Pankhurst, and Helen Bosanquet, were genuinely interested in helping the poor; they perceived that their fight for women's rights was intricately meshed with bringing attention to oppression of all varieties. These feminists understood the enormity of such a battle because, as *The Minority Report of the Poor Law Commission* (1909) said, one of the largest obstacles in overcoming the problem of unemployment and its resulting poverty was not so much persuading the middle and upper classes that poverty could be eradicated, but convincing them that the problem existed at all (Webb 2: 323). As an upper-class woman, gazing at a painting entitled *A Nineteenth-Century Madonna*, declares in *The Years That the Locust Hath Eaten*, "Really, that is too ridiculous!—a woman starving, and a dead child on her lap. Things like that don't happen in the nineteenth century" (201).

Like this painting, the two novels discussed here place the problem of the working poor directly in front of their middle-class readers' eyes. Holdsworth and Dixon are evidently operating within the long-standing tradition that women have the innate moral and compassionate temperament that obliges them to help the needy. This convention, embraced heartily by such women writers as mid-Victorian authors Elizabeth Barrett Browning and George Eliot (among others), has its origins, of course, in the eighteenth century, with writ-ers Mary Astell, Mary Wollstonecraft, and Hannah More espousing women's duty to charitably assist the poor, not only materially but spiritually as well.

The Years That the Locust Hath Eaten and *The Story of a Modern Woman* sincerely plead for justice for lower-class women, but their solution to the work-ing-class woman's problems is to impose middle-class values on her. These nov-els conceal a double edge: While struggling to reformulate the way people think about women and the poor, they also dangerously serve to reproduce the then current assumptions about those two groups. Ultimately, the woman writer's role in these two novels as a defender of women, especially lower-class women, is a precarious one precisely because the writer is middle class. She may sym-pathize with, empathize with, defend, and demand justice for the working-class woman, but her middle-class standing and her desire—even, need—to stay within middle-class boundaries often negates her efforts to help the working poor.

Yet these novels effectively locate the working poor's lot as a social problem within the range of middle-class help, particularly through the domestic-professional's guidance. Even though *The Years That the Locust Hath Eaten* and *The Story of a Modern Woman* end on seemingly dark notes, there is a glim-mer of optimism remaining, Holdsworth and Dixon entreating their readers to do what their protagonists could not: discover ways to change stultifying social conventions and conditions.

Although practically unheard of today, Annie E. Holdsworth's *The Years That the Locust Hath Eaten* was well received on publication in 1895, earning plau-dits from critics for its heroine Priscilla Momerie, a young married writer as "full of high aspirations, in the prime of youth and health, [and] animated by an enthusiasm for the masses who, in eyes like hers, are held to constitute the 'people'" (*Athenæum* 867). Holdsworth's novel is unique because it does what Rita S. Kranidis says many feminist novels do not do: "Characters in feminist novels often turn to the slums of London as sources of experience, wisdom, and growth toward independence, but those settings are rarely central to the narra-tives themselves" (69–70). By situating the action of *The Years That the Locust Hath Eaten* directly in a working-class neighborhood, Holdsworth reveals mul-tiple problems when middle-class ideology is administered upon the working-class poor, however well meant.

The Years That the Locust Hath Eaten is the story of a young writer who mar-ries the son of a country merchant, Dunstane Momerie, against her rector fa-ther's wishes. Ironically, Priscilla marries not for love, but for convenience: to avoid an arranged marriage to an older, landed gentleman, and because Dun-stane also wants to be a writer. Because they both plan on moving to London to pursue their respective careers, they decide to marry, believing two can live as cheaply as one. Although it is important for the domestic-professional writer to balance her personal and public lives, Holdsworth declares that a marriage based on utilitarian motives is not the means toward progress. The novel thus offers a domestic-professional critique of the institution of middle-class marriage, as well as an examination of the British class system as revealed through Priscilla's relationships with Dunstane and with the other tenants of their working-class apartment building.

Holdsworth's positioning of Priscilla as a professional writer acts as a metaphor for these critiques. As a young child and before she is married, Priscilla is consistently referred to as "unconventional," but the longer she is married, the more conventional—the more like the angel in the house—she becomes, allowing Dunstane to abuse her psychologically. Priscilla begins her writing career as a novelist but soon needs to write sensation stories to earn money to sustain herself, her newly invalid husband, and eventually their baby daughter. Her life is one of extremes, extraordinarily out of balance. As a single woman under her father's economic care, Priscilla sees writing as a way to use her imagination, but as a married woman her unceasing need to write for economic reasons leads her to believe she prostitutes herself by serial writing, as marriage also prostitutes her.

Priscilla's writing, despite late-Victorian propriety on the subject, reveals that a woman's sexuality is part of her art, whether she consciously acknowledges it or not: Priscilla's first novel, "A Parish Romance" (82), written while still a single woman, is a *"succès de scandale"* (22): one day "Priscilla awoke and found herself—yellow" (22). Ironically, the innocently named novel obviously (but not to Priscilla) is steeped with sexual innuendo. However, Holdsworth, as a middle-class writer, will not explicitly discuss sexual matters, nor allow her married heroine to seem sexual. But the novel that the unmarried Priscilla writes reveals a sexuality that suggests such feelings are innate and cannot be denied.

Holdsworth refuses to comment further on the content of the book, saying only that Priscilla was safe from critics in her little village because "Literature halted painfully and grudgingly at Frodsham" (22). The only person from Frodsham who reads the novel is Dunstane: "Her book had reached another soul. There was one who had read and not misunderstood her" (23). But although Holdsworth describes this connection as a spiritual one—from one soul to another—that book that touches Dunstane has a sexual power and lays a foundation for their friendship. Once Priscilla and Dunstane are married—and sexually active—that tension is transformed into a physical relationship, one with which perhaps neither is totally comfortable. Dunstane will eventually suffer from hysterical paralysis, and Priscilla, with her middle-class values of the wholesomeness of marriage, will transfer her ambivalent feelings about the reality of the institution onto her writing. Holdsworth equates marriage with a type of prostitution by making Priscilla feel that she is prostituting herself, not by any sexual acts with her husband, but by writing sensation stories for a living.

As a married woman forced to earn money for her husband, writing becomes a necessity, first for economic, then for psychological survival. Priscilla truly becomes "one of the masses," struggling to survive. Yet living among and becoming one of the working class impels her to write about the poor's condition, thus constituting her as a domestic-professional author. However, her situation is different than the other working-class women in the building because she maintains her conviction that she is still middle class and that Dunstane is failing her because he refuses to take on work he reasons is below him. Priscilla believes that her husband should be supporting her, but will not leave him because of her belief in the middle-class conventions of the dutiful wife; these conventions, with the added burden of her writing, eventually overwhelm and destroy Priscilla.

The Years That the Locust Hath Eaten locates the opposition between the ineffectual male (writer) and the domestic-professional female whose work attempts to make a difference. Dunstane Momerie is a literary descendant of George Eliot's Casaubon, vowing to write "The New Religion" that will change the world. But this work is nonexistent, as Dunstane, who places his "writing" above Priscilla's, constantly talks about the work, but never actually writes it. Additionally, although the philosophy behind his New Religion embraces the working class"—"Faith in one's self, in one's work, in one's future. . . . It was the worker who grasped immortality"—Dunstane cannot abide living among the working class in "this place [that] stamps me a poor man" (48, 47). His theories are platitudes"—"Poverty brought out the best in a man; endurance and fortitude were bread for the soul, to be bought without money"—clichés that middle-class people with money can afford to spout (51).

But although Dunstane refuses to believe it, he and Priscilla no longer are part of that class; they will learn what poverty actually does to people, grinding them down until it at last takes Priscilla's life. An important component in the Momeries' slide into poverty is Priscilla's pregnancy. When he learns Priscilla is to have a baby, Dunstane suffers an attack of neurasthenia.[2] The thought of actually having to start writing or take other paying work brings on his paralysis: "Dunstane dragged himself to a chair and fell forward on the table, his head on his hands. . . . But when he tried to rise his limbs slipped, and, groaning, he fell to the floor" (95, 97). He is horrified at the impending responsibility and that he will have to tutor to supply for his growing family.

Dunstane obviously hysterical paralysis as a result of his inability to assume responsibility and from his growing dependence on Priscilla as financial provider, whose periodical writing brings in the money that sustains them. Janet Oppenheim's analysis of male hysteria in Victorian times supports Holdsworth's damning characterization of Dunstane: "By withdrawing male victims from the public arena and relegating them to invalidism, nervous collapse underscored their lack of purpose, initiative, energy, and will. The depression that prostrated them thus denied their very claim to manhood" (151). But his paralysis also ends the couple's sexual relations, as the doctor claims "they'll never have another [baby]" (105), revealing Holdsworth's difficulty in trying to envision new role models for her readers while simultaneously avoiding a subject they may find distasteful. Therefore, paralyzing Dunstane offers Holdsworth a way to maintain her heroine in the role of the angel in the house, keeping Priscilla "pure" while also enabling her to develop into a domestic-professional.

Despite her portrayal of Priscilla as a "modern" woman capable of earning an income, Holdsworth still relies heavily on the middle-class notion that men should be the main providers for the family. She intimates that Priscilla should be allowed to earn her living as a writer, but that as a proper middle-class woman and wife, she should not necessarily have to do so. Holdsworth further implies that Dunstane *must* take on any work that brings in money. Dunstane's neglect of his "natural" economic responsibilities and his subsequent collapse expose him as the antithesis of the middle-class Victorian man. Holdsworth wants to alter gender constructs for women, but keep them in place for men. Thus, *Locust* partially fails as domestic-professional fiction because a new definition of manhood must be produced along with a newly created definition of womanhood.

If Dunstane and Priscilla's relationship is an examination of the class system, then it also scrutinizes the difficulty of escaping from those divisions in an effort to redefine gender constructs. Dunstane has married "up," and Priscilla, who loves the masses, consistently—though unconsciously—reminds him that he is indeed of a lower class than she: Priscilla's father, a country rector, is a gentleman; Dunstane's late father, a merchant, was not. The elder Momeries' situation foreshadows Dunstane and Priscilla's, because his mother ran the grocery business after his father became paralyzed. Even though the doctor blames Dunstane's paralysis on a "hereditary tendency" (103), it is apparent that both Momerie men cannot deal with a powerful, economically self-sufficient woman. Dunstane refuses to credit his mother for his university education, instead laying gratitude at the doorstep of a rich uncle and censuring his mother for dying while he was taking his exams: "'It was my uncle who sent me to Cambridge,' said Dunstane prosaically; 'he left the money for the purpose. He had faith in my abilities. . . . My finals were ruined by my anxiety for [my mother]. She died while I was taking the last paper'" (17–18). Now married to a woman of higher class than himself, Dunstane cannot handle its implications, which include reminding him that he comes from the working class.

Priscilla and Dunstane move into the Regent's Buildings for economic reasons, but interestingly, the majority of the neighbors with whom they most associate are also people whose occupations are ambiguous in terms of class labeling, perhaps accounting for their middle-class expectations and values: Stephen Malden, an artist and enlightened man who falls in love with Priscilla; Gertrude Tennant, an aspiring opera singer and the novel's New Woman, who is revealed to really only want marriage; and Miss Cardrew, Priscilla's former governess who now writes short stories for her living. Gertrude considers herself, Malden, and Miss Cardrew, as artists, to be "the aristocracy" of the building, "the people with something to live for" (32). Although these characters effectively constitute a late-Victorian type of "gentrification" of the Regent's Buildings, bringing their middle-class values and expectations into the tenement with them, their habitation also marks their economic liminality. They occupy a precarious position that can deliver them into the lower class at any moment.

An examination of Priscilla's relationship with these neighbors reveals the tensions inherent in the angel in the house image. Although Priscilla is a professional writer, Holdsworth consistently emphasizes her "angelic" qualities, especially her devotion to her duty as a wife. Malden, who falls in love with Priscilla and offers to elope to the Continent to save her from Dunstane's cruelty, serves to present the domestic-professional Priscilla as the antithesis of the New Woman, an instance of the separation between the "good" and the "bad" New Woman that often appears in domestic-professional fiction.[3] Priscilla momentarily considers his proposition, but she ultimately decides to stay with her husband, as convention wins out over feelings, even though she concedes, "Right is not best! ... And it is never happy. I have done right for these two years ... Do I look like a happy woman?" (228). Priscilla's comment implicitly acknowledges that her relationship with Dunstane has been less than satisfying, in all aspects. More important, she is saying that a relationship with Malden would happily include her sexuality, which late-Victorian middle-class society wants her to ignore.

After Malden temporarily leaves for Europe by himself, Priscilla puts that sexual tension and energy into writing *The Book of the Great City*, about the suffering of London's poor. But because she is not allowed to have a fulfilling personal life, her professional life also becomes unbalanced. Priscilla transforms into one of those she writes about: a working-class woman struggling to make ends meet, physically and emotionally suffocating under her burdens. Yet it is her own personal transformation that allows her to develop into a domestic-professional author who can change her community. Priscilla's writing thus extends her role as angel from in the house to out in society.

Miss Cardrew, Priscilla's former governess, is the other woman writer in *The Years That the Locust Hath Eaten*, "a spinster who mingled sentiment and fiction, and was known in literary circles as a purveyor of sensations" (20). She represents the single domestic-professional woman's problematic position in a society that does not want to acknowledge its "odd women," in George Gissing's words. "Cardie," as Priscilla calls her, is aware of the boundaries she is crossing with her writing and so holds to extreme conventions as if her adherence to such strictures puts her work effectively into the background. Cardie moves from one socially and economically liminal position as a governess to another as a writer. Because of her precarious social status, she consistently makes sure that she follows the rules of (middle-class) society: Comically, Cardie uses a footstool when Dunstane is home because "in a gentleman's presence a woman should be a creature without legs" (73). Other times she appears shocked at conversations that Priscilla or Gertrude engage in with Dunstane and Malden. However, despite her middle-class "delicateness" toward such conventions, Miss Cardrew's work encompasses writing sensation stories and romances. Middle-class hopes play a part in her willingness to debase herself temporarily as "a purveyor of sensations": "My book has sold beyond my most pleasurable dreams. Priscilla, my dear, I shall be able to live in the country ... and have a little shop" (260–61). Not totally comfortable with her liminality, Miss Cardrew still takes pride in her work, but also accepts it as part of her situation as a single, older woman with few choices.

Although Priscilla's relationships with the "aristocracy" of the Regent's Buildings are important to an examination of Holdsworth's critique of the class system, so is Holdsworth's attitude toward the working class and the middle class' responsibilities toward them. She is critical of the middle class' apparent obsession with cleanliness and its efforts to insist and expect that that obsession be shared by the working class. In *Imperial Leather: Race, Gender and Sexuality in the Colonial Contest,* Anne McClintock convincingly argues that the ideology of the middle-class woman as a creature of idleness was constructed upon the shoulders of the working class who labored to enable that idleness. Furthermore, the working class' labor needed to be hidden, as if to deny the existence of the dirt that needed their labor to clear it away. "In Victorian culture, the iconography of dirt became deeply integrated in the policing and transgression of social boundaries," says McClintock (153). She claims that the working class was feminized and racialized in order to contain it; that is, its labor was considered not as important as the business (masculine and middle class) sphere's, especially labor that occurred in the (domestic and feminine) household, and the tanned and/or grimy skin resulting from outside labor and dirty work served to racialize the working class—to make them "not white," so to speak.

The consistent themes of dirt and whiteness throughout *Locust* serve double duty: they reveal a feminist/socialist agenda, important to domestic-professional fiction, about the middle class's responsibility toward the working poor, but they also solidify class boundaries and prejudices, revealing a perhaps unavoidable trap for middle-class writers. Although Holdsworth does not explicitly racialize her working-class characters, the implication that they are another "species" in need of middle-class indoctrination appears in Holdsworth's constant employment of dirtiness and cleanliness. Her novel also reveals what I believe is a subliminal rejection of middle-class values through its treatment of "whiteness."

As critics such as bell hooks (166) and Louis Owens (44) have observed, whiteness, despite its traditional alignment with goodness and beauty, is often considered pernicious and dangerous to nonwhite cultures. In *Years,* the ideology of whiteness is transferred from race to gender, and it is an ideology that is particularly dangerous to middle-class women. Priscilla, white and middle class, wants to believe that she is "one of the masses" and wants to do something for their benefit, but as the conveyor of middle-class values to the Regent's Buildings, her "whiteness" foreshadows doom. Her middle-class values of cleanliness and order do little for the working-class tenants—they certainly do not improve their economic situation—but instead bring death to Priscilla herself. Throughout the novel the usual associations of whiteness with goodness and health are distorted and undermined. Repeatedly whiteness correlates to sickness and death. Whiteness in the Regent's Buildings comes not from leisure, but from stifling air and lack of sun, implying that whiteness/idleness is good only for the middle class. For workers, as well as the domestic-professional woman caught between classes, it is an unwholesome sign of unhealthiness, of too much work that drains the body of life-giving blood.

Priscilla's class ambiguity is apparent at the beginning of the novel with Chapter 1 titled "One of the Queen's Daughters." While the inhabitants of East London's Euston Road throng the streets in hopes of seeing "one of the Queen's darters ... going to the station" (5), Priscilla Momerie is moving into the ironically named Regent's Buildings. A conversation between several tenants about the two events consolidates Priscilla's blurred class status. As Mrs. Gibson and Gertrude Tennant discuss the Momeries, little Jimmy Gibson interjects with a question about the princess:

Gertrude laughed lightly. . . . "Do you know whose furniture that is coming in?"

"The new people at 30, I expect. They was to come in to-day. Newly married they are."

"Yes, I know. They are friends of Miss Cardrew's."

"Mother, mother! ain't she comin' now?"

"No, child. And I'm sure I wish she was, keeping me idlin' all day!" (6–7)

Although Jimmy's question refers to the royal daughter, Mrs. Gibson's answer pertains to both the princess and the similarly named Priscilla. In either case, waiting for either upper-class woman is a waste of time that a working-class woman cannot afford.

A further comparison between Priscilla and the queen's daughter emphasizes that Holdsworth is not totally comfortable with her middle-class protagonist crossing the line into working-class territory. Mrs. Gibson tells her son that he will be able to identify the princess because although "she will look just like common flesh and blood, ... she'll smile and bow, and p'raps she will 'ave a carriage and pair all to 'erself" (5). The first description of Priscilla's smiling eyes (8) reminds readers of Mrs. Gibson's description of royalty. Malden's question about Priscilla, "What is that girl doing in a place like this?" (8), could also be asked of the princess. Although Holdsworth sets up the premise that Priscilla's moving into a working-class tenement is admirable and worthwhile, she also suggests that ultimately it is just as absurd as if the queen's daughter were actually the one taking up residence in the buildings. The princess' cavalcade will be echoed ironically at the end of the novel by Priscilla's funeral procession:

"I suppose it's somebody grand wot they are takin' aw'y to be buried," [a woman] said. "They couldn't make more fuss for the Queen herself. I never seed such a crowd at a buryin' before."

"Nor I," said the woman beside her. "But lor! 'tain't nobody of no account. She were only a pore young woman wot lived in them workmen's dwellings." (306–7)

Moving into the Regent's Buildings, Priscilla brings along middle-class values about dirt and cleanliness, even if she herself has never before done housework. She finds cleaning to be a new experience; "it is very entertaining to manage a house" she tells her husband (40), something fun, not the work that it is to the working-class women who spend twelve-hour days at a factory, then come home to more work. If things are not cleaned, it is only because there are too many other responsibilities to which to attend. After cleaning her own apartment, Priscilla moves into the common areas: "Even the hall was swept and garnished. She had herself washed the flags of the passage" (9). Seeing her work more as spectacle than beneficence, "Priscilla had been disappointed that no one had gone by to admire her bare arms, and her hands in the dirty suds" (9). As Anita Levy points out, "The middle-class household model enabled analogical thinking by serving as a base from which to measure the deviance, and hence degeneration, of the poor and the undeveloped" (107). Coming from a bourgeois background, Priscilla is convinced that her work, as mere spectacle, is doing something for the working-class tenants of the building that they do not do for themselves and so is to be admired; she fails to realize that "bare arms" and "hands in the dirty suds" are the symbols of work that is an additional burden on women who already have too much to do. More important for my discussion of the domestic-professional, Priscilla needs to learn that her work must aim to do something, not be merely for show. She is helped in her education as domestic-professional by Mrs. Markham and Mrs. Gibson, who are the two major working-class characters in the novel.

Mrs. Markham and Mrs. Gibson not only play an important role in the domestic-professionalization of Priscilla, but also help to highlight Priscilla's fall from middle-class grace: all three women are responsible for the economic as well as the spiritual health of their families. Both Mrs. Markham and Mrs. Gibson work full-time jobs at a factory while raising numerous children with apparently no help from their husbands. In fact, Priscilla could be said to be in an even worse predicament, because Dunstane does not help around the house nor does he bring in a paycheck, the latter something Messrs. Markham and Gibson do, even if they mostly spend their free time at the local pub.

Additionally, Mrs. Markham's and Mrs. Gibson's plight as wives, mothers, and workers is emphasized by Priscilla's well-meaning but condescending attempts to make their lives better. Initially, Mrs. Markham and Mrs. Gibson do "not accept Mrs. Momerie as one of themselves" because they think her "a lady masquerading as a working woman" (41). Recognizing Priscilla not as a *real* working woman, but only one who "plays" at work, Mrs. Markham and Mrs. Gibson emphasize for the reader that at this point Priscilla is not a real domestic-professional in a position to change society. Her "masquerading" can be compared to the relationship between maid Hannah Cullwick and barrister Arthur J. Munby that McClintock analyzes in *Imperial Leather*, which in turn can shed light on the difficulties faced by a middle-class writer attempting to expose social wrongs.

Despite their class differences, Cullwick and Munby had a secret relationship, which included marriage, that lasted fifty-five years. Most interesting to biographers and cultural historians is the couple's fascination (McClintock refers to it as fetishism) with transgressing social conventions. Recorded by photographs, Cullwick would often either "cross-dress" up as a middle-class lady, blacken herself and pose as a male slave, or simply be photographed with the tools of her trade, all of which fascinated Munby. Cullwick's "masquerading," then, prompts McClintock to investigate the "difficult question of what kind of *agency* is possible in situations of extreme social *inequality*" (140). Although it is often assumed that the upper classes are more powerful vis-à-vis the lower classes, McClintock determines that the working class has a power of its own, enabling it to resist middle-class demands. The Cullwick-Munby alliance, on the surface, seems to be just another case of middle-class patriarchy exacting its demands, but McClintock reasonably shows that Cullwick held a particular type of power in the relationship, one that came precisely from being working class. For instance, Cullwick enjoyed the anonymity and safety that her working-class status conferred upon her in allowing her to walk the streets alone and undisturbed (177); she took pride in her work and the strength that it demanded (156–57); and, although Munby's lover and then wife, she always demanded that he pay her for domestic work (141).

McClintock questions agency in the novel, in which a middle-class person tries to impose her conventions and morals on the working class. That is, how is the duty of the domestic-professional impeded by her class status? Although not as explicit as in Cullwick's case, Mrs. Markham and Mrs. Gibson also hold a type of power unavailable to Priscilla while she maintains her middle-class beliefs. In Chapter 4, "Priscilla Makes Friends," Priscilla attempts to wash clothes for the first time in her life. This middle-class woman, who thinks that keeping house is "fun," obviously does not know what she is doing: "Washing was the easiest thing in the world; one only needed soap and water and muscles" (41–42). After watching Priscilla for a time, Mrs. Gibson and Mrs. Markham finally yield and show Priscilla how it is done: "You'll spile them fine things, Mrs. Momerie, mixing of them with dusters and kitchen towels. And you want hot water and washin'-powder. I never seed nobody wash clothes with scented soap before . . . You want soda and sunlight soap. Them tylet soaps ain't no good for clothes" (42). Despite the working-class accents that mark their class status, Mrs. Gibson and Mrs. Markham have, and revel in, a certain kind of superior knowledge well beyond Priscilla's sheltered experience; this knowledge not only enables them to survive in a gritty, unrelenting world, but also allows them a temporary inversion of the class hierarchy. Initially suspicious of Priscilla, they share their knowledge, not only of washing but of the degrading class system, giving her the first lesson in becoming a domestic-professional: Priscilla must learn to become an empathetic part of the systems she hopes to transform.

While they are working, they tell Priscilla the story of Jennie Pyke, a child who drowned in one of the washing tubs, kept full because "they was afraid of a water-famine; and they cuts off the water, all but two hours a day. So we was obliged to fill up tubs and jars to keep enough over the night" (43). The "they" that Mrs. Markham and Mrs. Gilbert are referring to are middle-class city authorities, and the very thing that is used to promote the middle-class value of cleanliness, the washing tub, ends up being an instrument of death. In the working-class women's eyes, it is middle-class administration that ultimately is the cause of the child's death; they have no doubts about who is to blame: "The coroner give it accidentally drownded, though Mrs. Pyke said 'twas the fault of the County Council" (44). Her middle-class sensibilities shaken, Priscilla flees, effectively leaving Mrs. Gibson and Mrs. Markham, the "real" working-class women, to do exactly what working-class women have always done: middle-class women's dirty work. Priscilla's later return with tea can be seen as an attempt to restore order from the chaos caused, not by the lower class's dirtiness, but by middle-class authority indirectly responsible for a child's death. Holdsworth may try to present Priscilla in the best possible light—as the one person who truly wants to help the lower classes—but her behavior is disturbing at times exactly because it imitates and perpetuates middle-class abuse of its responsibilities toward the lower classes. Only as she evolves into a domestic-professional, brought about by her involvement with these working-class women, can Priscilla's talent as a writer be channeled into appropriate venues.

A second scene that supports this argument and bears a close analysis appears in Chapter 18, "A Gift," when Mrs. Markham gives birth to twins. Mrs. Markham already has five children, a sixth baby recently dying because she had to go back to the factory only one week after giving birth, allowing Holdsworth to comment on some of the abuse workers faced in the factory system. Also central to the story at this point is that Priscilla's daughter, born prematurely, has died because of Dunstane's irresponsibility. The baby's name was to have been Beatrice, meaning "she that makes happy," but upon her birth, Priscilla named her Dolores ("sorrows"), nicknaming her "Dollie." Since Dunstane refuses to work, however, Priscilla alone shoulders the family's financial obligations with her writing. While she is out of the apartment, cashing a check received for one of her sensation stories, the baby stops breathing. Dunstane goes to get help, but as soon as he realizes he can walk, he collapses, allowing the baby to die rather than later explain how a paralytic walked. Dunstane blames Priscilla for being money hungry and out of their home when her daughter needed her.

The baby's nickname Dollie in effect becomes a symbol for dire consequences of middle-class desires. Whereas the death of Mrs. Markham's sixth child exposes the abusive regulations of factories toward their female workers, Priscilla's actions toward Mrs. Markham having twins uncomfortably suggests that it is permissible for a middle-class woman to take another woman's child. Dollie (particularly after her death) and Mrs. Markham's baby become the equivalent of "dolls," objects of material possession suitable for bargaining: "'Mrs. Markham,' Priscilla struck in, 'if you would give me one you should see *it* every day and nurse *it*, and have *it* when you liked, only you would let *it* live with me, and let *it* be my little baby, and let me have *it* to love and to ... '" (192; emphasis added). Priscilla's use of the word "it" to describe the baby reemphasizes in many ways that she is, as seen in the opening chapters of the novel, still "playing" house. The child is not a person to her, but a doll that places her in a maternal role, yet allows her to remain nonsexual.

Priscilla's nonsexuality is contrasted against Mrs. Markham's excessive fertility, thus again calling attention to the differences between the classes, "distinguish[ing] what [is] docile and desirable in a woman from what [is] degenerate and desirous" (Levy 109). With Mrs. Gibson's support, Priscilla persuades Mrs. Markham to give her one of the twins, one "dollie" replacing another. Their argument is that twins will produce twice the work for Mrs. Markham for which she does not have the time, considering the five children she already has and her factory job, which was responsible for the death of a sixth. Her initial dilemma is which baby to part with, the girl or the boy: "'I don't know as 'ow I could spare the little b'y. B'ys look after theirsels when they grows up. . . . I don't see as I can part with the gel. Gels is allus useful about a 'ouse'" (190–91). As Ellen Ross points out in *Love and Toil*, "Working-class mothers . . . more unsentimentally viewed their children in terms of the resources they required or contributed. They knew their love was vital to their children, but they acknowledged that young children meant hard work, which the children could later reciprocate" (129). As they grew, girls were an invaluable help with taking care of younger children and housework, and boys could get jobs to help the family financially. Both Mrs. Markham and Priscilla here view children as commodities: the former seeing them as eventual helpmates, the latter as something for her to care for so that she may continue fulfilling her maternal angel in the house role. At Mrs. Gibson's insistence, Mrs. Markham reluctantly relinquishes the girl.

Later in the day Mrs. Markham changes her mind and wants the child back, but it is very unsettling to the reader to see how Priscilla can "exchange" her dead child for another, a symbolic appropriation of the vitality of the working class by the "lifeless" middle class. Ironically, Priscilla, who sees herself as someone who wants to help the working poor, does so by imposing middle-class values. She is convinced that she can take care of the child better than Mrs. Markham, who has far too many children anyhow, or so she believes: "Her thoughts were bitter. Twins to Mrs. Markham, already overburdened with five, while she whose arms were empty must bear her desolation" (185). Although just as desperate for money as the working-class tenants, Priscilla conforms to the belief that she is still middle class, and so she also believes she should get what she wants, in this case, the child. It never occurs to her that she cannot financially provide for a child any better than the Markhams. After all, her natural child Dollie was born prematurely and unhealthy because of Priscilla's "writing incessantly . . . to keep her household together and put away a little fund for the time when she must be idle" (108). Additionally, Priscilla returns to her writing much sooner than she had wanted: "She must begin her work for the sake of the child. She understood now what made it possible for women like Mrs. Markham to go back to the factory so soon" (127). Losing Dollie and this second child, though heartbreaking for Priscilla, impels her to put her energy into her work; understanding of the poor results from experiencing their plight firsthand.

Her slide from middle class to working class *and* her progression as a domestic-professional writer are represented by the symbol she uses most often

to describe herself as a writer: the driver of a hackney. In the most obvious al-
lusion, Priscilla, as a writer of sensational short stories, sees herself as a "hack
writer," one who does as much as possible for as much money as possible, a situation in which many women writers found themselves. But the term "hackney" also reveals Priscilla's loss of class as well as her gain of insight. A hackney
was often a coach formerly belonging to the upper classes, but converted to a
for-hire vehicle and used mostly by the lower classes. Many times the aristocratic insignia was left on the coach (Pool 318). Priscilla internally wears the "insignia" of the middle class despite the fact that she is very much a working-class
woman. This tension, however uncomfortable it is for Priscilla, is necessary for
her development as a domestic-professional writer if she hopes that her writing
accomplishes any good for society.

At the end of the novel, worn out by the extremes in her life—writing her
short stories by day and her *Book of the Great City* at night—Priscilla dies. At
first, Dunstane, Malden, Gertrude, and Cardie plan to leave the building, but
then they decide to stay there, carrying out Priscilla's plan, as outlined in her
book, for alleviating the poor's burdens. Dunstane, ironically, forsakes writing
as he realizes his New Religion's fraudulence, realizing that his middle-class theories will not help the poor; he instead decides to use his knowledge to relieve
the poor's oppression, vowing "to teach ... as she wished" (304). Cardie and
Malden also agree to stay, assisting Dunstane because as Malden says, "We must
help each other for her sake" (305). But it is Gertrude who first resolves to
"remain in the Buildings, and try to carry on Priscilla's work" (303). The
domestic-professional woman's influence on the novel's New Woman is complete. Although Cardie warns her that "it will not be easy to fill our dear
Priscilla's place ... you cannot do what she did for them" (303), Gertrude, heed-
less now of her selfish ambitions for a singing career or marriage, will turn her
talents and compassion to aiding the weary and the ill of the Regent's Buildings,
suggesting that she will be the next domestic-professional.

Although Gertrude's reply to Cardie seems rather simplistic"—"She loved
them; and I will love them for her sake'" (303)—it contains the most basic of
Christian tenets: to love one another. Holdsworth's sincere statement touches
the heart of what many women writers thought was their duty, that love and
respect for all human beings was the keystone of building a just society. Unlike
Dunstane's unattainable idealism, this pragmatic feminism—a term I take from
Charlene Haddock Seigfried and Jane Duran—suggests several paradigms for
change, an essential feature of domestic-professional fiction. With their decision
to stay, Priscilla's friends make the first step in building that society. Thus,
Priscilla's goal as a domestic-professional writer has been achieved: people's attitudes have changed.

However, what Holdsworth leaves out is that the working-class tenants, such
as the Markhams and the Gibsons, have no choice. They must live in the Regent's Buildings because it is all they can afford. Their lives are little different
from what they were when Priscilla entered them. Holdsworth seemingly wants

to leave her readers with an optimistic ending, but the loose ends are disturbing. Priscilla is not rewarded. Instead the domestic-professional writer dies as a result of the extreme imbalance in her personal and public lives:

Her strength had lasted while the work lasted; now it was almost spent. The dailystories had become an insufferable burden; they did not bring in thirty shillings a week now. She kept the household together with difficulty ... only Dunstane did not notice that their comforts were fewer than of old. She denied herself bare necessaries, but a feverish excitement kept her up. She must see her book in print—that was still to live for. (260)

Priscilla, thinking her final manuscript has been rejected, crosses out its title, replacing it with *The Years That the Locust Hath Eaten* (279),[4] the biblical phrase that she feels sums up the past three years of her life: Her book "was like a live thing ... It had hands pushing her down into the ground, heaping failure upon her ... It had feet that danced upon her grave ... It had eyes that mocked her futile ambition" (278). Ironically, after Priscilla leaves her apartment, eventually collapsing and dying, a letter arrives from the publisher, asking only for a title change. Priscilla's whole being has been put into her writing, unlike the other domestic-professional authors discussed in this project, so when she thinks it is rejected, she gives up.

It is never shown what Priscilla actually writes in her short stories, her novels, or *The Book of the Great City*. But because Holdsworth gives her novel the same title as Priscilla's best effort, the text read can be seen as a mirror of her creation's: both are about the unacceptable state of the working poor. Since *Years* deals intimately with the ease with which the middle class can descend into the lower class, Holdsworth's rhetorical strategy is brilliantly revealed. She disguises the working poor's situation by placing her middle-class heroine in their position; her middle-class audience, who would recognize Priscilla as one of their own, could then more fully identify with the problems the lower classes faced. Although *Years* brings attention to the poor's plight, it also highlights the middle-class woman's. Despite her bravado about wanting to be "one of the masses," Priscilla can never fully assimilate because she clings to middle-class values. Her role as the angel in the house, ministering to all except herself, destroys any chance of survival outside of the middle class that created its ideology.

At the end of *The Years That the Locust Hath Eaten* the class system that destroyed Priscilla is still in place. But her novel has done some good, and in turn, Holdsworth's domestic-professional effort leaves the decision for change up to its readers. Holdsworth has given her readers the facts and details about the working-class poor's abominable situation, handing them the responsibility to do something about it.

Ella Hepworth Dixon's *The Story of a Modern Woman* employs a rhetorical strategy similar to that of *The Years That the Locust Hath Eaten*, balancing its domestic-professional woman precariously between the middle and working classes. If Dunstane Momerie is the literary legacy of *Middlemarch*'s Casaubon,

then Mary Erle, Dixon's writing protagonist, surely—as her name announces—
is a direct descendant of *Aurora Leigh*'s Marian Erle. Mary Erle is not, sexually
speaking, a fallen woman—although by the end of the novel she has an opportunity to become one—but she has fallen: on hard times and bad luck. Forced
by her father's sudden death and her small inheritance to support herself and
her younger brother, Mary turns to writing for periodicals, although her great
desire is to paint. Abandoned by the man she loves who marries another woman
for money and prestige, paralleled in the novel by the story of a working-class
girl jilted by her middle-class lover, Mary clings to the notion that he still loves
her. When, several years later, Vincent Hemming proposes that he leave his wife
and he and Mary elope to France, she denies him: Mary had promised her dying
friend Alison Ives that she would never knowingly hurt another woman. Like
Holdsworth, Dixon implicitly connects a woman's sexuality with her art, but
she ultimately declares, as Ann L. Ardis notes, that until Victorian society
changes its attitude about gender construction, the domestic-professional woman
will remain divided (107–112).

The Story of a Modern Woman is really the story of two modern women:
Mary and Alison. Alison confidently labels herself a modern woman, whereas
Mary seems to have the tag thrust upon her. The novel is also about a supposedly modern man, Vincent, who plans to write a book about women's education.
However, Dixon's characterization of Hemming leaves the reader thinking there
is little hope for women with either "old-fashioned" or "modern" men. All three
characters embody the desire to effect social change, but although the individual actions of Alison and Mary do lead to some change, Hemming's effort does
not, because his personal behavior contradicts his ideals. His hope for the "ame-
lioration of the English race" (115), like Dunstane Momerie's, is of little consequence because of his selfish conduct.

Mary Erle wants to be the modern, independent woman—in fact, she is forced
to be one because of her father's death, his small legacy, and the support of her
brother. But she also desires the conventional middle-class life as wife and
mother. Mary wants it both ways, as reflected in Dixon's description of her life
as "the nature of an experiment" (15). Dixon implies that progressive attitudes
about women's roles seem not only to have stopped but even to have been reversed. Mary was born in an in-between time, Dixon tells us, after the era when
women of the midcentury knew they were raised only to be good wives and
mothers and before the time "when parents [began] to take their responsibilities seriously" in educating and preparing their daughters for life, whatever it
may bring (15). Because of this, she is consistently torn and confused about her
feelings, a claim that most probably could be made about many late-Victorian
middle-class women.

By the time of her father's death, Mary is put into two roles that conventional
Victorian society deemed incompatible, but that many women had to fulfill: that
of the angel/mother *and* financial provider. As Julia M. Gergits notes, conservatives thought that women should passively stay in the home, but they were

often unable to do so because the men in their lives—fathers, husbands, and sons—had failed them financially: "If it is women's birthright to be protected by men and maintained in the home, as Ruskin and Patmore insist, the patriarchy has disinherited these women. They are left with no recourse: they must supply their own homes or starve" (110). The modern woman aspires to fulfill both duties, but Dixon ultimately concedes that such fulfillment is impossible while the patriarchal culture persists in defining stringent roles for women that ironically, as with Priscilla, make twice the work for women. Additionally, as was also shown in *The Years That the Locust Hath Eaten*, the preserving of middle-class values limits the opportunity for changing the social system. However, like *Years*, Dixon's novel is effective because it glaringly points out these defects.

Binding gender roles that leave little room for individuality are evidenced in several episodes involving Vincent and Mary. Before leaving for a year abroad to "collect materials for my book on the Woman Question" (80), Hemming asks Mary to consider marrying him on his return to England. Dixon describes the scene, which according to middle-class social conventions should be the high point of a young woman's life, as suffocating and imprisoning: "His hands, which held her two wrists as they stood there gazing at each other, felt like links of iron. In that one supreme moment Mary Erle tasted for the first time, in all its intensity, the helplessness of woman, the inborn feeling of subjection to a stronger will, inherited through generations of submissive feminine intelligences" (79). Ironically, this tableau will be repeated several years later; when Vincent proposes leaving his wife and running off with Mary, he again holds "her two wrists like a vice" (299). Hemming's status as a middle-class man allows him, with full social urging and approval, to break the bond he initiated with Mary to further himself politically and financially; yet Mary's position as a middle-class woman demands that she stay within the boundaries of respectable conventions or face dire consequences by rejecting them. Mary cannot win; Dixon suggests that middle-class society would either not accept her as a working wife or it would ostracize her as Hemming's mistress.

In her role of domestic-professional author, Dixon critiques the institution of middle-class marriage through Mary's situation: she he must adhere to the characteristics of the "angel," yet reap none of the economic rewards of marriage, an institution about which she has ambiguous feelings. Despite her initial reaction to his first marriage proposal, once Vincent is abroad, Mary, "of the order of women who idealise the absent" (113), grows increasingly fond and desirous of the romantic idea of marriage. As a little girl, Mary debated between wanting to be a "bride or an angel" (22), not realizing that Victorian conventions deemed the two inseparable. Her adult idealization of the absent corresponds with her childish idealization of marriage, her younger desire to be both bride and angel. This desire is then multiplied by the demands of work: "Lonely, tired, discouraged, she clung to the thought of their marriage with curious tenacity" (116). Mary longs for an escape from her responsibilities as sole provider for herself and her younger brother, an escape that Victorian society always promised young, middle-class women through the act of marriage. However, the flight that Hemming eventually offers her is not an option. As also evidenced in *Years*, the domestic-professional is a difficult role that not all can fulfill. Mary does not entirely accomplish it, but with the publication and success of *The Story of a Modern Woman*, Dixon does. Thus, though Mary seemingly fails, the function of domestic-professional fiction to incite social change is achieved through Dixon's narrative of Mary's story as a working woman writer.

Mary's writing is purely economically utilitarian: to earn enough money to live. Although she writes a novel, "a bit of real life" (183), Mary cannot find a publisher for it. Her life as a writer, where she teeters perilously on the brink of poverty, functions as the novel's critique of social inequity. A reviewer for *The Athenæum* complained, "It is an ungraceful habit to refer to any poor heroine as 'the girl' so many times on every page, and really at last suggests maid-of-all work associations" (770). But that is precisely Dixon's point. Although "by representing *what it was not* [i.e., not working class], the middle class defined precisely *what it was* and so secured its corporate identity" (Levy 24), in *The Story of a Modern Woman* class boundaries are blurred and transgressed economically as Mary clings to middle-class conventions and attitudes while slowly sinking into the economic distress of the working classes. Mary's degradation serves to question what happens to the individual's identity when one is labeled by a class distinction. Since a significant element of domestic-professional fiction is the recording of a woman's construction of her self, as with Priscilla's situation discussed earlier, Mary Erle's transformation to domestic-professional is based largely on her relationships with others, especially Alison Ives and Vincent Hemming, as well as her relationship to her writing.

Unlike *The Years That the Locust Hath Eaten*, in which the woman writer is the one who recognizes the plight of the poor and wants to do something about it, *The Story of a Modern Woman*'s social transformer is not Mary Erle, but her best friend Alison Ives, an upper-middle-class woman. Mary is too busy working to keep her head above water economically to worry about women in similar or worse conditions, whereas Alison has the time and the money to comfortably initiate her social reforms. Her special compassion is saving young working-class girls, and, interestingly, although Mary in many ways eventually fulfills that description, Alison never helps her financially. Middle-class conventions and politeness prevent Alison from offering, and Mary from asking for, help. But, like *Years*, the disturbing effects of the imposition of middle-class values on the working class are revealed. One could even go so far as to wonder if Alison's "help" is of consequence at all, as I will presently show.

Alison, the daughter of Lady Jane Ives, triumphantly refers to herself as a thoroughly modern woman. This "good" New Woman is set in opposition to the undesirable one, as evidenced in Dixon's description of Alison: "What attracted people at once was her intense womanliness, her utter absence of snobbery, her real desire to be in sympathy with her own sex" (58). However, Alison's upper-middle-class status allows her to forgo the usual societal commitments (when she wants), such as balls and country outings, to indulge in her passion for helping lower-class women, much to her mother's dismay. Lady Ives finds Alison's chosen avocation as social worker confusing and alarming: "In our time, balls and parties were supposed to suffice. But I can't get my child to take a proper interest in society" (243). Alison's and Lady Ives's differing definitions of "society" reveal the distinction between the "old" woman and the "modern" woman, as well as the "bad" and the "good" New Woman. The former envelops herself within a false atmosphere of frivolity, content, and intent on satisfying only herself, whereas the latter goes out into the world, determined to improve the poor's condition, thus improving society overall.

But although Alison is portrayed sympathetically by Dixon, she is also a problematic character. She first moves temporarily to the impoverished East End to do her work, but then decides to set up a young unmarried mother, Evelina, in an apartment in Mayfair. Alison's decision, on the surface, appears logical: "It seems to me that when one or two of us go and live down there we absolutely do no permanent good at all. The thing will be to bring the East End here. One by one, of course, just as we go there" (58). However, what she is saying, in effect, is that the working class must be immersed in middle-class culture, conventions, and values in order to improve.

When closely examined, Alison's "solutions" to Evelina's, and other unmarried girls', problems are somewhat questionable. Although she does persuade the baby's father to acknowledge his accountability and marry Evelina, Alison's main occupations seem to be taking "a lot of poor girls over [to] the National Gallery ... to explain Mantegna" (148, 150) and reading comic novels to them. Her reasoning for the latter is to "cultivate a sense of humour" in these girls: "It's what women ought to cultivate above all other things, especially, the poorer classes [she tells Mary]. With a keen sense of the ridiculous, they would never fall in love at all; and as to improvident marriages, they wouldn't exist" (64–65). Alison's attempts to encourage an appreciation of beauty in her charges reveal the influence of the Aesthetic Movement, particularly Oscar Wilde (for whom Dixon contributed a short story to the *Woman's World* when he was its editor), on Dixon's philosophy. In "The Decay of Lying," Wilde differentiates between improving the bodies and the souls of the poor: "We try to improve the conditions of the race by means of good air, free sunlight, wholesome water, and hideous bare buildings for the better housing of the lower orders. But these things merely produce health, they do not produce beauty. For this, Art is required" (983). However, Wilde is writing from a comfortable, male, middle-class position, and his supposition—like that of the entire Aesthetic Movement—that art can be separated from life questions the sociopolitical intention of literature that domestic-professional fiction advocates.

Dixon does not entirely reject Wilde's philosophy, but she believes that it is not enough merely to offer the poor "beauty." Where Alison fails, Dixon suggests, is that there is never any mention of a skill or trade she might be teaching these girls, something that socialist feminist Helen Bosanquet thought was imperative, not only for economic reasons, but also for domestic ones:

Those who argue that to make women industrially efficient will be to make them support their husbands in idleness, have quite overlooked the effect of a disciplined intelligence upon the choice of a girl who is not driven to seek an illusory refuge in marriage from poverty and hard toil. It is the girl who feels the alternative of a quiet independence open to her who chooses a good husband for herself and a good father for her children. (307)

Alison believes that solely by affecting middle-class conventions—developing a sense of humor—that Evelina's life will improve, yet Bosanquet proposes that it is the learning of a skill that will yield the same results. The description of Evelina's wedding reveals that Dixon believes that a balance between Wilde's aesthetic philosophy and Bosanquet's social theory are equally important in helping the working class.

After Alison dies, one has no idea whether her transformation of Evelina will significantly change Evelina's life. Dixon gives no clue that things will not look up on her wedding day. Mary reports to Alison, who cannot attend Evelina's wedding because of her illness, that the young girl's very middle-class-inspired decision to wear a white silk wedding dress, albeit secondhand, verged on the ridiculous. Alison's reply disturbingly reveals the culpability of her own schemes: "I think that it shows a certain vague hankering after the ideal—a sort of *élan* toward the unattainable" (258). By her own admission, Alison concedes that Evelina can only "hanker" after a middle-class way of life, but will never attain it. Like Holdsworth's novel, *The Story of a Modern Woman* acknowledges that the working class will remain the same as long as superficial solutions are offered for their problems. Moreover, those problems could easily envelop the middle class as well: if Evelina is raised out of her fallen status by marriage, Mary teeters on its edge when Vincent Hemming invites her to be his mistress.

Hemming's role as Mary's lover and jilt plays a significant part in Mary's fallen status; his character highlights the disparity between the learned man and the moral man. Although politically conservative, Hemming is solidly a middle-class gentleman with liberal ideas, including belief in higher education and the vote for women, and "he had a great deal to say on the future of the race, and of the necessity of maintaining a high ethical standard" (70–71). Hemming declares in a letter to Mary,

Were I, in short a man to whom personal happiness is paramount—I might have spoken more decisively in relation to a possible future together before I left England. But I am paying you no mean compliment, my dear Mary, when I tell you that I have every confidence that in you, as in myself, questions of vast importance rise superior to mere selfish considerations, and that in you, above all women, I have a sympathetic sharer alike of my ambitions, dreams, and hopes. (115)

Like Mary and Alison, Hemming is thoroughly affected by the British class system. Although he has the potential to be the new domestic-professional man, Vincent Hemming fails miserably because of his lack of morality. Selfish and ambitious to enter Parliament, these defects get the better of him and his ethics:

on his return to England he marries the daughter and heiress of a Lancashire manufacturing millionaire. Mary is left by herself to struggle on economically. Hemming's falling short as a domestic-professional man results in Mary being unable to fully develop her potential as a domestic-professional writer.

Yet Mary's struggle also reveals that she is continuing in her development as a domestic-professional, refusing to relinquish her moral foundation. Five years later, Vincent returns to Mary and begs her to run away to France with him, his argument for eloping self-serving: "You are above the prejudices of our false civilisation, you are capable of being a true woman, of giving up something for the man you love. . . . Other women—great women—have been strong enough, single-hearted enough, to do as much for the men they loved" (302–03). Hemming asks Mary to reject the middle-class conventions that force her to reject his offer, but he does not do so to shatter confining and oppressive strictures. He does so only for his own personal gratification. For all of his high-toned morality and supposed belief in women's abilities, Vincent's ultimate solution resounds with male chauvinism at its worst. Mary's refusal, seen by Ann L. Ardis as a rejection not of "sexuality per se but patriarchal culture's construction of sexuality, its normalization of erotic domination" (112), is an important step in Dixon's eyes of women taking control of their own lives and assisting other women in managing theirs, however painful it may be: "I can't, I won't, [says Mary] deliberately injure another woman. . . . Oh, the torture of women's lives—the helplessness, the impotence, the emptiness! . . . All we modern women mean to help each other now. We have a bad enough time as it is, . . . surely we needn't make it worse by our own deliberate acts!" (304). Mary's rejection of Hemming indicts him, and other men, for "injuring" women by their "deliberate," conscious acts, but it also locates her as another model of the domestic-professional woman for society to emulate.

Hemming and Dr. Dunlop Strange, Alison's suitor and a women's "nervous disease specialist" (100), are the men (many portrayed in fiction as doctors), who are in actuality "the symptoms of a diseased society" (Pykett 155). That is, both are "bad" New Men, blaming "the system" for their unhappiness and failing to acknowledge that they are part of the patriarchy that has made the rules. Strange, who works in a poor-women's hospital, wishes to marry Alison because "to get this woman for his wife would be the crowning act of a brilliantly successful career" (227–28). While visiting the hospital one day with Mary, Alison becomes attracted to "Case #27," a young girl dying of consumption after a failed suicide attempt by drowning. Alison finds out that the girl, whom Mary had seen several times in the park, was formerly Strange's mistress, a fact he endeavors to hide. Instead of admitting his part, Strange places ironic responsibility onto the girl: "Dear Miss Alison, those are terrible cases. They are cankerous evils, eating away the very life of our social system" (249).

Alison becomes almost obsessed with trying to help this nameless victim of Strange's carnality, and though she claims to be making new rules for society, her connection with "Case #27" exposes her weakness. Getting caught in the rain after numerous visits to the young girl's bedside, Alison contracts bronchitis and never recovers. Thus, Strange is ultimately responsible for the death of two women, "the lower-class woman he seduces and the middle-class woman he wishes to marry" (Pykett 155). But Alison's inability to recuperate is as much from her psychological deterioration at Strange's behavior as it is from her physical deterioration. In spite of her repeated declarations that she is the modern woman, Alison is as much as product of the "old" system as the young girl, and failure in love kills both of them. As with Priscilla, however, Mary's connection to someone less fortunate than herself continues her development as a domestic-professional, allowing her to survive.

Mary's recognition of "Case #27" as the young girl she saw waiting for a lover in the park parallels her fall into and her connection with the working class, which I discuss in more detail presently, but it is not the only time Dixon blurs class lines. At the beginning of the novel, after her father's funeral, Mary visits with one of her servants, who is upstairs sewing. This scene embodies Dixon's conviction that the angel in the house ideology is detrimental and dangerous to women of all classes. The adjectives used to describe the seamstress could also be used to describe Mary later as she toils at her writing and waits for Hemming:

The pale, pinkish light of a spring evening fell on a *drab-complexioned* girl, whose fat hand moved, as she sewed, with the *regularity of a machine*. . . . it was all *tame, monotonous, and regular as a clock*. She was *a docile, humble, uncomplaining creature*, who suggested inevitably *some patient domestic animal*. Her features, rubbed out and effaced with generations of servility, spoke of the small mendacities of the women of the lower classes, of the women who live on ministering to the caprices of the well-to-do. . . . As Mary looked at her, she was curiously reminded of many women she had seen: ladies, mothers of large families, who sat and sewed with just such an expression of *unquestioning resignation*. . . . Yes, they too were *content to exist subserviently*, depending always on someone else, using the old feminine stratagems, the well-worn feminine subterfuges, to gain their end. The woman who sews is eternally the same. . . . It was not so much a woman, but *The Woman at her monotonous toil*. (emphasis added; 13–14)

Dixon's representation of "The Woman," of any class, as the symbol of patriarchal oppression at the beginning of the novel augurs the many class transgressions and comparisons that follow in her story. Elizabeth Langland suggests that for much of the Victorian era, middle-class women, proscribed as "sexless" despite their roles of wife and mother, were represented as "guardians of spirituality," whereas working-class women were linked with "a dangerous sexuality" (71). But Dixon rejects even such dichotomous descriptions of spirituality or sexuality: what Mary learns is that women, middle or working class, are numbed and dehumanized by the patriarchal system.

Mary's descent into working-class life and adversity is also foreshadowed by a connection with the other working-class woman, the young "tawdry-looking girl" she sees in Regent's Park, "with restless eyes and a hard mouth, keeping a rendezvous with a lover who had not yet appeared" (129, 128). Like the sar-

donically named Regent's Buildings in *The Years That the Locust Hath Eaten,*
the name of Regent's Park in Dixon's novel emphasizes the ironic twist in Mary's
life. Instead of enjoying the fruits of a comfortable middle-class marriage—joining the "aristocracy" as a politician's wife—Mary must face the image of an impending lower-class life. Mary, though somewhat repulsed by the woman's
appearance and her pursuit, feels "drawn toward her"; soon "someone dressed
like a gentleman" joins her (129, 130). Later, Mary will learn that the man
"dressed *like* a gentleman," is really no gentleman in the truest sense, but Dunlop Strange, seducing "a respectable girl—a shop assistant" (260). Likewise, Vincent Hemming will try to seduce the respectable Mary and show himself also
to be the antithesis of what a gentleman is supposed to be. But, as Dixon alleges
with the characters of Strange and Hemming, the idea of the Victorian gentleman is badly in need of reconstruction.

Dixon makes the association between Mary and the girl even more obvious
the second time Mary sees her in the park while waiting futilely for Hemming,
who has just returned to England:

Yes, and there was the girl again, the girl with the hard mouth, whom she had seen the
winter morning, waiting, poor soul, for *her* lover. . . . The woman in her was dead; she
was past the stage of caring about her appearance. Despair was written on her face. . . .
No, he had not come, and in her glittering eyes one read the fact that in all human prob-
ability he never would. The girl with the hard mouth waited a long time, but finally she
disappeared down the Broad Walk. (153–54)

Although Mary considers her "a poor girl" waiting for someone who will not
come, little does she fathom that her lover also will not show that evening. That
night in bed, "the face of the girl she had seen twice in the Regent's Park rose
up again and again. And yet what had they in common?" (159). Mary's situation, the same as the shop clerk abandoned by her lover, will propel her into
also being "a poor girl," both emotionally and economically. Yet her domestic-
professional ethics will save her as similar situations destroy Alison and the
young girl.

Furthermore, Mary's father's failure to plan and provide for her future was
most probably grounded in his belief that Mary and Hemming would marry,
but Professor Erle also did not recognize Hemming's ambitious self-regard.
Mary is thus forced into becoming a working woman, but does not envision that
she will eventually become a working-class woman. The opportunity to work is
not entirely undesirable. Because of her original ambivalence toward Vincent's
marriage proposal, Mary views a career as positive, realizing that if she marries,
she must decide between being a dependent wife or an independent woman. She
associates Vincent's declaration that she has "the modern craze for work" with
its soul-saving possibilities: "It probably saves some of us from the madhouse"
(76). But when a "career" turns into a "job" that one requires just to make ends
meet, Mary learns that work also can drive one to the edge of madness and physical incapacity.

Mary's initial construction of herself as a domestic-professional with her brother to care for reveals the difficulty in assuming such a role. Her first foray into the writing profession is stressful but ultimately successful, a short story to accompany a sketch drawn by a friend: "But at last, after hours of torment, an idea came, and then the girl wrote steadily on with the easy facility of the amateur" (132). The story, interestingly, centers on class transgression, as a middle-class girl dresses as a maid to entice a young soldier. Mary, who writes the story in four days, is paid two guineas, and innocently believes that life as a writer will be smooth: "There were 365 days in a year, so that by writing a story or an article every four days she could earn something like two hundred pounds a year!" (138). But reality intervenes when she learns that her story was accepted not on merit, but because of the reputation of her scientist-father: "Your late father's name carries weight with a *certain* section of the public," the editor tells her (135). Trying to make it in a man's world, Mary discovers she succeeds only because of a man's name.

Dixon criticizes the middle-class adulation of convention as, even more to her chagrin as a writer, Mary learns that "her story was like everybody else's story" (133). As a woman, she is expected to be conventional, but as a writer, she needs to give the public something new. However, being a woman puts constraints on what is acceptable for Mary to write. When she submits a novel for serial publication that includes "a young man making love to his friend's wife," it is rejected on the grounds that "the public won't stand it. . . . They want thoroughly healthy reading" (221). Her male editor rejects the argument that her novel reflects "real life," proposing that Mary take his "'advice and stick to pretty stories. They're bound to pay best'"(223). But even though Mary is forced to take such action to support herself, Dixon refuses to do so, instead writing a novel such as *The Story of a Modern Woman*, which does present the realities of life that single women faced. Similar to Holdsworth's heroine, Mary fails at accomplishing social change through her writing, but Dixon's domestic-professional novel succeeds in presenting such problems to her public.

By the time Vincent returns to England, Mary is reporting for a ladies' periodical, *The Fan* (for which she writes three columns a month at a guinea per column), writing the above-mentioned novel to support her Oxford-bound brother, and authoring several freelance articles. Physically and emotionally beset by the profound "strain of writing" and "hours of insomnia" (190), she could easily pass for the sister of the young girl in the park. On the verge of a breakdown, Mary knows she has no choice but to push on with her work, for "if she gave up [her position on *The Fan*] for a month there would be a dozen women ready to snatch it from her" (190). Mary finds her life totally consumed by work, thus denying her an important part of the domestic-professional: an equilibrium in her life that affords her the opportunity to do something transforming for society. Since Mary cannot stabilize her life on her own, she turns to the male profession of medicine for a wholly unnatural remedy.

Middle-class advice comes from her physician Dr. Danby, who foolishly muses, "I should like to have all you young ladies living a healthy, out-of-door life, happily married, and with no mental worries" (215), as if being married and having no worries is mutually exclusive. Not much consolation for the working-class Mary, who has no other alternative but to take Danby's prescription of tonic: "the arsenic and strychnine—which sometimes for a week or two, seemed to give her a fresh lease of life." Even Mary recognizes the futility and absurdity of her circumstances: "We've got to be dosed with poisons to make us fit to sit at a desk and write—twaddle" (224).

Five years later, Mary's physical condition is not much better, nor has her economic situation eased. Vincent takes her "anæmic hand" and remarks "how thin and white you are! ... You can't be well" (296). Mary's white hands are a sign of her decline into the working class: "One works ... because one must," she tells Hemming. "And besides, ... I'm not a person of wealth and leisure like yourself" (297). As in *The Years That the Locust Hath Eaten*, whiteness here is negative, revealing not a middle-class woman's comfortable position, but instead exposing Mary's exertion to remain good and middle class. She rejects Hemming, and thus her decision as a working-class woman to hold onto middle-class values seals her fate: "Henceforward she was to walk alone, to fight the battle of life unaided—a moral starveling, whose natural instincts were to be pinched, repressed, and neatly trimmed in conformity with the rules of the higher civilisation" (273–74). Yet despite Dixon's disheartening description of her lot, Mary's personal decision reflects the domestic-professional's hope to transform society one person at a time.

After their father's funeral, at the beginning of the story, Mary had told her brother Jimmie: "There's London! We're going to make it listen to us, you and I. We're not going to be afraid of it—just because it's big, and brutal, and strong" (11). The city of London symbolically represents civilization, the middle-class civilization that "triumphs" when Mary rejects Hemming. Renouncing Vincent, although she still loves him, Mary returns to her work: "She had still to do the happy ending, the rapturous finale which the public demanded" (317). Yet Dixon as a domestic-professional novelist refuses to give her public that kind of ending, and she thus alters the traditional genre of the woman writer's novel. Echoing the former scene, she leaves Mary, alone and broken, looking out at the city "that lay stretched out at her feet; majestic, awe-inspiring, inexorable, triumphant London. Standing alone there on the heights, she made a feint as if to grasp the city spread out before her, but the movement ended in a vain gesture, and the radiance of her face was blotted out as she began to plod homeward in the twilight of the suburban road" (322). Despite Mary's editor saying that "The British public doesn't expect [novels] to be like life" (232), Dixon's own book was popular, indicating that the reading public wanted more than "pretty stories" from women writers. Dixon herself was somewhat bewildered at *The Story of a Modern Woman*'s success, calling it "a somewhat gloomy study of the struggles of a girl alone in the world and earning her own living. To my great surprise, it caught on at once" (*As I Knew Them* 136). However, some critics persisted in applying certain rules to women's writing.

Applauding the novel for not condescending to a current vogue in fiction of "self-assertive, heartless, sexless" heroines"—"the typical modern woman," the *Athenæum*[5] reviewer of *The Story of a Modern Woman* approvingly describes Mary as "a gentle ... failure in life." Making the same distinction between the "good" New Woman and the "bad" New Woman fairly common in domestic-professional fiction, this critic believes that the "modern" woman is unfeminine, wants nothing to do with the home, desires her own way, and most important, refuses to "meekly accept her *role* as a failure in life" (770). Mary Erle, from the reviewer's point of view, is an old-fashioned girl, the proverbial angel, the kind of woman whom middle-class women should aspire to be. But Dixon makes it clear that Mary is definitely a modern woman—the "good" New Woman—though she has mixed feelings about it. More important, Dixon emphatically declares that the modern woman is not much better off than the old-fashioned girl. Both types are still at the mercy of men for their well-being and happiness, whether those men be husbands or employers. In an essay, "Why Women Are Ceasing to Marry," Dixon postulates that it is not "from selfish reasons" (391) that modern women refuse to marry, but rather they "choos[e] the known evil, remain[ing] celibate rather than fly to others that they know not of" (395):

Possibly it was better for the race (if quantity, not quality, go to the making of a nation) when its feminine half was troubled by no such doubts, but married herself on the faintest provocation, and had no misgivings at rearing numerous progeny. On the other hand, it would seem certain that if woman continues to cultivate her critical faculties and her sense of humour—to exercise, in short her feminine prerogative of deliberate choice in the great affair of matrimony—that the standard of human felicity will be steadily raised, and the wedded state will shine forth in a different light to that in which it stands revealed to many thoughtful persons to-day. (396)

What makes her modern woman a better model, Dixon suggests, is that she has the courage, despite obstacles and asperities, to confront the difficulties of life so that women in the future may not have to do so.

The Years That the Locust Hath Eaten and *The Story of a Modern Woman* continue the tradition of women's writing as an attempt to benefit and improve society, a tradition that by the end of the nineteenth century had expanded into the larger arena of organized relief work. As Ann Rowell Higginbotham points out, "Much of this 'moral welfare work' was carried out by middle-class women who increasingly sought vocations in charitable work. These women served as missionaries to the poor, institutional visitors, and matrons of homes. Although charities ... were established and administered by both men and women, the supervision of women and infants became increasingly identified as work particularly suited to women" (86). Both novels feature women who at least try to initiate change, carrying on the feminine tradition of philanthropy, but like those who did professional charitable work, these domestic-professional authors attempt to do so within the male professional sphere.

However, the reader is left with the images of Alison and Priscilla dying, and Mary alone. These images serve to confirm that although women in late-Victorian England were encouraged to remain in "safe" areas such as the home and to do charitable work, there was in fact no safe region for women as long as current ideological structures remained in place. Yet these novels also explicitly remind us that, as Carol Gilligan explains, even though late Victorian women struggled with social conventions, their conflicts "demonstrate the continuation through time of an ethic of responsibility as the center of women's moral concern, anchoring the self in a world of relationships and giving rise to activities of care" (132). Furthermore, Holdsworth's and Dixon's positioning of a middle-class woman in a poor woman's situation chips away at the patriarchal infrastructure that fails to consider women's and the poor's condition, thus allowing the possibility for change in the future.

WORKS CITED

Ardis, Ann L. *New Women, New Novels: Feminism and Early Modernism.* New Brunswick: Rutgers UP, 1990.

Bosanquet, Helen. *The Strength of the People: A Study in Social Economics.* 1903. *The English Working Class.* Ed. Standish Meacham. New York: Garland, 1980.

Dixon, Ella Hepworth. *"As I Knew Them": Sketches of People I Have Met on the Way.* London: Hutchinson, 1930.

———. *The Story of a Modern Woman.* New York: Mershon, 1894.

———. "Why Women Are Ceasing to Marry." *Humanitarian* 14 (1899): 391–96.

Duran, Jane. "The Intersection of Pragmatism and Feminism." *Hypatia* 8 (1993): 159–71.

Gergits, Julia. "Women Artists at Home." *Keeping the Victorian House.* Ed. Vanessa D. Dickerson. New York: Garland, 1995.

Gilligan, Carol. *In a Different Voice: Psychological Theory and Women's Development.* Cambridge, MA: Harvard UP, 1982.

Gunn, Peter. *Vernon Lee: Violet Paget, 1856–1935.* London: Oxford UP, 1964.

Higginbotham, Ann Rowell. *The Unmarried Mother and Her Child in Victorian London, 1834–1914.* Diss. Indiana U. Ann Arbor: UMI, 1985.

Holdsworth, Annie E. *The Years That the Locust Hath Eaten.* New York: Macmillan, 1895.

hooks, bell. *Black Looks: Race and Representation.* Boston: South End, 1992.

Jones, Ann Rosalind. "Writing the Body: Toward an Understanding of *L'ecriture Feminine.*" *Feminist Studies* 5 (1981): 247–63.

Kranidis, Rita S. *Subversive Discourse: The Cultural Production of Late Victorian Feminist Novels.* New York: St. Martin's, 1995.

Langland, Elizabeth. *Nobody's Angels: Middle-Class Women and Domestic Ideology in Victorian Culture.* Ithaca: Cornell UP, 1995.

Levy, Anita. *Other Women: The Writing of Class, Race, and Gender, 1832–1898.* Princeton: Princeton UP, 1991.

McClintock, Anne. *Imperial Leather: Race, Gender and Sexuality in the Colonial Contest.* New York: Routledge, 1995.

Oppenheim, Janet. *"Shattered Nerves": Doctors, Patients, and Depression in Victorian England.* New York: Oxford UP, 1991.

Owens, Louis. *Other Destinies: Understanding the American Indian Novel.* Norman: U of Oklahoma P, 1992.

Pankhurst, Sylvia. *A Sylvia Pankhurst Reader.* Ed. Kathryn Dodd. Manchester: Manchester UP, 1993.

Pool, Daniel. *What Jane Austen Ate and Charles Dickens Knew: From Fox Hunting to Whist—The Facts of Daily Life in Nineteenth-Century England.* New York: Simon & Schuster, 1993.

Pykett, Lyn. *The "Improper" Feminine: The Women's Sensation Novel and the New Woman's Writing.* London: Routledge, 1992.

Ross, Ellen. *Love and Toil: Motherhood in Outcast London 1870–1918.* New York: Oxford UP, 1993.

Seigfried, Charlene Haddock. *Pragmatism and Feminism: Reweaving the Social Fabric.* Chicago: U of Chicago P, 1996.

Rev. of *The Story of a Modern Woman. Athenæum.* 16 June 1894: 770.

Webb, Sidney and Beatrice, eds. *The Minority Report of the Poor Law Commission, Parts I & II: The Break-Up of the Poor Law; The Public Organization of the Labour Market.* 1909. Clifton, NJ: Augustus M. Kelley, 1974.

Wilde, Oscar. *The Complete Works of Oscar Wilde.* 1966. New York: Harper & Row, 1989.

Rev. of *The Years That the Locust Hath Eaten. Athenæum.* 21 Dec. 1895: 867.

NOTES

1. I am indebted to Gail Turley Houston and Louis Owens for taking the time out of their busy schedules to read this essay; their insightful comments have improved it greatly.

2. Ironically, Holdsworth's life imitated her art. Three years after the publication of *Years,* she married poet Eugene Lee-Hamilton, half-brother of writer Vernon Lee (Violet Page) and a semi-invalid. According to Peter Gunn, his mother's "preoccupation with matters of heath, which in her reached a degree that may fairly be called neurotic, was at least part cause in [his] subsequent neurasthenia" (19). After his mother's death in 1896, Lee-Hamilton more or less miraculously recovered. Holdsworth and Lee-Hamilton had one child, a daughter, who died at age one, another similarity to Holdsworth's novel.

3. I investigate this occurrence in further detail in another, currently unpublished, article, "'A true as well as a new woman': Defining the New Woman in Feminist Fiction of the 1890s."

4. Joel 1.4 and 2.25: "That which the palmerworm hath left hath the locust eaten; and that which the locust hath left hath the cankerworm eaten; and that which the cankerworm hath left hath the caterpiller [sic]eaten"; "And I will restore to you the years that the locust hath eaten, the cankerworm, and the caterpiller, and the palmerworm, my great army, which I sent among you" (KJV).

5. Dixon's father, William Hepworth Dixon, was editor of the *Athenæum* 1853–69.

6

On the Face of the Waters

Flora Annie Steel and the Politics of Feminist Imperialism

LeeAnne Marie Richardson

No writer—not even Mr. Kipling—knows the life of the mixed population of the Anglo-Indian empire better than the author of *On the Face of the Waters*.
—*The Critic,* January 1897

Thus opens a review of Flora Annie Steel's *In the Permanent Way*, a collection of stories published one year after *On the Face of the Waters*. The evocation of Kipling here is predictable and unsurprising, but the assumption of equal familiarity with Steel's work speaks volumes about the effect of canon formation on literary history. Whereas Kipling has become virtually synonymous with literary representations of British colonial rule, Flora Annie Steel (1847–1929) has all but disappeared from the canon of writers on empire. And yet no writer— "not even Mr. Kipling"—can tell as much about the ideological work of competing fin de siècle literary genres, the intersection of colonial and patriarchal discourses, or the conflicted role of white women in the imperial project.

On the Face of the Waters (1896) represents Steel's fraught negotiation of the models presented by colonial adventure writers and New Woman novelists.[1] A reviewer for the *Pall Mall Gazette* writes of her novel that "Mrs. Steel has beaten Mr. Kipling on his own ground, India." The martial metaphor implies an adventure novel plot, which is driven by the need to subdue a competitor and fulfilled by conquering another's territory. *The Daily Chronicle*'s effusion that "Mrs. Steel gets fairly inside the Indian's skin, and looks out upon the life of that troublous fiery time through Indian eyes," however, indicates that this is *not* a typical adventure novel.[2] Steel has written an adventure novel that uses the genre's forms but interrogates its functions: The plot represents Indian culture but does not subordinate—or colonize—it. Appropriating the ideological strategies that characterize the New Woman novel, Steel revises the typical adventure narrative to challenge women's role in empire, reconsider racial hierarchies, and emphasize cooperation over colonization. The interplay of New Woman and colonial adventure fiction in this novel mirrors the dialogic representation of cultures Steel achieves: She implements aspects of both genres and produces a revisionist ideology of "feminist imperialism." Thus, *On the Face of the Waters* is a useful counterpoint—or even corrective—to the understanding of nineteenth-century imperialism proffered by the novels of Rudyard Kipling, H. Rider Haggard, Joseph Conrad, and E. M. Forster.

Notwithstanding, *Face of the Waters* does demonstrate several adventure conventions: Set in India at the time of the Mutiny, it features exotic situations, brave soldiers, and daring heroes. The dashing Jim Douglas, with the aid of his Indian servant Tara and her brother Soma, protect Kate Erlton in besieged Delhi. Kate's philandering husband has seen his mistress Alice Gissing killed by an Indian religious fanatic, and waits on the ridge above Delhi with the army for the opportunity to retake the city in a final climatic battle. But *Face of the Waters* is not quite an adventure novel. Although it resembles Kipling's *Kim* (1901) in important ways—Jim is a spy with a gift for disguise—it lacks a single protagonist who is identified as the locus of adventure, of power, of Western values. Moreover, many of Steel's women characters are like New Women (although, since the novel is set in 1859, they are not so named): independent, rebellious, critical of prevailing gender and sexual codes.

On the Face of the Waters displays the hallmarks of an adventure novel in its setting as well as its battle scenes, featuring bloody skirmishes, cannon fire, and the brave exploits of soldiers trying to hold the fort. Instigating warfare against racial others is typical of adventure heroes, such as G. A. Henty's Dick Humphries in *The Young Colonists* (1880), who becomes involved in the 1877–78 skirmishes that accompany Britain's annexation of the Transvaal; or the heroes of Rider Haggard's *Kings Solomon's Mines* and *Allan Quartermain*, who incite civil war; or the heroes of *She*, who kill natives with guns, spears, and—when necessary—their bare hands. Moreover, the male protagonists in *Face of the Waters* love battle for battle's sake: Like Rider Haggard's heroes, they feel that fighting and prevailing is what men do.[3] The battles and struggles for survival test the mettle of the men—and women—just as adventure is supposed to do. Indeed, because novels of the 1857 Mutiny were so popular at the end of the century, there is an entire subgenre of colonial adventure devoted to this event.[4]

Like many colonial adventure novels that purport to be nonfiction, Steel's makes claims to be a "scrupulously exact" example of "pure history" (*Face* v). Indeed the novelist claims that "I have not allowed fiction to interfere with fact in the slightest degree" (v). But most claims of documentary fact in adventure novels are meant to assure the reader that the hero really *is* as stalwart as the narrative demands him to be, that his adventures are within the realm of the possible, that the British national character possesses the mettle necessary to rule the empire. Significantly, Steel writes in her preface that her goal in writing from the historical record is to engender forgiveness. She writes that she has "tried to give a photograph—that is, a picture in which the differentiation caused by color is left out—of a time which neither the fair race or the dark race is ever likely to quite forget or forgive" (vi). Her hope is that the novel may bring each party understanding of the other, even if the events cannot entirely be forgotten.

Steel diverges from the norm in addressing her novel to a mixed-race audience. Most adventure novels assume an exclusively British audience (with the possible exception of Kipling, whose audience was initially Anglo-Indian, rather than British or native Indian) and seek to educate the men of England in the responsibilities of rule. Haggard dedicates *Allan Quartermain* to his son "in the hope that in days to come he, and many others boys whom I shall never know, may, in the acts and thoughts of Allan Quartermain and his companions, as herein recorded, find something to help him and them to reach to what, with Sir Henry Curtis, I hold to be the highest rank whereto we can attain—the state and dignity of English gentlemen." In an article called "The 'Imperialism' of Kipling and Stevenson," a *Review of Reviews* editor argues that "the influence of the popular novelist in molding the public sentiment is usually underestimated" (466). The reviewer accords great power to the adventure novel: "No other force in our time is so subtle, so powerful, and so far-reaching in causing millions of persons unconsciously to adopt the same ideals about certain courses of action" (466). Haggard and this reviewer clearly see this as a good and just revival of "the old Berserker blood of Englishmen" (466), but as a *Fortnightly's* reviewer cautions, "We had always supposed that a certain modesty and temperance of statement, a certain sobriety of intellectual tone, were among an English gentleman's typical traits. We had thought, too, that among the features notably absent from an English gentleman might be reckoned a gloating delight in details of carnage and horror and ferocity for their own ghastly sake" ("The Fall of Fiction" 325). The audience of Englishmen-in-training, it seems, favored carnage and domination. But Steel, who imagines Indians will read and appreciate her work, does not feature celebratory scenes of their massacre. She does not even focus on a single hero who might serve as a role model for British youth.

In fact, Steel strives to represent Indian subjectivity—a divergence from the adventure novel that contemporary reviewers often resented. Faulting Steel for "crowding her canvas" with Indians, one writer claimed that "their talk, their distinctive peculiarities of character and costume, their parts in the great tragedy which is taken as the ground plan of her story, are so abundantly described as occasionally to bewilder the inexperienced reader" (Lyall 428–29). Although this representation of Indian ways sets Steel apart from other adventure novelists, she nonetheless oscillates between racial pride and racial understanding. She is

caught in an ideological double bind: When she speaks in the voice of the Englishman (or woman), modern critics accuse her of racist, imperialist attitudes.
When she speaks in the voice of the Indian, they fault her for misunderstanding Indian culture or of colonizing the other. The question is not really "Is Steel
imperialistic or racist?" for even the Victorians most able to think outside of accepted constructs often betrayed their own racist ideology (from condescending
assumptions about the "noble savage" to advocacy of racial eugenics). The more
productive question would explore Steel's subversion of the traditional adventure narrative critiques in her culture's imperialist ideology (namely, masculine
superiority and strict racial hierarchies), and what it suggests about women's
conflicted role in empire building.

Steel's position as a woman, whose early childhood experiences made her
aware of the iniquities of strict gender roles, likely made her more receptive to
oppressive racial categories. Nonetheless, she remains a product of her culture
and, like Haggard and Kipling, displays unconscious racism in her fiction. But
Steel is less reductive than her male counterparts. Her negative characterizations
are countered by images of Indians who are true to their beliefs, brave, compassionate, and intent on doing their duty. Like the British characters, they have
flaws, hold prejudiced attitudes, and make mistakes in judgment. Neither race is
wholly "good" or wholly "bad." Steel's belief in British superiority is mitigated
by her respect for Indian culture and by her certainty that some aspects of Indian culture are superior. Indeed, in an 1897 interview, Steel expressed her ambivalence about British missionary influence in India, declaring, "I do not
honestly think we have much right to thrust our nineteenth-century religion,
with the civilization which it has called into existence, down the throats of a nation which in many ways seems to me more moral than we are" ("An Anglo-
Indian Novelist" 348–49).

In the very first pages of the novel, Steel makes clear that both Indian and British
perspectives will be represented. She opens with an event that was, for her, the
first step on the road to mutiny: the British annexation of Oude. Indians and Englishmen observe the auction of the deposed king of Oude's household goods; the
British are smug and the Indians embittered. The English bystanders believe, in
their insular fashion, that "the King, for some reason satisfactory to the authorities, had been exiled, majesty being thus vested in the representatives of the an-
nexing race: that is, in themselves. A position which comes naturally to most
Englishmen" (2–3). Unsurprisingly, the Britons are willing to assume both that
the Indian king is incompetent and that they are the appropriate alternative to native royalty. The situation "was simple also" to the Indians observing the auction:
"The King, for some unsatisfactory reason, had been ousted from his own. His
goods and chattels were being sold. The valuable ones had been knocked down, for
a mere song—just to keep up the farce of a sale—to the Huzoors. The rubbish—
lame elephants and such like—was being sold to them" (3). Steel stresses that the
Indians, far from being grateful for British rule, think that the British are the only
ones benefiting from the colonial relationship.

Moreover, Steel represents the mutual misunderstanding of the British and Indian characters in a way that shows that each has different reasons for thinking the ways she does, not that one is right and one is wrong. For instance, when the fighting in Delhi escalates, Kate wonders at Tara's "unnatural" calm: "Did she not know that *brave men on both sides* were going to their deaths?" (312).[5] For her part, Tara wonders that Kate, because she has given birth and seen life enter the world, should be so anxious about the possibility of death: "Did not the Great Wheel spin unceasingly? Let brave men, then, die bravely" (213). Even if this is a simplified version of "Eastern" and "Western" philosophies, it is nonetheless a recognition that each party has an comprehensible belief system, and it represents a refusal to demonize or infantilize non-British modes of thought.

Indeed, for Steel's characters, learning Indian ways is more than a technique of appropriation necessary to survival in dangerous times—as it is with Kim's knowledge of foreign ways and talent with disguises. Allen J. Greenberger, in *The British Image of India* (1969), writes that "The British in this period ... imagined that they had to reject everything Indian in order to retain their own individual identity and to succeed in what ever their endeavors might be" (19), and adventure novelists generally conformed to this program. But Steel represents native knowledge systems as a means of better understanding the self, the world, and others. During the siege of Delhi, Kate finds refuge in the garden of the Swami Sri Anunda. Kate, mired in Western ways, cannot imagine what she will do with herself, meditating in the swami's garden as "a devoted and repentant" (403) Hindu wife. Kate is agitated at the news of increased military action, and she is initially aware only of the material world, herself, and her troubles. But she discovers that "time slipped by with incredible swiftness. . . . And what a strange peace and contentment the life brought!" (403). Sri Anunda himself comes to Kate to tell her "The lesson is learned, sister" (413), for Kate has been through the process of discovering that "she was losing her grip on this world without gaining, without even desiring, a hold on the next. She was learning a strange new fellowship with the dream of which she was a part, because it would soon be past" (412). At the end of her fifteen days of meditation, Kate says, "I feel as if I had just been born" (419). Although this gloss on Eastern philosophy is hackneyed, it contrasts starkly with the prosaic soldierly concerns of a man such as Kate's husband, Major Erlton.

Most adventure novels valorize men such as Erlton, men with physical prowess but without learning or gifts of expression; Allan Quartermain is always half apologizing for his "blunt way of writing" because he is "more accustomed to handle a rifle than a pen" (Haggard, *King Solomon's Mines* 6). But Steel shows that this kind of unthinking and automatic response leads to misjudgment, violence, and massacre. When British troops make the "mistake" of firing on and killing twenty friendly Indian civilians—their own servants, including a woman—the colonel says, "There have been too many mistakes of that sort ... I wish to God some of us would think a bit" (326).[6]

Yet Major Erlton is an exemplary British soldier who "was up for the Victoria Cross" (426), and he does not want to dwell on complexities"—"for he hated thought" (386). Like the British military as a whole, he fails to understand India. An enormous country with a complex social and religious organization, it requires concerted effort and concentrated thought to take in. But when Erlton surveys the Indian landscape, he sees only the besieged city of Delhi and the enemies he imagines reside within. "That, to him, was India" (327). Steel highlights the limitations of his vision with a reminder that "millions" of Indians live in rural areas and are thinking only of the harvest; to them the British are merely "the claimer of revenue" (327), not enemies to attack. This complex picture is beyond Erlton's scope. Never "good at formulating his feelings into definite thoughts" (370), Erlton cedes responsibility for thinking to others. As he says to Kate, "you were always a oner at thinking. So—so you had better do it for both of us" (424).[7]

Erlton's willingness to let others think for him and to follow their directives links him with the stereotypical Indian native, and comparing him to Indian soldiers explodes many of the stereotypes. Although Erlton is not able to say why, he is "vaguely" glad that Colonel John Nicholson comes to head the siege of Delhi. That Nicholson "was the sort of man a fellow would be glad to follow" (370) is the best formulation Erlton can produce. If Indians are the "natural" followers, they are no more so than the typical British army officer, who shows a comparable eagerness to follow a strong leader. Erlton is Steel's primary example of British soldiery; his Indian counterpart is Tara's brother Soma (although Soma, as a sepoy, is not an officer). By comparison, the Rajput soldier's thoughtfulness and his ability to analyze his excruciating position between divided loyalties illustrates the complexity of British/Indian interactions, as well as the absolute superiority of some aspects of Indian culture.

Soma's trouble is that entertaining complex thought makes it difficult for a soldier to know where duty lies. He understands and appreciates his complex emotions and cannot be satisfied by having someone else think for him. So he is torn: He is from a long line of soldiers for whom loyalty to one's officers and confidence in the line of command is as highly valued as martial prowess. But he is also loyal to the Bengal army and his comrades there (including the ones who are court-martialed for refusing to use the new cartridges rumored to contain pork and beef tallow) because the Bengal army "was not—as a European army is—a mere chance collection of men ... but, to a great extent, a guild, following the profession of arms by hereditary custom from the cradle to the grave" (167). Before he witnessed the unjust and humiliating court-martial of eighty-five of his comrades, military law seemed just. Now, the British officers seemed profoundly unjust. Also at play is his respect for his commanding officer, Captain Craigie, who Soma knows to be honorable, brave, trustworthy, and an able leader. But Craigie too must obey his commanding officer—the officer responsible for jailing Soma's comrades.

Despite "the sweep and swing of her tale" and "the amplitude of its military march" ("The Novel of the Mutiny" 81), Steel often voices an anti-adventure aesthetic. Rebecca Saunders claims that "Steel wrote what may be thought of as a woman's adventure novel, inverting the elements of adventure so that her work remains that of a woman who could not glory outright in the emotions of adventure" (321). Steel's narrative is a critique of the adventure genre and its concomitant glorification of killing and oppression. It is not merely that Steel cannot "glory outright" but that she finds it necessary to question the "emotions of adventure" that cause unthinking violence. A detailed analysis of a key passage in the novel will demonstrate how Steel constructs typical adventure scenarios only to deflate their bellicose rhetoric of superiority and survivalism.

In a chapter of increasing tension, Kate is worried about Jim's long absence. He has been ill and still has not entirely recovered his strength. In a besieged city, traveling under disguise as an Afghan horse trader, he faces great peril, especially because his fatigue may cause lapses in his behavior and mastery of argot. As any adventure novelist would, Steel reminds the reader of all the dangers facing Jim, represents the anxiety of those waiting for him, and heightens the tension with presentiments of impending threat. During her anxious vigil, Kate is alone on the rooftop, still disguised as an Afghani horse trader's secluded wife. Because of her worry about Jim, when she hears footsteps on the stairs, she incautiously opens the door wide. Out hisses a voice of danger: "Salaam! Mem-sahib" (347). Is she discovered? Will she be killed? She retreats, but a figure slips past her. She is trapped. It is not danger, we learn; it is Alice's Mai, who according to Alice's last wish has been sheltering Sonny Seymour, the son of a British official.

But even the happy event of Sonny's arrival presages peril. Kate realizes that "There would be danger in English prattle" (350) and, indeed, Sonny calls out to her in English and only calls more loudly when she desperately tries to quiet him: "Steps on the stair, and Sonny prattling on in his high, clear lisp!" (351). The tension again mounts when Kate realizes that there are two people on the stair in a scuffle. Sonny is screaming in English; they are certainly discovered. Worse, Jim frantically shouts for Kate to open the door.

More adventure ensues when two men burst over the threshold, each fighting for supremacy. Jim, with "his knees to the ribs below them," calls for a knife or a revolver because "I can't hold——the brute long" (351). He "loosened one hand cautiously from the throat and held it out, trembling, eager" (352). This is the sort of scene that plays out again and again in adventure novels: The weakened hero valiantly finds new strength despite his infirmity in order to fight the native scoundrel, and when all seems lost finds a weapon to finally kill the source of danger. But Kate thwarts the conventional expectations associated with this plot strand when she refuses to hand over a knife, saying, "No! ... you shall not. It is not worth it" (352). She refuses to enable the adventure plot, to valorize survival if it means brutality, to associate honor with killing, to let the plot climax with violence and death.

The man turns out to be Tiddu, the old Baharupa who taught Jim the art of disguise. Tiddu had seen Jim in the market, in obvious difficulties from his recent illness, and insisted on seeing him safely home. Jim acknowledges that "but for Kate, he would have knifed the old man remorselessly. Even now he felt doubtful" (352). The conventional adventure plot would reinforce Jim's suspicions, would license his killing of the intruder to protect the heroine. But here, Tiddu becomes the more noble figure when he points out that Jim need not fear for Kate on his account. He will remember that Kate saved his life and will act accordingly. Unlike Jim, Tiddu and his tribe "know gratitude" (352); unlike Jim, Tiddu is too noble to attack someone who has aided and protected him.

Jim's anger stems from his feminized role. The adventure ideology—and the ideals of British masculinity that inform it—dictates that men not be weak or vulnerable (as Jim is after his illness). Autonomy and strength should be their hallmarks. Indeed, the adventure hero's typical role is the strong protector of innocent weakness. When Kate is missing from the rooftop, Jim cannot imagine that she will survive on her own. She is not an adventure hero; therefore she is weak and at risk. Jim's vision of male-female roles prompts him to claim that the "whole duty of man" is to "find and save Kate, or—*kill somebody*" (395). His first idea is to protect the innocent woman. But if he cannot, then killing an Indian—whether guilty of harming Kate or not—will do. To "*kill somebody*" is an appalling manifestation of the "whole duty of man," and Steel reveals the inadequacy of this vision by entirely deflating Jim's martial rhetoric.[8] The paragraph that follows Jim's declaration of intent underscores this: "Kate, however, had already been found, or rather she had never been lost" (395). Kate, we find, is entirely able to take care of herself, and Jim's idea of man's "whole duty" is entirely irrelevant.[9]

It is in the character of Kate that the New Woman enters the *On the Face of the Waters*.[10] Because the novel is set in 1857, Kate has little recourse to an established women's movement, discussions of the marriage question, or work for suffrage. Her intelligence, her reactions to events, her decisive action, and her dissatisfaction with her current state reflect the cultural climate of the novel's composition. As the novel opens, Kate is a New Woman in thought but an "old" one in deed. Her husband is thoroughly disreputable: He is openly having an affair, he gambles, and he cheats. Kate admits that "I do not love him" (21) but like many New Women after her, she feels trapped because all her options are equally disagreeable. She could leave her husband or have him dismissed from the army for improper conduct, but that would harm the son she sent to England "to keep him from growing up in the least like his father. And she had stayed with that father simply to keep with within the pale of respectability for the boy's sake" (14).

At this point in the novel, Kate is entirely mired in conventional English ways even though these conventions are what doom a divorced mother's son and license the sexual double standard. English domestic ideals are represented as her only comfort during what she regards as cruel exile from home and child. Initially, she plays the role of the *mem*,[11] living in a house with an English garden, desperately trying to grow English plants in the Indian climate. She does not mix with Indian society, because she does not know the language or understand the culture. And "what she did not understand" is what she "did not like" (10). She can imagine only that Indians are "uncivilized, heathen ... tied to hateful, horrible beliefs and customs" (10). Kate's growth as an autonomous woman is enabled and measured by her increasing respect for, understanding of, and participation in Indian culture.

Circumstances make Kate change her attitudes and her actions. The rising in Meerut coincides with Erlton's letter that he is divorcing her because Alice is pregnant by him. Ironically, his chivalrous desire to protect women explains his career-ruining decision to divorce. He knows that Kate not only condemns him, but also is smart and strong enough to thrive without him; she will be upset only insofar as his decision affects their son. Erlton respects this, but he has a more pressing concern: "It isn't as if he were a girl, *and the other may be*" (182). So Kate is left to fend—and, most important, to think—for herself. She "was trying to understand what it all meant; really—deprived of her conventional thoughts about such things" (222). Kate initially sees Alice only as "the woman at whom other women held up pious hands of horror" (223)—rightly. But then she realizes that it is merely by conventional standards that she has any cause to blame Alice.[12] Kate does not love Erlton and is not physically attracted to him. Alice has, in essence, picked up something that Kate did not want. Viewing the situation against the grain of convention, Kate muses, "What wrong had [Alice] done to one who refused to admit the claims or rights of passion? What had she stolen, this woman who had not cared at all?" (234). All Alice had "stolen" was "motherhood; and that was given to saint and sinner alike" (234).

Steel hereby rejects the assigned role of women in the colonial project: bearing the sons of empire. As Rosemary George notes, women's only *national* role before voting was motherhood; this is true in the colonies as well, for there women cannot vote, serve in the Indian Civil Service, or join the army. John MacKenzie explains that the eugenics and motherhood movements of the late-Victorian and Edwardian eras were suffused with imperialism. Disturbed by a falling birth rate, and the revelation during the Boer War of the physical inadequacy of a third of all recruits, "The majority of Fabians, together with the leading Liberal imperialists, supported a programme to keep mothers at home, educate them in motherhood, encourage 'eugenic' marriage, and provide State inducements to procreation, nutrition, and health" (159). In Steel's rendering, the exalted nature of women's maternal role in maintaining the nation's standards becomes a mere biological reality. Motherhood as an imperial imperative and a eugenic duty is incompatible with something freely given to "saint and sinner alike." For Steel, motherhood is allied with the sacred—Kate's strongest bond is with her absent child and with Sonny, who brings hope into her Indian life—but not with a woman's political and national duty.

Kate's emergence as a heroine coincides with her falling away from British domestic ideology. In her role as *memsahib*, Kate was superior to all things Indian, but trapped by circumstance and circumscribed by convention. This changes when she is left on her own to escape from the cantonment in Delhi, which is overrun with insurgent sepoys. She is safely hidden in a dark niche near the gate, but tempted to leave her haven for the mercy of a quick and certain death. The idea of having a chance to change, to survive, to prosper, however, spurs her to save herself. "Chance! There was a spell in the very word" (256). Kate takes her chance, so successfully that "none would have guessed that a woman, full of courage, ay! and hope" (256) was steeling herself for her final escape. When Kate ventures out, she finds a blanket and wraps herself "in ayah's fashion" with skirt and veil (268), "so, boldly, she slipped out of the corner, and made for the gate, remembering to her comfort that it was not England where lonely woman might be challenged all the more for her loneliness. In this heathen land, that down-dropped veil hedged even a poor grass-cutter's wife about with respect. What is more, even if she were challenged, her proper course would be to be silent and hurry on" (268). This is the first time she realizes the advantage of being a woman in India, the place she previously disregarded as merely "heathen" and in all ways inferior to England.

Kate next stumbles upon Jim, who saves her with a daring ride through throngs of fighting men. Steel once again engages the adventure genre, complete with wild war whoops and derring-do. But when Jim stops to contemplate how best to keep Kate safe, the reader sees again the folly of his idea of "the whole duty of man." Jim decides that he and Kate cannot continue moving from place to place without a set plan of action:

To begin with, Kate's nerves could not stand it. She was brave enough, but she had an imagination, and what woman with that could stand being left alone in the dark for twelve hours at a time, never knowing if the slow starvation, which would be her fate if anything untoward happened to him, had not already begun? He could not expect her to stand it, when three days of something far less difficult had left him haggard, his nerves unstrung. (280)

His concern for the state of Kate's nerves (which ironically reveals the delicacy of his own) is gallant, but unnecessary. The woman for whom mere "chance" is a call to action will not sit still waiting for "slow starvation." Indeed, during Jim's subsequent illness, the formerly helpless Kate learns enough of Indian language and customs to take care of herself. This, however, is a source of discomfort to Jim, who finds he is no longer needed in the protector's role:

You've learned everything, my dear lady, necessary to salvation. That's the worst of it! You chatter to Tara—I hear you when you think I'm asleep. You draw your veil over your face when the water-carrier comes to fill the pots as if you had been born on a housetop. You—Mrs. Erlton! If I were not a helpless idiot I could pass you out of the city to-morrow, I believe. It isn't your fault any longer. It's mine ... It gets on my nerves—my nerves! (331)

He is in the position Kate had been in, waiting for care, unsure of what is happening around him, and unable to effect any change in the outcome. But Jim lashes out irritably, unable to bear the strain the way Kate does.

Kate's placidity is not caused by some sort of natural passivity; she is merely too strong to waste her energies fretting and complaining. Instead, she learns Hindi, studies Indian culture, and prepares for the time when she may be able to take her chance. When Kate claims that the presages of military actions they have heard are not fearful to her but "a great relief," Jim is offended, stressing how much more relieved he, as a man, must necessarily be. He claims that "women can scarcely understand what inaction means to a man" (299). Jim's statement reveals how little he understands women's need for agency, and how much his culture imposes women's supposed desire to be guarded by a strong man. Kate's personal experience with "long weary hours of waiting" (299) tells her differently.

Kate finally gains the opportunity to think and act for herself, which prompts her to be "interested in her own adventures, now that she had, as it were, the control over them" (400). Control over her life and actions brings her alive. Ironically, she achieves this control by joining a community of women.[13] Unlike Jim, who wants to *kill somebody*," Kate finds her course of action in appealing to the common humanity—the common womanhood—of those around her. Unable to regain the rooftop from which she escapes, Kate decides to "throw herself on the mercy" (377) of Newâsi, the Indian widow princess. "I am ... a woman like yourself" (378), Kate exclaims. It is not just that both are women: Both are spirited, independent, strong-minded women. The narrator points out that "Abool-Bukr had been right when he said that Kate Erlton reminded him of the Princess Farkhoonda da Zamâni [Newâsi]. Standing so, they showed strangely alike indeed, not in feature, but in type; in the soul which looked out of the soft dark, and the clear gray eyes" (378). Instead of killing the other to find action and affirm one's own right to act (as Jim would do), Kate sees the womanhood, the humanity of the other, and finds herself affirmed. The New Woman's adventure is to find empowerment not by stepping on but by walking with the other.[14]

Inasmuch as Kate proves to be thoroughly independent and capable, Jim's proclamations about women are clearly wrongheaded. Indeed, he is fallible, flawed, and often mistaken. Far from the perfect hero, Jim does not have complete understanding and often makes irrational responses. When impatient or angry, his "sheer animal hatred" (294) and his "arrogance and imperious temper" (294) cause him to lash out and make sweeping statements such as "women [are] trivial creatures" (294). In calmer moments, as when he is when reasonably discussing policy, he says the opposite. The conventional adventure hero, by contrast, is always strong (even in weakness: *Ayesha* has Holly and Leo recovering from exhaustion, but the text also stresses that any other men would have been killed by their experience), always accurate in his analysis of the situation, always successful in achieving his goal. Jim's success, on the other hand, comes in changing his goal. He does not find and save Kate, nor does he *"kill somebody."* Kate persuades him to understand success differently: Success is not global domination, but local victory.

Benita Parry demonstrates how the adventure paradigm can colonize the reader's reactions to a novel when she claims that the struggle in *On the Face of the Waters* is "between 'aimless, invertebrate discontent' and 'law and order,' as savagery challenges civilization" (119). To be sure, Jim does use the offensive description "aimless, invertebrate discontent" to refer to the sepoys' (in)actions. But the novel's events prove not only that his characterization of the Indian soldiers is wrong, but that his analysis of how events will play out is mistaken as well. Moreover, Jim's harsh words refer to a specific situation, not to some conception of the Indian national character. He is annoyed at being proved wrong, and he responds with invective when angry. He had told the British commanders that they had not yet seen a serious insurgency because India's Hindu and Muslim populations were so divided against each other that they would not unite against a common enemy. But the beef and pig tallow rumored to be in the new gun cartridges are abhorrent to members of both religions, and Jim is sure that this development will bring on a mutiny (141). This is why he declares it "d—d inconceivable folly and tyranny" (170) on the part of the British leadership when eighty-five sepoys are put before the court-martial and sentenced to ten years' hard labor for refusing to fire the new cartridges.

But the eighty-five are shackled in front of the assembled native troops, and still the sepoys obey their British officers. Jim's initial anger is at the British army officers: "this business has strained the loyalty of the most loyal to the uttermost; and we deserve to suffer, we do indeed" (171). Indeed, the insistent superiority of the generals infuriates him: "Why can't we admit boldly ... that the cartridges are suspicious? That they leave the muzzle covered with a fat, like tallow?" (171). (Jim himself indulges in this British superiority when he calls the Indians "children—simple, ignorant, obstinate" [192]. But rather than an example of Steel's racism, it illustrates her continual emphasis on his mistaken judgments).

Jim's sympathy for the sepoys turns to anger at them when they "fail" to react to injustice the way he would. The troops quiescently watch their comrades being shackled; they march the prisoners off toward the stockade without incident. When they reach the jail without an uprising, Jim is disgusted: "If this intolerable tyranny failed to rouse action there could be no immediate danger ahead ... he felt that a handful of resolute men ought to be able to hold their own against such aimless invertebrate discontent. He felt a vague disappointment that it should be so. . . . They were a poor lot who could do nothing but talk!" (173). At this moment, his assessment appears high-handed. But it ultimately reflects on the British. The sepoys do rebel[15] and the British fail to act for several days. Instead of fighting the rebels, British officers sound the retreat to ensure the safety of the European cantonments. All is quiet there, but the British soldiers remain on the parade ground all night (200). The men talk of action, but they do not act; their officers will not permit it, even refusing requests to ride the thirty miles to Delhi to give warning of the unchecked rebellious sepoys headed their way. We discover that the British are "a poor lot who could do nothing but talk!"

With no information about the state of affairs in Meerut, the British army in Delhi "was paralyzed by that straining of the eyes for a cloud of dust upon the Meerut," hoping for help or news. Kate, a "mere woman," is "weary of the deadly inaction" (251) and is prevented by the Anglo-Indian social structure from doing anything but watch British men fail to act on their opportunities: "the long hours had dragged by uselessly" (253). When troops are finally assembled to retake Delhi, it is nearly *four months* after the initial uprising at Meerut. Even at the end of the century, this version of events was not the accepted one in Britain. A. C. Lyall's *Edinburgh Review* essay castigates Steel's fictional account of "serious history" because it is not flattering to the British national character: "She very plainly intimates that nothing but culpable inaction and want of energy prevent instant pursuit by a force from Meerut of the mutineers" (430).

Steel's narrative method—and the main locus of her divergence from the typical adventure novel—is most effectively illustrated in a passage in which she refers to British "Men" and Indian "Murderers." The narrator relates how the British troops finally attack Delhi after holding siege for four months, saying, "*to the three thousand marching upon Delhi that cool dewy night ...* there were but two things to be reckoned with in the wide world: Themselves—Men. Those others—Murderers" (307; emphasis added). Steel clearly indicates that she is recording the thoughts of "*the three thousand marching upon Delhi*," but she is often misunderstood because she is employing free indirect discourse. Parry quotes this "Men/Murderers" section to prove that Steel believes that the mutineers are savage, aggressive criminals (120). But again, this is not Steel's viewpoint, nor does she represent it as a justified, virtuous, or commendable one. It is the intention of the novel, as Steel writes in her introduction, to mingle viewpoints, to be the recording camera rather than the partisan analyst.[16]

Steel's harshest critics seek proofs of her imperialism in two nonfictional sources: her autobiography, *The Garden of Fidelity*, and her co-authored book of Indian housekeeping, *The Complete Indian Housekeeper and Cook, and Practical Recipes for Cooking in all Its Branches* (with Grace Gardener). But the deployment of this evidence often betrays insensitivity to genre considerations. A novel that proposes to promote understanding between the races will not have the same tone or emphasis as one purporting to help Anglo-Indian women manage their Indian servants. That Steel recommends a "high-handed dignity in dealing with those who for thousands of years have been accustomed to it" (*The Garden of Fidelity* 133) does not reflect well on Steel, but neither does it provide adequate proof that Steel's *novels* recommend a "high-handed dignity" with Indians.

Rosemary George discusses the female Indian romancers as if their novels were ideologically and generically identical to Steel's. Her primary argument is that the "lady novelists" of India—she singles out Maud Diver, Alice Perrin, and Steel—represented women's complicity with the imperial project through their authoritative tone and their characters' racial superiority:

What is remarkable about these novels and guidebooks is the confidence of the female authorial voice. The ideological proximity of this genre with the other discourses of imperialism constructs "the Englishwoman"—a female subject who is firmly anchored as a "full individual" through her racial privileges. . . . their writing represents a coherent, unified bourgeois subjecthood. (61)

Steel's representations of racial difference are actually *less* mired in images of Brits' superiority and dark-skinned degradation than a novel such as Thackeray's *Vanity Fair*. Thackeray's casual racism, his way of expressing racial stereotypes to comic effect, his Sambos and Schwartzes, represent a level of British imperial racism far beyond that of *On the Face of the Waters*. Steel's novel is, unarguably, compromised by her limited vision of other races, her Western perceptions of Indian philosophy and society, her pride in the work of empire to educate, to influence, and to effect what she saw as progress. But Kate's subjectivity is less "firmly anchored" in her identity as a British woman who is superior to women of color than George suggests, for her coming to full consciousness of her powers is based in her interaction *with* Indians, not in her control *over* them.

George further argues that women's status as "exiles" gives them access to power, for in the colonies, "'not belonging' was one's only avenue to unified and autonomous subject status. Being white and English was what marked the imperialist as the fortunate outsider. And as such, it was a status shared equally by English men and women and was therefore erased as a possible site of gender struggle" (62). George's vision of gender equality in the colonies (at least in terms of exile status) is not supported by Steel's fictional recounting. Alice embraces Indian society and understands more Hindi than Herbert Erlton; Jim has an Indian "wife" and thus has a far more intimate knowledge of Indians than Kate has; Kate, as the typical Anglo-Indian wife, initially stays at home and shuns the society of natives. She does not understand any Indian languages, and thus cannot understand the people or the society around her. Steel's own experiences as the wife of an Indian civil servant reveal her status as "more in exile" than her husband. In her autobiography Steel recounts that she did not wish to be an outsider, but rather to participate in administrative activities with her husband. As a woman, however, she was strongly discouraged from doing so. Women, even with their measure of authority over native servants, were more exiled than men from Indian society.

Following Nancy Armstrong's assertion that "such writing as the [eighteenth-century] conduct books helped to generate the belief that there was such a thing as a middle class with clearly established affiliations before it actually existed," George is arguing that reading the next century's Indian romances and guidebooks establishes that "the modern *politically authoritative* Englishwoman was made in the colonies: she was first and foremost an imperialist" (37). In essence, because she represents herself as such, the memsahib in India *is* politically empowered and authoritative. This is a problematic assertion, however, because women had no institutionalized political power, they were largely dependent on their husbands, and the "freedoms" of Anglo-Indian society also involved a great deal of constraint.

One of the tropes that British feminists invoked to demonstrate Indian women's debasement was the zenana or harem. As Antoinette Burton points out, "Seclusion was thought to be the equivalent of degradation, and harem life 'dull and vacuous to the last degree'"(66). Ironically, seclusion is one of the hallmarks of women in Anglo-Indian society, and the stereotypical image of the memsahib is a woman who is a "small-minded, social snob who tyrannically rules over a household of servants and refuses to associate with Indians" (Sharpe 91). Such a woman spends her days in intrigues, idleness, and gossip. British women were in their own kind of zenana, secluded from Indian society, shuttled off to hill stations in hot weather, barred from mixing in native Indian society. Their measure of authority over natives was accompanied by a great measure of imposed restrictions over self. British men, in striving to protect "their" women from Indian culture, confined women to the home with little to do (without even children to care for) and thus impelled them into the superficial, flirtatious, frivolous life for which they then criticized the stereotypical memsahib.

The similarity between British and Indian women extends beyond their physical separation from men; they share a similar ideological function in relation to men. Jenny Sharpe notes that central to both cultures are notions of women's honor, which reflect on masculine identity: "Both British and Hindu codes venerate womanhood as an institution to the extent of devaluing women's lives" (102). British ideals of death before dishonor and the Hindu practice of *suttee* means that women prove their worth—and the nation's valor—by dying. Indeed, to a lesser extent, Kate sacrifices herself to her husband to conform to demands for feminine domestic virtue. This domestic virtue, however, produces a pagan religion, one that is not god-centered but husband-centered. Kate's "cult of home was a religion to her" (22), but she does not even have the satisfaction of truly believing in it. Her salvation, her way of coping with her intolerable situation, is convincing herself that she does believe. Supposedly civilized pressures to conform to social and religious customs are as strong as those that compel Tara to burn on her husband's funeral pyre. Tara is drugged by her family, and is therefore willing to passively accept her fate as suttee. Jim Douglas pulls her off the pyre, and she suffers the same long-standing torment of daily life that Kate Erlton does: stifling all emotion and thought of a future in order to live through the present.

Tara and Kate have more in common than their self-abnegation. Most critics, however, claim that Tara and Kate function as opposites, with Tara acting to show what Kate is not. Saunders's comment that "In contrast to Tara's sexuality is Kate's transcendence of it" (312) is misleading, because Steel goes to great lengths to demonstrate how alike Tara and Kate are in their repressed sexuality. Tara is largely desexualized; as a widow, she is true to her husband's memory by denying her sexual self. Steel's Indian women are not, as her critics charge, uniformly obsessed with sexuality and passion. Like Kate, who "refused to admit the claims or rights of passion" (234), Tara's cry of suttee is her call to self-repression. Tara can crush the desire roused by the lovemaking between Jim and Zora with this cry; far from being sex-obsessed, she can deny passion easily. But Tara finds it much more painful to distance herself from the camaraderie and easy contact between Jim and Kate. Zora never engaged with Jim "as an equal," as Kate does. "And, strangely enough, the familiar companionship—inevitable under the circumstances—roused her jealousy more than the love-making on that other terraced roof had done. *That* she understood. *That* she could crush with the cry of suttee. But *this*—this which to her real development seemed so utterly desirable; what did it mean?" (347). Tara's heart aches at her separation from society, but it did not ache at her lack of physical passion.

Indeed, the eventual emergence of Kate's sexuality (long denied because of her abhorrence of her husband) realigns her symbolic affiliation from Tara to Zora. Jim's plan is for Kate to "pass as his wife—his sick wife, hidden, as Zora had been, on some terraced roof" (281), and although she initially balks at his request to wear Indian dress and jewelry, Kate learns to play the role with consummate skill. Her connection with Zora is established as soon as Jim puts one of Zora's bracelets on her: He attaches a "gold fetter" to her wrist and she feels an "odd thrill" (285) of sexual attraction. Jim recognizes an affinity with Zora in Kate's interest in dress and appearance. She "wished so much for a looking-glass just now, to see how I looked" in her native dress that Jim "felt an odd resentment in recognizing that Zora would have said the words as frankly" (284). The women are so alike in some respects that he has a "vague feeling he had done all this before" (284).

Alice Gissing, too, is likened to Zora. Both lose a child in its infancy, both are sexually uninhibited, and both are "bought" by men. Zora is literally bought by Jim from "a house of ill-fame, as he would have bought a horse, or a flower-pot, or anything else which he thought would make life pleasanter to him" (28). Alice found "wealth in the person of Mr. Gissing" (53) after the death of her first husband, who she had chosen for the "good looks which had attracted her" (53). Alice cannot understand the social dictates that admonish her for employing her "knack of making most men happy" (229). Like Zora, she is unsullied by her socially questionable alliances with a man and she remains "strangely, inconceivably unsoiled" (56) by the so-called "sin" in which she indulges. Zora, too, is unmarried to the man with whom she is intimate, but "was a good woman for all that" (285).

Saunders writes that Alice must be killed because "Steel here is as much the tool of imperialism as any memsahib. Alice is sacrificed to women's larger role of helping Englishmen control Indians. The sacrifice of Alice shows an urge for women to deny their victim status and identify with men" (314) rather than celebrate their personal freedom. But Alice does die as a victim. A religious revolutionary kills her when she interferes in his attempt to reclaim the parrot unfairly taken from him by a British officer. Sonny, who is holding the parrot, is saved by Alice's noble deed, but Alice does not join with men against the Indians; the events leading to her death begin with the action of the British military establishment. She dies saving the life of a small child not only to prove that she is, and always has been, a good woman (despite what conventional morality might deem her) but also because her culture cannot accommodate the new morality suggested by her character. Although she is a married woman, pregnant by another woman's husband, she is not portrayed as evil, morally corrupt, or contagious. But there is no course of action she can take without causing damage to some innocent party. Like many New Woman novels, social roles have not caught up with new attitudes, so there is no "happy" ending possible for women who defy conventions.

Steel's perspective here is realistic rather than racist: She acknowledges the racial conflict between the British and the Indians. Erlton, when out driving with Alice, accidentally strikes and kills an Indian child with his horse. Alice responds that she "should have been much sorrier if it had been a white baby" (63). When the doctor withholds agreement, she replies, "People say, of course that it is wicked not to feel the same toward people whether they're black or white. But we don't. And they don't either" (63).[17] Alice cuts off his "sententious" (64) answer, asking, "I wonder what your wife would say if she saw me driving in your dog-cart?" (64). The doctor is stymied, because "The one problem was as unanswerable as the other" (64). Sex relations are like race relations—fraught and mystifying. Steel does not see a solution on the horizon, although her quest for mutual understanding, respect, and toleration will go a long way toward realizing the goal of racial and sexual equality.

Even Jim Douglas, flawed as he is, realizes that differences between the British and the Indians are cultural rather than racial. He wants to father a white boy not because the child will resemble him physically, but because he will resemble him culturally. A white boy would be educated in English institutions, mix in English society, and would thus "inherit familiar virtues and vices, instead of strange ones" (357). Jim knows full well that both nations have their full share of virtues and vices. The British are not superior in their behavior; their behavior is merely familiar.

The New Woman adventure novel aims to fulfill the ideal of social understanding and reveal the shortcomings of sexual and political imperialism. A woman who discovers her own powers and self-reliance through an "adventure" goes outside her known world for help coping with and finding answers to her perilous situation. She eschews violence and killing, and instead of defining herself in opposition to a racial other, sees herself in solidarity with the other. As Hafzan, a maid of the Mogul court at Delhi, says, "God save all women, black or white, say I!" (279). Conventional adventure novels feature supposedly knowing men, who describe events in terms of race. Wise women in New Woman adventure novels try to look beyond race. In constant dialogue with the adventure genre it often mimics but more often critiques, On the Face of the Waters creates new possibilities for women of all colors. Read in conjunction with the novels of imperialism, Steel's narrative problematizes British colonialism and offers an alternative to imperialist conquest.

unlike "Mister," Sahib is used after the surname: Smith Sahib). The term *sahib* became more widely used the longer Europeans were in India, and eventually came also to mean "White Boss/Leader" or, more generally, "European man." Thus, *memsahib* means lady boss or white woman. But memsahib gained a pejorative connotation among Europeans in India to refer to a frivolous, gossiping, idle, sequestered wife. The phrase "playing the mem" most definitely draws on the latter connotation. Mem and Memsahib could be used interchangably; they mean the same thing, and, as far as I am aware, there isn't a major difference in connotation. The specific meaning would depend on context rather than on whether the short or long form is used.

12. I do not claim, however, that Alice "becomes a model for Steel of appropriate female behavior" (308) as Saunders does.

13. Kate Flint identifies one of the purposes of New Woman fiction as generating and consolidating this type of community. The letters received by Sarah Grand, George Egerton, Mona Caird, and Emma Frances Brooke "testify to their popularity among woman readers, and to the influence of their work in the growing feminist movement The 'New Woman' fiction, far more even than the sensation novels earlier in the century, may be said to have created and consolidated a community of woman readers" (305).

14. The result of Steel re-viewing colonial romance through feminist eyes is a New Woman's adventure novel. This scene is reminiscent of Ella Hepworth Dixon's *Story of a Modern Woman* (1894), which climaxes with Mary Erle's decision that "I can't, I won't, deliberately injure another woman. Think how she would suffer! Oh, the torture of women's lives—the helplessness, the impotence, the emptiness! ... All we modern women mean to help each other now. We have a bad enough time as it is ... surely we needn't make it worse by our own deliberate acts!" (255).

15. And not just for nonpolitical reasons. The discontent had been fostered for some time, from the annexation of Oude, to the public shackling of soldiers and the rumors of animal tallow not addressed. Indeed, Steel opens the novel with the aftermath of the Oude annexation to show the discontent among the Indian people of all castes it has caused. Soma reveals that sepoys are disillusioned by the move: "Now that Oude was annexed, [the British] took away [from the sepoys] the extra leave due to foreign service" (31). Soma tells Jim that "the current jest" in the regiments is "that the maps were tinted red— i.e. shown to be British territory—by savings stolen from the sepoy's pocket" (31).

16. Saunders suggests that passages such as these reveal "the lurid quality of Steel's writing" (314). The passage Saunders quotes, however, represents the anguished thoughts of the young soldier Mainwaring at Alice Gissing's death. Steel demonstrates that Mainwaring (who naively believed Alice a model of angelic virtue) feels the need to avenge Alice's death, but Steel herself is not advocating revenge. She continually stresses that atrocities are committed on both sides. Brantlinger avoids these bald misreadings, noting that "Steel enters into the thoughts and feelings of a variety of characters, both British and Indian, often without maintaining a distinct narrative voice. It is therefore not always possible to separate her judgments from those of her characters" (220–21).

17. This is the sort of remark that sets the critics afire. But note, Steel is not saying this—her character is.

7

Re-reading the Domestic Novel

Anne Thackeray's The Story of Elizabeth

Helen Debenham

Anne Thackeray's[1] *The Story of Elizabeth*, published anonymously in *The Corn-hill Magazine* from September 1862 to January 1863 and shortly afterward in book form, attracted what could seem a surprising amount of notice for a brief and very simple tale. Its story is familiar: The moral trial and chastening of a frivolous young girl, Elizabeth, known as Elly, who is frustrated in love, undergoes suffering and illness, and must choose between rival suitors. At the start a "foolish woman" who "revolt[s] against the wholesome doctrine" by not embracing "the hard lesson of life" (1), Elly eventually earns happiness once she has "learned to endure and to care for others, and to be valiant and brave" (192). The fact that the authorship of this "every-day story" ("Popular" 266) was well known in the literary circles of London partly explains the attention. Any work by the daughter of one of the most celebrated authors of the day was bound to be noticed. Certainly the only adverse review, a stinging attack in the *Athenæum*, owed more to that journal's long-running antagonism to William Makepeace Thackeray than to the claimed defects of the novel itself (Jewsbury 552–53).[2] Partisanship, however, cannot wholly explain the enthusiasm with which others greeted the work. "One of the most remarkable of our recent novels" and "the lightest, brightest, cleverest, little book that has been published in a long time," wrote the reviewers in *Victoria Magazine* and *Fraser's* respectively ("Literature" 95; "Popular" 269), and in *Blackwood's* Margaret Oliphant praised at length its "vivid force of line and colour" and the "daring reality" of its heroine (Oliphant 171, 179).[3] Rhoda Broughton later described how, as a young woman, she came upon *Elizabeth*'s "wonderful novelty and spring-like quality" with "astonished delight" and was inspired by it to begin her own more "sensational" career (Ritchie, *Letters* 118), and as late as 1875 an unknown person cared sufficiently to commission Lawrence Alma Tadema to paint a study of "Miss Thackeray's 'Elizabeth'" (Swanson 184).[4]

For another twenty years Anne Thackeray continued to produce fiction, five novels and four volumes of short stories in total that, though never best-sellers, attracted high praise from discerning readers. Her third novel, *Old Kensington* (1873), was ranked by many next to *Middlemarch* as the outstanding novel of its year, and George Eliot herself more than once mentioned the novels of "Miss Thackeray" (with some of Trollope's) as the only fiction she read.[5] In the 1880s changing literary fashions and her own inclinations led Thackeray to turn increasingly to nonfiction, memoirs, and introductions, which were also much admired and not just by her own generation. Robert Louis Stevenson and Henry James were among her devoted admirers, and in 1940 Siegfried Sassoon found that "her descriptions of Italy made [him] *ache* with envy" and long to have known her (81). None of this was enough to ensure her lasting reputation, and where she has been remembered throughout the later twentieth century, it has usually been as her father's daughter, occasionally as the step-aunt of Virginia Woolf,[6] and as a source of information about other Victorians.[7] The recent rise of critical interest in Victorian fairy tales has brought some of her short stories back into view with sympathetic readings especially from Nina Auerbach and U. C. Knoepflmacher. In general, however, Thackeray's literary fate, at least as far as the fiction is concerned, was pronounced by Virginia Woolf and subsequently reinforced by her biographer, Winifred Gérin. Woolf travestied her step-aunt's achievements in *Night and Day* (34)[8] and, even in her official eulogy, discouraged closer acquaintance by carefully qualified praise. Declaring Thackeray "brilliant" but "naturally or wilfully deficient" in "precisely those qualities of concentration and logical construction" that the novel demands, she continues: "It is true that the string does not always unite the pearls; but the pearls are there, in tantalizing abundance—descriptions, sketches of character, wise and profound sayings, beyond the reach of any but a few modern writers, *and well able to stand the ordeal* of printing together in some book of selections" (qtd. in Gérin, Appendix A, 284; emphasis added).[9] Gérin, more simply determined to read the life as a paradigmatic Victorian development from youthful error to triumphant maturity, flatly asserts that she "never mastered the art of plot-construction" and that her "real gift" lay in the later work (viii). Unfortunately, the authority of their pronouncements has rarely been seriously questioned.

Oliphant herself was unimpressed by the plot of *The Story of Elizabeth:* "The narrative, such as it is, gets too much for the author. It tangles about her hands, and embarrasses her, and rather puts her out in her work; but still she gets through with it in a confused way" (176). Yet for her the merits outweighed the defects: "the faculty which can execute a series of little pictures so vivid and life-like, and which has the mind to conceive, and the courage to utter, so singular a disclosure of the secrets which lie within that mist of virginal sanctity and supposed angelhood in which the heart of a pretty girl is veiled from close inspection, is one of no small power and promise" (178). That there might be a connection between the originality of conception and the "confused" plotting is something neither she nor Woolf considered. In other ways, however, Oliphant and her fellow enthusiasts challenge modern readers to recapture the novelty and freshness they discerned in *Elizabeth*, and to comprehend its significance for our understanding of mid-nineteenth-century literature. Their praise has perhaps been disregarded because the domestic romance has tended to fall outside the categories modern criticism deems interesting, and, especially in recent feminist scholarship, has been overshadowed by the sensation fiction of writers such as Mary Braddon and Ellen Wood whose works, along with the fierce critical denunciations they inspired, offer more obviously fertile ground for the exploration of contemporary ideologies. *The Story of Elizabeth* was reviewed alongside *Lady Audley's Secret, Aurora Floyd, East Lynne*, and others in both *Blackwood's* and *Fraser's*, and in both its virtues were explicitly contrasted with sensation's "vices." Oliphant is now so frequently cited as the voice of orthodox "outraged femininity" deploring sensation's treatment of "woman and the feminine" (Pykett, *Feminine* 7) that it is easy to overlook her evident skepticism about "supposed angelhood," with all the idealized constructions of femininity that phrase implies, and her enthusiastic endorsement of Thackeray's demystification of feminine "secrets." What all reviewers of *The Story of Elizabeth* remarked upon, even the viciously antagonistic Geraldine Jewsbury in the *Athenæum*, was the tone that set this novel apart from others of its kind. Wit and humor (sarcasm and mockery in Jewsbury's eyes) make it much more than mere "sunniness and Victorian conventionality" (Boyd 78). Such a work does not need to be overtly subversive to extend our understanding of textual play and intertextuality in the period or our appreciation of the ways in which women's writing can negotiate contemporary ideologies.

The plot of *Elizabeth* blends familiar with some unfamiliar ingredients, the mix being further complicated by fairy tale elements and an unusual Parisian setting. Elly Gilmour, first met as a lighthearted eighteen-year-old, is deliberately separated from her prospective lover, Sir John Dampier, by her mother. Caroline Gilmour, a widow of thirty-six when the novel starts, also loves John. She prevents him from proposing to Elly and then marries a French Protestant pastor, Stephen Tourneur, in a fit of pique. Elly, transferred to a confined life in Paris, is desperately unhappy and behaves badly in consequence. She is on the verge of agreeing to marry Tourneur's worthy but awkward son, Anthony, as a means of escape when John reappears, sees her misery, and secretly takes her out a few times to cheer her up. Recognized by an acquaintance at the opera, John claims they are engaged, to cover the indiscretion, but then tells Elly he is already promised to his wealthy cousin Laetitia. Elly falls seriously ill. During her convalescence in the care of John's kindly aunt, Miss Jean Dampier, she reassesses her behavior and rejects both a chance to marry the repentant John because she does not want to hurt Laetitia and a proposal from John's cousin Will.

Back in Paris she tries to lead a more actively good life until John, who has always really preferred her, reappears, freed from his engagement by the discovery that Laetitia and Will are in love.

There are no subplots and few minor characters. The work was initially conceived as a long short story, and in early page proofs it comes to a conclusion after Elly's illness, with a brief paragraph announcing that she recovered, reformed, and later married John's cousin. Encouraged by friends to change this ending, Thackeray extended the work from three to five installments in the *Cornhill*.[10] Even so, the whole, amounts only to about 53,000 words, or one small volume in Victorian terms. Such brevity helps to explain the speed and directness of the narration, the absence of "padding" that reviewers saw as part of its charm. If the rewritten ending looks like a conventional reward, more particularly as the novel has declared from the outset the necessity of disciplining feminine excess into dutiful submission, closer reading suggests a different reason, one that helps to explain Thackeray's "unsatisfactory" plots: Rather than being simply "tangled" or "confused," her work explores the lack of correlation between plots and everyday life and thus, at a fundamental level, questions the structures of cause and effect that form the moral foundations of Victorian realism.

Foregrounding its conclusion is just one of the ways in which this novel draws attention to genre, highlighting the conventions of romance and reform that will be gently undercut as the novel progresses. Elly is simultaneously the stereotypical heroine, such as appears in "half a dozen" Royal Academy paintings every year (18), with "great soft eyes and pretty yellow hair, and a sweet flitting smile that came out like the sunlight" (2), and also, in Oliphant's words, "the most daring sketch of a troublesome girl which we remember to have seen; ... naughty to an extent which no heroine of our acquaintance has yet attempted; she is cross, she is disobedient, she is sullen and perverse; and even, perhaps the most unpardonable sin of all, she is untidy" (171). Such ordinariness, for contemporary readers Elly's most unusual quality, clashes with and problematizes the narrative context in which she is placed, making the conventional framework a site of contest between a "real" woman and the fictional and ideological constructions permitted her. Thackeray does not explore alternatives to the romance plot. Indeed she seems happy to accept the idea that love is "the only possible interpreter" of female lives.[11] But she does interrogate its meaning by showing how much it "hangs precipitously on chance."[12] Throughout, the text keeps the reader aware of the contingency of narrative in ordinary life and hence the contingency of the ideology that the reform and marriage plot inscribes. Only a series of coincidences propels the story to its moral and marital conclusions: John Dampier reappears in the nick of time to prevent Elly from accepting Anthony's proposal; "unlucky chance" (102) ensures that Monsieur Tourneur discovers Elly's visit to the opera; Elly accidentally finds a note that implies that Laetitia loves John; an inadvertent disclosure by Will precipitates the final unraveling of who loves whom. Most tellingly, in a plot supposedly predicated on the necessity of reform, had John not been prevented from seeing Elly on a crucial day at the start of the story, "he could not have helped speaking to her and making her and making himself happy in so doing," and "Elly, with all her vanities and faults, would have made him a good wife" (15) without having to reform at all. Although the narrator immediately expresses uncertainty whether "happiness is the best portion after all," conventionally justifying the heroine's forthcoming trials, the weight of the narration denies a correlation between unhappiness and goodness. The sternly ascetic Stephen Tourneur, a charismatic preacher, undeniably has "the loftier spirit" (160), which Elly can respect; Will Dampier, also a clergyman, who "enjoy[s] life and all its good things with a grateful temper, and [makes] most people happy about him" (159), does her far more good.

The text everywhere balances its demonstration of the contingency of ideological narratives with an awareness of their power to control women's behavior. Elly has internalized, and the other characters collude in seeing, the romance plot as *the* narrative, of marriage and reform, that must construct her character and control her life. Together they offer an almost textbook, and often very funny illustration of Paul De Man's contention that "it is very difficult not to conceive of one's past and future existence as in accordance with temporal and spatial schemes that belong to fictional narratives and not to the world," even though the effect of such narratives "upon the world may well be all too strong for comfort" (362). This is most vividly and humorously demonstrated during Elly's illness, that inevitable illness of a heroine caught in transgression and frustrated in love. Elly, lying on what all sentimentally assume to be her deathbed, makes appropriate speeches of remorse and forgiveness; John is split between conventionally proper "regret" and the uncomfortable (for him and for conventionally proper readers) realization that her death "would be a horrible solution to all his perplexities" (118), while in the kitchen down below, Françoise, the cook, "who ha[s] never taken such a bad view of Elly's condition as the others, and who strongly disapprove[s] of all this leave-taking, [tells] Miss Dampier that if they wanted to kill her outright, they need only let in all Paris to stare at her" (119). Françoise's pragmatism both highlights the artificiality of the scene in the room above and points to its potential danger: In real life a seriously ill person might indeed die if subjected not only to the treatment customary in literature but also to the weight of spectator expectation. (It is typical of Thackeray's work that she gives this deflationary role to a servant, who is allowed, even in her very brief appearances in the story, an individuality that escapes the rigid class boundaries of most English fiction, one of various ways in which the French setting permits and naturalizes difference from the English norm.)

Other less life-threatening instances of "life" following art help to expose and redefine the connections between the decorums of "proper" femininity and the fictions of romance plotting. As a good Victorian heroine, Elly knows no distinction between friendship with a man and love. Exhilarated by her temporary escape from her stepfather's house, she assumes that John must share her newly discovered feelings, that "if he [is] the other half of her life, surely, somehow, she must be as necessary to him as he was to her," that "he care[s] for her still, she knew he [does]" (73). "And," the narrator continues, signaling the limitations of Elly's maidenly vocabulary, "her instinct [is] not wrong; he [is] sincerely and heartily her *friend*" (73, emphasis added).[13] Before long Elly finds the perfect justification for her planned indiscretions when Françoise tells her that "good people live for others." "Whom had she ever lived for but herself? Ah! there [is] one person whom she would live and die for now. Ah! at last she [will] be good" (90). She also strictly observes, in the completed novel, the convention that a woman loves once only, though the text makes alternatives clear. Elly's entrapment within the ideological narratives of "proper" femininity is matched by that of Anthony within the discursive confines of his puritanical upbringing, which make him an impossible husband for her, despite his being "head over heels in love" (78) and intrinsically far superior to John. John likens him to "the bear" with whom "the princess in the fairy tale" goes off (72), forgetting that fairy tale bears often turn out to be princes. Faint echoes in Elly's relationship with Anthony of other unsuccessful literary pairings reinforce the sense that Thackeray is playing with genre, setting the persuasively normal reality of her characters against the strenuously heroic virtues and vices of Jane Eyre and St. John Rivers, or Maggie Tulliver and Philip Wakem.

John is still more difficult to stereotype than Elly and Anthony, a fact that disconcerted contemporary reviewers, who wanted to read him, as Elly does, as a hero, a "St. Michael Killing the Dragon" of her dreary life, similar to the picture she observes in the Louvre (83). His sheer ordinariness, even more remarkable than Elly's, complicates his ostensible narrative function not least because of Thackeray's wry humour. Introduced as "careful, as men mostly are, and want[ing] to think about his decision [whom to marry] and ... anxious to do the very best for himself in every respect—as is the way with just, and good, and respectable gentlemen" (7–8), John continues kind, confusedly egotistical, and splendidly vacillating between Laetitia, with "a house in the country and money at her bankers," and the "wayward, charming, beautiful" and poor Elly (8). He insists that Elly must not marry Anthony, then, on finding "his advice so quickly acted upon," is "glad and sorry, but I think," says the narrator, "that he would rather have been more sorry and less glad, and have heard that Elly had found a solution to all her troubles" (80). His ambivalence mounts to a climax when, provoked to rage by his mother (hardly a heroic motive for matrimony), he determines to jilt Laetitia and propose to Elly:

[N]ow that the die is cast, now that after all these long doubts and mistrusts he had made up his mind, somehow new doubts arise. He wonders whether he and Elly will be happy together? He pictures stormy scenes; he intuitively shrinks from the idea of her unconventionalities, her eagerness, her enthusiasm. He is a man who likes a quiet life, who would appreciate a sober, happy home—a gentle, equable companion, to greet him, to care for his tastes and ways, to sympathize, to befriend him. Whereas now it is he who will have to study his companion all the rest of his life; if he thwarts her she will fall ill of sorrow, if he satisfies her she will ask for more and more, if he neglect her—being busy, or weary, or what not—she will die of grief, if he wants sympathy and common sense she will only adore him. (151–2)

The modern reader may be reminded of George Bernard Shaw's (or perhaps more accurately Lerner and Loewe's) Professor Higgins, worrying about "letting a woman in his life." Jewsbury was enraged: "[T]he man who causes all the dire misery and mischief that goes on [is] a shallow, selfish, idle man, entangled with three women, to one of whom he is affianced; to none of whom he is in earnest; and the story of his levity and reckless pursuit of his own amusement is told with an unconscious indifference that is startling" (552).[14] Others were more politely puzzled by him: "We wish she could have chosen some one better and nobler than a mere pleasant, good-natured, well-meaning, gentleman-like man of the world" ("Popular" 269). That John is an inadequate hero is, of course, the point: He will not be a bad husband, and in fact will probably be a reasonably good one, but it is impossible to assimilate his genial normality into the usual categories of reward or punishment.

If gentle humor softens most of Thackeray's exploration of social fictions to the point that contemporary readers responded to the "freshness" without entirely recognizing its cause, in one area of the novel the shock of the "real" was far too strong for them. This was the depiction of Elly's mother as her rival and enemy in love, "a subject which is, or ought to be, quite inadmissible for a novel" and "trenches on the sin of incest," according to Jewsbury (552). Oliphant, Thackeray's most enthusiastic reviewer, was equally upset: "There are some things which may be matters of fact and yet are inherently false, unlawful, unnatural, and unfit for the use of the artist" (173). Oliphant struggles at some length with the differences between "fact" and "truth," between, on the one hand, her recognition that "there are bad mothers" and that having either mother or daughter "magnanimously make a holocaust of her heart and give up the sublime lover," as the "literature of self-sacrifice" might dictate, is "foolish, weak and impracticable," and, on the other hand, her painful conviction that the situation Thackeray presents "upsets all the foundations of life, and makes love itself hideous" (174). Her only comfort is that the author "fails altogether in carrying [this part of the plot] out" and "break[s] down in the unfinished sketch of the jealous mother" (174). The impassioned jumble of gender, morality, and aesthetics in Oliphant's complaint suggests that the issue here comes close to the heart of mid-Victorian debates about realism, already inflamed by the emergence of sensationism, and certainly that there is something more in the representation of Caroline than the incompetence, or at best immaturity, Gérin discerns in the novel (129). Thackeray's "fault" was generic transgression, destabilizing a seemingly simple domestic romance by introducing into it a sexually passionate, thirty-six-year-old, "unmotherly" mother, a figure incompatible with the customary gendered discourse of realism that "prescribe[d] both how women [might] represent and how women [might] be represented" (Pykett, *Sensation* 33).[15]

Caroline Gilmour-Tourneur is in some respects the most remarkable figure in the novel. In the fairy tale framing of Elly's story she is troped as the wicked (step)mother, angry that the mirrors now declare her beauty eclipsed. Her moments of despairing passion find her with the red gown and "wild-falling" hair of a fallen woman (12). Thackeray, however, likes to invert the maxims of fairy tales[16] and Caroline's "wickedness" is typically muted by authorial sympathy. Despite her "black eyes and black hair," she and her daughter are "too much alike, too much of an age" (4), and having found that "people whom she had known, and who had admired her but a year or two ago, seemed to neglect her now and pass her by, in order to pay a certain homage to her daughter's youth and brilliance," Caroline has "suddenly" grown "old," feeling that "the wrinkles were growing under her wistful eyes, and that the colour was fading from her cheeks" (4–5). That she has genuinely loved John over a period of years and with, in the novel's most bitter irony, an intensity Elly will never equal, gives her a pathos and, briefly, a voice unique among nineteenth-century fictional mothers. She marries Tourneur for the power his position will give her and so that John "will learn that others do not despise me, and I–I will lead a good life" (35). For a time she flourishes, spending "her whole days doing good, patronizing the poor, lecturing the wicked, dosing the sick, superintending countless charitable communities" (47) and snubbing previous acquaintances, but these consolations are only temporarily satisfying and she largely fades from view when a more positive maternal figure is needed. At the end the narrator records simply that she "looks haggard and weary; and one day when I happened to tell her I was going away, she gasped out suddenly—'Ah! what would I not give——' and then was silent and turned aside. But she remains with her husband, which is more than I should have given her credit for" (194). The lack of a firm resolution to Caroline's story underlines the novel's equivocation about orthodox closure, which unsettled contemporary reviewers and later aesthetes alike. "We do not know whether the picture is true to nature," wrote the novelist George Moore about *The Story of Elizabeth* in 1921, airily dismissing what was most important to mid-Victorians, "but we know that it is true to art; our objections do not begin till her marriage, which seems to us a jarring dissonance, the true end being the ruin of Elly and the remorse of her mother" (169).[17] (He would have been appalled to know how much more conventional he now sounds than Thackeray does.)

As should have been evident from the passages quoted so far, a key factor in Thackeray's play with orthodoxy is her narrative voice. Seemingly earnest, a little naïve, her narrator is consistently engaged and intrusive. She chats to the reader, asking questions, offering alternatives, sharing opinions. Throughout she carries the weight of moral commentary, so clearly promised in the opening paragraph, interpreting, chiding, and sometimes pleading for Elly with a particularly feminine-seeming version of that kind of "author-ity" that, in Richard Pearce's summary, "derives from tradition, or a canon and way of reading, established by the class whose authority the authorial voice reflects and perpetuates when it addresses (or inscribes) its readers as members of his presupposed narrative community" (16). "I cannot help being sorry for her," remarks the narrator, as Elly weeps after her pretty clothes are denounced in a prayer meeting organized by her stepfather, "and sympathizing with her against that rigid community down below; and yet, after all, there was scarcely one of the people whom she so scorned who was not a better Christian than poor Elizabeth" (46). The balance between sympathy and moral "correctness," between frivolity and rigidity, is neatly judged to invoke that *via media* of moral good sense and fair play on which English realism prided itself. That Elly's ordeal takes place in Paris adds chauvinist emphasis to this appeal. Yet the careful art in placing words and details for the maximum seemingly artless effect hints that the narrator is, in Luce Irigaray's terms, "mim[ing] the role imposed upon her" (108). The same qualities of self-effacing diffidence and charitableness that inscribe the narrative voice as "properly" feminine, and so give it the right to speak with moral confidence, also undermine its authority. So well does Thackeray counterfeit the tone of normative femininity that it comes as little surprise toward the end of the novel when the previously omniscient narrator appears in person as an old friend of Miss Jean Dampier and so like her as to be almost indistinguishable from her. Together they offer a clear commentary on the processes of plot construction.

Miss Dampier, the "only good female character in the novel," in Jewsbury's eyes (552), is a sporadically interfering but largely ineffectual "fairy godmother," her role as determiner of fates indicated by her omnipresent knitting ("What is it you want me to do?" cries John, early on. "Drop one, knit two together" she replies [9]). Although she ironically praises John for his "well-regulated heart" and "noble self-denial" in giving up Elly for whom he cares in favor of Laetitia with her "50,000£" (8), she shares his ambivalence: "She really wanted John to marry his cousin, but she was a spinster still and sentimental; and she could not help being sorry for pretty Elizabeth" (9). Her most positive actions are rescuing the sick Elly from Paris and caring for her in convalescence, when she takes on the nurturing role Caroline has abandoned (again, it is notable that Thackeray avoids the clichéd reconciliation of mother and daughter over the sickbed). What Miss Dampier cannot do is to resolve the dilemmas and reward all the deserving in any realistic way. Shortly after telling John of Elly's decision that he must stay with Laetitia, she is seen "sitting in the window and the sunshine, knitting castles in the air." She says, "Suppose he does not take this for an answer? Suppose Laetitia has found someone else, suppose the door opens and he comes in, and the sun shines into the room, and then he seizes Elly's hand, and says, 'Though you give me up I will not give up the hope of calling you mine,' and Elly glances up, bright, blushing, happy" (161–62). "Only a fat, foolish old woman," the narrator calls her, excusing these "follies" (162), but this is, of course, in effect how the novel will end. Miss Dampier's resemblance to the implied author, who has relied so heavily on chance to motivate her plot, is unmistakable. Neither woman can simultaneously satisfy her emotional and her moral impulses without recourse to chance or lapsing into blatant "fairy tale" sentiment. To miss these associations, simply to label Thackeray's structures as defective, is to miss the point that the text is burlesquing conventional plots, not failing to produce one. The touch is always very light, the mockery gentle; hence, a possible alternative reading of Miss Dampier's function in the novel's interrogation of Victorian realism—seeing her as an image of women's power, marginalized by patriarchal systems, able to help Elly but not to control her fate—seems somewhat too dark. The closing stages of the novel find the two old women, narrator and authorial avatar, sitting together in the twilight, sighing at the reflected glow of the young lovers' finally achieved happiness. Gentle satire connects their caricatured spinsterly sentimentality to the whole process of closure. Theirs is a kindly world, in general a desirable world of virtue rewarded, but not one attainable outside fiction or through the sequences of cause and effect espoused by realism. The authoritative discourse that informed the novel's opening moral premise finally dissolves into a sentimental idealism.

What Victorian readers admired most about *The Story of Elizabeth* was precisely what George Moore disdained to know: its "truth to nature *as it is,* and not as it might become under all kinds of strange and false aspects" ("Popular" 129). Modern readers, also, have at times resisted seeing this as a virtue. As well as the vivid life-likeness of the characters, Thackeray's contemporaries praised especially the evocation of Elly's misery in Paris: "in no novel or history do we ever remember to have met with any narrative so startlingly distinct and real as this account of [Elly's] life in a house which has absolutely no attraction for her, whose occupations and pleasures are all utterly distasteful" (Oliphant 175). Victorian critics were happy to assume, as was indeed the case, that this part of the narrative was based in very real knowledge. Because of their mother's unfortunate madness, Thackeray and her sister spent much of their girlhood in Paris with their grandparents, an arrangement that, despite mutual affection, led to tempestuous clashes as the young Anne, in particular, resisted her severely religious grandmother's "serious efforts to turn them into little Calvinists" (Gérin 15). The house and the street described in *Elizabeth* are those the family lived in, and Stephen Tourneur's preaching is modeled on that of Paster Adolphe Monod, a leading Calvinist to whose confirmation classes the two girls were sent (much to their father's fury when he heard). For Gérin these facts point only to "lack of inventive power" (127)—a charge, incidentally, often leveled at women writers—and she jumps to the assumption that Thackeray "was probably no more than seventeen when she began" the novel (127).[18] This, surely, is as reasonable as assuming that Charlotte Brontë began *Jane Eyre* at ten. Without claiming that Thackeray is Brontë's equal in genius, it is worth noting that Brontë's own critical reputation suffered for some time because her work was seen as too autobiographical, a fact now often seen as underlying its strength. As long as the use of biographical material is seen as a defect, Thackeray's artistry will also remain undervalued—an unhappy childhood does not automatically lead to successful authorship.

The use in *The Story of Elizabeth* of biographical experience of another kind, less obvious to contemporary readers, might superficially support Gérin's views. The mother-daughter rivalry clearly recalls that between Lady Castlewood and her daughter Beatrix in William Thackeray's *The History of Henry Esmond* (1852), the first of his novels for which Anne acted as amanuensis. This work in turn recalls William's intense and ultimately unhappy relationship with Jane Brookfield. She, though a good friend to the Thackeray girls even after her break with their father, obviously threatened for a time to usurp the role he had always insisted they play as his companions in the place of his absent wife.[19] It takes little psychological ingenuity to read in *The Story of Elizabeth* some residual suppressed rivalry and wish fulfilment on Anne Thackeray's part. However, *Elizabeth*'s total inversion of another treatment of the mother-daughter theme cannot be so easily dismissed as mere copying or biographical determinism, demanding instead to be read as deliberate rewriting. Richard Monckton Milnes' "Unspoken Dialogue" was published in the second number of the *Cornhill* (194–97). In this trite poem a mother—"Four decades o'er her life had met / And left her lovely still" (194)—and daughter dispute their right to the same man. The mother resents her daughter's greater loveliness and virtue; the daughter fears that the mother plans to ensnare her in "pleasure of the clam'rous town / And vanity's mean strife" and so to her ruin her chances of gaining "one whom she can prize / At once with an adoring mind and with admiring eyes" (195). Notions of maternal duty and recollections of her first husband fail to move the mother until she turns to prayer. Immediately "her hard pride [is] turned to shame/her passion to remorse." When she finally leaves her daughter free to meet the suitor,

> Her heart by holy grace had cast
>
> The demon from its core,—
>
> And on the threshold calm she pass'd
>
> The man she loved no more. (197)

In complete contrast, Elly's bitter resentment at being removed from city pleasures into the austerely moral French Protestant household and Caroline's unending self-chosen purgatory question both Milnes's prurience and the moral simplification in William Thackeray's novel that justifies Esmond's final choice by Beatrix's unworthiness. To see *Elizabeth* as dialogue with these earlier works rather than copy not only grants Anne Thackeray the agency and artistry otherwise denied her, but also foregrounds the cultural work of intertextuality. It may, for example, cast new light on a third version of the mother-daughter relationship that appeared in the *Cornhill* in 1864–66, that of Hyacinth and Cynthia Kirkpatrick in Elizabeth Gaskell's *Wives and Daughters*.

Finally, some of Woolf's most subtly insidious praise hints that all of this is mere accident. In the obituary she merges her step-aunt's personality and writing in the image of "a garden" where "the bird of the soul raised an unpremeditated song of thanksgiving for the life it had found so good" (Gérin 284), whereas Mrs. Hilbery, we are told, "wrote as easily as a thrush sings" (Woolf, *Night and Day* 34). Frances Thomas makes clear both the ideological under-pinning of such imagery and how it demeans a woman writer when, in response to William Rossetti's presentation of his sister, Christina, as "a purely sponta-neous song-bird, one who composed from momentary inspiration, and with lit-tle revision," she sarcastically observes that "a woman writer must be feminine, passive, self-abnegating and her writing must be spontaneous; for a woman to struggle, even to think, about what she did, detracted from that delicious spon-taneity. William did not want the world to think he had a monster for a sister" (157). Anne Thackeray knew from personal experience that the effects of this particular "fictional narrative" could be "too strong for comfort." William Thack-eray had foreshadowed her dilemma when he wrote of his then nine-year-old daughter, "I am afraid very much she is going to be a man of genius. I had far sooner have had her an amiable and affectionate woman" (Ritchie, *Letters* 21). He did, nonetheless, bring her up expecting to be a writer and to support her-self and her sister. Anne Thackeray was at times throughout her life torn be-tween the conflicting demands of being a "genius" and being a "woman" and she had notoriously chaotic habits as a writer.[20] As this study has endeavored to show, she also produced works of art.

WORKS CITED

Auerbach, Nina, and U. C. Knoepflmacher, eds. *Forbidden Journeys: Fairy Tales and Fan-tasies by Victorian Women Writers.* Chicago and London: U of Chicago P, 1992.

Borowitz, Albert. "The Unpleasantness at the Garrick Club." *Victorian Newsletter* Spring 1978: 16–23.

Boyd, Elizabeth French. *Bloomsbury Heritage: Their Mothers and Their Aunts.* London: Hamish Hamilton, 1976.

Clarke, Norma. *Ambitious Heights: Women, Friendship, Love: The Jewsbury Sisters, Fe-licia Hemans and Jane Carlyle.* London: Routledge, 1990.

Debenham, Helen. "*The Cornhill Magazine* and the Literary Formation of Anne Thack-eray Ritchie." *Victorian Periodicals Review* 33.1 (Spring 2000): 81–91.

De Man, Paul. "The Resistance to Theory." *Modern Criticism and Theory: A Reader.* Ed. David Lodge. London: Longman, 1988.

Eliot, George. *The George Eliot Letters.* Ed. Gordon S. Haight. New Haven: Oxford UP, 1954–56. 7 vols.

Gérin, Winifred. *Anne Thackeray Ritchie: A Biography.* Oxford: Oxford UP, 1981.

Hill-Miller, Katherine C. "'The Skies and Trees of the Past': Anne Thackeray Ritchie and William Makepeace Thackeray." *Daughters and Fathers.* Ed. Lynda E. Boose and Betty S. Flowers. Baltimore: Johns Hopkins UP, 1989. 361–83.

Howe, Suzanne. *Geraldine Jewsbury: Her Life and Errors.* London: Allen, 1935.

Irigaray, Luce. "This Sex Which Is Not One." *New French Feminisms: An Anthology.* Ed. Elaine Marks and Isabelle de Courtivron. Brighton: Harvester, 1985.

Jewsbury, Geraldine. "New Novels." *Athenæum* 25 Apr. 1863: 552–53.

"Literature of the Month." *Victoria Magazine* May 1863: 95.

MacKay, Carol Hanbery. "Hate and Humor as Empathetic Whimsy in Anne Thackeray Ritchie." *Women's Studies: An Interdisciplinary Journal* 15 (1988): 117–33.

Milnes, Richard Monckton. "Unspoken Dialogue." *Cornhill Magazine* Feb. 1860: 194–97.

Moore, George. *Confessions of a Young Man.* London: Heineman, 1928.

Oliphant, Margaret. "Novels." *Blackwood's Edinburgh Magazine* Aug. 1863: 68–82.

Pearce, Richard. *The Politics of Narration: James Joyce, William Faulkner and Virginia Woolf.* New Brunswick: Rutgers UP, 1991.

"The Popular Novels of the Year." *Fraser's Magazine* Aug. 1863: 253–69.

Pykett, Lyn. *The "Improper" Feminine: The Woman's Sensation Novel and the New Woman's Writing.* London and New York: Routledge, 1992.

———. *The Sensation Novel from* The Woman in White *to* The Moonstone. Plymouth: Northcote, 1994.

Ritchie, Anne Thackeray. *Anne Thackeray Ritchie's Journals and Letters.* Commentary and notes by Lillian F. Shankman. Ed. Abigail Burnham Bloom and John Maynard. Ohio State UP, 1995.

———. *Letters of Anne Thackeray Ritchie.* Selected and edited by her daughter Hester Ritchie. London: John Murray, 1924.

———. *The Village on the Cliff.* London: Smith, 1867.

Sassoon, Siegfried. *The Best of Friends: Further Letters to Sydney Carlyle Cockerell.* Ed. Viola Meynell. London: Rupert Hart Davis, 1956.

Stephen, Leslie. *Sir Leslie Stephen's Mausoleum Book.* Oxford: Clarendon, 1977.

Swanson, Vern G. *The Biography and Catalogue Raisonné of Lawrence Alma Tadema.* London: Garton in Association with Scholar, 1990.

Thackeray, Anne. *The Story of Elizabeth, Two Hours, and From an Island.* The Works of Miss Thackeray. London: Smith, Elder, 1886

Thackeray, William Makepeace. *The History of Henry Esmond.* London: Smith, 1852.

Thomas, Frances. *Christina Rossetti: A Biography.* London: Virago, 1994.

Woolf, Virginia. *The Essays of Virginia Woolf.* Ed. Andrew McNeillie. Vol. 3. London: Hogarth, 1988. 3 vols.

———. *Night and Day.* 1919. London: Hogarth, 1938.

———. *The Question of Things Happening: The Letters of Virginia Woolf.* Vol. 2. Ed. Nigel Nicolson. London: Hogarth, 1975.

———. *A Room of One's Own.* 1929. London: Hogarth, 1978.

NOTES

1. Anne Isabella Thackeray, born 1837, became Mrs. Richmond Ritchie in 1877 and Lady Ritchie when her husband was knighted in 1907. She published under various versions of these names. Like most of her fiction, *The Story of Elizabeth* was published before her marriage; therefore, in this paper I refer to this author by her maiden name.

2. Published anonymously, in accordance with *Athenæum* policy, the review was written by Geraldine Jewsbury. The journal's antagonism to William Thackeray was part of a long-running dispute among the friends and supporters of Charles Dickens and William Thackeray, which flared into active hostility as a result of what is known as the Garrick Club affair in 1858, but which has its roots more deeply in literary rivalries.

Jewsbury's review reactivated the ill feeling to such an extent that it has been considered a contributory cause of William's death at the end of the year. For a fuller account see Albert Borowitz 16–23.

3. Oliphant may not have known who the author was when she first read it. Anne Thackeray's sister, Harriet (known as Minny), wrote to her father in September 1863 that it was not "anyone who knows us" who wrote the review. She goes on: "Mr Blackwood told me that he heard [Mrs Oliphant] praising it one day & instantly told her to write a review of it" (Ritchie, *Journals* 95).

4. Swanson's statement that the painting is a portrait of Anne Thackeray herself is incorrect.

5. See Eliot VI: 123 and 418. See also IV: 209.

6. Leslie Stephen's first wife was Minny Thackeray. Virginia was the daughter of his second marriage, to Julia Duckworth.

7. Carol Hanbery MacKay has done much valuable work on Thackeray, principally on the nonfictional material. She deals more with fiction in "Hate and Humor as Empathetic Whimsy in Anne Thackeray Ritchie" (117–33). An important recent addition to the available biographical material is *Anne Thackeray Ritchie's Journals and Letters*.

8. Mrs. Hilbery, the mother of the heroine in Woolf's second novel (first published in 1919), writes copiously in "brilliant" and "lightning-like" bursts of inspiration but never completes anything (34). Woolf's formal denial that there are more than "touches of Lady Ritchie in Mrs Hilbery" is belied by her manifest glee in a later letter to Vanessa: "My only triumph is that the Ritchies are furious with me for Mrs Hilbery and Hester [Anne Thackeray's daughter] is writing a life of Aunt Anny to prove that she was a shrewd, and silent woman of business." See *Question* 406, 474.

9. The obituary originally appeared in the *Times Literary Supplement* 6 March, 1919: 123. It is also reprinted in Volume 3 of *The Essays of Virginia Woolf* (13–19). See also "The Enchanted Organ" in the same volume (399–400).

10. For more detail about the rewriting see my "*The Cornhill Magazine* and the literary formation of Anne Thackeray Ritchie."

11. Virginia Woolf's complaint about the representation of women in earlier fictions appears in *A Room of One's Own* (137).

12. Shankman sees this only as a fault (Ritchie, *Journals* 67).

13. Thackeray explores the limitations of "feminine" discourse more fully in her second novel, *The Village on the Cliff* (1867).

14. In some, almost certainly coincidental, ways *The Story of Elizabeth* parodies aspects of Jewsbury's last and most serious love affair, with Walter Mantell, in which Jewsbury experienced what it was to be an older woman unrequitedly in love with a younger man possibly engaged to his cousin, and to discover the joys and discontents of power. Despite this, and her customary disdain of men, Jewsbury needed to believe Mantell worthy of her love. (See Howe and Clarke.) Whether or not Jewsbury consciously recognized the parallels, this aspect of Thackeray's novel is unlikely to have appealed to her, and a personal motive helps to explain the otherwise inexplicable intensity of her venom in the review.

15. My use of the term "proper femininity" throughout this paper follows the definitions established in Pykett's work.

16. For example, describing Elly's refusal to try to conform to her restricted life in Paris, Thackeray compares her with Cinderella's sisters, who "cut off their toes and heels,

and could not screw their feet in [to the shoe], though they tried ever so. Well, they did their best; but Elly did not try at all" (43).

17. Moore compares Thackeray with George Eliot to the latter's disadvantage, though his opinion that "a woman cannot become a man" colors his judgment (169).

18. It also contradicts Thackeray's later claim that, on her father's instructions, she wrote nothing between the ages of fifteen and twenty-two or -three, which Gérin earlier cites without query (118). However, as I suggest in my "*The Cornhill Magazine* and the Literary Formation of Anne Thackeray Ritchie," there is reason to doubt that this was entirely true.

19. Katherine C. Hill-Miller provides a good brief analysis of William's relations with his daughters in "'The Skies and Trees of the Past': Anne Thackeray Ritchie and William Makepeace Thackeray" (361–83).

20. Leslie Stephen complained that "[s]he wrote fragments as thoughts struck her and pinned them (with literal not metaphorical pins) at parts of her MS till it became a chaotic jumble, maddening to the printer" (14).

8

"I Am Not Esther"

Biblical Heroines and Sarah Grand's Challenge to Institutional Christianity in The Heavenly Twins

Jennifer M. Stolpa

The Heavenly Twins (1893), like Sarah Grand's other novels, is not often read today and is given minimal critical attention in comparison with the works of other Victorian women novelists and with those of Grand's late-Victorian male contemporaries. Grand's novel deserves a larger readership and more scholarly attention because of its value as a literary text that engages readers with strong characterization, narrative experimentation, and intriguing story plots; as a critical text that offers insights into gender studies; and as a cultural text that offers insights into the Victorian period not found in the present canon.

If the test of whether a long-neglected novel warrants a larger readership is its ability to move modern audiences and provide an enjoyable reading experience, *The Heavenly Twins* offers the same potential for success now that it enjoyed upon its first publication. Although Grand struggled to find a publisher for the novel, in part because of its frank treatment of syphilis and its condemnation of the sexual double standard that threatens the heroines' well-being, once published, it enjoyed great commercial success. Reprinted six times in England during the first year, sales reached 20,000. In America, at least five times as many copies were sold in the first year (Kersley 72–73). The novel continued to be a popular success, reissued in 1897, 1899, 1901, 1904, 1912, and 1923 (Bonnell, "Legacy" 470), and was translated into a number of languages, including Russian and Finnish (Kersley 91).

The novel's early commercial success is not surprising. Aside from the controversial issues it discusses (always a potential selling point), the novel is alternately humorous and poignant, allowing its readers to laugh at the titled twins' youthful antics while challenging its readers to rebel against the restrictions placed upon the female characters' intellectual and spiritual development. Grand's novel tells the story of three young women, Evadne Frayling, Edith Beale, and Angelica Hamilton-Wells. Evadne's potential and Angelica's intellectual brilliance are all but lost to the public world because of the restrictions placed upon women's sphere of activity. Two of the women, Evadne and Edith, are forced to submit to parental authority even though that authority is leading them to marry morally corrupt and syphilitic men; once married, they are expected to submit to their husbands despite the men's failings.

The novel potentially resonates with a modern audience because of continued debates about the connection between gender and particular characteristics or limitations. Despite its relevance to modern discussions, the 1992 reprint of the novel by Ann Arbor Paperbacks has sold fewer than 2,000 copies to date (McCarthy). Far from its popular success in the 1890s, the novel is apparently not even gaining widespread classroom use. This is perhaps because Victorian scholars first need to reassess the novel's value as a literary, critical, and cultural text. Once the novel is closely reevaluated and its importance to the literary period established, sales and readership of the novel will certainly rise.

I am not the first in recent years to argue that neglect of *The Heavenly Twins* is unjustified. In reprinting the novel in 1992, the University of Michigan argued that it offers modern scholars another accessible example of New Woman fiction. In the introduction to this reprint, Carol A. Senf cites the novel's popularity in England and America at the time of its original publication, the novel's appeal to feminist scholars of New Woman fiction, and the respect accorded the novel by significant literary figures such as Mark Twain and George Bernard Shaw as reasons why more students of Victorian literature and gender studies should read the novel. Stanley Weintraub's "George Bernard Shaw Borrows from Sarah Grand: *The Heavenly Twins* and *You Never Can Tell*" briefly explores Shaw's open respect for Grand's novel, which he argues is reflected in character similarities, the quotation of a few lines, and the presence of certain lines of thought in his 1895 play *You Never Can Tell*.[1]

Teresa Mangum's *Married, Middlebrow, and Militant: Sarah Grand and the New Woman Novel* (1998) also strives to revive interest in Grand's works. Mangum points out that *The Heavenly Twins* offers insights into the New Woman figure, gender performance, the unjust submission of women to husbands and fathers, and the sexual double standard in the Victorian period. Moreover, Mangum says that she is reassured of the novel's importance "not by conventional academic accolades but by the enthusiasm, seriousness, and personal commitment with which my undergraduate classes respond to Grand's *The Heavenly Twins*" (219).

This summary of Mangum's text on Grand might lead those unfamiliar with Grand's work to believe that the significant aspects of her novels have already been thoroughly discussed. One reason certain Victorian women's novels are neglected is that they may be considered one-dimensional. For example, a novel that is overtly religious or contains characters who discuss their beliefs frequently may be labeled as religious propaganda, pertaining to a particular de-nomination. Indeed, most Victorian works contain clerical characters and refer-ences to religion, and many novels of the period were preoccupied with questions of faith and doubt. Unfortunately, many authors whose texts focus almost ex-clusively on religious issues (Charlotte Yonge, Mrs. Humphry Ward, Felicia Skene, Elizabeth Missing Sewell) are considered noncanonical. In part because these texts have not been more carefully examined, additional insights into the novels' presentations of gender, poverty, divorce, the legal system, or any num-ber of other issues have been lost.

This is the case with Grand's *The Heavenly Twins*. Although the text's pre-sentation of gender identity issues has been illuminated by Mangum, the com-plexities of such episodes as Angelica's decision to take on the identity of her male twin in the section "The Tenor and the Boy—An Interlude," for example, have certainly not been exhausted. I cannot hope to engage in a complete re-assessment of the novel in the space of this essay. However, before I explore in some depth one particular aspect of the novel that has long been ignored, its treatment of women within Christianity, I wish to briefly address three other significant aspects that illustrate the breadth of themes within the novel still awaiting critical attention.

First, Grand frequently discusses the merits and flaws of eighteenth- and nine-teenth-century fictional and nonfictional works, including texts such as Henry Fielding's *Tom Jones*, works by Thomas Carlyle, Elizabeth Gaskell's *Ruth,* and late-Victorian novels by Rhoda Broughton and Ouida. Grand comments on these other texts, especially on the sexual double standard many of them explore, from the perspective of a New Woman novelist. Grand examines the effects such varying works have on Evadne's education and development. For instance, she contrasts the views of Evadne and her father on the morality of Tom Jones. In doing so, Grand offers a critical view of Fielding's canonical work, providing evi-dence that some women of the late nineteenth century looked upon established masterpieces as open to criticism because of their support for a patriarchal soci-ety. Grand anticipates twentieth-century feminism's direct commentaries on male-authored visions of women's sexuality, offering a similar indictment of certain male texts. A close examination of this and other intertextual references would enrich our understanding of how late-nineteenth-century writers viewed their literary ancestors.

Second, the novel's numerous references to music by Schubert and Wagner, as well as the recurring refrain from Mendelssohn, "He, watching over Israel, slumbers not, nor sleeps," calls for an analysis of Grand's response to certain composers as well as a study of the novel's interdisciplinary approach to cre-ativity in musical and narrative composition. Grand's use of the recurring re-frain from Mendelssohn is identified as significant to the text as a whole by Mary Patricia Murphy in her dissertation, "Timely Interventions: Gender, Temporal-ity, and the New Woman" (1997). Murphy examines how the clock that sounds the refrain is used to mark important times within the lives of different characters. In *Rebellious Structures: Women Writers and the Crisis of the Novel 1880–1900*, Gerd Bjørhovde also alludes to the possibility that the chime may help Grand structure the narrative and accentuate particular moments. However, Grand's concern with the refrain not just as words but as *music* is evident in her repeated transcription of the bars of music that accompany the refrain.

Third, Grand's experimentation with narrative styles makes her concern with musicians' creativity and formal style more significant. Grand employs a number of different narrative techniques: the use of footnotes to correct information in Book One, "Childhoods and Girlhoods," as if the text were an accurate representation of historical truth; the interpolation of the story of "The Tenor and the Boy—An Interlude," which at first appears to have little relevance to the stories of Evadne, Edith, and Angelica; the brief experiment with a form of stream-of-consciousness narrative style in Chapter Six of "Mrs. Kilroy of Ilverthorpe"; and the abrupt shift in Book Six, "The Impressions of Dr. Galbraith," to a first-person, quasi-scientific account from the perspective of one of the characters. Each of these styles addresses issues that have been central to the study of narrative throughout the history of the novel, including history versus fiction, the potential for accurate representation, the utility of multiple perspectives, and the effects of untrustworthy narrators.

Several critics have explored Grand's narrative style and the shifts in narrative voice within the novel. John Kucich, in "Curious Dualities: *The Heavenly Twins* (1893) and Sarah Grand's Belated Modernist Aesthetics," refers to the novel's inclusion of a variety of styles, such as "cyclic repetition, micro-realism, and plot disjunction to frustrate the momentum of linear narrative" (199). In more depth, Marilyn Bonnell's "Sarah Grand and the Critical Establishment: Art for (Wo)man's Sake" explores the novel's narrative structure as a response to the aesthetic and realist movements of Grand's time. Kucich and Bonnell's studies are valuable, but have hardly exhausted the potential responses to Grand's use of varying narrative forms.

The novel also treats with some significance the issue of institutional Christianity's teachings about women. Grand's own interest in various Christian denominations and other religions, as well as doctrinal disputes in general, appears to have begun early in her married life, while she traveled with her military husband in the Far East (Kersley 37). Exposure to Eastern religions would have allowed Grand to compare and contrast the doctrines and beliefs of various religious systems. At some point, Grand was led to see the Bible and institutional Christianity as bound by the culture in which they were written and developed. For example, as noted in the diaries kept by her devoted friend Gladys Singers-Bigger, when Sarah was in her seventies and eighties, Grand allegedly said on 19 June, 1934, that "as against accepting the whole of the Bible as inspired, she quoted certain bloodthirsty passages in Leviticus which she could not accept" (qtd. in Kersley 260). Such a comment is in part a result of the nineteenth-century Higher Criticism of the Bible as a text written by human individuals (men), and not God. It also indicates that Grand thoughtfully examined Christianity and the Bible and was aware of the major theological arguments of the time.

Grand would also have known about the ways in which biblical passages were used by both men and women to promote women's submission to and dependence on men. Throughout most of the history of institutional Christianity, passages such as the Genesis story of Eve's part in original sin or Paul's letters on the public silence of women have been used to argue that women's submission is in fact divinely ordained.

Throughout the history of Christianity there have also been individuals who, like many modern day Christian feminists, argued that Christianity's true roots call for women's equality, not subordination. Those who study such proto-Christian feminist thought in the nineteenth century focus much more attention on American women writers' resistance to patriarchal Christian ideals than on British women writers' explorations of the same issues. For example, in its survey of women's active and independent presence within Christianity and theological discussions, Rosemary Radford Ruether's *Women and Redemption: A Theological History* (1998) contains chapters describing medieval women mystics, women in the Renaissance period and seventeenth-century Protestantism, American women of the nineteenth century, and twentieth-century Western European feminist theologians. The revised edition of Elizabeth A. Clark and Herbert Richardson's *Women and Religion: The Original Sourcebook of Women in Christian Thought* (1996) similarly skips over British women of the nineteenth century. The lack of attention to Victorian women's interest in theological discussions may be the result of a perception that British women of the time contributed little to such discussions, at least not as openly and frequently as their American counterparts. However, a number of publications from the period demonstrate the opposite. Nonfictional works by England's Julia Kavanagh, Florence Nightingale, Catherine Booth, and Frances Power Cobbe question Christian institutional endorsement of a binary gender ideology that relegated women's activities only to a private sphere of influence.[2]

Additionally, novels such as *The Heavenly Twins* affirm the presence in England of proto-Christian feminist thought. Like Victorian women novelists such as Charlotte Brontë, Anne Brontë, Charlotte Yonge, Elizabeth Gaskell, Felicia Skene, Margaret Oliphant, and George Eliot, Grand uses the opportunity of fiction, a form of writing seen as acceptable for women, to study religion and theology, subjects many clergymen (and laypeople) thought were beyond women's capabilities. Although some Christian denominations encouraged laywomen to read and apply the Bible to their own lives, the systematic study of theology, what John Ruskin referred to in "Of Queen's Gardens" as the "one dangerous science for women" (143), was generally considered inappropriate for women.[3] Furthermore, Grand's novel contrasts with many nineteenth- and even some early-twentieth-century novels that used religious arguments to support an ideal of womanhood as passive and submissive, and to perpetuate ideals of separate spheres for women's and men's activities (Rowbotham 84–85). Instead,

Grand condemns such abuses of Christian ideas, arguing that liberation from a binary gender ideology is inherent in Christianity.

Grand's work is indeed one of the strongest fictional forays into theology by a Victorian woman writer. In the novel, Grand distinguishes between the practices of Christian churches and the egalitarian roots of pre-Pauline Christianity. She explores how Church authorities manipulate biblical texts to maintain women's submission to husbands and fathers. Simultaneously, Grand points to biblical heroines who demonstrate women's power, physical prowess, strength, leadership, and independence. Grand counters the ideal of wifely submission, extolled by the clergy as divinely ordained, with images from the Bible that offer very different role models for women. She seeks not only to demonstrate the androcentrism of institutional Christianity, but to uncover biblical stories that restore to Christianity the power to liberate men and women from gender-restricted roles.

Grand alludes to female biblical figures who transcend stereotypical gender boundaries; these allusions reinforce critical readings of the novel as feminist in its questioning of gender stereotypes. Grand even refers to the male and female Creator, which she says is mistranslated in Genesis as "He." In the "Proem," Grand's preface to her novel, she refers to "Elohim," the spirit that signifies "the union to which all nature testifies, the male and female principles which together created the universe, the infinite father and mother, without whom, in perfect accord and exact equality, the best government of nations has always been crippled and abortive" (xliii).

The controversial nature of such a statement in the late nineteenth century is borne out by the continued resistance to the idea of a deity combining male and female more than one hundred years later. Like Sarah Grand, modern Christian feminists who argue in favor of such a vision of a Christian God continue to meet opposition within certain denominational hierarchies.[4] Although Grand does not return in her novel to this idea of the gendered nature of God, the novel continually challenges the theological stance of Christian institutions and their clergy.

Ideala, one of the minor characters in *The Heavenly Twins* who is prominent in the novel's prequel (Grand's *Ideala* [1889]), points out the disparity between what the clergy teach from the Bible and the behavior they prescribe for women. Arguing that the clergy "do a great deal of harm," Ideala says to a clerical character, "You preach the parable of the buried talents, and side by side with that you have always insisted that women should put theirs away" (*Heavenly* 266). Angelica, disguised as "the boy" in her escapades with the Tenor, later echoes Ideala's choice of scriptural passages; "I hope to live, however, to see it allowed that a woman has no more right to bury her talents than a man has" (453). Whereas Ideala and Angelica criticize the clergy for dismissing the true meaning of such biblical passages, Evadne's mother presents the opposite argument. She tells Evadne, "read your Bible properly" and stop "quoting Scripture too, for your own purposes" (106). It is apparent in the novel that in order to read the Bible properly, Evadne must agree with the interpretations set forth by the male clergy.

Grand is always careful to distinguish between her challenge to the Christian hierarchy and a true Christian ethic that is unpolluted by church politics. Grand differentiates between "the clergy," busily doing their work, and "Christianity ... [which] was much neglected" (355). The disparity between what the clergy teach and what the Bible teaches is again brought forward in dialogue between Mr. St. John, the representative of the Church of England within the novel, and Mrs. Malcolmson, whose voice within the novel supports women's equality. Mr. St. John says clearly, "What can be more admirable, more elevating to contemplate, more powerful as an example, than [a woman's] beautiful submission" (179). Mrs. Malcolmson argues that such rhetoric, what she refers to as "poetry of the pulpit," has extolled women's "helpless condition under the pompous title of 'beautiful patient submission'" for too long. Moreover, Mrs. Malcolmson insists that such rhetoric represents not the law of God given to man, as Mr. St. John argues, "but the law of [man's] own inclinations" (181).

Grand does not limit herself to female voices alone, but includes male characters who recount ways in which biblical passages have been misinterpreted, abused, or manipulated to match the desires of the male authorities within institutional Christianity. Sir Shadwell Rock, an esteemed London physician, disdains the use of particular images of women to support the "clerical theory" that woman "is a dangerous beast, to be kept in subjection, and used for domestic purposes only" (638–39).

Additionally, one of the title's twins, Diavolo, disagrees with his grandfather on the generally accepted interpretation of the story of Adam and Eve. Whereas his grandfather, the duke, proclaims that "it was a woman, my boy ... who compassed the fall of man," Diavolo argues that after careful study the story proves to have several different interpretations. First, Diavolo argues that the Genesis story does not prove that women are weak, "for you see, the woman could tempt the man easily enough; but it took the very old devil himself to tempt the woman." Second, Diavolo suggests that "it happened a good while ago" and is perhaps no longer accurately told nor perfectly applicable to modern women. Third, he suggests that the devil may likely have reached Adam first and Eve "'got it out of him'" because of her curiosity; thus the blame belongs to both. Finally, dismissing the Edenic story because of its age and dubious interpretations, Diavolo declares that there is no doubt about the redemption. It was a woman who managed that little affair. And, altogether, it seems to me that, in spite of the disadvantage of being classed by law with children, lunatics, beggars, and irresponsible people generally, in the matter of who has done most good in the world, women exceed the mark. (261). Diavolo's views on women have been aided by growing up with his twin, Angelica, whose intelligence, strength, and determination surpass his own. Through this male character, Grand challenges one of the major arguments used to support women's submission to men—their weakness and blame for original sin.

Grand's reevaluation of the Bible's diverse range of models for women can be seen in a number of similar passages. One passage exemplifies the passive images of virtue, often embodied in Mary, which began in the nineteenth century

to supplant images of Eve as a warning about women's potential for sinful behavior. Another passage overtly contrasts these ideals of passivity and subordination with biblical heroines whose activity, often violent, offers a model of
resistance to injustice. The effects of these sets of images on Edith and Angelica, respectively, illustrate Grand's challenge to institutional Christianity's manipulation of particular female images.

The first passage describes Edith's room at home, which is filled with images
that have helped to form her sense of self. Elaine Showalter's brief discussion of
The Heavenly Twins in *A Literature of Their Own* argues that Edith represents
the "Old Woman" in a New Woman's novel, for she is "steeped in religion and
the feminine mystique" (206). Showalter does not further discuss what "religion" is for Edith, but a close reading of the text demonstrates that it is a particular form of institutional Christianity that Grand blames for Edith's
sufferings. More specifically, Edith is "steeped" in carefully chosen religious images of women as passive, virtuous mothers.

The images deemed suitable for Edith, the daughter of the bishop of Morn-
ingquest, include photographs and engravings of a number of religious works from
the Renaissance. Hanging in her room "there was a 'Virgin and Child,' by Botticelli, and another by Perugini; 'Our Lady of the Cat,' by Baroccio; the exquisite
'Vision of St. Helena,' by Paolo Veronese; Correggio's 'Ecce Homo'; and others
less well-known" (*Heavenly* 158).[5] Taken as a whole, the pictures are said to provide the young Edith with a model of "freshness and serenity" to contemplate
(158). Although at first Edith's devotion to such images appears exemplary, Grand
later depicts the way this devotion leads to a disastrous marriage and Edith's death.

Considered individually, each work represents facets of the same ideal of womanhood—one that would encourage Edith's religious sensibilities toward submission, passivity, and chastity. First, Botticelli's *Virgin and Child* may refer to
any number of his paintings of Mary and the infant Christ. Botticelli's images
of the Virgin Mother, popular in the nineteenth century, invariably portray her
as singularly attentive to her child, or as humbly averting her gaze from both
the Christ child resting in her arms and those who view her portrait.

Similarly, Perugino's *Madonna and Child* (1500) is one of many paintings
with similar subjects and titles to which Grand may be referring. Pietro Perugino's images of the Virgin, typical of many Renaissance works, portray a woman
who is idealized, to stress her virtue and devotion, and at the same time made
more familiar, to emphasize her humanity (Abbott 53). Although women were
thus able to see Mary as a role model, "they were simultaneously reminded of
the gulf which separated the impossible ideal from their own flawed lives" (53).
Most of Perugino's portraits of Mary reinforce cultural ideals of woman as a
model of beauty, as a compassionate, reserved, and devout woman, and as a
mother, first and foremost (57, 64).

Almost all of Federico Barocci's works focus on religious subjects. *Virgin with
Kitten* was completed some time before 1577 and portrays a very domestic scene,
a technique Barocci frequently used in an attempt to reach the minds and hearts

of "simple people" (Pillsbury 255). The virgin's soft, round features complement
the two cherubic children she holds on her lap. While the children's attention is
drawn toward a kitten pictured in the lower left, the virgin looks down at one
child, eyes once again humbly, perhaps submissively, averted from the viewer's
gaze. A man in the upper right observes the domestic scene. The virgin capably
cares for the two lively children, whose hands stretch in different directions,
while still maintaining a look of peace on her face.

There are two versions of Paolo Veronese's *Vision of St. Helena,* one now in
Rome and the other in the National Gallery in London (Orliac 108). The differences between the two center on St. Helena's dress; although she is clearly a
member of the upper class in both, within the painting now in Rome she wears
a crown and is more richly dressed. In both, two cherubs approach St. Helena,
carrying the cross she is reported to have seen in her vision. As the focus of both
portraits, St. Helena's eyes are closed, either asleep or in a prayerful trance. Both
depict her as passively receiving the vision. Furthermore, a reference to St. Helena directs attention to a female role model who is reverenced primarily for her
devoted and prayerful life, as well as her influence over her son Constantine the
Great. The ideal of womanhood expressed both in Veronese's paintings and in
St. Helena's story is one of passive influence rather than independent activity.

Correggio's *Ecce Homo* (c. 1520) depicts the adult Christ immediately after
receiving his sentence of death. Pontius Pilate looks on from the upper left, his
expression pleading impotence, while a soldier in the far right looks intently at
Christ. Mary, positioned at the bottom left, has fainted and lies back in the arms
of St. John, identifiable because of the red and green colored clothing generally
attributed to him in Renaissance paintings (Ekserdjian 163).

This individual consideration of the paintings found in Edith's room illustrates their presentation of an ideal woman as the joyful mother, with emphasis placed on qualities such as patience, resignation to suffering, submission,
passivity, dependence, and weakness. Taught by these images, Edith is later unable to reconcile her own marriage to Sir Mosley Menteith with what has been
her ideal. Her husband's syphilis is passed on to her son, whose resultant sickly
nature destroys the joy she might have felt at the birth of her child. Despite her
husband's sexual infidelity before and during their marriage, Edith can consider
nothing except submission. As Edith returns to her parents' home, suffers from
mental and physical illness, and eventually dies, Grand condemns not only a
sexual double standard that excused Sir Mosley Mentieth's behavior, but also
the models provided to Edith.

After Edith's marriage, she is faced with her husband's open flirtations with
other women. Grand makes it clear what is to blame for Edith's mental and emotional death: "Edith had been robbed of all means of self-defence by the teaching which insisted that her only duty as a wife consisted in silent submission to
her husband's will" (*Heavenly* 280). Upon returning to the room she had as a
girl, Edith finds that while nothing there has changed—the paintings remain—
there has been a "direful difference in herself" (284).

Angelica, a witness to the devastating effects of Edith's unfortunate marriage, dreams one night of the potential resistance women could offer to those who would force their subordination to fathers and husbands, regardless of the moral character of such men. The imaginative freedom of the dream allows Grand to present Angelica's opposition to the authority of men throughout history who would dictate women's submissive position, including "Caesar, Pan, Achilles, Hercules, . . . Lancelot and Arthur, . . . Henry VIII, Richelieu, Robespierre, Luther, and several Popes" (294). Within Angelica's dream, clergymen insist that they disseminate the word of God directly. They tell her that to question her natural masters within society—fathers, clergymen, husbands—is to go against God. As the dream continues, Angelica confronts religious leaders such as the Roman Catholic pope and cardinals, as well as archbishops from the Church of England.

Within her dream, Angelica cries out to all women, attempting to encourage their active resistance to ideals of womanhood that require submission and self-abnegation: "'I am not Esther, most decidedly! But I am Judith. I am Jael. I am Vashti. I am Godiva. I am all the heroic women of all the ages rolled into one, not for the shedding of blood, but for the saving of suffering.' They did not understand her a bit, however, they were so dazed, and they all looked askance at her. 'I see,' she said, 'I shall have to save you in spite of yourselves'" (296). Apart from the reference to the nonbiblical Lady Godiva, who opposed her husband's ideas and used her body to fight against his high taxation of the poor, Angelica reclaims as role models for women the strong, active, independent, and often fierce female fighters against oppression who are found within the Bible. Having seen the result of Edith's education into submissive female models within Christianity, Angelica's list of biblical heroines serves as a reminder to women that the stories that are *not* taught by the clergymen offer a vastly different image of true womanhood, women's proper sphere of activity, and gendered characteristics.

An analysis of Angelica's impassioned speech can be enhanced by comparing it with one significant contemporary of Grand's novel, *The Woman's Bible*, which was compiled and written by Elizabeth Cady Stanton and a number of other prominent American women in the 1890s. *The Woman's Bible* was a strong form of feminist theology because of its assertion that biblical women have not been properly interpreted by church authorities, nor adequately represented in sermons and theological discourses.[6]

The first model cited in Angelica's speech, that of Esther, she rejects. In place of this she calls on the ideal of resistance that the biblical Vashti represents. Teresa Mangum argues that Grand is referring to "the actress Vashti, who had such a hold on the Victorian imagination" (132). However, given the biblical nature of all but one of the references, Lady Godiva, it is probable that Grand's reference is to the biblical Vashti. There is further evidence of Grand's familiarity with the biblical story of Vashti in a passage from *The Beth Book* (1897), in which a defiant Beth refuses to cater to her classmates' desires, paraphrasing the biblical passage: "'Twas not for this I left my father's home! / Go, tell your class, that Vashti will not come" (300).

The Book of Esther begins with this story of how Esther replaced Vashti in the king's favor. King Ahasuerus is host to the powerful princes from all of the surrounding areas, and they feast for seven days, drinking "royal wine in abundance" (Esth. 1. 7). When the king calls on Vashti, the queen, to come before the assembly of princes and show her beauty, Vashti refuses. Angered, the king is advised to dismiss Vashti and "give her royal estate unto another that is better than she," for if he does not, all men in his kingdom will suffer similar indignities from their wives because of Vashti's model of rebellion (Esth. 1.15–19). The king banishes Vashti and names Esther as queen. Esther's acceptance of a subordinate role to the king in the remainder of the book contrasts with Vashti's earlier rebellion.

As a result, Vashti's strong egalitarian image of woman has appealed to feminists much more than Esther's submissive image (Niditch 122). This appears to have been the case with the women who compiled and wrote *The Woman's Bible*. Commenting on Vashti's refusal and attributing various reasons for it, Lucinda B. Chandler writes that "she had a higher idea of womanly dignity than placing herself on exhibition as one of the king's possessions" (Stanton et al. 2: 86). She did not choose to be seen as "an exhibit" or as the king's property to do with as he pleased (2: 87). Rather, Vashti represents "the growth of self-respect and of individual sovereignty" among women (2: 87). Stanton's response to the story of Vashti, "I have always regretted that the historian allowed Vashti to drop out of sight so suddenly" (2: 90), expresses a frustration similar to that of Angelica in *The Heavenly Twins*. Although Angelica has clearly read the story of Vashti's disobedience, it is a model of womanhood that the clergy ignore in favor of the more submissive Esther.

Although Stanton interprets Esther's later obedience to the king as "a show," a "good policy" of behavior she has learned from Vashti's misfortune (2: 89), a close reading of the Book of Esther reveals that the predominant image of the title figure is as "the most naturally beautiful, humble, and subservient of women at the court" (Niditch 122). As a result, Angelica calls on Vashti, not Esther, to serve as a model for her own behavior. Within the biblical story, Vashti's decision not to appear before the drunken revelers is neither condemned nor praised by the narrator; however, Vashti has successfully judged for herself what actions are appropriate, rather than submitting without hesitation to her husband's will. This is a powerful model for Angelica. She has witnessed the effects of the passive Christian role models provided to Edith, whose unquestioning obedience to her father and her husband leads to her death.

The second biblical heroine Angelica calls upon is Judith. The apocryphal Book of Judith describes the torment of the town of Bethulia by the enemy general, Holofernes. Cut off from food supplies and weakened by famine, the people of Bethulia persuade the elders of the city to surrender to Holofernes if God does not rescue them in the next several days. Judith, a widow respected in the town, calls the elders to a meeting and criticizes them for their lack of faith. Judith later goes to the enemy camp and uses her great beauty to gain entrance to

Holofernes' tent. After feasting with Holofernes, who becomes drunk, Judith decapitates him with his own sword, takes the head back to Bethulia, and persuades her people to attack while the enemy is weakened by this loss.

Margarita Stocker has followed the many representations of Judith throughout history in *Judith, Sexual Warrior: Women and Power in Western Culture* (1998); and Susan Ackerman places Judith's story within the context of other biblical heroines in *Warrior, Dancer, Seductress, Queen: Women in Judges and Biblical Israel* (1998). Both Stocker and Ackerman provide detailed analyses of the Judith story and its interpretations. Ackerman suggests that although Judith's beheading of Holofernes is often remembered, her role as "the mastermind whose strategies lead to the defeats of both Holofernes and his Assyrian army" in the later battle is often forgotten (51). As a warrior and leader, Judith is a wise counselor who is willing to fight for God, to defend the covenant, and to stand up for the oppressed (62–63). Stocker argues that because Judith is able to accomplish what she does in part because of her physical beauty, described in the Bible as a purposeful gift from God, the ideas of Eve and the "dangerous sexual lure of womankind" are overturned. In Judith, God is "not above using sexuality to vanquish the pagan and save the chosen people" (Stocker 3). Furthermore, God carries out this plan through a woman—one who opposes the city's elders, who plans and carries out a dangerous mission, and who acts in ways that overturn patriarchal images of women as meek and submissive.

Stocker writes that whereas Esther is little more than a "domesticated consort and trophy wife" who has influence only over a husband rather than direct control over events, Judith exercises power and control over her own future and the future of her community (12–13, 21). Because of her independence, Judith was used throughout the Reformation and in the early nineteenth century as a model for the rebellion of either a lay believer against a Roman Catholic hierarchical church, or of an English patriot against the hierarchical politics of his country (133, 138). When such models of rebellion were no longer necessary to the Church of England or useful to those who opposed the monarchy, such images of Judith were no longer used. Instead, to fit with the ideal of womanhood as pious, devout, humble, and subordinate, the figure of Judith was either praised for remaining a widow and attaining a form of new virginity through celibacy, or gradually demonized in the Victorian period (139).

Thus, as Angelica reclaims Judith as a role model for women, Grand contests the increasingly popular images of Judith as a woman bent on revenge. Many late-Victorian texts portray Judith as a woman who would kill even her husband to serve her own interests (Stocker 153). However, it is clear that Grand does not wish to propose that women engage in physically violent acts. Angelica calls upon women such as Judith as role models because of their willingness to fight against oppression. Grand is not calling on women to literally rise up and decapitate their husbands. Rather, Grand calls on women to metaphorically rise up and symbolically decapitate patriarchy by asserting their own right to define their sphere, activities, and potential.

The next image of woman, Jael, was even more troublesome for Victorians than Judith.[7] Jael's assassination of the warrior Sisera, despite her heroism and the importance of her action to her people, was considered "revolting under our code of morality" to Elizabeth Cady Stanton. Stanton argued that Jael deceived Sisera and killed him after he entered her tent under the "guise of hospitality" (2: 20). Jael does welcome Sisera into her tent and tells him to "fear not" (Judg. 4.18), providing him with water and a place for him to sleep. Her decision to take a nail and hammer, striking the nail into his temple and fastening it to the ground (Judg. 4.21), was difficult for Stanton to reconcile with any ideal of womanhood.

Conversely, Grand cites Jael along with Judith and Vashti as seemingly equal examples of heroic biblical women. Indeed, her positive interpretation of Jael's courage and heroism against an oppressor is in agreement with many modern interpretations of the story. Susan Ackerman writes that within the context of the Book of Judges, Jael's actions support other evidence that she is a religious functionary taking part in a religious war. The idea of Jael as a "'most blessed' assassin need not stand in conflict with a portrayal of 'most blessed' Jael as a nurturer and sustainer" (91). Ackerman argues that Jael's first duty as a religious functionary in her society is to the nurturance and maintenance of her own community. This takes precedence over any other obligations of hospitality. Because her people are engaged in a holy war declared by God, and because Jael's privileged relationship with God has allowed her to learn that it is God's will that Sisera be killed, Jael's response is consistent with her portrait as a "mother of Israel." Like other biblical heroines, Jael's warrior actions are encompassed by her role as protector of the Israelites.

In contrast with the modest and humble women portrayed in the paintings in Edith's room, the biblical heroines to whom Angelica refers in her dream present an image of biblical women as public leaders, strong warriors, and active opponents of oppression. After Angelica awakens from her dream, Grand continues to explore the battle over whether the Bible represses or liberates women. When Angelica sees fresh evidence of Edith's madness, she seeks out the bishop's presence as comfort. Resting his hands on the Bible, the bishop waits "patiently until [Angelica] should have calmed herself" (*Heavenly* 298). The presence of the Bible, which the bishop believes will move Angelica toward the quiet calm it instilled in his daughter, seems only to heighten Angelica's distress. As she paces the floor, her dream seeps into her wakened consciousness. Fully awake, Angelica replies again to the cardinal from her dream who insisted that he knew "'the Sacred Duties of Wife and Mother'" (298). She calls him a "meddling priest" who does *not* understand the position and sacred roles of wife and mother. Although Angelica does not directly confront the bishop himself at this point, her statements oppose his attempts to use the Bible to squelch her resistance to certain patriarchal ideas about women and marriage that are embodied in Edith.

Angelica turns the tables and uses the Bible as a weapon against men, specifically against the man who has caused Edith such hardship. Although the bishop

stumbles to express Edith's strident desire for Sir Mosley Menteith to leave the
house, Angelica does not hesitate: "Seizing the heavy quarto Bible from the table,
she flung it with all her might full in his face. It happened to hit him on the
bridge of his nose, which it broke" (301). Using the Bible as a literal weapon
against Menteith calls to the reader's mind once again the ways in which men
have used the Bible as a weapon against women to restrict their full development. Angelica later considers it "poetical justice" to have used the Bible in this
way and refuses to feel regret (302). Afterward, when the bishop condemns her
actions, Angelica castigates him for his inability to maintain the "woman's
sphere" in such a way as to prevent the harm that has come to Edith (302–03).
Although at first she hesitates to speak, Angelica reminds herself that "I am
Jael—I am Judith … I must speak!" (300).

    In addition to contrasting with the role models for women found in the paint-
ings in Edith's room, Angelica's dream raises questions about the earlier passages regarding Edith. First, several of the artists Grand chose to place within
Edith's room also painted portraits of Judith. Botticelli's works include several
depictions of Judith, either with the head of Holofernes or returning with his
sword after slaying him. Bloody images of Holofernes' headless corpse would
hardly have been deemed appropriate for a young woman's bedroom, yet it is
intriguing that within the oeuvre of the artists Grand places in Edith's bedroom
are contrasting models for women—the passive Mary and the active, heroic Judith. The existence of these other works points to the choices the clergy make
to hinder knowledge of strong biblical heroines. Veronese also portrayed Judith
holding the head of Holofernes in two different portraits. In these works, however, Judith is humbly looking down at her servant or at the ground, not at the
head or the viewer. Far from triumphant, the image attempts to reconcile Judith's actions with the image of a submissive woman.

    Second, although within the text it is assumed that Edith has descended into
madness, the stories of Judith and Jael challenge this diagnosis. Her own words
suggest that the description is used only because her response cannot be recon-
ciled with an image of true womanhood as passive, subordinate, and submissive.
Edith tells her mother

"I am quite, quite mad!" she said. "Do you know what I have been doing? I've been murdering him! I've been creeping, creeping, with bare feet, to surprise him in his sleep; and
I had a tiny knife—very sharp—and I felt for the artery"—she touched her neck"—"and
then stabbed quickly! and he awoke, and knew he must die—and cowered! and it was all
a pleasure to me. Oh, yes! I am quite, quite mad!" (304)

Edith decides that she must be mad, for such behavior—even the desire for
such behavior—is antithetical to her vision of what a woman is to be. However,
her cries of insanity come only pages after Angelica's dream in which Jael is set
forth as a potential role model. Edith imagines creeping up on her husband,
stealthily finding a way to murder him, and stabbing him in the artery, rather
than in the temple as Jael does. Like Jael, Edith would use her tormentor's com-

fort in her presence to induce him to sleep so that she could overpower and kill him. Within the context of the Renaissance paintings of the Virgin Mother and St. Helena, Edith's thoughts are symptoms of insanity, for no sane woman could possibly have such a desire. In contrast, within the context of Angelica's dream, and within the context of the biblical heroines Angelica refers to, Edith's thoughts are signs of heroism, of striking out against the suffering endured by women taught to be submissive daughters, wives, and mothers.

The two sets of contrasting images of biblical women, in addition to characters' direct challenges to institutional Christianity, illustrate the ways in which Grand's text espouses ideas now integral to Christian feminism. Grand's insistence that we examine the ways in which gender is inculcated through particular images further supports interpretations of her novel's sociological study of gender formation and identity. Furthermore, Grand's reevaluation of certain biblical heroines points out that the presence of religious references does not automatically signify acceptance of the institution's patriarchal norms. This suggests that other women's novels from the Victorian period that may have been neglected because of seemingly repressive religious content could and should be reexamined more carefully so that as scholars of the period we become fully aware of their religious complexities.

In her presentation of biblical heroines, Grand exposes polarities of Christian ideals and what is taught in the name of Christianity; of women's passive acceptance of subordination and women's resistance to oppressive systems. The very title, *The Heavenly Twins*, calls upon readers to carefully examine both sides to any image. The twins of the title represent dualities of male and female, emotion and action, good and bad. Even in their names, Angelica and Diavolo, the twins are reminiscent of heavenly angels and dastardly devils. Despite the apparent simplicity of this polar opposition, the two characters rarely live up to their names' expectations, nor do their actions fit traditional male or female roles. Grand's novel repeatedly presents the reader with doubled perceptions and challenges gender dualities. Her novel questions established perceptions, and so it is sadly ironic that it has so long been perceived by literary critics as an unimportant work. It is time to challenge this perception and recognize the value and significance of Grand's novel to the Victorian canon.

WORKS CITED

Abbott, Katherine R. Smith. "Defining a Type: Perugino's Depictions of the Virgin Mary." *Pietro Perugino: Master of the Italian Renaissance.* Ed. Joseph Antenucci Becherer, et al. New York: Rizzoli International, 1997.

Ackerman, Susan. *Warrior, Dancer, Seductress, Queen: Women in Judges and Biblical Israel.* New York: Doubleday, 1998.

Bjørhovde, Gerd. *Rebellious Structures: Women Writers and the Crisis of the Novel 1880–1900.* Oslo: Norwegian, 1987.

Bonnell, Marilyn. "The Legacy of Sarah Grand's *The Heavenly Twins:* A Review Essay." *English Literature in Transition* 36 (1993): 467–78.

———. "Sarah Grand and the Critical Establishment: Art for (Wo)man's Sake." *Tulsa Studies in Women's Literature* 14 (1995): 123–48.

Booth, Catherine. "Female Ministry; or, Woman's Right to Preach the Gospel" 1859. *Victorian Women Writers Project Library.* Indiana University. 15 Sept. 2002. <http://www.indiana.edu/~letrs/vwwp/booth/ministry.html>.

Clark, Elizabeth A. and Herbert Richardson. *Women and Religion: The Original Sourcebook of Women in Christian Thought.* Rev. ed. New York: Harper, 1996.

Cobbe, Frances Power. "The Fitness of Women for the Ministry." *Theological Review* 13 (1876): 239–73.

———. "Woman's Work in the Church." *Theological Review* 2 (1865): 505–21.

Ekserdjian, David. *Correggio.* New Haven: Yale UP, 1997.

Grand, Sarah. *The Beth Book: Being a Study of the Life of Elizabeth Caldwell Maclure, A Woman of Genius.* 1897. New York: Dial, 1980.

———. *The Heavenly Twins.* 1893. Ann Arbor: U of Michigan P, 1992. 3 vols.

———. *Ideala.* 1889. New York: Optimus Printing, 1894.

Johnson, Elizabeth A. *She Who Is: The Mystery of God in Feminist Theological Discourse.* 1992. New York: Crossroad, 1997.

Kavanagh, Julia. *Women of Christianity, Exemplary for Acts of Piety and Charity.* NewYork: D. Appleton, 1852.

Kersley, Gillian. *Darling Madame: Sarah Grand and Devoted Friend.* London: Virago, 1983.

Kucich, John. "Curious Dualities: *The Heavenly Twins* (1893) and Sarah Grand's Belated Modernist Aesthetics." *The New Nineteenth Century: Feminist Readings of Underread Victorian Fiction.* Ed. Barbara Harman and Susan Meyer. New York: Garland, 1996. 195–204.

Mangum, Teresa. *Married, Middlebrow, and Militant: Sarah Grand and the New Woman Novel.* Ann Arbor: U of Michigan P, 1998.

McCarthy, Ellen, Acquiring Editor for Ann Arbor Paperbacks. Telephone Interview. 16 Sept. 2002.

Murphy, Mary Patricia. "Timely Interventions: Gender, Temporality, and the New Woman." Diss. U of Iowa, 1997.

Niditch, Susan. *War in the Hebrew Bible: A Study in the Ethics of Violence.* New York: Oxford UP, 1993.

Nightingale, Florence. *Cassandra and Other Selections from Suggestions for Thought to the Searchers After Religious Truth.* 1860. Ed. Mary Poovey. New York: New York UP, 1992.

Orliac, Antoine. *Veronese.* Trans. March Chamot. Ed. André Gloeckner. London: Hyperion, 1940.

Pillsbury, Edmund P. "Federico Barocci." *Dictionary of Art.* Ed. Jane Turner. Vol. 3. London: Macmillan, 1996. 253–58.

Rowbotham, Judith. *Good Girls Make Good Wives: Guidance for Girls in Victorian Fiction.* Oxford: Blackwell, 1989.

Rowlette, Robert. "Mark Twain, Sarah Grand, and *The Heavenly Twins.*" *Mark Twain Journal* 16.2 (1972): 17–18.

Ruether, Rosemary Radford. *Women and Redemption: A Theological History.* Minneapolis: Fortress, 1998.

Ruskin, John. *Sesame and Lilies*. 1868. Philadelphia: Henry Altemus, n.d.

Senf, Carol A. Introduction. *The Heavenly Twins*. 1893. Ann Arbor: U of Michigan P, 1992. vii–xxxvii.

Showalter, Elaine. *A Literature of Their Own*. Princeton, Princeton UP, 1977.

Stanton, Elizabeth Cady, et al. *The Woman's Bible*. 1895. Boston: Northeastern UP, 1993.

Stocker, Margarita. *Judith, Sexual Warrior: Women and Power in Western Culture*. New Haven: Yale UP, 1998.

Weintraub, Stanley. "George Bernard Shaw Borrows from Sarah Grand: *The Heavenly Twins* and *You Never Can Tell*." *Modern Drama* 14 (1971): 288–97.

NOTES

1. See also Robert Rowlette's note on the respect Mark Twain had for the novel: "Mark Twain, Sarah Grand, and *The Heavenly Twins*" (1972).

2. For specific examples of prose works by these women that challenge institutional Christianity see Julia Kavanagh's *Women of Christianity, Exemplary for Acts of Piety and Charity* (1852), Florence Nightingale's *Cassandra and Other Selections from Suggestions for Thought to the Searchers After Religious Truth* (1860), Catherine Booth's "Female Ministry; or, Woman's Right to Preach the Gospel" (1859), and Frances Power Cobbe's "The Fitness of Women for the Ministry" (1876) and "Woman's Work in the Church" (1865).

3. Ruskin's "Of Queen's Gardens" was the lecture later published with "Of Kings' Treasuries" in the book *Sesame and Lilies*.

4. For example, see Elizabeth Johnson's *She Who Is: The Mystery of God in Feminist Theological Discourse* (1992). Johnson explores feminine images of the Christian God throughout history and logically argues for more expansive images of God. Her work is still considered controversial within many Christian denominations.

5. I have maintained Grand's spelling of Perugini and Baroccio within the quotation, but my own references contain the agreed-upon modern spelling of Perugino and Barocci. Grand's reference to "Our Lady of the Cat" undoubtedly refers to Barocci's *Virgin with Kitten*.

6. All biblical references and quotations not taken directly from Grand's novel are based upon the edition Stanton and her co-authors used. I have chosen this version and translation because it is one that would have been accessible to Grand.

7. For an example of the complicated representations of Jael in Victorian women's fiction, see Margarita Stocker's discussion of Charlotte Brontë's *Villette*, in which she argues that Jael represents for Lucy Snowe "woman's internalization of patriarchy." See Stocker's *Judith, Sexual Warrior: Women and Power in Western Culture* (125).

9

Dinah Mulock Craik

Sacrifice and the Fairy-Order

Robyn Chandler

Dinah Mulock Craik (1826–87) is best known to modern readers as the author of the best-selling *John Halifax, Gentleman* (1856), a novel whose dramatization of the social and political triumph of the middle classes is usually read as no more than an uncritical and cliché reflection of mid-Victorian bourgeois ideology, "unqualified in its rejoicing" (Brantlinger 119). Throughout her career, however, Craik practiced and promoted energetic interventions in—rather than simply celebratory reflections of—contemporary theological, social, political, and aesthetic debates. Craik wanted to make rather than mirror history; she had a lifelong concern with the realization of a new social order based on a liberal version of Christianity that emphasized tolerance and equality for all. As Sally Mitchell shows in her excellent introduction to Craik's life and work, Craik grappled with controversial issues of the day and presented often radical solutions to inequitable situations. Her openness to experimentation carried over, at times, into her poetics, most notably with *A Life for a Life* (1859), a novel whose gendered dual narration is at once an expression of "separate spheres" and an undermining of its exclusivity.

With *A Life for a Life* Craik cast subjection as "the great question of our time," a question that existed on both a social and cosmic level. Published nearly a decade earlier, the domestic novel *Olive* (1850) might be less aesthetically innovative than *A Life*, but with it Craik developed her heroine—a crippled artist who saves the soul of a doubting clergyman—into the inheritor of the nineteenth century's cultural and religious capital.

Olive (1850) is the story of a female Romantic artist who is also a Victorian angel. Ostensibly *Olive* is the story of the journey from Art to Religion, from

Romanticism to Romance, from the realm of "fairy" to the domain of the "angel in the house." Although *Olive* begins as a female *Künstlerroman*, the "deformed" (and therefore unmarriageable) Olive Rothesay devoting herself to a life of art and filial devotion, it mutates halfway through into what Margaret Maison has called a "feeble rescue story" (219) with Olive, "feeling less of an artist and more of a woman," transferring her dedication to the saving of the doubting Reverend Harold Gwynne's soul. Olive not only saves Harold's soul for Christianity, but also redeems his faith in womankind. With his love "the curse of hopeless deformity" (1: 32; ch. 3) is lifted and Olive is reabsorbed into the domestic, into marriage and (step)motherhood.

A text that initially reads as religiously and politically conservative also reads as theologically and politically innovative. The "male doubter saved by the influence of a good woman" plot was adopted enthusiastically by women novelists and thus came to characterize the novel of doubt, and *Olive* was one of its first expositions. *Olive* is also less conventional than it may initially appear in another sense: Embedded within the increasingly conventional plot is a feminist soteriology, and although the novel is a classic, but fictionalized, instance of the nineteenth-century feminization of religion in Ann Douglas' sense, involving an alliance between women and the clergy, this is an alliance located *outside* the church. Craik, in effect, creates a new "religious field" and situates it in the debatable ground provided by "fairy," using both the plots and imagery of the genre and its standing as a highly contested cultural narrative. *Olive* exploits this debatable ground to conduct an investigation into the representation of Christianity and its relationship to knowledge and to institute the female angel/artist as the midcentury inheritor of "religious capital" who achieves the redemption of patriarchy. Like Elizabeth Langland's mid-Victorian domestic manager who controls cultural capital, this hybrid creature is the new possessor of religious capital because she has the power of representation.[1] Olive represents Christianity—in herself and as an artist/fairy teller.

Both as embodiment and artist, Olive's power of representation does not simply reflect but interrogates Christianity, a function made clear from the very genesis of both the character and the novel. Born at Stirling, the home of national heroes, Olive's deformed body poses the ultimate question, her nurse Elspie (the first of the text's fairy godmothers)[2] wondering over the newborn: "'God forgie me—but why did He send ye into the waefu' warld at a'?' It was a question, the nature of which has perplexed theologians, philosophers, and metaphysicians, in every age, and will perplex them all to the end of time" (7: 12–13; ch. 1). That Olive embodies the answer to the question she poses is prefigured in her mother's dream after which she is named, a vision of a "child-angel—with a green olive-branch in its hand," which leads the significantly named Sybilla through perils to "a beautiful valley," touching her hurts with the olive branch and healing them, and revealing itself at last as her daughter (1: 27; ch. 2).

Olive's prophetic role is akin to that of the Romantic artist, that "ironic child" credited by the poet Novalis with the writing of the "true fairy tale"[3]:

[Olive] had never even heard of Wordsworth; yet, as she listened to the first cuckoo note, she thought it no bird, but truly "a wandering voice" ...

She had never heard of Art, yet there was something in the gorgeous sunset that made her bosom thrill; and out of the cloud ranges she tried to form mountains such as there were in Scotland, and palaces of crystal such as she read of in her fairy tales. No human being had ever told her of the mysterious links that reach from the Infinite, out of which, from the buried ashes of dead Superstition, great souls can evoke those two mighty spirits, Faith and Knowledge; yet she went to sleep every night believing that she felt, nay, could almost see, an angel standing at the foot of her little bed, watching her with holy eyes, guarding her with outspread wings.

O Childhood! beautiful dream of unconscious poetry; of purity so pure, that it knew neither the existence of sin nor of its own innocence ... Blessed Childhood! ... hidden therein, lay the germs of a whole life. (1: 97–8; ch. 7)

Although formally untutored, Olive conjoins a Romantic education through the Book of Nature with the necessary exposure to Christian revelation, "the faith she had been taught by Elspie" (1: 274; ch. 7), who "coming from the debatable ground between Highlands and Lowlands, had united to the rigid piety of the latter much wild Gaelic superstition" (1: 68–9; ch. 5). The faith of the debatable ground, then, is an amalgam of the Romantic and the Evangelical, the heretical and the orthodox, through and with which the "ironic child" must lead the way; luckily Olive's "usual childish games [include] piecing disjointed maps" (1: 117; ch. 9).

As Nina Auerbach and U. C. Knoepflmacher note, of course, all Victorian women were theoretically "ironic children": "if they were good, they never grew up" (1). Olive is the embodiment of this fairy tale "ironic child": "She looked less like a child than a woman dwarfed into childhood" (1: 56; ch. 5). As such her deformity "represents her very womanhood" (Showalter 28), that is, the Victorian construction of womanhood, the burden of which Olive assumes in a *Pilgrim's Progress*-like journey through "the various phases which compose that strange and touching mystery—a woman's life" (1: 13; ch. 1). Craik's specifically female Christian is both an everywoman and marked by difference, like her famous contemporary in the prototypical *Jane Eyre*, of which, as Cora Kaplan notes, *Olive* is "both a companion and a countertext" (xx), Craik "reworking some of the narrative elements of the much noticed, controversially received" novel, and providing "a related but alternative blueprint for female subjectivity" (x-xi).[4] In an obvious echo of Jane Eyre whose recognition of her heterogeneity is mediated through representations—the "reading" of her specular image in the haunted red-room according to her nurse's tales—Olive is also typed as the denizen of the fairy tale. Olive has "a spectral air," she is "the sort of being renowned in elfin legends, as springing up on a lonely moor, or appearing by a cradle-side; supernatural, yet fraught with a nameless beauty" (1: 57; ch. 5).[5] Olive's first ball is the site for the recognition and naming of difference; a rite of passage that should mark her inclusion within normative femininity in fact signifies her radical otherness, giving her the "first shock of her bitter destiny" (1: 213; ch. 14). Looking toward the Camelot of love and marriage the "curse" comes upon her. As they gaze into a mirror together, Olive's friend Sara (herself representative of normativity as will be discussed below) "helps" her to understand why she "seem[s] different from other girls." Sara speaks the male gaze; her simultaneous assertion and denial, emphasis and ellipsis, both render such aberrant femininity visible and consign it to the negative realm, to the realm of the unspoken: "'it does not signify to me ... . But perhaps with strangers, especially with men, who think so much of beauty, this defect— ... I did not say that it was a positive *deformity*" (1: 181–82; ch. 12).

Later, Olive is driven to momentary doubt, feeling herself locked within the specular logic of the Calvinist fairy tale:

She saw in herself a poor deformed being, shut out from all natural ties ... How hard seemed her doom! If it were for months only, or even years; but, to bear for a whole life this withering ban—never to be freed from it, except through death! And her lips unconsciously repeated the bitter murmur, "O God! why hast thou made me thus?"

It was scarcely uttered before her heart trembled at its impiety. And then the current of her thoughts changed. Those mysterious yearnings which had haunted her throughout childhood ... returned to her now. God's immeasurable Infinite rose before her in glorious serenity ... . She felt ... that her poor deformed body enshrined a living soul. A soul that could look on Heaven, and on whom Heaven also looked—not like man, with scorn or loathing, but with a Divine tenderness that had power to lift the mortal into communion with the immortal. (1: 189–91; ch. 13)

"Fairy" and Olive's "vivid fancy" (1: 189; ch. 13) thus provide the possibilities: For critique and for an alternative to the predestined narrative; the "true fairy tale" is a way to lift one's gaze from the mirror and into the freedom of Heaven. "Fairy" also provides Craik with the negative pole of her gender critique, although Craik is "writing against the grain of prejudice that informed the work of her more illustrious and better-remembered peers"[6] with her inversion of the valences of monstrous and "ideal" forms as expressed in the relationship of Sybilla Rothesay, the "fairy apparition" (1: 47; ch. 4) to her daughter's "spectral air." Sybilla is the woman as object, "a flesh-and-blood fairy—a Venus de Medici transmuted from the stone" (1: 17; ch. 1). Although seriously neglecting her infant daughter, Sybilla opposes herself to the monstrous, refusing to name the golden-haired Olive after her Rothesay ancestors. Among these "awful women" is Lady Isobel, whose lover being slain by her brother "laid a curse on all the line who had golden hair, and such never prospered, but died unmarried and young" (1: 23; ch. 2).

Sybilla, like her daughter, has been rendered monstrous by the objectification forced on women by ideology: in her case, a restrictive feminine education (1: 39; ch. 3) that had taught her to consider "beauty as the greatest good" (1: 32;

ch. 3). Sybilla is punished with blindness, befitting both her excessive aestheticism and her Sibylline nature. Her prophetic dreams at Olive's birth are realized: The reawakening of Sybilla's maternal affections brings her "nearer to heaven than she had ever been in her life" (1: 185; ch. 13), and at the time of her death the Sibyl is "growing quite an angel" (2: 297; ch. 13). In a revision of Jane Eyre's dream wanderings burdened with the feeble child whom she at last lets fall, before Jane herself falls into the ruins of Thornfield (Brontë 309–10), Olive, the child-angel ("mother unto [her] mother," 1: 307; ch. 18), has indeed led the fairy safe "through many troublous ways" (2: 313: ch. 14).

In order to draw her angel-artist, Craik must redeem womankind from normative femininity, from the extremes of both the excessively Romantic—Sybilla—and the prosaic—Sara, the product of the conduct book. Sara speaks the male gaze, the relativity of women; she is one of "the class from whence are taken the lauded 'mothers, wives, and daughters of England" (1: 154; ch. 11), for whom Sarah Ellis, the preeminent early Victorian ideologue of domesticity, wrote. *Olive* is an early example of Craik's revision of Ellis' "relative creature," most clearly expressed in Craik's own highly successful conduct book, *A Woman's Thoughts About Women* (1858), in which Craik reworks Ellis' imagery of the fairy order and the angel. Ellis' contention in *The Women of England* that "the cultivation of moral habits" (5) is a necessary precursor to "the development of the Christian character" (4) suggests the role conduct books in general played in secularizing Evangelical values,[7] and a brief analysis of Craik's 1858 reformulation helps clarify *Olive*'s use of these motifs in contradicting the secularizing tendencies of conduct book femininity.

Craik's weaver of "the fairy Order" is the "happy woman," a direct descendent of Ellis' earlier "ministering angel" "whose peculiar charm is that of diffusing happiness." The considerate and caring household management Ellis' domestic angel undertakes gives the *impression* that "the fairy order ha[s] been at work" (Ellis 202–03, 196). Craik's "fairy Order" expresses truth, demonstrating the links between things, by disentangling "the tangled threads" showing "a clear pattern through the ugly maze," justifying "the ways of Providence" (*A Woman's Thoughts* 187–88). Ellis' "fairy order," on the other hand, is a "fairy story," an artifice. It denies the true links between things. As Langland explains, Ellis' "fairy order" works with "Providence" to mystify mistress/servant relations (75–76).[8] Although Craik herself evokes Providence in respect to class positioning, she also allows for class mobility, and, more important in this context, she emphasizes the "one common womanhood" of mistress and servant under Providence (*A Woman's Thoughts* 123–24) against Ellis' denial of natural ties, "except what necessarily implies authority and subjection" (184), a mercenary reality that the "fairy order" is designed to disguise. Accentuating this difference, in *Olive* the class-based fairy order is rejected, and delineated instead as the closest of natural ties, an expression of the "maternal and filial bond" (1: 306; ch. 18). Because of Olive's behind-the-scenes organization, for example, it seems to Sybilla that "everything arranged itself, as under an invisible fairy hand ..."

(1: 308; ch. 18). Craik's "happy woman" of *A Woman's Thoughts* is the Miltonic poet, justifying the ways of God to men. Moreover, she is synonymous with her text: The metaphorical "fairy Order" embodies order, she is "a living justification of the ways of Providence." Ellis' domestic "angel" is duplicitous; despite the rhetoric of embodiment, "her peculiar charm" seems less that of the Christian body than that of a Duessa, self-consciously manufacturing her artificial "fairy order." Craik's Sara is "fair and fause, fair and fause" (3: 109; ch. 6), ensnaring Harold Gwynne with "the enchantments of a beautiful woman" (1: 263; ch. 16), while speaking of her preexisting engagement, "her violated troth," "in a cold, businesslike manner" (1: 272; ch. 17). Sara's mercenary and duplicitous attitude to love and marriage is punished with an early death.

Craik substitutes a Christian materialism for the ultimately mercenary materialism of the conduct book heroine, delineating a spiritual economy that, ironically, incorporates the "world" banished by the conduct book. Although Ellis suggested "fancy millinery" and "engraving" as in no way threatening "the seclusion of domestic life, and the delicacy of the female character" (346), Ellis' "angel" casts the veil of the "fairy order" to maintain the fiction of the home as a private, feminine sphere, divorced from matters of production. Craik, by showing Olive engaged in fine art and foregrounding her financial motive for doing so, highlights feminine production in the home and maintains its links with the "public" as well as the domestic economy. The disastrous marriage of Olive's parents is largely a result of their inhabiting separate spheres, "two parallel lines, which would never, never meet!" (1: 124; ch. 9), and leads to an economic disaster from which only their daughter's domestically based labor can save them; the next generation unite love and labor at Morningside, "a wishful, progressive fantasy of love and work" (Kaplan xx). Whereas *Olive* recalls Mary Wollstonecraft's *Vindication* in many particulars—Sybilla's superficial education and maternal hostility, Angus's arrogance and tyranny, for example—Craik's delineation of "a REVOLUTION in female [and male] manners" is grounded in a Christian materialism.

According to the writer and critic Mrs. Oliphant, however, it was not Wollstonecraft but "the invasion of *Jane Eyre*" with its "wild declaration of the 'Rights of Woman' in a new aspect" that had resulted in the "most alarming revolution of modern times" ("Modern Novelists" 557). *Olive's* reinscription of *Jane Eyre* was an attempt by a woman writer, herself "touched by the spirit of Jane Eyre" ("Modern Novelists" 560), to recuperate both the female text and the female reader from the wilder excesses produced by "Jane Eyre fever."[9] Craik's soteriology demands the heroine be freed from the shackles of normative femininity; Brontë's Byronic female, however, is rejected. Craik's murder of the artificial Ellisian "angel" and her conversion of the Sibyl together allow her to resurrect a purified form of the "heroine in white muslin, the immaculate creature who was of sweetness and goodness all compact, [who] had lasted in the common lines of fiction up to [the] time" of *Jane Eyre* in 1847, and to whom *Jane Eyre* had given, "for the moment, the *coup de grace*" (Oliphant,

Women Novelists 17). Through "fairy" Craik transmogrifies the *Quarterly Review*'s "personification of an unregenerate and undisciplined spirit" (Rigby 173)—Jane—into "a visible angel of peace" (2: 266; ch. 12)—Olive. Although Olive shares Jane's feelings of "silent revolt against [her] lot,"[10] she immediately quashes such feelings as "impious" (e.g. 1: 190; ch. 13 and 1: 274; ch. 17). Whereas the child Jane cannot obey the demand for "perfect submission and stillness" that would liberate her from the haunted red-room, Olive is "unlike a child, in whom are the springs of anger and revenge," having preternaturally learnt "to suffer and be silent" (1: 67; ch. 5). In an episode clearly designed to be read against Jane's red-room experience (and the death of Helen Burns) Craik begins her reassertion of the equation of faith and freedom. Alone in bed with her dying nurse the child Olive is beset with "awful thoughts of death and the grave," "children's fancies about 'ghosts' and bogy." These terrors, significantly occurring in a passage, lead her to God. Unlike Jane shut in the red-room, who attempts to maintain silence, "fearful lest any sign of violent grief might waken a preternatural voice to comfort me, or elicit from the gloom some haloed face, bending over me with strange pity" (Brontë 48), Olive recites the Lord's Prayer. From her experience of increasing strength as she reiterates "Deliver us from evil," she learns "that mighty faith 'which can move mountains'; that fervent boldness of prayer with the very utterance of which an answer comes." By reciting her magic incantation, the bogy is transformed into "the Angel of that child ... beside her ... teach[ing] her in faint shadowings the mysteries of her life to come" (*Olive* 1: 105–9; ch. 8). Jane's anticipation of the spirit of Mr. Reed, on the other hand, is an "idea, consolatory in theory, [that] I felt would be terrible if realized," and results in "a species of fit" when she believes she hears "the rushing of wings" (Brontë 50, 49). Paradoxically, then, it is Jane "Rechristianized," refeminized, avoiding "complaint," who is released from confinement.[11]

Craik gives Olive Jane's desire for "more vivid kinds of goodness," for "action." Although Olive begs admittance and apologizes for trespassing in realms guarded by patriarchy,[12] rather than railing she wins through her own efforts (2: 53; ch. 3) "exercise for [her] faculties, and a field for [her] efforts as [her] brothers" have. Becoming a governess is written out of the realm of possibility (Olive's chance of a fulfilling career is ironically furthered by her lack of education), and Jane's artistic dabblings become with Olive a full-fledged professional career.

What initially reads as an apology for her femininity and a properly passive approach—"Woman as I am, I will dare all things—endure all things. Let me be an artist!" (2: 52; ch. 2)—can, of course, equally be read as a declarative statement, for Olive is "a woman ... at once gentle and strong, meek and fearless, patient to endure, heroic to act" (1: 287–88; ch. 17). Olive's body signifies this radical ambivalence, identified by Poovey as a quintessential female Romantic literary strategy of accommodation, "a code capable of being read in two ways: as acquiescence to the norm and as departure from it ... " (*The Proper Lady* 41). Olive's "deformity"—which at once condenses and displaces femininity—allows her to transcend the constraints of gender, essentially limitations of form: "That sense of personal imperfection which she deemed excluded her from a woman's natural destiny, gave her freedom in her own" (2: 58; ch. 3). She uses her "difference" to claim the female artist as Romantic heroic exile: "I, too, am one of these outcast; give me then this inner life which is beyond all!" (2: 52; ch. 2).

Craik establishes her angel-artist as heir to the male romantic artist. Olive's tutor, the painter Michael Vanbrugh, models himself on Michelangelo, the archetypal artistic genius, "the one among [us artists] who was himself above humanity, Michael the Angel!" (2: 48; ch. 2). Like Olive, Michael is cursed with physical imperfection. But unlike Olive, Vanbrugh's monstrosity links him to the demonic: he is an "ogre," "an ascetic and a misanthrope" (2: 141; ch. 7 and 2: 25; ch. 2 he is a creature of the Calvinist fairy tale, a "gigantic warrior, guarding the shrine of Art" (2: 40; ch. 2) from women:

I said that it was impossible for a woman to become an artist—I mean, a *great* artist ... Not only a painter, but a poet; a man of learning, of reading, of observation. A gentleman ... A man of high virtue, or how can he reach the pure ideal? A man of iron will, unconquered daring, and passions strong—yet stainless. Last and greatest, a man who, feeling within him the divine spirit, with his whole soul worships God! (2: 48–9; ch. 2)

But the patriarchal archangel overreaches himself, vowing to "out-do Providence; I, with my hand, will continually create beauty" (2: 9; ch. 1). He believes the male advantage in art is that men, as the narrator reminds us, "can trample on all human ties" whereas women are bound by "the heart and affections ... with everlasting links" (2: 54; ch. 3). As the narrative and imagery make clear, however, it is the violence of the Romantic gaze that imprisons women by fashioning them in its image. Michael paints Olive "in the painful attitude of a 'Cassandra raving'" (2: 13; ch. 1), Sybilla as *Alcestis* (who literally sacrificed her life for her husband), and Olive as her grieving mother. He proposes marriage so that he can take Olive to Rome (significantly on the proceeds of the sale of *Alcestis*), his "design" to "make of [Olive] such an artist as no woman ever was before"; she will be to him "'like a child" (2: 156; ch. 7). Victorian women artists were often trained like sons to work in the family business; as adults they often married another artist. Thus entering into such a childlike/marital relationship with the patriarch would be in keeping with a typical nineteenth-century female artist's professional development. It also, however, demonstrates the Romantic specularity noted by Anne Mellors in which woman exists for the Romantic lover or poet as no more than a mirror image of himself (2: 156; ch. 7). Olive rejects such patriarchal reproduction. She refuses Michael, holding that to marry without love would be "a heavy sin" (2: 158; ch. 7); that the wages of such a sin might literally be death is suggested by the demise of Michael's sister Meliora, who had accompanied her brother to Rome and starved in the garret while he went out and painted.

Meliora (whose "indigent father's anticipation of a bequeathed fortune had caused her rather eccentric christian name," 2: 26; ch. 2) is Olive's second fairy godmother: "the most hopeful little body in the world … wherever she went, she always brought 'better things'—at least, in anticipation" (2: 26; ch. 2). Meliora is another fairy tale narrator: of "consolatory proverbs" and of artistic mythology, telling "all the stories of little peasant-boys who have … risen [through art] to be the companions of kings" (2: 28; ch. 2). As Susan Casteras explains, the myth of origin was part of the Victorian "cult of male genius," and was represented as a principally male transaction—between "boy wonders" and "older, protective males"—wherein "the female is backgrounded and her impact displaced onto the feminized boy geniuses whom she has helped to nurture" (139, 143). In a sleight of hand typical of both Craik and the fairy tale itself, Meliora simultaneously inhabits this male myth and, partly through the manipulation of its conventions, is herself instrumental in creating a new female myth of origin. From her position in the background Meliora foregrounds the female artist, telling tales of the female artistic tradition (2: 30; ch. 2) and acting as "Cinderella's godmother" to Olive's painting career. In a neat inversion of the myth of origin, Olive is effectively a "masculinized girl genius," Michael conceding that "though you are a woman, you have a man's soul—the soul of genius" (2: 152; ch. 7).

In this new female myth of origin both body and soul are acknowledged. Meliora embodies the true "fairy order" in the domestic and the artistic spheres, demonstrating that matters of production are not opposed, as Michael (and Mrs. Ellis) would have it, to the creation of the artistic "fairyland" (2: 50–1; ch. 3). Whereas Vanbrugh paints "grand pictures, which nobody bought" (2: 10; ch. 1), making his only sales to the traditional upper-class market, Olive represents the nineteenth-century trend away from classical and toward English literary sources and domestic subjects, subjects that appealed to the growing middle-class market, who were often with little or no classical education and indifferent to such themes (as demonstrated by the purchaser's desire to have Olive's allegorical *Charity* double as a family portrait, 2: 103; ch. 5). What Michael dismisses as the "paltry gold" that "women always think of" (2: 113; ch. 5) is revealed as a veritable fairy currency: "a Danaë-stream [poured] into Olive's lap" by "the beneficent little fairy … Cinderella's godmother." This is Olive's annunciation, confirming her inheritance of the power of representation.

Within the true fairy order these "elfin coins" are the (Sybilline) leaves on which Christian destiny is written, heralding the female angel-artist as the savior of her race. The money enables Olive to "redeem" her dead "father's honour" by paying his debts (2: 93–4; ch. 4). Later, responding to a posthumous request to "Atone [her father's] sin!," Olive must find and care for Christal Manners, his illegitimate daughter. Olive's "holy work" is to take up this "cross" of patriarchal/paternal failure (3: 197–98; ch. 10). As her name suggests, Christal Manners, like Sybilla, is the product of a Rousseauesque education and her

"Parisian feet" cannot manage "the hateful labyrinths of the muddy road" (2: 168; ch. 13 and 2: 186; ch. 9).

Although Olive thus embraces self-denial, to "feel less of an artist and more of a woman" (2: 242; ch. 11) does not, in fact, result in her martyrdom, but is rather an escape from male Romanticism's materialization of women and the total self-abnegation it demands of them. Michael's idolatrous attitude toward forms effectively "reduced the womenkind about him to the condition of perfect slaves" (2: 150; ch. 7). The female Christian artist is juxtaposed with the male genius as pagan, as violent idolater; Michael feels "like Parrhasius of old, who exulted in his captive's dying throes, since upon them his hand of genius would confer immortality" (2: 50; ch. 2). His neglect of "paltry gold" ensures that, with respect to Meliora, and the underpaid and starving model for his *Cleopatra*, Celia Manners, mother of Christal, this becomes horribly and literally true. At the time of *Olive*'s writing the dyad of idolatry and female abjection was associated with Roman Catholicism (and by extension the Oxford Movement). Sybilla may well be "happy to think my child is safe with me, and not carried off to Rome" (2: 242; ch. 6). Eschewing "the City of Art" (2: 152; ch. 7) recoups feminine suffering for the true City of God, where the female artist may live and thrive; as already noted, "to endure" is the prerogative of the artist as much as the loving woman. Olive's rejection of the "painful attitude" of Cassandra allows her to rise "from the ashes of dead superstition" as Cinderella, as Florence Nightingale's female Christ, the "Saviour of her race" (Nightingale 227) the new possessor of religious capital.

In part, then, fairy's debatable ground is a midcentury strategy, a way to include the Romantic and feminine with the hegemonic Evangelical stress on Scripture and individual judgement while avoiding associations with Ritualism/Popery. Or, as Harold Gwynne puts it, a way of allowing Olive to speak both "graceful—poetical" religion (2: 178; ch. 7) that is also "plain reasonable words— not like the vain babblers of perverted creeds" (2: 321; ch. 14). Fulfilling the promise of her childhood, Olive has effectively become Vanbrugh's "great artist"; she is now "Not only a painter, but a poet," sharing with the now blind Sybilla "vivid pictures painted by Olive's eloquent tongue" (2: 162; ch. 8). As a successful artist, the possessor of religious capital, the "ironic child" enters the "new era" (2: 168; ch. 8) ready to debate with the doubting clergyman, Harold Gwynne, and, with her body and her text, to replace the "wornout forms of religion."

Harold Gwynne, as not only a doubter, but a doubting clergyman, and a scientist to boot, is by definition linked with the monstrous, "an infidel!," "Satan" (2: 274; ch. 7), a "wizard or a magician" (2: 110; ch. 5). Harold is a Carlylean figure, a Victorian doubting everyman whose very desire for truth has led him into skepticism (2: 285; ch. 13): "doubts came upon my mind," says Harold, "as they will upon most young minds whose strivings after truth are hedged in by a thorny rampart of old, worn-out forms" (2: 278–79; ch. 12). Although Harold has made his own way from Atheism (3: 337; ch. 16) to Deism, believing in "the one ruling Spirit of the universe—unknown, unapproachable," this leaves him still trapped in the Carlylean Centre of Indifference where there is no fear or hope and "God, Heaven, Immortality—are ... meaningless words" (2: 277; ch. 12). Harold is effectively trapped in the past: His compromise is that of the eighteenth century, his preaching "a plain moral discourse—an essay such as Locke or Bacon might have written" (2: 196; ch. 9). He is, like Sara, trapped in the prosaic; without specifically Christian truth, there can be no poetry, no new clothes, only plain discourses and meaningless words.

The "poetical" is (literally) crucial to the new dispensation. Whereas Michael, as the Romantic artist who travels to Rome, overstates the importance of form, Harold, the Romantic doubter, bearer of the Protestant spirit "who must find out the truth for myself" (3: 33; ch. 2), understates it. Christian forms are not all to be discarded as so many old clothes. Revelation is the Christian idea rendered as forms, the mysterious link between body and text, the incarnation, the Word of God. Harold must be returned from "the Infinite Unknown, into whose mysteries the mightiest philosophers may pierce and find no end," to "the God mercifully revealed, 'Our Father which is in heaven'—He to whom the poor, the sorrowing, and the ignorant may look, and not be afraid" (2: 265; ch. 12). To guide Harold through "the wild labyrinth" (3: 47; ch. 3), the angel-artist uses the religion of "the debatable ground," "a faith that taught the peace of resting childlike beneath the shadow of that Omnipotent Will, which holds every tangled thread of fate within one mighty Hand, which rules all things, and rules them continually for good" (1: 274; ch. 17).

But to the "ironic" clergyman a "debatable ground" means a questionable one: "Can one love Him," asks Harold, "when one does not fully know?" (2: 248–49; ch. 11). Paradoxically, Harold prevents his young daughter, Ailie, from "resting childlike," by keeping her in "perfect ignorance of the first principles of Christianity" (2: 178; ch. 8), "deem[ing] it inexpedient that the feeble mind of a child should be led to dwell on subjects which are beyond the grasp of the profoundest philosopher" (2: 179; ch. 8). The consequent debate between the "ironic child" and the "ironic" clergyman over the child's education recalls Ellis' subordination of religious instruction to the "cultivation of moral habits," and is central to Craik's exploration of the politics and poetics of religious literacy.

The debate begins when Harold overhears Olive's attempt to explain death and immortality to the child who is playing on her mother's grave. While acknowledging "the great beauty of a woman's religion" and that Olive's "way of putting the case was graceful—poetical," this is said in a "half-sarcastic, half-earnest way" (2: 178; ch. 8). The clergyman upholds the patriarchal prerogative: "a father is the best guide of his child's faith!" Olive, the Sunday-school teacher, knows she is standing on questionable ground, apologizing "for speaking so freely" of theology to "a clergyman—in this place too" (2: 176, 180; ch. 8).

But Olive continues the debate at a later date, contending that "You hid from her [Ailie] the true faith; she will soon make to herself a false one." Harold responds:

Nay, what is more false than the idle traditions taught by ranting parents to their offspring—the Bible travestied into a nursery tale—heaven transformed into a pretty pleasure-house—and hell and its horrors brought to frighten children in the dark. Do you think I would have my child turned into a baby saint, to patter glibly over parrot-like prayers, to exchange pet sweetmeats for missionary pennies, and so learn to keep up a debtor and creditor account with Heaven? ... I would rather see her grow up a heathen.

But ... would you have her die as she is now, utterly ignorant of all holy things?

Would I have her die an infant bigot—prattling blindly of subjects which in the common course of nature no child can comprehend? Would I have her chronicled in some penny tract as a "remarkable instance of infant piety," a small "vessel of mercy," to whom the Gospel was revealed at three years old? (2: 251–52; ch. 11)

The debate is an allegorical set-piece, concentrating Craik's theological, social, and political explorations into the opposed figures of the Sunday-school teacher and the clergyman and their disputatious discourse itself, a rehearsal of the eighteenth-century debates over children's education, exploiting the complex political history of fairy and its polysemous nature. Alan Richardson shows how the late-eighteenth-century debates over suitable children's literature were implicated in the "politics of literacy" and demonstrates that the accepted historical narrative of these debates is a seriously deficient and in fact politically inverted account. The accepted account shapes the debates into a gendered narrative in which male Romantics (seen as Radical promoters of fairy and the imagination) won out over that "cursed Barbauld crew" of mainly women writers (seen as Conservative advocates of reason and didacticism). However, not only was religion involved in the "antifairy side," complicating its typing as perpetrator of an arid rationalism, but it was the Rationalists, and some Evangelicals, who were politically Radicals; Wordsworth and Coleridge had become social and political conservatives. Fairy was not brought into the mainstream as an agent of subversion; it was fairy's perceived conservatism that helped it become acceptable as children's literature, as did its appropriation to the purposes of the eighteenth-century educationalists (Richardson 112–27). Although by the 1850s the question of propriety was largely settled in favor of fairy, the debate continued, given fresh relevance by changes in the perception of the nature and status of mythology. Although the *kunstmärchen* or invented fairy tale had become popular, fairy also represented the popular survival of the "remnants of ancient religious systems, the mental offspring of deep-thinking sages." Fairy functioned as a central trope of domestic ideology and the ideology of gender; it also united the discourses of literature and religion, the study of fairy described by one practitioner as "the philosophy of popular fiction" (Keightly 512). As Dickens' "Frauds on Fairies" demonstrates with its "politically correct" feminist version of Cinderella,[13] the earlier gendered narrative continued to inform midcentury discourse, highlighting issues of truth, representation, and the authority to speak, what might be called the politics of religious literacy.

To some degree Olive inverts the accepted gendered valences of the debate, aligning herself with "that clear demonstration of reason which forces conviction" (2: 285; ch. 13) yet, ultimately, revalorizing the "idle traditions" and the "nursery-tale." To Harold these are figures for falsity with which he satirizes the extremes of Evangelical child rearing (which he is, ironically, guilty of himself. Ailie suffers the superficial observation of forms, forced to keep an Evangelical Sunday without the Christianity [2: 200–1; ch. 9]). By extension, Evangelicalism itself is accused of parody. Olive is also aware of the "frightful profanities of that cant knowledge which young or ignorant minds acquire, and by which the solemn, almost fathomless mysteries of Christianity are lowered to a burlesque" (2: 244; ch. 11).

Craik is aware of the potential disapproval and/or ridicule that could greet religious fiction, in particular that written by women,[14] and the Evangelical child is also a satirical figure for "woman's religion." Craik distances her own text from traditional female religious genres: Here the "penny tract" is burlesqued, she has already parodied the domestic allegory.[15]

Simultaneously, the patriarch's ambivalent, ironic attitude to "woman's religion" is being routed, the Sunday-school teacher beginning the process of converting the cleric. The "debatable ground"—of "nursery tales," of a child's religious education—is a woman's "place." Being outside the church, in the graveyard, Olive is breaking no Pauline injunction, and as Harold himself points out, what better place to discuss death and immortality (2: 180; ch. 8).

It is the site of another death, that of the keeper's young son, that precipitates Harold's confession of his doubt and confirms Olive's position and that of "nursery tales." In the keeper's woodland cottage "strong bold men, who feared none of the evils of life, became as feeble as children before the awful power of Death." Like babies before their mother/nurse, "man" is left "poor, weak, and naked before his God" (2: 262; ch. 12). Only the angel can show the way in the face of death; the clergyman, like the Romantic artist, is himself allied with death. Whereas the painter killed "embodied hope," the doubting cleric's specifically masculine rejection of "human affections" is accompanied by his violent (albeit accidental) crushing of an autumnal butterfly, an image equally rich in analogical associations (3: 51; ch. 3). Like Vanbrugh, Harold enforces confinement on the powerless. Both Ailie with her "utterly untaught mind" (12: 175; ch. 8) and the keeper John Dent with his accusal—"I know naught about Him, parson— ye never larned me"—have been condemned by Harold to religious illiteracy. Harold, in so disenfranchising women and the working class, is guilty of the ultimate abuse of power, rendering subjects powerless in the face of death. Harold preaches submission to Providence, typing God as a judge and legislator. Again, such subjection is revealed to be wrong.

Harold is himself religiously illiterate, reduced to asking Olive for guidance; even then he cannot speak on "God—heaven—immortality" (2: 262; ch. 12). As Harold has already, unwittingly, prophesied, Olive is "a far better apostle than the clergyman" (2: 254; ch. 11). The "good woman" (2: 265; ch. 12) is confirmed as the possessor of religious capital, rightfully usurping the abusive cleric: "now the sceptre seemed torn from his hand—he was a king no more" (2: 269; ch. 12).

Olive herself soothes the savage breast of the half-naked "sturdy woodsman ...
almost giant-like in height and bulk" (2: 257; ch. 12), who, half-crazed with grief
for his dead son, prompts another man to consider "the devil's got un" (2: 260;
ch. 12). In exorcising Dent's violent potential, Olive, "a visible angel of peace"
(2: 266; ch. 12), is filling the social role previously administered by male clergy,
unifying and reconciling the classes. This is achieved not through submission to
oppression, but through subjection to a loving father: "the God mercifully revealed, 'Our Father which is in heaven'—He to whom the poor, the sorrowing,
and the ignorant may look, and not be afraid" (2: 265; ch. 12). On the walk home
through the forest, Harold at last reveals himself as a heathen in clerical clothing, but is, like Dent, managed by Olive's passive agency:

there came to Olive, in the place of fear, a strong compassion, tender as strong, and pure
as tender. Angel-like, it arose in her heart, ready to pierce his darkness with its shining
eyes—to fold around him and all his misery its sheltering wings. He was a great and
learned man, and she a lowly woman: in her knowledge not worthy to touch his gar-
ment's hem—in her faith able to watch him as from Heaven. (2: 269; ch. 12)

Faith is Olive's "great argument"; it is "a spiritual sense that may even transcend knowledge," (3: 30; ch. 2) an attribute of the poet, of the fairy-artist. Clearly
Harold would be better to close his *Sartor*, and open his *Cinderella*, for out of
the "ashes of dead Superstition" rises Cinderella/Olive, the figure who incorporates faith and knowledge. Again, Craik distinguishes her feminization of religion from Brontë's reputedly "anti-Christian composition" (Rigby 173). In Jane
Eyre's adult dream of the red-room, the "light that long ago had struck me into
syncope" becomes the moonlike goddess figure "Mother," warning Jane away
from temptation and confirming her flight from Rochester (346). In the "night
when one might faintly dream what the world would be, if the infidel's boast
were true, and *there were no God*" (2: 266; ch. 12) *Olive's* moon rises strongly
against heterodoxy: "lifting itself out of the horizon's black nothingness ... like
an immortal soul" (2: 282; ch. 12), forming a counterpart to Olive's angel-like
compassion, and beneath which Olive girds herself for the saving of Harold's
soul (2: 286–87; ch. 13). Both the moon and angel images have the neuter pronoun; the effect in the latter image at least is to transcend the constraints of gender. Nevertheless, it is in the "pure, beautiful life of a Christian woman" that one
gains an immediate apprehension of Truth. "Sometimes I tried to read ... the
morality of Jesus ... and it struck me how nearly you approached to that divine
life which I had thought impossible to be realized," writes Harold to Olive (3:
27; ch. 2). Like the "fairy Order" Olive embodies truth, her revelation, continues Harold, conveyed "less in words" than in "The silent teaching of [her] own
life" (3: 36; ch. 2).

The "silent voice of a Christian's life" (2: 291; ch. 13), however, also has a textual manifestation, albeit in a strangely labyrinthine manner. Chapter 34 is a
condensed version of the text's theology, written in epistolary format. Only
Harold's letters are cited, despite the fact that the chapter outlines Olive's creed.

Craik repeatedly reminds *her* reader that Harold is quoting from Olive's letters to him, repeating Olive's theology back to her.[16] In part this literary tactic is a strange subterfuge to get the male to speak the female text, thus validating it. Having Harold Gwynne as narrator allows Craik to have a woman's theology not only spoken by a male voice, but "written" by a clergyman (albeit an infidel!). By using the epistolary form, and reiteration and indirect reportage, Craik foregrounds Olive's theology *as a text*, effectively setting it alongside the other texts in Harold's theological library; the library is another, specifically textual, figure of the "debatable ground": "a vast mass of polemical literature, orthodox and heterodox, including all faiths, all variations of sect. Mahomet and Swedenborg, Calvin and the Talmud, lay side by side; and on the farthest shelf was the great original of all creeds—the Book of Books" (1: 253; ch. 16). The clergyman is thus learning from the Sunday-school teacher's text and Craik concludes the chapter with a carefully ungendered apologia that nonetheless accentuates the validity of women's theology:

Following whither our subject led, we have gone far beyond the bounds usually prescribed to a book like this. After perusing the present chapter, you may turn to the title-page, and read thereon, "Olive: a *Novel*." "Most incongruous—most strange!" you may exclaim. Nay, some may even accuse us of irreverence in thus bringing into a fictitious story those subjects which are acknowledged as most vital to every human soul, but yet which most people are content, save at set times and places, tacitly to ignore. There are those who sincerely believe that in such works as this there should never once be named the Holy Name. Yet what is a novel, or, rather, what is it that a novel ought to be? The attempt of one earnest mind to show unto many what humanity is—ay, and more, what humanity might become; to depict what is true in essence through imaginary forms; to teach, counsel, and warn, by means of the silent transcript of human life. Human life without God! Who will dare to tell us we should paint *that*? (3: 37–8; ch. 2)

The novel announces itself as "debatable ground," the narrator preempting the readers' response—"Most incongruous—most strange"—to a seemingly irreverent and yet in fact prophetic text; a text like Novalis' fairy tale. Like Harold's library it holds seemingly disparate texts in balance and writes women's texts into the field of religion, into "truth."

The library relates all texts "orthodox and heterodox" back to "the great original of all creeds—the Book of Books" (1: 253; ch. 16), "the book on which ... every form of religion is founded" (3: 27; ch. 2), a library in itself. As in Harold's library, within this meta-library is contained "the revelation ... as clear and distinct from the mass of modern creeds with which it has been overladen" (3: 27; ch. 2), "that lore—at once the most simple and most divine—the Gospels of the New Testament" (3: 4; ch. 1). "Simple" perhaps, but true religious text is both plain and poetical, and, again using the allegory of the child's education, Craik emphasizes that "imaginary forms" are crucial to the experience of truth.

Now and then—once in particular she remembered—old Elspie fell asleep; and then Olive turned to her favourite study, the Book of Revelations [*sic*]. Childlike, she terrified herself over the mysterious prophecies of the latter days, until at last she forgot the gloom and horror, in reading of the "beautiful city, New Jerusalem."

She seemed to see it—its twelve gates, angel-guarded, its crystal river, its many-fruited tree—the Tree of Life. Her young but glowing fancy, unable to separate truth from allegory, created out of these marvels a paradise, material in itself. She knew not that heaven is only the continual presence of the Eternal. Yet she was happy; and in her dreams she never pictured the land beyond the grave, but there came back to her, as though the nearest foreshadowing of its deep, holy rest, the visions of that Sunday afternoon. (1: 281–82; ch. 17)

The child's reading of Revelation is valorized. As she had regarding gender ideology (and as briefly noted above), Craik exploits the "debatable" nature of "fairy," using it as both a critique and model of Christianity. She distinguishes the "mystic horrors of Calvinistic predestination," for example, from the truth of Providence, figured as a giant Fate (1: 274; ch. 17). Truth and falsity are often so juxtaposed, using fairy-lore in the place of the equally ambiguous, but more controversial, "myth." Fairy-lore, the "nursery tale," is also used to hold truth and allegory in tension and with the child's reading of Revelation, Craik's earlier dismissal of parody, of burlesque, is rescinded. To be understood on earth "the solemn, almost fathomless mysteries of Christianity [must be] lowered," "the Bible [is necessarily] travestied into a nursery tale," brought within the domestic. Craik is arguing that revelation itself is "debatable ground": a logical resolution of the form/truth debate is impossible and faith in the Incarnation demands the two be held in tension.

Craik draws on the "orthodox and heterodox" texts of the library—fairy lore, biblical lore, and the works of Swedenborg (who believed the soul became more childlike as it progressed in spiritual wisdom)—to show that the salvation of Harold lies in his achieving "ironic childhood." The ironic clergyman, where the gap between truth and form produces satire and hypocrisy, must be reborn as an ironic child, where truth is incarnate. Harold must learn to read as a child, as Olive and her mother do every night, the last few chapters of Revelation: "the blessed words, the delight of her [Olive's] childhood—telling of the heavenly kingdom, and the after-life of the just" (2: 300; ch. 13).

This infantilization is brought about by the fairy-teller. As Harold begins to regain faith, as his "mind echoes [Olive's] words," "a child-like peace [is] creeping into [his] heart. All human affections are growing closer and dearer" (3: 34; ch. 2). Brontë symbolically emasculates Rochester by blinding and crippling him in the fire at Thornfield; in the fire at Olive's home Craik infantilizes Harold: "His whole face seemed softened and spiritualized" and "With childlike helplessness there seems to come a childlike peace" (3: 313–14; ch. 15). This peace is achieved because Harold had "learnt from [Olive] that holy faith which conquers death"; Olive is his "life's good angel" (3: 316; ch. 15). While Harold is making his "love-confession" he lies on Olive's breast like a child (3: 321; ch. 15) and she "love[s] him at once with the love of mother, sister, friend, and wife" (3: 322; ch. 15).

Human love and desire are the proofs of Providence: "Can you believe in human love, yet doubt the love of Him who is its origin?" asks Olive. "Can you think that He would give the yearning for the hereafter, and yet deny its fulfilment? That what He made good He will not make happy, and what He makes happy He will not make immortal?" (2: 321; ch. 13). Theology is ultimately a matter of feeling, not abstract knowledge: Olive opposes the maternal and filial bond to Harold's question, "can one love him when one does not fully know?" (2: 248–49; ch. 11) by rhetorically asking "can such love end with death?" (2: 325; ch. 13).

Craik's ultimate image of divine love is the married couple. Her language and imagery blends sexual and religious desire and satisfaction into a seamless whole: "Fulfilment" is found in "the still, sacred love of marriage. And, however your modern heart-infidels may doubt, and your free-thinking heart-desecrators scoff, *that* is the true love—the tie which God created from the beginning, making man and woman to be one flesh, and pronouncing it 'good'" (3: 355; ch. 17).

Olive achieves an equally Christian and fairy-tale ending. Through the auspices of Olive's aunt Flora Olive and Harold respectively inherit the house at Morningside (a reference to Bunyan's House Beautiful from where can be seen the Delectable Mountains) and a legacy. This allows them to marry (skipping the bourgeois practicalities of income) and confirms their residence in "debatable ground," here revealed as Beulah, on the borders of heaven. *Olive* concludes with a tableau of the "true man and woman, husband and wife," the man having been led by the fairy along the winding road to the summit of the Braid Hills where (like Christian on the Delectable Mountains) they look "up to Heaven to guide their way" (3: 376; ch. 17).

Though it is Olive who has led them to within sight of the city of Revelation and "[sent] the cobwebs out of [Harold's] brain," something of the Ellisian fairy's duplicity seems to come into play: "Olive never let him see how skilfully she did this lest his man's dignity should revolt at being so lovingly beguiled" (3: 373; ch. 17). The arts of fairy, reconfigured as Christian, enable a feminine apocalypse; the "debatable ground" also allows opposing readings of *Olive*, a truly radical ambiguity. The borders of heaven are something of a social blueprint: The final redemption of patriarchy is reliant on female emancipation. Flora's will allows Olive to enter marriage as an equal, for example, and nonbiological motherhood is validated (and fairy's evil stepmother banished). Through her own desire, and confirming the angel-artist's usurpation of the conduct-book heroine, Olive is now the rightful mother of Sara's daughter, Ailie. Moreover, at the time of her marriage Olive, as Kaplan contends, is clearly "an established artist" (xx). Possibly misled by the apocalyptic burning of Olive's studio (which is less a purification of impropriety than a necessary stage in the progression toward paradise), but also by the ambiguities of Craik's text as she attempts to prevent male "revolt," several critics, including Paula Gillet and Denise Denisoff, believe Olive's marriage signifies the end of her art career. Olive goes about "her little

household duties" with her "artist-soul" intact, however, and even if it is more
of a struggle, as Craik does not fail to note, the angel-artist continues to produce. Moreover, Olive's time is being taken up not simply by domesticity but
also by her implied study of science (3: 356–57; ch. 17).

Olive, both "orthodox and heterodox," has saved an erring clergyman by leading him out of the fold and into debatable ground. Unsurprisingly Harold's re-
constructed faith is not strictly orthodox: "his faith was now the Christian
faith—even, in most points, that of the Church—still, there was in his nature a
stern simplicity which somewhat cast aside forms" (3: 330; ch. 16). To "somewhat cast aside forms" allows Romanticism without Romanism, a Protestant
Romanticism. Bernard M. G. Reardon writes that

Romanticism ... marked a re-evaluation of religion as an experience the authenticity of
which must be sought within itself. If such authenticity could not, primarily at least, be
found there it would be found nowhere. Abstract argument, as essentially extrinsic to
the experience itself, was unavailing. Faith has its roots in feeling and intuition, of which
theological doctrines can never be more than an imaginative symbolism, historically determined. (*Religion* 29)

"Feeling and intuition" being traditionally feminine qualities, the elevation
of the feminine is also a Romantic trait, and one accentuated by Craik. The Christian God (or his text) and Olive (and her text) are the two new sources of authority for faith. Olive recommends, "I follow no ritual, and trust no creed,
except so far as I find it in the Holy Word" (2: 322; ch. 14). But a deceptively
simple economy of faith is revealed as a highly complex grammar of assent, as
Olive (and Craik) leads her readers directly to that part of the Holy Word where
interpretation is particularly fraught, and then promotes an "ironic" reading in
which allegory is necessary to truth, and the "fairy" necessary to faith.

Craik's narrative transforms the female child and its congenitally deformed
body—exemplum of the evangelical doctrine of original sin and its specifically
female provenance (the Rothesay women with yellow hair are emblematic of
the curse of Eve)—converting it via the fairy tale into a sign of grace. Moreover,
this female "ironic child" is an agent of Providence, a tracer of the "threads of
guidance" (3: 198; ch. 190) who replaces law with "lore" and takes over the patriarch's role: "her father's desk [is] now her own" (1: 313; ch. 18).

Over the next decade, Craik established her own right to write at this desk.
Her 1859 novel *A Life for a Life* was written by "'The Author of John Halifax'
... a public figure with a stature equaled by few women of her generation, who
could speak her thoughts with the assurance that they would be read and regarded because she had written them" (Mitchell, *Dinah* 99).

A Life for a Life tells the stories of Dr. Max Urquhart, an army surgeon with
a skeleton in the closet, and Theodora (Dora) Johnston, a vicar's daughter no
longer in her first youth and beginning to despair of ever answering the question "What am I to do with my life?" (110; ch. 12). In the best domestic tradition, the novel traces the vicissitudes of their courtship, and because, rather late

in the piece, Max is discovered to have murdered Dora's dissolute brother many years previously (albeit under conditions of great provocation), these are not negligible. Max confesses to the murder and is imprisoned for three months. There is a happy ending for the star-crossed lovers, however; as the preface describes it, *A Life* is the story of "a man-slayer ... finally ... loved by and married to his victim's own sister" (iv), both parties finally forgiven by the victim's father. In a similar vein *A Life* also features a seducer finally loved by and married to the mother of his child: Dora's elder sister's fiancé, Francis, and the Johnstons' ex-servant girl, Lydia. The novel ends with Max and Dora emigrating to Canada to begin a new life, but intending to return.

Along with her controversial subject matter Craik utilized an innovative dual narrative structure, alternating Dora's journal, "Her Story" with Max's journal, "His Story." Craik developed *A Life*'s innovative poetics to address contemporary hermeneutical and representational crises, exploring the notion of "sacrifice—of "A Life for a Life"—as it related to midcentury gender ideology and theology, and was played out in topical debates on the Crimean War, Atonement Theology, capital punishment and penal reform, "Fallen women," and women's work. Craik wove all these discourses, and dramatizations of her nonfiction work, *A Woman's Thoughts about Women*, into the novel she came to consider her best work.

A Life opens in the immediate aftermath of the Crimean war, and immediately signals a crisis of representation, part of the "crisis of faith generated by the unprecedented publicity that accompanied the Crimean war" (Poovey, *Uneven Developments* 169).

What a time it was—this time two years ago! How the actual romance of each day, as set down in the newspapers, made my old romances read like mere balderdash: how the present, in its infinite piteousness, its tangible horror, and the awfulness of what they called its "glory," cast the tame past altogether into shade! Who read history then, or novels, or poetry? Who read anything but that fearful "Times?"

   And now it is all gone by—we have peace again; and this 20th of September, 1856, I begin with my birthday a new journal. (1–2; ch. 1)

Far from being "all gone by," Craik's text is itself a discursive battleground, into which the violence of individual and cultural history implodes in the form of diseased and broken bodies. Disrupting the narrative, *A Life*'s bodies/embodiments—whether real or "ghastly imaginations" (116; ch. 13), whether Max's soldier patients or, most disruptive of all, Dora's murdered brother—break the surface of the text itself (e.g., 143; ch. 15), demanding to be read. Existing literary forms are entirely unable to deal with the "actual romance of each day" and Craik repudiates the traditional novel form for the overlapping diaries of Max and Dora. Despite the rejection of fictional "balderdash," it is the private, subjective account that carries the symbolic weight of new life, picking up the torch lit by the *Times* war correspondents, who published an alternative to the officially sanctioned military narrative. By the novel's conclusion it is clear that the private domestic narrative itself—as expressed by Dora and Max—has effectively and affectively replaced all public or institutional narratives.

Craik parallels the crisis of faith in military and political authority and the midcentury crisis of faith in theological discourse. Issues of representation and authority were equally at stake in this latter crisis, also precipitated by the democratization of the discourse—in the press, the "grass-roots" activities and publications of dissenting religious groups, for example, and, of course, literature such as Craik's. *A Life* participates in English theological debate of the 1850s, documenting the shift in sensibility from the economic and forensic frame of reference that dominated hegemonic Evangelical ideology of the first half of the nineteenth century. At midcentury, liberal theologians such as Benjamin Jowett began to reject the idea of a vicarious bloody sacrifice inflicted upon Christ by his loving Father, the idea that Christ was thus paying the debts of humanity in suffering for their sins. Jowett wrote in 1855 that "the only sacrifice, atonement, or satisfaction, with which Christ has to do, is a moral or spiritual one; not the pouring out of blood upon the earth."[17] The implications of cruelty and waste in such critiques (and those aimed at doctrines of eternal punishment) were given some urgency by contemporary events. Craik was by no means the only one to consider the relationship between a supposedly Christian nation and its military exploits, a relationship highlighted by the ostensibly religious nature of the Crimean war (the original quarrel was between France and Russia over the right to protect Christian holy sites). Nor was she the only one to attempt to read the resulting carnage according to the ultimate narrative of sacrifice: as a holocaust, a reading that would itself reflect back onto the Atonement narrative. The Crimea had a casualty rate of more than 17 percent, with more than 78 percent of these fatalities caused by disease, and in 1856 Florence Nightingale wrote,: "I stand at the altar of the murdered men, and while I live, I fight their cause" (qtd. in Woodham-Smith 259). Craik similarly uses the typology/iconography of the sacrificial victim to criticize the Establishment. Indeed, in the first part of the novel the critical voice is largely that of actual public record both in its tone and targets—attacking military and governmental institutions and their culture, a culture Craik suggests is damagingly male and nondomestic.[18]

As a kind of cross-dressed Nightingale (complete with a lamp; ch. 14), Dr. Max Urquhart's experiences and observations as an army surgeon in the Crimea result in his campaigning for sanitary and barracks reform in the face of military indifference. It is not the Horse Guards, however, but a Church of England clergyman, Theodora's father, whom Craik represents as supporting "the pouring out of blood upon the earth," the Old Testament type of the Atonement—the father who would sacrifice his own son (74; ch. 7), who has in fact written his own son out of history: "blotted out—as if he never had existed" (e.g., 139; ch. 15). To the Reverend Mr. Johnston "the law of the land—[is] the law of God" and "God's law is blood for blood. *Whoso sheddeth man's blood, by man shall his blood be shed.*" To interpret the text otherwise is to "blaspheme" (164; ch.

16). In this combination of the "Mosaic" and "Calvinistic" (263; ch. 27), the Reverend Mr. Johnston, politely described as "classical" (44; ch. 5), is a typical representative of his cloth, who are less politely described as "droning out 'words, words, words,' when bodies and souls perish in thousands round them," and "splitting theological hairs" (43; ch. 5). Max notes wryly it is "no wonder" the army chaplain "prefers Moses and the prophets to the New Testament ... 'He that taketh the sword shall perish by the sword!' would sound particularly odd in a military chapel" (39; ch. 5). Craik further suggests the pre-Christian and "primitive" origins of blood sacrifice by situating her brother's murder at Stonehenge and allying dogmatism with "the blind obstinacy of a brute" (123; ch. 14).

Craik complicates such dogmatism by making her hero a murderer, one who (like the soldier) takes as well as saves lives and is himself cast as a martyr. Craik's is a profoundly Christian sensationalism, using paradox to unsettle and reveal the text's bourgeois secret as the ultimate mystery, the dead male body, the violence at the center of a religion of love, at the heart of Christian culture, a violence in which all Christians are implicated. Like the liberal theologian Jowett, Craik privileges the "moral and spiritual" sacrifice, but Craik's rejection of the traditional understanding of the Atonement is not a rejection of physicality/materiality.

Craik wrote in *A Woman's Thoughts* that "there are no such distinctions as 'secular' and 'religious'" (183) and *A Life*'s "strange theology" chooses to "bring God's truth into all the circumstances of life" (363; ch. 37) through a sophisticated co-opting of secular discourse. On one level *A Life* is a Christian allegory reworking biblical types of the Atonement into a highly contemporary narrative, and in ultimately rejecting the blood sacrifice Craik replaces the sacrificial victim with the Physician as her central male type of the Atonement, heeding the words of Matthew 9:12–13 that "They that be whole need not a physician, but they that are sick ... go ye and learn what that meaneth, I will have mercy, and not sacrifice: for I am not come to call the righteous, but sinners to repentance." Craik writes this traditional type into the context of mid-century professionalization. She redefines medicine as a moral occupation and denies the clerical ownership of theology. While not going so far as to suggest the physician as a replacement for the clergy—note her use of "amateur" below—in terms of the theological paradigm of progressive revelation (155; ch. 16) the Physician takes over the preacher's interpretative authority precisely because he is located at the interface of sacred and secular, and has the cure of both body and soul (e.g., 157; ch. 16). Dr. Urquhart describes himself as "an amateur demonstrator of spiritual anatomy" (18; ch. 3), and his theological understanding is supported rather than threatened by scientific discourse:

[H]e believed moral and physical evil to be so bound up together, that it was idle to attack one without trying to cure the other. He thought, better than all building of gaols and reformatories, or even of churches—since the Word can be spread abroad without need of bricks and mortar—would be the establishing of sanitary improvements in our great towns, and trying to teach the poor, not how to be taken care of in workhouses, prisons, and hospitals, but how to take care of themselves, in their own homes … . "The doctor" has, of all persons, the greatest influence among the poor.(161; ch. 16)

Despite Urquhart's distaste for institutions he later works as Gaol Surgeon to a "great prison," "a model of its kind, on the solitary, sanitary, and moral improvement system" (290; ch. 31). The "separate system" was, in fact, promoted by Victorian Evangelicals; it was understood to prevent moral contamination and introduce new opportunities to minister to the individual (Tomlinson 129). That sin has a pathology and is therefore curable is crucial to *A Life*'s "strange theology;" however the "one clear doctrine, namely, that any sin, however great, being repented of and forsaken, is by God, and ought to be by man, altogether pardoned, blotted out, and done away" (155; ch. 16) was criticized by the *Christian Remembrancer* for the idea that repentance abrogated all punishment.[19] Craik represented the "separate system" as more Utilitarian than Christian and as inimical to reformation, reducing humanity to "a herd of brute beasts," "their bodies well looked after, but their souls—they might scarcely have any! They are simply Nos. 1, 2, 3, and so on, with nothing of human individuality or responsibility about them" (290; ch. 31).

The popularity of the "separate system" at mid-century was in response to the threat posed by the criminal body. As Christopher Hamlin notes, all "brands" of mid-Victorian pathology share a common "image of how the pure was corrupted by contact with impurity and in the process transformed into a replica of impurity that would perpetuate further corruption" (389). The criminal body was a new and pressing problem for the mid-Victorians: Due to the simultaneous rejection of traditional methods of disposal (death and transportation) society was having to consider the ongoing relationship between this body and the larger social body for the first time.

The most prominent mid-century image of a shared moral and physical pathology, however, was the prostitute: "a canker on the body politic whose presence was necessarily contaminating" (Levine 81). She was also seen more specifically as a canker on the military: As a result of the drive for reform brought about by the Crimean exposé some medical men and army officials began to push for contagious diseases legislation as early as 1857, legislation which was to protect soldiers by inspecting and confining prostitutes. The "fallen woman" was thus "ætiologically" implicated in Crimean discourse, as a scapegoat for the state of the army. The mid-century fallen woman is also, of course, another type of the sacrificial victim: Prostitution being, as the anti-Contagious Diseases legislation activist Josephine Butler would later characterize it, a "costly and impious sacrifice of souls."[20] Like the images of military victory, the physician, law and debt, the "fallen woman" is at once a biblical type and a contemporary debate.

Although Craik's Lydia Cartwright is not yet, strictly speaking, a prostitute, she is definitely a "kept" woman and her "rescue" demonstrates the shift away from patriarchal law. The Reverend Johnston initially intends to cut Lydia and her child out of the Christian body, so "that they may carry their corruption elsewhere" (298; ch. 32). Under this old transactional and "bloody" understanding, Lydia would of necessity have become a prostitute (289–90; ch. 31) or have starved. Her illegitimate child would have become an innocent scapegoat, inevitably and irrevocably a "reprobate" (299; ch. 32), fallen in the theological sense: "It is written, *The seed of evil-doers shall never be renowned.* The sinless must suffer with the guilty" (298; ch. 32). Under the truly Christian reading of atonement as practised by Theodora, however, the transaction is replaced by love, and death by life: The prostitute is "reborn" as a mother and a wife, the fallen woman is as she whose *"sins which were many, are forgiven, for she loved much"* (334; ch. 35). The infant scapegoat is reborn as a "scapegrace" (334; ch. 35), one who will be the salvation of his father (331; ch. 34).

Craik has turned the Crimean ætiology on its head: It is Lydia's seducer, the ruling-class Francis Charteris, almost Governor of "a lovely West Indian Island" (179; ch. 17), who is one of those "worse than murderers, for they destroy both body and soul" (286; ch. 30). Urquhart, the narrative's actual murderer, is instrumental in the salvation of Lydia. His espousal of a single moral standard for men and women, "the Christian principle of love and marriage" (289; ch. 31), is contrasted with Charteris' duplicitousness. Charteris' moral double-standard (280–81; ch. 30) is proof of his unfitness to rule. The single moral standard (which campaigners would use to argue against the Contagious Diseases Acts) also defines Urquhart in opposition to post-Crimean medical discourse. Again, Craik coopts rather than simply rejects secular discourse, reconciling medicine's "happy hooker" (who according to Dr. Acton's influential 1857 study saved herself by marrying respectably) with the martyred victim of the rescue workers. Lydia does end up happily married, but this only occurs through the agency of Atonement. Unlike her lover, Lydia is "of the very best" of the working-classes, a characteristic, Craik had written in *A Woman's Thoughts about Women* (1858), shared by many "Lost Women," as was the failure of her employers to protect her from a predatory male (191–92; *A Life* 297–98, ch. 32).

Craik's earlier nonfictional work is a crucial intertext for *A Life* more generally: The novel dramatizes many of Craik's earlier essays on the "Woman Question." "Her Story" is Theodora's quest to discover the significance of her name, to understand in what sense she is "'the gift of God' ... —what for, and to whom?" (3; ch. 1). Like Nightingale's "Cassandra," Theodora believes that "women as well as men require something to do" (96; ch. 10), but her inability to answer the question "what am I to do with my life?" (110; ch. 12), pushes her into invalidism and ultimately the desire for death. But Max reminds her self-destruction is wrong, for God demands that we present our "bodies [as] a living sacrifice ... which is [our] reasonable service" (Rom.12.1); we are put on earth "to do good work" (221; ch. 13). As Craik wrote in *A Woman's Thoughts,* we all have the "heaven-given honour of being [among] the Workers of the world," an honor with which we fulfil "the duty of self-dependence" (90, 77, 181ff). Theodora, in fact, is also a murderer, culpable of the "great sin" (as Craik wrote in her essays in terms reminiscent of *Cassandra*), "the massacre of Old Time," "the only mortal gift bestowed equally on every living soul, and excepting the soul, the only mortal loss which is totally irretrievable" (67).

Craik's essays promoted self-dependence for women "in this curious phase of our social history" when marriage is no longer the sole end of a women's existence (77), stressing that "the patient must minister to herself" (69). That the turning point for Theodora's health is her betrothal to her physician (she is God's "gift" to Max) and that marriage is *A Life*'s final model of Atonement (258; ch. 27) does not negate this, for Craik represents marriage as an equal relationship in which Theodora also ministers to the body and spirit of Max (359 ff; ch. 37)— the patient and the physician are interchangeable. Marriage is premised on a single moral standard (289; ch. 31) and a unity of purpose and labor (369; ch. 37). Marriage is the closest type of Atonement because real atonement is divine love, and, as in *Olive*, human love partakes of the divine (187; ch. 19). Craik explicitly states that Max's marriage with Dora is a sign of divine forgiveness and itself replaces Max's previous "method of atonement": his fallacious "economic" interpretation of a life for a life (258; ch. 27) under which his life was "owed" (e.g. 186; ch. 18). Craik stresses that lives are linked through love not an economic or forensic nexus: The debt or duty is transformed into a gift or offering, the debtor becomes a lover, prostitution becomes marriage, punishment becomes forgiveness.

With its parallel his- and her-stories ultimately resolved into marriage (at-one-ment), *A Life for a Life* formally embodies the binary logic based on sexual difference that was fundamental to nineteenth-century culture. Simultaneously, the text does undermine the notion of separate spheres by documenting a process of feminization (the novel concludes in the feminine voice), and breaking down the distinctions between men and women. In *A Woman's Thoughts* Craik privileged the relationship between women and the divine based on the female capacity for suffering, writing of "*a woman*— ... the creature who, with all her imperfections, is nearer to heaven than man, in one particular—she 'loves much.' And loving is so frequently, nay, inevitably, identical with suffering, either with, or for, or from, the object beloved ... " (179); however, "it is the divine law that we should *all*, like our Master, be 'made perfect through suffering" (187; emphasis added). As Sally Mitchell notes, Craik "applies to a guilty man many conventions typical of writing about the unchaste woman ... . [Max] is virtually a seduced innocent" (*Fallen* 115), literally driven to murder. That is, Max is paralleled with Lydia, rather than her seducer, and aspects of his story are drawn directly from Craik's own chapter on "Lost Women" in *A Woman's Thoughts*. While Craik wrote of the opposition of men and women that it was a "difference [that] will for ever exist" (*A Woman's Thoughts* 158), she also asked: "do we not continually find womanish men and masculine women? and some of the finest types of character we have known among both sexes, are they not often those who combine the qualities of both? Therefore, there must be somewhere a standard of abstract right, including manhood and woman, and yet superior to either" (73). But Craik's were ultimately feminine standards. In both *Olive* and *A Life* patriarchal law is replaced by feminized lore; the clergyman is instructed by the daughter.

Craik argued that in order for Christianity to survive in the modern world it must be brought within the domestic, and, conversely, that the redemption of patriarchy was reliant on female emancipation. In *Olive* Craik intervened in the politics of religious and aesthetic literacy, using the debates between Romantics and Evangelicals over fairy tale and children's education in order to delineate the relationship between women and truth and creativity, and coopt the female text into the library of cultural master texts. Craik's revolution negotiated a position between the radical position on gender and religion as offered by Charlotte Brontë's *Jane Eyre*, and Craik's own critical reading of the conservative figure of the domestic woman as promoted by the contemporary conduct book. Her resulting figure of the female artist-fairy is Nightingale's desired "Saviour of her Race," a utopian woman who will revitalize modern culture, who will redeem social and religious patriarchy through her body and text.

With *A Life* Craik moves the question of Sacrifice—the theological meeting-place of the sacred and the secular and a crucial constituent of the feminine in mid-century gender ideology—to centre-stage. She asks "the great question of our time" (155; ch. 16) within the tradition of Domestic Realism, aligning actual political, social and theological "events." In response to contemporary hermeneutical and representational crises she has the domestic engulf the public, the subjective voice replace the institutional narrative, and history be subsumed into herstory. *A Life* is resolutely topical; if, finally for Max and Dora, "everywhere was Home" (370; ch. 37), then the home is a public and present domain. Craik's novel is, in fact, an exposé of "the skeleton in the closet" of mid-century bourgeois domesticity, and, given that "everywhere was Home," the State. The fallen woman was something of a mid-century fetish and one expects to find her outcast body as a model for the new Christianity with its social emphasis. Few, however, rewrote domesticity and indeed the social body more generally around the impure woman, let alone the convicted murderer. George Eliot's *Adam Bede*, for instance, *A Life*'s rival in lending library popularity in 1859, expels Hetty Sorrel from the social body. But for Craik atonement demands the "living sacrifice," and thus the reincorporation of the transgressive body.

Craik's Christian sensationalism self-consciously usurps more than that "portion of the preacher's office" Henry Mansel would shortly accuse sensation novels of taking (482), for, wrote Craik, "undeniably, the modern novel is one of the most important moral agents of the community ... the preacher may preach to his thousands; but the novelist counts his audience by millions." The novelist is "treading dangerous ground" for "Fiction ... is the truth of life itself. He who dares to reproduce it"—and Craik makes sure we understand her use of the "superior pronoun" is inclusive—"is a Prometheus who has stolen celestial fire." The "true novel-writer," however, "has a right to do" so, for "Like the fairy Order in the nursery tale," Craik's new model woman, the novelist "can see the under threads that guide the pattern" of "the tremendous web of human life" ("To Novelists" 442–43), and, as Olive has made clear, a woman's place *is* "debatable ground."

WORKS CITED

Auerbach, Nina and U. C. Knoepflmacher, eds. *Forbidden Journeys: Fairy Tales and Fantasies by Victorian Women Writers.* Chicago: U of Chicago P, 1992.

Brantlinger, Patrick. "The Entrepreneurial Ideal." *The Spirit of Reform: British Literature and Politics, 1832–1867.* Cambridge, MA.: Harvard UP, 1977. 109–27.

Brontë, Charlotte. *Jane Eyre.* 1847. Ed. Q. D. Leavis. Harmondsworth: Penguin, 1981.

Casteras, Susan. "Excluding Women: The Cult of the Male Genius in Victorian Painting." *Rewriting the Victorians: Theory, History, and the Politics of Gender.* Ed. Linda M. Shires. New York: Routledge, 1992. 116–46.

Craik, Dinah Mulock. *John Halifax, Gentleman.* London: Hurst and Blckett, 1856.

———. *A Life for a Life.* 1859. London: Hurst and Blackett, n.d.

———. *Olive; and, The Half-Caste.* 1850. New York: Garland, 1975. 3 Vols.

———. "To Novelists—and a Novelist." *Macmillan's Magazine* 3 Apr. 1861: 441–48.

———. *A Woman's Thoughts about Women.* 1858.

Craik, Dinah Mulock, and Christina Rossetti. *Maude; On Sisterhoods; A Woman's Thoughts about Women.* Ed. Elaine Showalter. London: Pickering, 1993.

Davidoff, Leonore, and Catherine Hall. *Family Fortunes: Men and Women of the English Middle Class, 1780–1850.* London: Hutchinson, 1987.

Denisoff, Denise. "Lady in green with novel: the gendered economics of the visual arts and mid-Victorian women's writing." *Victorian Women Writers and the Woman Question.* Ed. Nicola Diane Thompson. Cambridge Studies in Nineteenth-Century Literature and Culture. Cambridge: Cambridge UP, 1999. 151–69.

Dickens, Charles. "Frauds on the Fairies." 1853. *A Peculiar Gift: Nineteenth Century Writings on Books for Children.* Ed. Lance Sodway. Harmondsworth: Penguin-Kestrel, 1976. 111–18.

Douglas, Ann. *The Feminization of American Culture.* New York: Knopf, 1978.

Ellis, Sarah Stickney. *The Women of England, Their Social Duties, and Domestic Habits.* London. 1839. Victorian Women Writers Project. Ed. Perry Willett. 5 Feb. 1999. Indiana U. 13 June 1999. http://www.indiana.edu/~letrs/vwwp/ellis/womeneng.html.

Fryckstedt, Monica C. *Geraldine Jewsbury's Athenaeum Reviews: A Mirror of Mid-Victorian Attitudes to Fiction.* Acta Universitatis Upsaliensis. Studia Anglistica Upsaliensia 61. Uppsala, Swed.: Uppsala Universitet, 1986.

Gillett, Paula. *Worlds of Art: Painters in Victorian Society.* New Brunswick, NJ: Rutgers UP, 1990.

Hamlin, Christopher. "Providence and Putrefaction: Victorian Sanitarians and the Natural Theology of Health and Disease." *Victorian Studies* 28 Spring 1985: 381–411.

Helsinger, Elizabeth K., Robin Lauterbach Sheets and William Veeder. *The Woman Question: Society and Literature in Britain and America, 1837–1883.* Vol. 2. New York: Garland, 1983.

Kaplan, Cora. Introduction. *Olive and The Half-Caste.* By Dinah Mulock Craik. Oxford: Oxford UP, 1996. ix–xxv.

Keightley, Thomas. *The Fairy Mythology, Illustrative of the Romance and Superstition of Various Countries* 1828. New edition 1850. London: George Bell, 1878.

Langland, Elizabeth. *Nobody's Angels: Middle-Class Women and Domestic Ideology in Victorian Culture.* Ithaca: Cornell UP, 1995.

Levine, Philippa. *Feminist Lives in Victorian England: Private Roles and Public Commitment.* Oxford: Blackwell, 1990.

Maison, Margaret. *Search Your Soul, Eustace: A Survey of the Religious Novel in the Victorian Age.* London: Stag-Sheed, 1961.

Mansel, Henry. "Sensation Novels." *Quarterly Review* 113 Apr. 1863: 481–514.

Mellors, Anne K. *Romanticism and Gender.* New York: Routledge, 1993.

Mitchell, Sally. *Dinah Mulock Craik.* Twayne's English Authors Ser. 364. Boston: Twayne, 1983.

———. *The Fallen Angel: Chastity, Class and Woman's Reading, 1835–1880.* Bowling Green, Ohio: Bowling Green UP, 1981.

Nightingale, Florence. *Cassandra and Other Selections from Suggestions for Thought.* Ed. Mary Poovey. London: Pickering, 1991.

Oliphant, Margaret. "Modern Novelists—Great and Small." *Blackwood's* 77 May 1855: 554–68.

Oliphant, Mrs., et al. *Women Novelists of Queen Victoria's Reign: A Book of Appreciations.* 1897. n.p.: Folcroft, 1969.

Poovey, Mary. *The Proper Lady and the Woman Writer: Ideology as Style in the Works of Mary Wollstonecraft, Mary Shelley, and Jane Austen.* Chicago: U of Chicago P, 1984.

———. *Uneven Developments: The Ideological Work of Gender in Mid-Victorian England.* London: Virago, 1989.

Reardon, Bernard M. G. *Religion in the Age of Romanticism: Studies in Early Nineteenth-Century Thought.* Cambridge: Cambridge UP, 1985.

———. *Religious Thought in the Victorian Age: A Survey from Coleridge to Gore.* 2nd ed. London: Longman, 1995. Rpt. of *From Coleridge to Gore.* 1971.

Richardson, Alan. *Literature, Education, and Romanticism: Reading as Social Practice 1780–1832.* Cambridge Studies in Romanticism 8. Cambridge: Cambridge UP, 1994.

Rigby, Elizabeth. Rev. of *Vanity Fair* and *Jane Eyre. Quarterly Review* 84 Dec. 1848: 153–85.

Sellar, W. Y. "Religious Novels." *North British Review* 26.51 Nov. 1856: 216.

Showalter, Elaine. *A Literature of Their Own: British Women Novelists from Brontë to Lessing.* Rev. ed. London: Virago, 1982.

Stoneman, Patsy. *Brontë Transformations: The Cultural Dissemination of Jane Eyre and Wuthering Heights.* London: Prentice Hall/ Harvester Wheatsheaf, 1996.

Swartz, David. *Culture and Power: The Sociology of Pierre Bourdieu.* Chicago: U of Chicago P, 1997.

Tomlinson, M. Heather. "Penal Servitude 1846–1865: A System in Evolution." *Policing and Punishment in Nineteenth Century Britain.* Ed. Victor Bailey. London: Croom Helm, 1981. 126–49.

Warner, Marina. *From the Beast to the Blonde: On Fairy Tales and Their Tellers.* London: Vintage-Random, 1995.

Woodham-Smith, Cecil. *Florence Nightingale: 1820–1910.* London: Constable, 1950.

NOTES

1. Langland is using Bourdieu's notion of class as a group defined through cultural representation, sees women as the producers/controllers of such representations, and believes that "In this dimension of cultural currency as opposed to economic capital, women

dominated Victorian society" (7). I go back to Bourdieu's associated notion of "religious capital" (in some senses, via Weber's idea of "religious interest," the genesis of concepts of symbolic power and cultural capital), again defined as being accumulated and exercised through the power of representation, and consider women as the new possessors and producers of the same, as demonstrated by the mid-century text. Although at this time "religious capital" is still closely related to "cultural capital" in a way that would eventually cease to be possible following the Darwinian "revolution" of 1859, I want to highlight the need to distinguish these forms of power; a distinction necessary to account for *Olive's* particular delineation and location of its "religious field" in relation to other contemporary arenas. My concept of the "debatable ground" owes something to Bourdieu's concept of "field" which is used, as Swartz explains, "to designate competitive arenas where other forms of capital (e.g., symbolic, cultural, social) as well as economic capital are invested, exchanged, and accumulated" (44).

2. Olive's fairy godmothers are also the Theological Virtues of faith, hope, and charity and the three (Christian) graces Aglaia (Brilliance), Euphrosyne (Joy), and Thalia (Bloom). Elspie and Sybilla together are Faith or Aglaia (Brilliance), Meliora is Hope and Joy, and Aunt Flora (Bloom) is Charity. These three structure and unify *Olive*, each presiding over a separate stage of Olive's development. All three give Olive gifts that lead to her fairy tale ending—Elspie, faith; Meliora, hope, specifically a painting career; and Flora, a house.

3. "A true fairy tale must also be a prophetic account of things—an ideal account. . . . A true writer of fairy tales sees into the future. [Fairy tales are] confessions of a true, a synthetic child—of an ideal child. (A child is a good deal leverer and wiser than an adult—but the child must be an ironic child.)" (Novalis; qtd. in Warner 188)

4. *Olive* is an early instance of the myriad retellings of *Jane Eyre*, many of which are documented in Patsy Stoneman's *Brontë Transformations: The Cultural Dissemination of* Jane Eyre *and* Wuthering Heights.

5. Jane Eyre sees herself as "like one of the tiny phantoms, half fairy, half imp, Bessie's evening stories represented as coming out of lone, ferny dells in moors, and appearing before the eyes of belated travellers . . . ." Recollecting her experience the adult Jane recognizes that she was "a discord in Gateshead Hall; I was like nobody there . . . a heterogeneous thing . . . a useless thing . . . a noxious thing . . . " (Brontë 46 and 47).

6. Here I have borrowed Kaplan's description of Craik's intervention in mid-century racial discourse (xxv).

7. See Davidoff and Hall esp. ch. 3.

8. This ideological motif is also found outside Ellis' texts; Langland notes that Brontë's Rochester prefers to identify Jane Eyre as a fairy rather than as his employee (76 n9).

9. E. P. Whipple, "Novels of the Season," *North American Review* 67 (1848): 355–56, qtd. in Showalter 139–40.

10. The *Jane Eyre* quotations are from Jane's famous feminist outcry that opens chapter 12 (Brontë 141).

11. Even Olive's stepsister Christal Manners—the counterpart of Adèle (in her parentage and Parisian style), Bertha Mason (in her murderous attempt on Olive), and also, in her failure "to wrestle with an angry spirit" (184) the child Jane—is offered the possibility of redemption. Even within an "almost . . . demon" (288) lurks the possibility of "a lingering angel" (292).

12. Here art and religion, as discussed below.

13. While Dickens' immediate critical target is George Cruikshank, whose retold fairy tales promoted temperance, Dickens' retelling of Cinderella burlesques the "Woman Question" in particular. Cinderella (a member of the Juvenile Band of Hope since the age of four) goes off to the ball dressed in "rich sky-blue satin pantaloons gathered at the ankle" (115), courtesy of her fairy godmother (a confirmed free-trader). Upon marriage to her Prince (a Total Abstainer) Cinderella becomes a dictator who gives women the vote, gaining them entry into public life but, consequently, disenfranchisement from love.

14. For disapproval, see, for example, W. Y. Sellar:

> Those who have most earnestly studied disputed questions of doctrine and philosophy, who have felt the serious duty of rightly and honestly using their reason in the pursuit of truth, who have learned to despise sophistry and rhetoric on moral as well as intellectual grounds, would not, even had they the power, condescend either to trifle in this way with their deepest convictions, or to take advantage of the idle hours and weaker susceptibilities of their readers. (216)

For ridicule, see George Eliot's delineation of the "most pitiable of all silly novels by lady novelists ... what we may call the *oracular* species—novels intended to expound the writer's religious, philosophical, or moral theories" (148).

15. *Charity,* see above.

16. See esp. bottom 222.

17. "On Atonement and Satisfaction," qtd. in Reardon, *Religious Thought* 247.

18. See ch. 11, esp. 101.

19. "Our Female Novelists," 38 [1859]: 308; qtd. in Fryckstedt 69.

20. "Address at Croyden" (3 July 1871); qtd. in Helsinger et al. 163.

10

Marie Corelli

"The Story of One Forgotten"

Brenda Ayres

For two decades she was the most popular woman novelist in the world (Bullock xv), the "best-selling novelist of her generation" (Bigland 11). One of her biographers claims that while Queen Victoria was alive, Marie Corelli was the "second most famous Englishwoman in the world" (Masters 6). Her best-seller, *The Sorrows of Satan* (1895), went through sixty editions with immediate sales that exceeded any British novel to date.[1] According to another biographer, this novel made her name as familiar as Charles Dickens to most English readers (Bullock 117), and it became known as the first actual best-seller in England (Federico 7; Ransom 80). Half of all of her novels were world best-sellers, selling more than 100,000 copies each year (Casey 163).[2] One of her most ardent fans was the queen herself. The novelist's fame having gained a friendship with the prince of Wales, Corelli was the only writer invited to attend his coronation (Bullock 103–4)

To date nine books have been written on Corelli, the latest being in 1999 and 2000,[3] with a number of other significant criticism published about her works.[4] This volume and recent attention indicate her continuing importance as a Victorian woman and writer. However, the only thing upon which her biographers and critics agree is that they cannot agree upon Corelli's life or the quality of her writing. The novelist was dedicated to generating a stream of fiction which included not only thirty novels[5] in thirty-seven years, but also fiction about her life, especially about her parentage and age. As far as the biographers can determine, perhaps the year was 1855 when Mary (or the Scottish equivalent, Minnie) Mackay was born, perhaps the illegitimate daughter of a journalist, Dr. Charles Mackay, LL.D. Mackay was a one-time colleague of Dickens (Bullock 5)

and a neighbor to George Meredith. After the death of his wife, when Minnie
was ten years old, he married her mother. Following a string of frustrated governesses, Minnie was sent to a convent school, but which and where, no one
knows for sure.

Her first pseudonym was Rose Trevor (Masters 56), but by the time she sold
her first novel, she had taken the name of a famous Italian musician, Arcangelo
Corelli. That novel was *A Romance of Two Worlds* (1886), an instant best-seller,
published, according to Corelli, when she was still a teen although she was actually thirty-one. It is difficult to reconstruct Marie Corelli—not just her life
but also her views on gender as well as a critical assessment of her work. When
Corelli, being rather litigious, appeared in court, she apparently had no difficulty
lying under oath about her age. It is no wonder that biographers have had an
arduous task in piecing together an accurate profile. Regardless, disturbingly, all
of the male *and* female biographers (except for the work done most recently by
Teresa Ransom and Annette Federico)[6] have been preoccupied with Corelli's
physical presence, marital status, and passion for animals and flowers[7]—all conveyed negatively. Instead of remaining unbiased in their focus on the novelist
and her writing, they resort to ad hominem. George Bullock, for example, frequently tells the reader that Corelli was "squat and tubby." Brian Masters postulates that she wore too-tight underwear, which caused her to need an operation
later (66). Even a female biographer takes a jab, describing her "almost as broad
as she was long" (Bigland 226). More than once all of the biographers mention
that she dressed more like a young girl—than what? A fright of fifty? Such details have been selected by people who are judging a writer by a different set of
signifiers than if they were referring to a man, and they are failing to treat professionally another professional. Did Corelli write the way she did because she
had a "dumpy little figure"? Did she perceive herself as always being youthful?
Actually several of her novels did voice a belief that science could find a way to
prevent aging. Yet, none of the biographers, except the two most recent (Ransom and Federico) justify their choice of physical detail in relationship to her
writing. This sort of bias undermines for me any assessment that these biographers have made on her literary work. Furthermore, this bias is not much different from what was levied against most of the women writers of the nineteenth
century, and especially against Corelli by her contemporaries in the press. This
is the sort of bias, in my opinion, that has caused many worthy novels by Victorian women to become stories of those forgotten.

There has been too long a history of criticism flaring ad hominem and sim-
plistically reading text with a certain set of expectations formed by critics who
valued novels by males and devalued novels by females. Especially in the hey-
day of Corelli's novels with the New Woman movement, much of the criticism
against her was sexist. Federico, the latest author of a book-length treatment of
Corelli, suggests that one of the reasons the novelist lied and dressed as to appear hyperfeminine was for public relations. After all, the *Westminster Review*
touted her as "the greatest genius of self-advertisement" (1906). Federico ex-

tensively argues that Corelli lived in a new era of book marketing, in which publicity sold the books. Early on, Corelli learned of the acrimony male critics bore, not just to her works but also to her person (14). The turn of the century faced a multiplicity of sexual and class complexities (such as Oscar Wilde's indictment for "gross indecencies") a reaction against what was perceived as a feminization of the culture caused by the volume of novels written by women as well as the emergence of the New Woman novel. Conversely, many were alarmed by the masculinization from industrialization, science, technology, capitalization, imperialism, and war. Others blamed the rise of decadence in society on the aristocratic who had the unchecked and ungovernable power and privilege to wield immorality. Still others looked to the anachronistic aristocracy to return life to the old ways. These were the waters through which Corelli had to navigate. Federico rightly describes Corelli and her work as a "blend of masculine militancy and feminine mellifluousness" (110); to compensate for her inflammable prose, she dressed as if she were an ingenue, this to check the critics (who, once they met Corelli in person, often expressed their surprise that she did not look like a militant, bluestocking man hater), to appear the part of an anti-New Woman, and to sell an image of herself that in turn, sold her books. At times she was descendant of aristocracy and dined with royalty. At other times, she was just middle class or even less—a poor lost orphan. She chose whatever image seemed to work for public relations, her publisher, and her critics. Ransom suggests another reason why Corelli might have lied often and worked at projecting a youthful image: to throw off those same dogged critics who seemed determined to expose her illegitimate birth status, one that would have still carried a stigma at the end of the century (4).

Unfortunately, the Masters biography did not consider such contexts, but just as its predecessors, perpetuated sexism in its portrayal of Corelli. Continuing his misplaced focus on her character, Masters has the further audacity to assume that she was a prude about sex and thought it a revolting subject (236–38). He neglects to provide any evidence of such views. Janet Casey likewise assumes that Corelli "cherished her role as a Victorian woman who must necessarily recoil from any discussion of a frankly sexual nature and politely avoid the sordid and the radically unconventional" (165). Masters deduces that she must have had such great physical needs in that she had no husband; instead, she lavished her love on animals and flowers (236–43).

The first assumption is baffling insofar as all of Corelli's heroines and villainesses are passionate and physical[8]—unlike many female characters in canonized works. Mary Dean in *The Treasure of Heaven* is only part angel in the house: a truly good, self-denying, nurturing woman who supports herself and had supported her dying father. The other part of her is self-reliant and capable of taking care not only of herself but also of the men in her life. They don't protect her, provide for her, or define her. Mary rescues David Helmsley, who, unbeknownst to her, is the richest man in the world. He had abandoned his wealth to travel the roads of England to seek out a kindlier people than he had known among his peers. Indeed the poorest of the poor share what little they have with him. In the middle of a raging storm, he nearly dies from hunger, depression, and cold when the physically strong Mary drags him to her cottage.

As he recovers, he learns that she is thirty-four and prefers to remain single. Besides that preference, she is single because "Providence ... persuad[es] men generally to choose thriftless and flighty women for their wives, and to leave the capable ones single" (291). Mary Dean performs all the duties within and without the house, seemingly in no need of a husband. When Dave finally dies and leaves all of his money to Mary, another man, one who has come to love her, refuses to marry her because he despises wealth and it hurts his pride that she has money and he does not. Nevertheless she knows that he is a good man who would do good things for needy people if only he had money. To remove herself as an obstacle to his doing good work, she decides to throw herself into the sea, thereby leaving him the wealth. Her beloved comes to her rescue and professes his love. Mary Dean is an independent, intelligent, content, strong—emotionally and physically—robust woman full of passion and courage, and with rosy cheeks. The reader is made aware of her physicality.

In addition to strong women, Corelli rarely withholds description of passion between men and women. The following is Alwyn's experience in kissing the beautiful Edris in *Ardath*:

Ah! ... what divine ecstasy,—what wild and fiery transport filled him then! .. Her kiss, like a penetrating lighting-flash, pierced to the very centre of his being,—the moon beams swam round him in eddying circles of gold—the white field heaved to and fro, ... he caught her waist and clung to her, and in the burning marvel of that moment he forget [*sic*] everything, save that, whether spirit or mortal, she was in woman's witching shape, and that all the glamour of her beauty was his for this one night at least, this night which now in the speechless, glorious delirium of love that overwhelmed him, seemed like the Mahometan's night of Al-Kadr, "a better than a thousand months!" (86)

These are not the words of a prude or one who believed sex to be vulgar. Rather, Corelli believed that sex was a heavenly passion, a "chief joy, if not the only one of life" (*Treasure* 48).

The next assumption that Masters makes is that because Corelli never married, she was sexually frustrated. What follows is his judicious opinion of her and women in general:

Unconsciously, her lust for power, her wish to control other people, to manipulate events, to have the last word, all derived from a need to replace the sexual love denied her ... Women without men usually have overweening ambition, coupled with a ruthless determination to satisfy it. Deprived of the primitive function which is their right, they spend their lives trying to show the world that they too can achieve something. (238)

Whether or not Corelli ever had a serious love affair cannot be agreed upon by her biographers, although Ransom provides a persuasive history of Corelli's love for Arthur Severn, who treated her abominably. Regardless, she did not marry, although her books preached to women that they were to obey men and although she stopped obeying men altogether when her father died. On the subject of marriage she made this statement: "I have three pets at home which together, answer the same purpose as a husband ... I have a dog which growls in the morning, a parrot which swears all the afternoon, and a cat which comes home late at night" (qtd. in Bullock 200). In *Jane*, the heroine is content to be single and is quite productive as a result. In *Romance*, Zara, who believes that her soul mate is not on earth and believes that to marry without a union of the souls is reprehensible, thwarts the attentions of a prince. At one point when he attempts to force himself upon her with what could only turn into a rape, she smites him with the electricity that flames within her own spirit. In *Ziska: The Problem of a Wicked Soul*, this reader is not clear who is the possessor of the wicked soul. Princess Ziska is a woman who had been betrayed in another life by a man whom she deeply loved. In fact, because she got in the way of his ambition, he killed her. Tellingly Corelli wrote: "Men always murder—morally if not physically—the women who love them too well" (119). In an act of revenge, Ziska kills her current lover, who is really the reincarnation of her murderer from that former life. Mavis in *The Sorrows of Satan* desires love but is content to remain single. She is never lonely, she says, but finds great and satisfaction in her solitude and work as a writer, which is assuredly the voice of Corelli.

When the biographers pitch her as a frustrated, overweight, middle-aged woman who must be miserable because she never married and had children, they bank on a miscalculated and unprofessional accounting of Corelli's life. When Bullock complains about her split infinitives, her problem with French adjectives, her melodrama and sentimentality (xv)—at a time when melodrama and sentimentality were considered art forms, and today are respected as cultural signs—and when he glibly infers that because many of her characters seem to be both superhuman and disappointing, Corelli must have had an inferiority complex (66)—and when Masters complains of her "ultra clichés," "exuberant style," and lack of careful characterization (13–15), none of these criticisms, or what the other biographers have to say, persuade me that Corelli has not penned literature worth reading in the twenty-first century.

Yet, aside from a plethora of criticism by her contemporaries as well as her biographers, several of them applauded her ability to tell a story. The first Corelli novel I read was *Thelma: A Society Novel* (1887). Set in Norway, the narrative is as rich as any in the current Victorian canon:

Midnight,—without darkness, without stars! Midnight,—and the unwearied sun stood, yet visible in the heavens, like a victorious king throned on a dais of royal purple bordered with gold. The sky above him,—his canopy,—gleamed with a cold yet lustrous blue, while across it slowly flitted a few wandering clouds of palest amber, deepening, as they sailed along, to a tawny orange. A broad stream of light falling, as it were, from the centre of the magnificent orb, shot lengthwise across the Altenfjord. . . . Absolute silence prevailed. Not even the cry of a sea-mew or kittiwake broke the almost death-like stillness.(2)

Not only are the details fresh and vivid (she was praised by many Norwegians for her description of a country that she had never visited), they establish tone and mood, and provide signs for the novel's theme. This was not the writing of a "feminine twaddler."[9]

The discovery of a grotto, which holds the sarcophagus of a dead woman named Thelma, is unsurpassed in gothic narrative. I was riveted to the story. As for passion, Corelli's *Thelma* was no usual, sentimental love story told by a blue-stocking spinster to ingenues dreaming of happy marriages and romance. So powerfully conveyed is the passion that one man comes to feel for an intelligent, physically strong (she rows her own boat), and beautiful Norwegian maid, and so wickedly passionate is the Reverend Dyceworthy for that same maid, that the novel was banned in several libraries, which certainly must have embarrassed Corelli, who constantly denounced prurient novels by her contemporaries.

Masters also praised Corelli: "She ignored the literary fashions of the day, loathed naturalism, had a remarkable instinct for dramatic tension, and above all an extraordinary unbridled imagination"; he must have written this after reading Corelli's second novel, which was, coincidentally the second novel of hers that I read. *Vendetta: The Story of One Forgotten* (1886), intrigues from cover to cover with its dramatic tension. Supposedly based upon a true story according to the author's preface, one Count Fabio Romani, thought dead by cholera, is buried alive in the family vault. His awakening among the bones of his ancestors is as deliciously macabre as Poe. After Romani digs himself out of the vault, he learns that his wife had been having an affair with his best friend and that she treats their daughter without a single beat of motherly love in her cold bosom. Later her total disregard of the child will result in the child's death. As Stella dies in her father's arms, I sobbed aloud with sorrow and anger, just as Corelli had meant for me to do. Romani works his revenge on the two lovers in a tightly woven, carefully plotted narrative. And then in perfect Victorian convention, an earthquake—God's judgment—befalls the contessa (Romani's wife), and with much gory bloodletting, the bad woman dies, her hand quivering out from beneath a rock.

But the reader is left haunted by something said earlier in the novel: "What is the usual fate that falls even to the best woman? Sorrow, pain and petty worry, unsatisfied longings, incompleted aims, the disappointment of an imperfect and fettered life" (206). *Vendetta* is no typical Victorian sensational or sentimental novel that clearly delineates good and evil.

After this delightful reading, I wondered why I had never heard of Corelli before. It was then I decided to write this essay for the *Silent Voices* collection, about a woman who represented so well the maligned writers of the nineteenth century that I thought deserved recognition in my own age. That is also when I decided to use *Vendetta*'s subtitle: *The Story of One Forgotten*. Corelli's works are representative of many Victorian women writers who once knew fame from their writing but somewhere along the way got buried alive. However, they still can articulate perceptions of the period crucial to current scholarship of Victorian culture. Their demonstration of literary quality needs to be reassessed as well.

Then I read *Ardath* (1889). I must say this was one of the most painful readings of my career. I thought I would never finish it. All the while I was thinking, "Oh, this is why I never heard of Marie Corelli. I could never get my students to read this thing." Ironic to my project, the novel's subtitle is *The Story of a Dead Self:* Perhaps certain novels do live out their life spans and should be left to the decline and fall of a once thriving empire, just like Babylon in *Ardath*—except it was Corelli's conviction, as illustrated in *Ardath*, that people, including Babylonians, never die.

To Corelli, *Ardath* was her masterpiece. And the Reverend William Gladstone, three-time prime minister of England, was so moved by it that he called upon Corelli, leaving his wife to wait in the carriage while he told the novelist that the work was "a magnificent conception," and that he considered her "a great power to move the masses and sway the thoughts of the people" (qtd. in Bigland 109).

Ardath starts out with great promise. Following a quote from Keats' *Endymion* comes this:

Deep in the heart of the Caucasus mountains [*sic*] a wild storm was gathering. Drear shadows drooped and thickened above the Pass of Dariel,—that terrific gorge which like a mere thread seems to hang between the toppling frost-bound heights above and the black abysmal depths below,—clouds, fringed ominously with lurid green and white, drifted heavily yet swiftly across the jagged peaks where, looming largely out of the mist, the snow-capped crest of Mount Kazbek rose coldly white against the darkness of the threatening sky. (5)

Such lyrical prose goes on for three lovely pages. Then Corelli satirizes ethnocentric English tourists (which she does even better in the opening of *Ziska*),[10] continuing to provide fresh narrative and insights. Afterward, the pages grow long when a British poet and atheist, Theos Alwyn, debates the existence of God and meaning of the universe with a monk, Heliobas.[11] This subject continues much later in the novel between Alwyn and Zabâstes and halts the fiction. Nevertheless, Corelli addresses some key issues that preoccupied many a thoughtful mind at the end of the century, such as science and education, hedonism and religion, science and nature, reasoning and emotion, art and emotion—all deliberated upon by Matthew Arnold in *Culture and Anarchy* and elsewhere. However, Corelli puts such debate into the mouth of seemingly real people who are directly affected by their own and each other's views and/or their unresolved conflicts. Albeit perhaps inappropriate for a novel, regardless of how didactic many novels were allowed to be, Corelli's treatise is intelligent, passionate, and urgent, and it casts clearly all sides of the debates.[12]

Ardath's plot leaps forward when Alwyn is transported to Al-Kyris of 5000 B.C. There he meets the poet laureate, Sah-lûma, who the reader soon comes to realize is a reincarnation of his former self. The egotistical Sah-lûma is also the incarnation of his narcissistic self.

Part of Corelli's *fin de siècle* appeal is that she weaves into her plot ideas of automatic writing, magnetic healing, reincarnation, soul transmigration, and mesmerism as if they were scientific procedures. Knowledge and practice of these paranormal phenomena were widespread but still quite controversial. In both her century and ours, many fundamentalists have considered these to be forbidden acts of the occult. Yet many important people did accept them and not just as religious practices. Even Mark Twain came to believe in magnetic healing (Goldsmith 69), a significant point in that Twain visited Corelli in 1907 and they must have exchanged theories and experiences on the subject. Even more people could not reconcile religion/the supernatural/the spiritual with science. However, to Corelli there were no conflicts between them unless people believed in one to the exclusion of the other. It is not surprising in an age of telephones, telegraphs, and other uses of electricity, plus the knowledge of atoms, that people such as Corelli came to be convinced that the basis of the entire spirit world was electricity, that one could pass one's own electricity into another to bring healing, give knowledge, and transport to another body or time or world. And it is no wonder that Corelli held that these ideas were securely grounded in science. They were definitely grounded in history in that the ancient Greeks had used magnets to heal (Goldsmith 20).

Their offering of an alternate belief that united science and spirit is one reason Corelli's novels were so successful. Hers were a strident backlash to the decreasing influence of religion close to the end of the century. In every novel she deals with this subject to the degree that "nothing could have exceeded the passion with which she attacked moral lapses, whilst championing the purity and going to the rescue of the weak. She had the zeal of a missionary, the declamatory methods of an evangelist, and she captured the loyalty of her readers at one sitting" (Bullock 45). Many of her works appealed to three kinds of people: "the sentimental Christian who was attentive to the moral tonics of fiction, the enthusiastic student of science or of psychic forces who attempted to expand the boundaries of the mind, and the sober members of the working class who would benefit from a steady fare of exotically forbidden stories promising material rewards for virtue" (Kowalczyk 851).

I was not thinking about all of this while making my way through *Ardath*. I just assumed that Alwyn's transport to Babylon and his resulting love/hate relationship with Sah-lûma was a clever, psychological probing into his self. Corelli herself thought it a profound, psychological novel (Masters 82), although the critics did not share this opinion. Read as an introspection, including complexities of one's multiple gender perceptions and sexual desires within self (except when Corelli enters the novel and preaches against evil women), the ideas in the novel and how they are presented are fascinating, original, visionary, and brilliant.

A nexus of gender indices is readily apparent in this description of Alwyn's meeting of Sah-lûma: "of his own superior height and superior muscular development—but what were these physical advantages compared to the classic perfection of Sah-lûma's beauty?—beauty combining the delicate with the vigorous, such as is shadowed forth in the artistic-conceptions of the god Apollo. His features, faultlessly regular, were redeemed from all effeminacy by the ennobling impress of high thought and inward inspiration" (102). At other times, Corelli does not dismiss Sah-lûma's feminine features nor Alwyn's feminine attraction to Sah-lûma: "The idea that any evil fate was in store for the bright, beautiful creature, whom he had, oddly enough, learned to love more than himself, moved him to an almost womanish apprehension" (251). His absolute submission to this man whom he has come to idolize so that he constantly does the other's bidding against his own better judgment is behavior more to be expected from a Victorian woman. Now Corelli would have the reader know that their mutual attraction is simple brotherhood and companionship (104), and certainly, in reconciling one with one's self, one would hope to experience these bonds. Regardless, there is more:

As [Alwyn] spoke Sah-lûma regarded him intently,—Theos met his gazed [sic] frankly and unflinchingly. Surely there was some singular power of attraction between the two! ... for as their flashing eyes again dwelt earnestly on one another, they both smiled, and Sah-lûma, advancing, proffered his hand. Theos at once accepted it, a curious sensation of pleasure tingling through his frame, as he pressed those slender brown fingers in his own cordial clasp. (104)

Of course, once a reader understands that Sah-lûma is Alwyn in a former life, the magic and chemistry can be explained in other than homoerotic terms, but why should they? Even if Alwyn falls in love with himself, why can it not be a homoerotic love, especially if he is finding within himself the "other" whom he had never known nor loved before? Here, whether Corelli intended it or not, is the male, as Richard Dellamora finds him in Victorian culture, as both subject and object of desire at the same time (1); for Alwyn to love Sah-lûma is to say that Sah-lûma loves Alwyn, and that they are one and the same. Yet neither is exactly a rigidly defined Victorian male. In Denis de Rougemont's theory of heterosexual love, the man comes to love in the female, the spiritual and mystical—"his true *self*" (104); therefore, he is not really in love with the "other" so much as he is in love with the other side of himself. De Rougemont argues that at its base, passion is narcissistic. When one falls in love with another and that love is reciprocated, it is a positive validation of self. It confirms that one must be wonderful if someone else thinks so. The more wonderful the partner is, the more wonderful, then, the other must be or else the partner would not value the other as much. Ultimately, the purpose of loving is not altruistic, for the betterment of the other, but for self-aggrandizement. Love between two equals—and Alwyn and Sah-lûma are definitely equals—is "an enrichment, each enlarging himself through the other" (Firestone 145). Love is blind: The beloved is perfect, and the "I" seen through the eyes of the beloved is perfect as well; therefore, the "I" thinks he is perfect too. Men fall in love with their own projected image (Firestone 153).

Obviously these tenets would be at odds with most nineteenth-century novelists who emphasized death of self in both Christianity and in marriage. Re-

gardless, here in Corelli is her Alwyn, a Victorian man who has denied God and
come to the end of his own life. He is supposed to die to himself and be born
again in Christ. Yet he has met himself, and instead of denying the love for himself, he comes to value it: "In his Dream of a single night, he had loved the brilliant Phantom of his Former Self more than his own present Identity" (396).
This is a remarkable psychological and philosophical insight: That a man, to come
to know and love his real self, has to meet a "Phantom," a "Specter," "an
ephemeral Shadow-Existence." There he finds the Keatsian "hope beyond the
shadow of a dream." This is a reality more vivid than reality itself because it has
become knowable.

Even more exciting about this revelation is that the other self is androgynous.
Alwyn's response to self is often masculine and feminine at the same time.

Terry Eagleton's theory is quite apropos to explain this dynamic. He describes
the Jane/Rochester romance in *Jane Eyre* as an enactment of "curious rhythm
of sexual attraction and antagonism, and in a series of reversals of sexual roles"
(30–31). This is an accurate analysis of the developing relationship between
Alwyn and Sah-lûma. Eagleton observes that a man, to attract one of the "opposite sex," attempts to become a woman (i.e., Rochester's disguise as a female
Gypsy). The gender change allows him to gain a better understanding of what
it means to be female and indicates a willingness to become feminized to join
with the feminine (31). At times Sah-lûma is feminine—with his curls, his tunic,
his artistic sensitivities, and his unabashed physical closeness with Alwyn. All
the while, the women in his court and throughout the city are madly in love
with him, but he does not return their love (although he does share in their ado-
ration for himself). He is passionately seduced by a woman of extraordinary
beauty and evil, the high priestess, Lysia. Alwyn is also seduced by her. This is
no love triangle, though. It is much more complicated in that Alwyn is sometimes jealous of Sah-lûma's love for Lysia, not just because he desires Lysia, but
because he desires Sah-lûma. Sah-lûma experiences the same sort of jealousy
for Alwyn.

Quite simply (or not), Alwyn comes to a love for himself—for his androgynous self. *Ardath*, despite some of its tedious narrative, is a greater romance than
the typical paradigm: Boy loves girl, boy can't get girl, boy finally gets girl (or
girl gets boy). Significantly, the novel's subtitle, "The Story of a Dead Self," de-
parts from Victorian conventions of preaching the virtues of dying to self. Instead, the novel begins with a character who is dead to himself, but will end up
alive and in love with himself, and thereby capable of truly loving others.
Kierkegaard said that all true love begins with the true self.

Unfortunately, most biographers and critics have failed to appreciate the original perspectives that Corelli offers as products of the Victorian period, during
a time when gender identities and religious dogma were questioned. Critics have
also expressed ambivalence toward the quality of her writing. Upon reading her
first novel, *The Romance of Two Worlds* (1886), Oscar Wilde wrote her, "You
certainly tell of marvellous things in a marvellous way" (qtd. in Masters 60 and

Ransom 36). The novel was also praised by Wilkie Collins (Masters 60) and the queen of Italy (85). Queen Victoria herself asked for a presentation copy and invited Corelli to lunch. On the other hand, a critic pronounced it "pure bosh" (qtd. in Bigland 78). Despite the mixed reviews, no one can dispute the wide readership Corelli enjoyed and the powerful effect of her novels. Passages were often quoted from the pulpit. Many credited *Wormwood* (1890) for Switzerland's initiating severe regulation of drinking and France's control of absinthe (Masters 108). In the United States, a new church was created, founded on the doctrines presented in *Romance* as well as a new town in Colorado called Corelli City (Masters 94, Bigland 110). Hundreds of babies born after *Thelma* were named after its eponymous character, whose name was created by Corelli (Ransom 41, 44).

Popularity aside, most critics, myself included, agree that the novels exhibit a drastic unevenness of information, logic, and narrative craft, which might account for the ambivalent and conflicting reviews. George Bullock (and many of Corelli's critics) complained about her blunders in detail, the famous being in *Barabbus*, in which she unluckily assumed that Judas would have had a sister, Judith, with a surname of Iscariot. A newspaper mocked the novel with the headline "Now Barabbus was a rotter."[13] One *Morning Post* reviewer described her writing as "full-blooded Turkey carpet style"; and another, "impeccably bad taste" (qtd. in Masters 12). Most biographers and critics agree that her writing is excessive, verbose, and heavy-handed, without balance. She simply wrote all that came to mind without selective elimination or craft.[14]

After having read a dozen or so of Corelli's novels, I trudged through much of the same bog, so that I felt as if I were walking in circles. Corelli, through the thirty-seven years of her writing, rarely diverted from themes, even if she determined not to produce any two books that would be "the least alike."[15] Her novels were her podium for some very relentlessly strong opinions. Americans, for example, were crude, superficial, and materialistic. Clergy were the greatest enemies of Christianity. Jews were moneymongers. The Italian countryside was a wasteland. Paris, if not all of France, had no morals at all. Libraries were "centres for infectious diseases." *The Master Christian* attacks Catholicism, as do many of her other novels.[16] She often accused the clergy of being in league with the devil. The one theme that predominated was the "New Woman" and what she perceived that accompanied this movement as a relaxed morality and dissolution of family and church. Behind the decadent woman were salacious novels, hers being the exception.

According to her, women had lost their morals because they read such books as Hardy's *Tess* (1891), Dowie's *Gallia* (1893), Egerton's *Keynotes* (1893) and *Discords* (1894), Grand's *Heavenly Twins* (1893), Brooke's *A Superfluous Woman* (1894), Iota's *The Yellow Aster* (1894), and Allen's *The Woman Who Did* (1895). She lambasts all of these novels by name. But the one writer who was the real downfall of humanity to Corelli was Swinburne (*Sorrows* 327). Yet, strangely, Corelli's first chapter in *Thelma* begins with an epigraph from Swinburne: "Dream by dream shot through her eyes, and each Outshone that last that lighted." She often railed Ouida (Bullock 110) as did many who were tired of her "shocking romances" (qtd. in Bigland 76). However, in the spring of 1890, Corelli wrote an article for *Belgravia Magazine* entitled "A Word about Ouida," in which she championed "the greatness" of Ouida's work (Bigland 117–18).

These contradictions are not nearly as baffling as are Corelli's views on women. Time and time again she said she was not a suffragette. She believed "A woman who really loves a man ... governs him unconsciously to herself, by the twin powers of sex and instinct. She was intended for his help-mate, to guide him in the right way by her finer forces" (*Treasure* 404). Women who sought equality with men, as typified by Honoria Hatwell-Tibkin in *My Wonderful Wife,* smoke cigars and wear pants and receive these kind of reactions: "Ye Gods! My wife Looked Like a Man!"[17] But Corelli was not saying that women were incapable of exerting power and influence. Women naturally had "keen instinct, close observation, and large sympathies"; they ought "to produce greater masterpieces than men" (*Wife* 22). In many ways, women were superior to men, according to Corelli, and should help men behave themselves and evolve into higher forms of being. At other times, Corelli seemed to contradict herself, such as in this passage: "When women voluntarily resign her position as the silent monitors and models of grace and purity, down will go all pillars of society"; England will become as barbaric as those other nations that are "anti-Jesus" (*Wife* 41–42). Notwithstanding this strong warning, Corelli was no silent monitor. In fact, she was the first woman invited to lecture at the Royal Society of Literature (Bullock 143).

If one were to conclude that Corelli was conflicted, it would not come as a surprise to any Victorian reader familiar with those novelists who spoke loudly against the "New Woman" and women's rights.[18] Having a voice with which to speak publicly appears contradictory to the notion that women should not have a place in the public sphere. The inconsistencies are reason enough to value what Corelli has written, providing further insight into a Victorian culture (then and now) that wants it both ways for women: the silence and the voice, the submission and the exertion. Janet Casey appreciates that Corelli "reflects the confusion of an entire generation of women, a generation confronted at once with the suffragette movement and the decline of the feminine ideal as perceived in the Victorian age" (164). Her writings appealed to women who were confused because she herself, and her characters could exhibit a feminist spirit couched in a "fundamentally conventional Victorian ideology" (166).

Yet, perhaps Corelli and her work were not conflicted and confused about gender. *Sorrows,* like *Ardath,* is a fascinating satire, often dialectical, on gender perceptions. The protagonist, Geoffrey Tempest, marries a woman who is superbly beautiful, but hard-hearted, manipulative, unfaithful, and mean. Tempest, a writer himself, jealous of the success of another writer, Mavis Clare,[19] believes that no woman writer is capable of logic or "correct opinion." That he is terribly mistaken about the capabilities of Mavis becomes obvious, so obvious that Corelli must be challenging gender standards that men have set for women as reductive and unacceptable. Mavis' reasoning in her discussions with Tempest is thoughtful and intelligent, supported by literary and philosophical allusions, and not induced by emotion, in contrast to Tempest's dialogue and behavior throughout the entire novel.

Once he meets Mavis, despite her prominence as an author and her independence as a woman, he learns how sweet, pure, honest, simple, and disciplined she is. He comes to regret and resent his marriage to Sibyl. Although the reader is not to sympathize with Sibyl, Corelli does tell her story: She has had no choice but to marry Tempest because he is a millionaire, and although her father is titled, they have been desperately poor. All the while she loves Tempest's best friend, Lucio Rimânez (who turns out to be Satan). When her husband realizes her unhappiness, he excuses it as mere hysteria, a female condition. In response, Sibyl screams:

Hysteria!—nothing else! It is accountable for everything that moves a woman's nature. A woman has no right to have any emotions that cannot be cured by smelling-salts! Heartache?—pooh!—cut her stay-lace! Despair and a sense of sin and misery?—nonsense!—bathe her temples with vinegar! An uneasy conscience?—ah!—for an uneasy conscience there is nothing better than sal volatile! Woman is a toy—a breakable fool's toy; and when she *is* broken, throw her aside and have done with her—don't try to piece together the fragile rubbish! (271)

Then, sparing the reader no possible error in understanding, Corelli has Sibyl declare herself his property, a piece of goods that he purchased (160–61). Lucio/Satan, who has had a long history of experience and knowledge of relationships between men and women, has this to say: "Myself, I prefer the barbaric fashion of old times, when rough savages fought for their women as they fought for their cattle, treated them as cattle, and kept them in their place, never dreaming of endowing them with such strong virtues as truth and honour!" (293). If this is not Corelli mischief enough, she has him remind Tempest that biblical patriarchs, like Abraham, took two to three wives and a handful of concubines, and Abraham was "the very soul of virtue according to sacred lore" (31). None of this endorses a gender ideology in which a woman is to submit herself to a husband and that husband is to have absolute authority over her. All the while that Sibyl seems to be an anti-ideal in contrast to the feminine Mavis, the problem begins with the male who thinks he can treat women like possessions and status instead of thinking, feeling human beings who have needs of their own. And, even as Mavis dresses in ruffles, serves tea, surrounds herself with flowers and adoring animals, and is solicitous to her guests, she is a strong-minded, strong-willed woman who has definite opinions of which she exercises no reserve in expressing to men who might disagree with her. In fact, she, unlike Tempest, is able to identify Lucio as Satan and to resist his allures. Her character has more faculty than does Tempest's.

Besides transversing and obfuscating gender ideals, another reason it is neither easy nor appropriate to pigeonhole Corelli's gender politics is that, despite her proselytizing about how a woman should be a helpmate, she did not see gender as polarized as the critics suppose. In several novels, she refers to God as being both male and female. For example, from *The Soul of Lilith:* "There are two governing forces in the Universe ... one, the masculine, is Love; the other, the feminine, is Beauty. These Two, reigning together, are God—just as man and wife are One ... When God made man in His Own image, it was as Male and Female" (136). If Corelli could see the male and the female within the same spirit, it is not surprising that her characters conflate gender and confound conventional notions of male/female identities. To Corelli, there is only one identity: It is male and female combined. Peripheral to that identity are power, politics, and personalities—all of which would be unnecessary if people realized their complete selves as male and female, equally balanced and fused into one harmonious whole. At least, this was her ideal: Restrictive gender roles were the evils of the world. Notwithstanding, the solution was not for women to act like men, or vice versa. They were to transcend this world to a state of pure femaleness and maleness that could unite into one complete whole, like God.

This perception is demonstrated in *A Romance of Two Worlds.* The nameless female protagonist meets Zara for the first time and relates, "Never shall I behold again any face or form so divinely beautiful!" (1: 185). And then she describes in detail the woman's figure, throat, complexion, eyes and lashes, hair, and clothes. From that point on, Corelli furnishes many more intimate scenes where the two women kiss and touch each other, but she reminds the reader that such displays and feelings are simply in the spirit of sisterly love. Regardless, these scenes voyeuristically depict Zara as the object of desire, not just for the reader but also for the female narrator. For instance, in one scene the narrator enters Zara's boudoir to find her sleeping: "her hair scattered loosely on the pillows," her "delicately tinted cheeks," her "lips tenderly red, like the colour on budding apple-blossoms in early spring"—parted to show small white teeth. Her night-dress is slightly undone, which slightly reveals and disguises her neck and "rounded bosom" (2.88). These are sensual details noted by the female narrator written by a female novelist. Brian Masters insists that Corelli was not a lesbian, despite her long-term, interdependent relationship with Bertha Vyver. This woman, a friend from youth, lived with Corelli for forty-seven years (276–78). Regardless of any other implications, Corelli's most cherished and enduring relationship was with another woman with whom she a domestic consanguinity. Homosexuality, heterosexuality, and bisexuality are tags that simply fail to explain and identify relationships between people and gender perceptions. Reductive signifiers are ineffective in discussing Corelli's novels. An excellent case in point is *A Romance of Two Worlds.* This is the story of a woman who begins a spiritual quest to know something greater than herself, not much unlike many of Corelli's readers who had abandoned the security of religion. What she discovers is the greatness of her self-existence. In part she learns this through her relationship with Zara. On one hand, Zara is a superior being and exists exteriorly. Subconsciously the narrator may desire her sexually, to bond with her to a degree of intimacy and sense of completion possible through sexually merging with another. On the other hand, Zara is a fully realized woman, the epitome of what the narrator desires to be herself. Her desire to unite with Zara is a desire to unite with her own most female self. To love Zara is to love womanhood as it is ideally and spiritually embodied in Zara.

Therefore, when Corelli laments the unsexing of women, she is not opting for a traditional status quo for women. She believes that women, as women, can enjoy a sphere of influence, power, and freedom that is forfeited if they try to behave as men. Clearly in *My Wonderful Wife!* Corelli denounces women for dressing like men, as did many men who seemed to be threatened by this practice. In the late half of the century, women were rebelling against constrictive clothes that bound them physically and politically. Although the wife, Honoria, is quite radical in behavior and ideas, such as believing marriage to be an outdated institution, she represents many freethinkers of the day who hoped for an alternate social order. Corelli does seem to participate in a backlash of indignation. However, what is not clear is why Corelli objects so much to women dressing as men. After all, Honoria's public lecture on why women should dress like men, as Federico has noted, has been written with much more logic than satire. She has Honoria's husband say, "I want to see the *womanly* side of your nature—the gentleness, softness, and sweetness that are all in your heart, I am sure, if you would only let these lovely qualities have their way, instead of covering them up under the cloak of an assumed masculine behavior" (32). As symbolized here with the cloak and the covering, the point is not just that women should not dress as men to imitate them, but that women should not abdicate their female self. "It will be a bad, a woful [sic] day for England when women as a class assert themselves altogether as the equals of men," the weary husband/Corelli asserts, "for men, even at their best, have vile animal passions, low desires, and vulgar vices that most of them would be bitterly sorry to see reflected in the women whom they instinctively wish to respect" (33). Women are better than men, so why lower one's self to be like a man?

Corelli conveys a similar sentiment in *The Treasure of Heaven:* "A woman who really loves a man ... governs him, unconsciously to herself, by the twin powers of sex and instinct. She was intended for her help-mate, to guide him in the right way by her finer forces" (404). And later: "Mary, if there were more women like you, there would be more men!—men in the real sense of the world—manly men, whose love and reverence for women would make them better and braver in the battle of life" (432).

This, however, is a womanly ideal, which Corelli espouses in an age when she finds very few women who live the ideal or even value the ideal. Instead, the typical woman to Corelli is as Helobias describes:

As a rule, women are less sensitive than men. There are many of your sex who are nothing but lumps of lymph and fatty matter—women with less instinct than the dumb beasts, and with more brutality. There are others who adding the low cunning of the monkey to the vanity of the peacock, seek no other object but the futherance of their own designs, which are always petty even when not absolutely mean. (*Romance* 160)

Corelli did not have much better things to say about men either. Through
Honoria in *Wonderful Wife,* Corelli launches a diatribe, the gist of which can be
found in almost every one of her novels: "Don't talk of your sex, my dear boy,
as though they were all romantic knights-errant of the olden time, because
they're not! They're nasty fellows, most of them ... and as for their admiration
of all those womanly qualities ... they'll run after a ballet dance much more
readily than they'll say a civil word to a lady" (223–24).

The true unsexing is explained in *Delicia* (1900):

The woman who paints a great picture is "unsexed"; the woman who writes a great book
is "unsexed"; in fact, whatever woman does that is higher and more ambitious than the
mere act of flinging herself down at the feet of man and allowing him to walk over her,
makes her in man's opinion unworthy of his consideration as a woman; and he fits the
appellation of "unsexed" to her with an easy callousness, which is unmanly as it is des-
picable. (ix)

Corelli was not simply outspoken about women's dress and vote; she was outraged at how short both genders failed to live up to their ideals. Her ideas about
gender politics evolved, as did the century. All along she believed that women could
be lawyers, doctors, educators, writers—that these professions should not be gender specific, and more important, that they should be opened to women so women
could bring about reforms that could benefit their own sex (*Free Opinions* 178).
In fact, when she needed a major operation, she turned to Dr. Mary Scharlieb, the
first woman to graduate with an M.D. from London University. Just like many
women, once women were given professional opportunities during World War I
and proved their capabilities, Corelli changed her mind about the vote for women:
"By every law of justice they should have the vote—and I who, as a woman, was
once against it, now most ardently support the cause" (qtd. in Ransom 201).

Corelli had much to say about the end of a great century and the beginning
of a new one fraught with turbulence, and not just about changing roles for men
and women. She saw herself as "an inspired interpreter of the Divine Will" (Bullock 52). Her criticism, as well as her correctives, was deemed by many of her
readers a voice of one anointed to speak to a generation of backsliders. She was
a prophetess at a time when her readers wanted to be told simply what was
wrong with their lives and how to fix it. Yet they were people torn within themselves, determined to dismantle Victorian morality and to reassert it at that same
time. She "carved her niche in fiction as a moralist, enhanced it with the myth
of the romantic artist of mysterious origins, and excited her audience with her-
metic lore and pseudoscientific formulae which became emblems implying that
divine providence was no longer patient with a culture dying because of its formalism and hypocrisy" (Kowalczyk 851). Masters speculated that Corelli's work
was so well received by the public because the public consisted of a "suburban
intelligence whose demands were pitched much lower" than were the educated
reader prior to 1870. They were literate but not very intelligent. "Marie held
her audience spellbound, hypnotised, because she shared their prejudices, and

could be relied upon to be second-rate even at her best," he deduced (291). Certainly he did not give Corelli or her readers much credit.

He was not alone. Most critics have refused to give Corelli's work a serious place in literature. In 1930 Q. D. Leavis wrote, "The high-level reader of Marie Corelli ... is impelled to laugh, so ridiculously inadequate to the issues raised is the equipment of the mind that resolutely tackles them, and, on the other hand, so absurdly out of proportion is the energy expended to the objects that aroused it (for instance, in Marie Corelli's novels, female smoking and low-cut gowns)" (qtd. in Casey 163). The passing of forty years after this criticism did not improve her ratings but did augment the cultural value of her work: "Of course, she isn't a great novelist, she isn't even a good one. But her books are of interest because they clearly reflect opinions, wishes, likes and dislikes of the nineteenth century and the early years of the twentieth. If you want to know that the man on the Clapham omnibus thought of life during those years, Marie Corelli's books will help to tell you" (Lucas 283).

Similarly Richard Kowalczyk values what her novels can tell his readers of the 1970s about culture at the turn of the previous century: "its common feelings, moral preferences, and psychological needs." But then with too much assurance and patronizing he concludes, "No one questions the judgment literary history places upon Corelli's works ... her career allows us to understand popular culture at the turn of the century" (851).

Corelli's works did experience a revival in the 1950s and '60s. In 1953 Bigland explained why she values Corelli's novels: "Despite their melodrama, their sticky sentimentality, their fantastic theories on anything from religion to electricity, they mirror a spacious, elegant way of life which has gone for ever"(16). The 1950s and '60s, with its postwar backlash against Communism and the women's movement, was not too dissimilar to Corelli's period of post-Victorianism. The passing of an "elegant way of life," meaning morality, order, and stability, was at the crux of most of Corelli's writing and explains the resurgence of readership. This explanation does not do Corelli's work justice either.

A miserly and shortsighted obituary appeared in the *London Times* the day after her death (21 April, 1924): "Even the most lenient critic cannot regard Miss Corelli's works as of much literary importance" (qtd. in Casey 163). Yet at her death, *Romance* was in its 38th edition, *Barabbas*, 54th; *Thelma*, 56th; and *Sorrows*, 60th (Scott 251). Regardless of the fact that she was publishing right up to the end and even afterward, with film companies wanting to buy film rights to nine of her novels (Ransom 156), Corelli was a story that many people wanted to forget, especially her male critics, especially her detractors who believed that the Victorians had nothing of value to say that would help the survivors of that the twentieth-century wars. But her voice could never be forgotten. Her battles with the male press opened the way for other successful women writers in the twentieth century (Federico 169). Documented in their biographies, her writings influenced James Joyce, George Orwell, and Willa Cather (9). R. B. Kershner credits Corelli with pioneering the modernist period (10).

Whether Victorian or modern, feminist or antifeminist, popular or literary, Corelli passed away almost an entire century ago, and we have come to learn that we do not know all that the Victorians had to say about anything, especially about the complexities of gender relationships and of finding purpose and contentment and knowledge about one's own existence. These are the very inquiries of Corelli's novels that offer some unique perspectives not to be found in the current Victorian canon. It is well worth our while to open the vaults and reconsider Corelli's value.[20] Hers was a unique period that had done away with its Victorian corsets in favor of bloomers, all the while anxious about a God, in which one could not believe, who would strike at any moment. In Corelli's world, the good were still rewarded and the evil foiled. Unlike her Victorian predecessors, she was busy redefining good and evil, relevant to her own decades. She was no Victorian revivalist; she was a Victorian survivor who made it into the twentieth century and helped many others to do likewise. Federico has noticed a recent resurrection of Corelli's work with the rise of New Age spirituality (150). If readers will not forget Corelli, if she has something to say about both her age and ours and has been heard in the past and is being heard in the present by readers, why do critics and scholars persist in assuming she has nothing worth hearing?

WORKS CITED

Adcock, A. St. John. "Marie Corelli: A Record and an Appreciation." *Bookman* 26 (1909): 59–78.

Alcoff, Linda. "Cultural Feminism versus Post-structuralism." *Feminism and Philosophy: Essential Readings in Theory, Reinterpretation, and Application.* Ed. Nancy Tuana and Rosemarie Tong. Boulder, CO: Westview, 1995. 435–56.

Bigland, Eileen. *Marie Corelli, The Woman and the Legend.* London: Jarolds, 1953.

Bullock, George. *Marie Corelli: The Life and Death of a Best-Seller.* London: Constable, 1940.

Casey, Janet Galligani. "Marie Corelli and Fin de Siècle Feminism." *English Literature in Transition* 35: 163–78.

Corelli, Marie. *Ardath; The Story of a Dead Self.* 1889. New York: Lupton, n.d.

———. *Barrabus.* London: Methuen, 1893.

———. *Free Opinions Freely Expressed.* London: Constable, 1905.

———. *Jane.* London: Hutchinson, 1900.

———. *The Master Christian.* London: Methuen, 1900.

———. *The Murder of Delicia.* London: Skeffington, 1896.

———. *My Wonderful Wife!* (1890). New York: Lovell, n.d.

———. *A Romance of Two Worlds: A Novel.* 2 vols. London: Bentley, 1886.

———. *The Sorrows of Satan.* 1895. Oxford: Oxford UP, 1996.

———. *The Soul of Lilith.* London: Bentley, 1892.

———. *Thelma: A Society Novel.* 1887. New York: Hurst, n.d.

———. *The Treasure of Heaven: A Romance of Riches.* London: Constable, 1906.

———. *Vendetta: The Story of One Forgotten.* 1886. New York: Street and Smith, n.d.

———. *Wormwood.* London: Methuen, 1890.

———. *Ziska: The Problem of a Wicked Soul.* London: Methuen, 1897.

Dellamora, Richard. *Masculine Desire: The Sexual Politics of Victorian Aestheticism.* Chapel Hill: U of North Carolina P, 1990.

De Rougemont, Denis. *Love in the Western World.* Princeton: Princeton UP, 1956.

Eagleton, Terry. *Myths of Power: A Marxist Study of the Brontës.* New York: Barnes, 1975.

Federico, Annette R. *Idol of Suburbia: Marie Corelli and Late-Victorian Literary Culture.* Charlottesville, VA: UP of Virginia, 2000.

Felski, Rita. *The Gender of Modernity.* Cambridge, MA: Harvard UP, 1995.

Feltes, N. N. *The Literary Capital and the Late Victorian Novel.* Madison: U of Wisconsin P, 1993.

Firestone, Shulamith. *The Dialectic of Sex: The Case for Feminist Revolution.* New York: William Morrow, 1970.

Goldsmith, Barbara. *Other Powers: The Age of Suffrage, Spiritualism, and the Scandalous Victoria Woodhull.* New York: Knopf, 1998.

Keating, Peter. Introduction. *The Sorrows of Satan.* 1895. Oxford: Oxford UP, 1996. ix–xx.

Kershner, R. B. "Joyce and Popular Literature: The Case of Corelli." *James Joyce and His Contemporaries.* Ed. Diana A. Ben-Merre and Maureen Murphy. New York: Greenwood, 1989. 52–58.

Kowalczyk, Richard L. "In Vanished Summertime: Marie Corelli and Popular Culture." *Journal of Popular Culture* 7 Spring 1974: 850–63.

Lawrence, Arthur H. "Miss Marie Corelli." *Strand* 16 (1898): 17–26.

Lucas, John. "Marie Corelli." *Great Writers of the English Language: Novelists and Prose Writers.* Ed. James Vinson. New York: St. Martin's, 1979. 283.

Masters, Brian. *Now Barabbas Was a Rotter: The Extraordinary Life of Marie Corelli.* London: Hamilton, 1978.

Ransom, Teresa. *The Mysterious Miss Marie Corelli: Queen of Victorian Bestsellers.* Phoenix Mill, UK: Sutton P, 1999.

Scott, William Stuart. *Marie Corelli: The Story of a Friendship.* London: Hutchinson, 1955.

Stead, W. T. "'The Sorrows of Satan'—and of Marie Corelli." *Review of Reviews* 12 July–Dec. 1895: 453–64.

Stuart-Young, J. M. "A Note upon Marie Corelli by Another Writer of Less Repute." *Westminster Review* 167 (1906): 680–92.

NOTES

1. Publishing history can put this figure into perspective: prior to 1895, novels came out in three expensive volumes, the famous triple deckers, purchased by libraries from which people would borrow them. *The Sorrows of Satan* was one of the first novels to be published in a single volume and offered at a low price. Not only were the libraries purchasing copies, but so was her reading public. *Sorrows* sold 25,000 copies in its first week, and 50,000 in the next seven (Keating x–xi).

2. Compared with Hall Caine, who sold 45,000; Mrs. Humphrey Ward, 35,000; and H. G. Wells, 15,000 (Masters 6); and more than Rudyard Kipling, Arthur Conan Doyle, and H. G. Wells combined (Casey 163).

3. Kent Carr, *Bijou Biographies*, vol. 8 (London: Henry J. Drane, 1901); R. S. W. Bell and T. F. G. Coates, *Marie Corelli; the Writer and the Woman* (London: Hutchinson, 1903); Bertha Yvers, *Memoirs of Marie Corelli* (London, Alston Rivers, 1930); George Bullock, *Marie Corelli: The Life and Death of a Best-Seller* (London: Constable, 1940); Eileen Bigland, *Marie Corelli, The Woman and the Legend* (London: Jarolds, 1953); William Stuart Scott, *The Story of a Friendship* (London: Hutchinson, 1955); Brian Masters, *Now Barabbas Was a Rotter: The Extraordinary Life of Marie Corelli* (London: Hamilton, 1978); Teresa Ransom, *The Mysterious Miss Marie Corelli; Queen of Victorian Bestsellers* (Phoenix Mill, UK: Sutton, 1999); and Annette Federico, *Idol of Suburbia: Marie Corelli and Late Victorian Culture* (UP of Virginia, 2000).

4. See Adcock, Alcoff, Casey, Felski, Feltes, Keating, Kershner, Kowalczyk, Lawrence, Lucas, Stead, and Stuart-Young.

5. In addition to those listed in Works Cited: *The Silver Domino* (1892), *The Mighty Atom* (1896), *Cameos* (1896, which included a rpt. of *My Wonderful Wife!*), *Boy* (1900), *Temporal Power* (1902), *God's Good Man* (1904), *Holy Orders* (1908), *The Devil's Motor* (1910), *The Life Everlasting* (1911), *Innocent* (1914), *The Young Diana* (1918), *My Little Bit* (1919), *The Love of Long Age* (1920), *The Secret Power* (1921), *Love and the Philosopher* (1923), *Open Confession: To a Man from a Woman* (1925).

6. Ransom's work is the most inclusive and useful of all of the biographies, with wonderful summaries and insights into all of Corelli's work. References to Corelli's life are tied to the works. Federico offers refreshing, critical, feminist and cultural theories about Corelli and her works, but is not as comprehensive as Ransom.

7. She always had a dog or several dogs and was quite fond of the ponies she drove. As for flowers, Masters says that she kept seventy vases with fresh blooms changed twice a week at her house in Stratford-upon-Avon (2).

8. Federico would not agree with this assessment. From her reading, Federico interprets Corelli's perception of passion (and conventional marriage) as being menial pursuits. Spiritual transcendence was the only way to find freedom (and Federico reads Corelli's notion as freedom from restrictive gender roles). See ch. 4.

9. This is a pejorative term given to a typical female novelist by the main character in *The Sorrows of Satan* (Tempest). This is before Tempest admits that novelist Mavis Clare is a genius; hence Corelli satirizes male criticism of female writers.

10. *Ziska* begins: "It was the full 'season' in Cairo. The ubiquitous Britisher and the no less ubiquitous American had planted their differing 'society' standards on the sandy soil watered by the Nile, and were busily engaged in the word of reducing the city, formerly called Al Kahira or The Victorious, to a more deplorable condition of subjection and slavery than any old-world conqueror could ever have done."

11. Heliobas appears in a number of Corelli's novels. He is Corelli's genius "scientist" who can control energy and drugs to induce transmigration of the soul and to prevent aging.

12. See especially 251–63 and 474–78.

13. From which Brian Masters borrowed his biography's title.

14. Although according to Masters, she made painstaking revisions and employed great patience and deliberateness in writing (56, 249).

15. Intentions written in a letter to her first publisher, George Bentley, 1887 (qtd. in Federico 98).

16. Except curiously in *Romance*, in which Zara and her brother are Catholic as well as spiritually advanced in the use of personal electricity, potions, baths, and soul travel.

17. The title to Chapter 2, *My Wonderful Wife!*

18. I am thinking here of Augusta Evans Wilson, who, in many ways was an American counterpart to Corelli.

19. Although heatedly refuted by Corelli, Mavis Clare is clearly a self-portrait (Keating xii).

20. Henry Miller, in a 1976 article in *The New York Times Book Review*, also urged a reassessment of Marie Corelli. See Masters 305–06.

Bibliography

Abbott, Katherine R. Smith. "Defining a Type: Perugino's Depictions of the Virgin Mary." *Pietro Perugino: Master of the Italian Renaissance.* Ed. Joseph Antenucci Becherer, et al. New York: Rizzoli International, 1997.

Abraham, William J. *Canon and Criterion in Christian Theology from the Fathers to Feminism.* Oxford: Clarendon, 1998.

Abrahams, Beth-Zion Lask. "Grace Aguilar: A Centenary Tribute." *Jewish Historical Society of England* 16 (1952): 137–48.

Ackerman, Susan. *Warrior, Dancer, Seductress, Queen: Women in Judges and Biblical Israel.* New York: Doubleday, 1998.

Ackroyd, Peter. *Dickens.* New York: Harper, 1990.

Adburgham, Alison. *Silver Fork Society: Fashionable Life and Literature from 1814 to 1840.* London: Constable, 1983.

Adcock, A. St. John. "Marie Corelli: A Record and an Appreciation." *Bookman* 26 (1909): 59–78.

Aguilar, Grace. *The Days of Bruce: A Story from Scottish History.* New York: Burt, 1852.

———. "History of the Jews in England." *Essays and Miscellanies. Choice Cullings from the Manuscripts of Grace Aguilar.* Ed. Sarah Aguilar. Philadelphia, 1853. History of Women, reel 237, no. 1157.

———. *The Jewish Faith: Its Spiritual Consolations, Moral Guidance, and Immortal Hope … .* Philadelphia: Sherman, 1853.

———. *The Perez Family. Home Scenes and Heart Studies.* London: Routledge, 1891. 1–94.

———. *Sabbath Thoughts and Sacred Communings.* London: Wertheimer, 1853.

———. *The Spirit of Judaism.* Ed. Isaac Leeser. Philadelphia: No. 1 Monroe Place, 1842.

———. *The Vale of Cedars; or, the Martyr.* New York: Appleton, 1880.

———. *Woman's Friendship: A Story of Domestic Life.* London: Groomridge and Sons, 1850.

———. *The Women of Israel; or Characters and Sketches from the Holy Scriptures and Jewish History Illustrative of the Past History, Present Duties, and Future Destiny of the Hebrew Females, as Based on the Word of God.* London: Routledge, 1889.

Alcoff, Linda. "Cultural Feminism versus Post-structuralism." *Feminism and Philosophy: Essential Readings in Theory, Reinterpretation, and Application.* Ed. Nancy Tuana and Rosemarie Tong. Boulder, CO: Westview, 1995. 435–56.

Alderman, Geoffrey. *Modern British Jewry.* Oxford: Clarendon, 1992.

Altmann, Alexander. "The New Style of Preaching in Nineteenth-Century German Jewry." *Studies in Nineteenth-Century Jewish Intellectual History.* Ed. Alexander Altmann. Cambridge, MA: Harvard UP, 1964.

Anderson, Amanda. "George Eliot and the Jewish Question." *Yale Journal of Criticism* 10 (1997): 39–61.

"An Anglo-Indian Novelist: Interview with Mrs. F. A. Steel." *American Monthly Review of Reviews* 16 (1897): 348–49.

Anley, Charlotte. *Miriam; or, the Power of Truth. A Jewish Tale.* 5th ed. London: J. Hatchford, 1836.

The Anti-Maynooth Petition. A Tract for the Times by a Delegate to the Anti-Maynooth Conference. Anti-Catholicism in Victorian Britain. 1845. Ed. E. R. Norman. New York: Barnes, 1968.

Appleton, Elizabeth. *Private Education; or a Practical Plan for the Studies of Young Ladies With an Address to Parents, Private Governesses, and Young Ladies.* 1815. London: Colburn, 1816.

Ardener, Edwin. "The 'Problem' Revisited." *Perceiving Women.* Ed. Shirley Ardener London: Malaby, 1975.

Ardis, Ann L. *New Women, New Novels: Feminism and Early Modernism.* New Brunswick: Rutgers UP, 1990.

Armstrong, Nancy. *Desire and Domestic Fiction: A Political History of the Novel.* 1987. New York: Oxford UP, 1989.

Arnstein, Walter. *Protestant Versus Catholic in Mid-Victorian England: Mr. Newdegate and the Nuns.* Columbia: U of Missouri P, 1982.

Ashton, Dianne. "Grace Aguilar and the Matriarchal Theme in Jewish Women's Spirituality." *Active Voices: Women in Jewish Culture.* Ed. Maurie Sacks. Urbana: U of Illinois P, 1995. 79–93.

———. *Rebecca Gratz: Women and Judaism in Antebellum America.* Detroit: Wayne State UP, 1997.

Auerbach, Nina, and U. C. Knoepflmacher, eds. *Forbidden Journeys: Fairy Tales and Fantasies by Victorian Women Writers.* Chicago: U of Chicago P, 1992.

Barbour, John. *The Bruce.* . Edinburgh: Canongate, 1997.

Barker, Juliet. *The Brontës.* London: Phoenix, 1995.

Basham, Diana. *The Trial of Woman: Feminism and the Occult Sciences in Victorian Literature and Society.* London: Macmillan, 1992.

Beaty, Jerome. "*Jane Eyre* and Genre." *Genre* Winter 1977: 619–54.

———. *Misreading Jane Eyre. A Postformalist Paradigm.* Columbus: Ohio State UP, 1996.

Beeton, Isabella. *Book of Household Management.* 1861. London: Chancellor, 1994.

Bigland, Eileen. *Marie Corelli, The Woman and the Legend.* London: Jarolds, 1953.

Bjørhovde, Gerd. *Rebellious Structures: Women Writers and the Crisis of the Novel 1880–1900.* Oslo: Norwegian, 1987.

Blessington (Gardiner), Marguerite, Countess of. *The Governess.* 1839. Paris: Baudry, 1840.

Bonnell, Marilyn. "The Legacy of Sarah Grand's *The Heavenly Twins:* A Review Essay." *English Literature in Transition* 36 (1993): 467–78.

———. "Sarah Grand and the Critical Establishment: Art for (Wo)man's Sake." *Tulsa Studies in Women's Literature* 14 (1995): 123–48.

Booth, Catherine. "Female Ministry; or, Woman's Right to Preach the Gospel" 1859. *Victorian Women Writers Project Library.* Indiana University. 15 Sept. 2002. <http://www.indiana.edu/~letrs/vwwp/booth/ministry.html>.

Booth, Charles. *The Life and Labour of the People of London.* 1902. 5 vols. New York: Angus M. Kelley 1969.

Borowitz, Albert. "The Unpleasantness at the Garrick Club." *Victorian Newsletter* Spring 1978: 16–23.

Bosanquet, Helen. *The Strength of the People: A Study in Social Economics.* 1903. *The English Working Class.* Ed. Standish Meacham. New York: Garland, 1980.

Boyd, Elizabeth French. *Bloomsbury Heritage: Their Mothers and Their Aunts.* London: Hamish Hamilton, 1976.

Braddon, Mary Elizabeth. *Lady Audley's Secret.* 1862. Oxford: Oxford UP: 1987.

Brantlinger, Patrick. "The Entrepreneurial Ideal." *The Spirit of Reform: British Literature and Politics, 1832–1867.* Cambridge, MA: Harvard UP, 1977. 109–27.

———. *Rule of Darkness: British Literature and Imperialism, 1830–1914.* Ithaca, NY: Cornell UP, 1988.

Bredsdorff, Elias. *Hans Christian Andersen: The Story of His Life and Work, 1805–75.* New York: Scribner, 1975.

Brissenden, R. F. *Virtue in Distress: Studies in the Novel of Sentiment from Richardson to Sade.* New York: Macmillan, 1974.

Bristow, Amelia. *Emma de Lissau; A Narrative of Striking Vicissitudes and Peculiar Trials; With Notes Illustrative of the Manners and Customs of the Jews.* 2nd ed. London: Gardiner, 1829. 2 vols.

Brontë, Anne. *Agnes Grey.* 1847. London: Penguin, 1988.

Brontë, Charlotte. *Jane Eyre.* 1847. Ed. Q. D. Leavis. Harmondsworth: Penguin, 1981; London: Oxford World's Classics, 1985.

Buckley, Julia. *Emily, the Governess: A Tale.* London: n.p., 1836.

Bullock, George. *Marie Corelli: The Life and Death of a Best-Seller.* London: Constable, 1940.

Bulwer Lytton, Rosina. *Very Successful.* London: Whittaker, 1856.

Burton, Antoinette. *Burdens of History: British Feminists, Indian Women, and Imperial Culture, 1865–1915.* Chapel Hill: U of North Carolina P, 1994.

Carey, Rosa Nouchette. *Only the Governess.* 1888. London: Macmillan, 1920.

Carnell, Jennifer. E-mail to Lucy Sussex. 14 Dec. 1999.

Casey, Janet Galligani. "Marie Corelli and Fin de Siècle Feminism." *English Literature in Transition* 35: 163–78.

Casteras, Susan. "Excluding Women: The Cult of the Male Genius in Victorian Painting." *Rewriting the Victorians: Theory, History, and the Politics of Gender.* Ed. Linda M. Shires. New York: Routledge, 1992. 116–46.

Cawelti, John. *Adventure, Mystery and Romance: Formula Stories As Art and Popular Culture.* Chicago: U of Chicago P, 1976.

Cazamian, Louis. *The Social Novel in England: 1830–1870.* Trans. Martin Fido. Boston: Routledge and Kegan Paul, 1973.

Cesarani, David. *The Jewish Chronicle and Anglo-Jewry, 1841–1991*. Cambridge: Cambridge UP, 1994.

Chance and Choice, or, the Education of Circumstances. Tale I. The Young Governess. London: Parker, 1850.

Charlotte's Governess. London: Stevens, 1902.

Cheap, Eliza. *The Nursery Governess*. London: Seeley, 1845.

Clark, Elizabeth A., and Herbert Richardson. *Women and Religion: The Original Sourcebook of Women in Christian Thought*. Rev. ed. New York: Harper, 1996.

Clark, Suzanne. *Sentimental Modernism*. Bloomington: Indiana UP, 1991.

Clarke, Norma. *Ambitious Heights: Women, Friendship, Love: The Jewsbury Sisters, Felicia Hemans and Jane Carlyle*. London: Routledge, 1990.

Clifton, Irene. *The Little Governess*. London: Partridge, 1900.

Cobbe, Frances Power. "The Fitness of Women for the Ministry." *Theological Review* 13 (1876): 239–73.

———. "Woman's Work in the Church." *Theological Review* 2 (1865): 505–21.

Collins, Philip, ed. *Dickens: The Critical Heritage*. New York: Barnes and Noble, 1974.

Collins, Wilkie. *Antonina; or, the Fall of Rome*. New York: Peter Fenelon Collier, n.d.

Cooper, Anthony Ashley. "State and Prospects of the Jews." *Quarterly Review* 63 (1839): 166–92.

Corelli, Marie. *Ardath; The Story of a Dead Self*. 1889. New York: Lupton, n.d.

———. *Barrabus*. London: Methuen, 1893.

———. *Free Opinions Freely Expressed*. London: Constable, 1905.

———. *Jane*. London: Hutchinson, 1900.

———. *The Master Christian*. London: Methuen, 1900.

———. *The Murder of Delicia*. London: Skeffington, 1896.

———. *My Wonderful Wife!* (1890). New York: Lovell, n.d.

———. *A Romance of Two Worlds: A Novel*. 2 vols. London: Bentley, 1886.

———. *The Sorrows of Satan*. 1895. Oxford: Oxford UP, 1996.

———. *The Soul of Lilith*. London: Bentley, 1892.

———. *Thelma: A Society Novel*. 1887. New York: Hurst, n.d.

———. *The Treasure of Heaven: A Romance of Riches*. London: Constable, 1906.

———. *Vendetta: The Story of One Forgotten*. 1886. New York: Street and Smith, n.d.

———. *Wormwood*. London: Methuen, 1890.

———. *Ziska: The Problem of a Wicked Soul*. London: Methuen, 1897.

Craik, Dinah Mulock. *Bread upon the Waters: A Governess's Life*. 1852. Leipzig: Tauchnitz, 1865.

———. *John Halifax, Gentleman*. London: Hurst and Blckett, 1856.

———. *A Life for a Life*. 1859. London: Hurst and Blackett, n.d.

———. *Olive; and, The Half-Caste*. 1850. New York: Garland, 1975. 3 Vols.

———. "To Novelists—and a Novelist." *Macmillan's Magazine* 3 Apr. 1861: 441–48.

———. *A Woman's Thoughts About Women*. 1858. London: Hurst, n.d.

———, and Christina Rossetti. *Maude; On Sisterhoods; A Woman's Thoughts about Women*. Ed. Elaine Showalter. London: Pickering, 1993.

Croly, George. *Salathiel the Wandering Jew; A Story of the Past, the Present, and the Future*. New York: Funk, n.d.

Crowe, Catherine. *Aristodemus*. Edinburgh: Tait, 1838.

———. *Men and Women: or, Manorial Rights*. London, 1843.

———. *The Night Side of Nature*. London: Newby, 1848.

————, trans. *The Seerest of Prevorst; Being Revelations Concerning the Inner-life of Man, and the Inter-diffusion of a World of Spirits in the One We Inhabit.* By Justinus Andreas Christian Kerner. London: J. C. Moore, 1845.

————. *Spiritualism and the Age We Live In.* London: Newby, 1859.

————. *The Story of Lilly Dawson.* London: Colburn, 1847.

————. *Susan Hopley; or, The Adventures of a Maid-servant.* 1841. London: Nicholson, n.d.

Cumberland's Minor Theatre. London, n.d.

Cvetkovich, Ann. *Mixed Feelings: Feminism, Mass Culture, and Victorian Sensationalism.* New Brunswick: Rutgers UP, 1992.

Davidoff, Leonore, and Catherine Hall. *Family Fortunes: Men and Women of the English Middle Class, 1780–1850.* London: Hutchinson, 1987.

Debenham, Helen. "The *Cornhill Magazine* and the Literary Formation of Anne Thackeray Ritchie." Ritchie *Victorian Periodicals Review.* 33.1. Spring 2000: 81–91.

Dellamora, Richard. *Masculine Desire: The Sexual Politics of Victorian Aestheticism.* Chapel Hill: U of North Carolina P, 1990.

De Man, Paul. "The Resistance to Theory." *Modern Criticism and Theory: A Reader.* Ed. David Lodge. London: Longman, 1988.

Denisoff, Denise. "Lady in Green with Novel: the Gendered Economics of the Visual arts and Mid-Victorian Women's Writing." *Victorian Women Writers and the Woman Question.* Ed. Nicola Diane Thompson. Cambridge: Cambridge UP, 1999. 151–69.

De Rougemont, Denis. *Love in the Western World.* Princeton: Princeton UP, 1956.

Dickens, Charles. *Bleak House.* London: Penguin, 1985.

————. *The Christmas Books.* Vol. 1. London: Penguin, 1987.

————. *Dombey and Son.* New York: Penguin, 1977.

————. "Frauds on the Fairies." 1853. *A Peculiar Gift: Nineteenth Century Writings on Books for Children.* Ed. Lance Sodway. Harmondsworth: Penguin-Kestrel, 1976. 111–18.

————. *The Letters of Charles Dickens.* Vols. 2, 3, 5–7. Clarendon, Oxford, 1974–93.

————. *Oliver Twist.* New York: Penguin, 1986.

————. *Our Mutual Friend.* New York, Penguin, 1986.

————. *Speeches.* Ed. K. J. Fielding. Oxford: Clarendon, 1960.

Disraeli, Benjamin. *Sybil.* London: Longmans and Co., 1920.

Dixon, Ella Hepworth. *"As I Knew Them": Sketches of People I Have Met on the Way.* London: Hutchinson, 1930.

————. *The Story of a Modern Woman.* New York: Mershon, 1894.

————. "Why Women Are Ceasing to Marry." *Humanitarian* 14 (1899): 391–96.

Douglas, Ann. *The Feminization of American Culture.* New York: Knopf, 1978.

Duran, Jane. "The Intersection of Pragmatism and Feminism." *Hypatia* 8 (1993): 159–71.

Dyos, H. J. *Exploring the Urban Past.* Ed. David Cannadine and David Reeder. Cambridge: Cambridge UP, 1982.

Eagleton, Terry. *Myths of Power: A Marxist Study of the Brontës.* New York: Barnes, 1975.

Edgeworth, Maria. "The Good French Governess." *The Bracelets and The Good French Governess.* London: Houlston, 1868.

Eisen, Arnold M. "Secularization, 'Spirit,' and the Strategies of Modern Jewish Faith." *Jewish Spirituality: From the Sixteenth Century Revival to the Present.* Ed. Arthur Green. *World Spirituality: An Encyclopedic History of the Religious Quest,* Vol. 4. New York: Crossroad, 1987.

Ekserdjian, David. *Correggio.* New Haven: Yale UP, 1997.

Eliot, George. *The George Eliot Letters.* Ed. Gordon S. Haight. New Haven: Oxford UP, 1954–56. 7 vols.

Elizabeth, Charlotte. *Judah's Lion.* London: Seeley, 1870.

Ellens, J. P. "Which Freedom for Early Victorian Britain?" *Freedom and Religion in the Nineteenth Century.* Ed. Richard Helmstadter. Stanford, CA: Stanford UP, 1997. 87–119.

Ellis, Markman. *The Politics of Sensibility: Race, Gender, and Commerce in the Sentimental Novel.* Cambridge: Cambridge UP, 1996.

Ellis, Sarah Stickney. *The Women of England, Their Social Duties, and Domestic Habits.* London, 1839. Victorian Women Writers Project. Ed. Perry Willett. 5 Feb. 1999. Indiana U. 13 June 1999. <http://www.indiana.edu/~letrs/vwwp/ellis/womeneng.html>.

Endelman, Todd M. *Radical Assimilation in English Jewish History 1656–1945.* Bloomington: Indiana UP, 1990.

———. "The Social and Political Context of Conversion in Germany and England, 1870–1914." *Jewish Apostasy in the Modern World.* Ed. Todd M. Endelman. New York: Holmes, 1987. 83–107.

Engels, Friedrich. *The Condition of the Working Class in England.* Trans. and ed. W. O. Henderson and W. H. Chaloner. Oxford: Basil Blackwell, 1958.

"The Fall of Fiction." *Fortnightly Review* 1 Sept. 1888: 324–36.

Farjeon, Benjamin L. *Aaron the Jew. A Novel.* 3rd ed. London: Hutchinson, 1896.

Federico, Annette R. *Idol of Suburbia: Marie Corelli and Late-Victorian Literary Culture.* Charlottesville, VA: UP of Virginia, 2000.

Felski, Rita. *The Gender of Modernity.* Cambridge, MA: Harvard UP, 1995.

Feltes, N. N. *The Literary Capital and the Late Victorian Novel.* Madison: U of Wisconsin P, 1993.

Ferris, Ina. "From Trope to Code: The Novel and the Rhetoric of Gender in Nineteenth-century Critical Discourse." *Rewriting the Victorians.* Ed. Linda Shires. New York: Routledge, 1992.

Fielding, Sarah. *The Governess, or, Little Female Academy.* 1749. London: Oxford UP, 1968.

Finestein, Israel. "Anglo-Jewish Opinion During the Struggle for Emancipation, 1828–58." *Jewish Society in Victorian England: Collected Essays.* London: Valentine Mitchell, 1998. 1–53.

———. "Jewish Emancipationists in Victorian England: Self-Imposed Limits to Assimilation." *Anglo-Jewry in Changing Times: Studies in Diversity 1840–1914.* London: Valentine Mitchell, 1999. 82–101.

Firestone, Shulamith. *The Dialectic of Sex: The Case for Feminist Revolution.* New York: William Morrow, 1970.

Flint, Kate. *The Woman Reader, 1837–1914.* Oxford: Clarendon, 1994.

Forster, John. Rev. of *Susan Hopley, or Circumstantial Evidence,* by Catherine Crowe. *Examiner* 28 Feb. 1841: 132.

Foucault, Michel. "What Is an Author?" *The Foucault Reader.* Ed. Paul Rabinow. Middlesex: Penguin, 1984.

Fowler, Alistair. *Kinds of Literature: An Introduction to the Theory of Genres and Modes.* Oxford: Clarendon, 1982.

Fryckstedt, Monica C. *Geraldine Jewsbury's Athenaeum Reviews: A Mirror of Mid-Victorian Attitudes to Fiction.* Acta Universitatis Upsaliensis. Studia Anglistica Upsaliensia 61. Uppsala Sweden: Uppsala Universitet, 1986.

Galchinsky, Michael. *The Origin of the Modern Jewish Woman Writer: Romance and Reform in Victorian England.* Detroit: Wayne State UP, 1996.

Gallagher, Catherine. *The Industrial Reformation of English Fiction.* Chicago: U of Chicago P, 1985.

Garnett, Richard. "Catherine Crowe." *Dictionary of National Biography.* Vol. 5: 237.

Gaskell, Elizabeth. *Letters.* Ed. J. A. V. Chapple and Arthur Pollard. Manchester: Manchester UP, 1966.

———. *North and South.* Ed. Angus Easson. New York: Oxford UP, 1992.

George, Rosemary Marangoly. *The Politics of Home: Postcolonial Relocations and Twentieth-Century Fiction.* Cambridge: Cambridge UP, 1996.

Gergits, Julia. "Women Artists at Home." *Keeping the Victorian House.* Ed. Vanessa D. Dickerson. New York: Garland, 1995.

Gérin, Winifred. *Anne Thackeray Ritchie: A Biography.* Oxford: Oxford UP, 1981.

Gillett, Paula. *Worlds of Art: Painters in Victorian Society.* New Brunswick, NJ: Rutgers UP, 1990.

Gilligan, Carol. *In a Different Voice: Psychological Theory and Women's Development.* Cambridge, MA: Harvard UP, 1982.

Glatzer, Nahum N. "The Beginnings of Modern Jewish Studies." *Studies in Nineteenth-Century Jewish Intellectual History.* Ed. Alexander Altmann. Cambridge, MA: Harvard UP, 1964. 27–45.

Gogmagog-Hall; or, the Philosophical Lord and the Governess. London: Whittaker, 1819. 3 vols.

Goldsmith, Barbara. *Other Powers: The Age of Suffrage, Spiritualism, and the Scandalous Victoria Woodhull.* New York: Knopf, 1998.

"The Governess Question." *English Woman's Journal* Nov. 1859: 163–70.

Governesses' Benevolent Institution. *Reports of the Board of Management, 1843–1853* London: Brewster, 1844–54.

Grand, Sarah. *The Beth Book: Being a Study of the Life of Elizabeth Caldwell Maclure, A Woman of Genius.* 1897. New York: Dial, 1980.

———. *The Heavenly Twins.* 1893. Ann Arbor: U of Michigan P, 1992. 3 vols.

———. *Ideala.* 1889. New York: Optimus Printing, 1894.

Greenberger, Allen J. *The British Image of India: A Study in the Literature of Imperialism, 1880–1960.* London: Oxford UP, 1969.

Greg, W. R. "The False Morality of Lady Novelists." *National Review* 8 (1859): 144–69.

Gunn, Peter. *Vernon Lee: Violet Paget, 1856–1935.* London: Oxford UP, 1964.

Haggard, H. Rider. "About Fiction." *Contemporary Review* 51 (1887): 172–80.

———. *Allan Quartermain.* 1887. London: Collins, 1955.

———. *Ayesha: The Return of She.* 1905. North Hollywood, CA: Newcastle, 1977.

———. *King Solomon's Mines.* 1885. Ed. Dennis Butts. Oxford: Oxford UP, 1989.

———. *She: A History of Adventure.* 1886. Ed. Daniel Karlin. Oxford: Oxford UP, 1991.

Hall, Anna Maria (Mrs. S. C. Hall). *The Governess. A Tale. Stories of the Governess.* London: Governesses' Benevolent Institution, 1852.

Hamilton, E. P. *The English Governess in Russia.* London: Nelson, 1861.

Hamlin, Christopher. "Providence and Putrefaction: Victorian Sanitarians and the Natural Theology of Health and Disease." *Victorian Studies* 28 Spring 1985: 381–411.

Hare, Augustus and Julius. *Guesses at Truth: By Two Brothers.* From the 5th London ed. Boston: Ticknor, 1861.

Harris, Daniel A. "Hagar in Christian Britain: Grace Aguilar's 'The Wanderers.'" *Victorian Literature and Culture* (1999): 143–69.

Heighway, Osborn W. Trenery. *Leila Ada, The Jewish Convert. An Authentic Memoir.*
    Philadelphia: Presbyterian Board of Publication, 1853.
Helsinger, Elizabeth K., Robin Lauterbach Sheets, and William Veeder. *The Woman Ques-
    tion: Society and Literature in Britain and America, 1837–1883.* Vol. 2. New York:
    Garland, 1983.
Henty, G. A. *The Young Colonists.* 1880. New York: Mershon, 1880.
Higginbotham, Ann Rowell. *The Unmarried Mother and Her Child in Victorian Lon-
    don, 1834–1914.* Diss. Indiana U. Ann Arbor: UMI, 1985.
Hill-Miller, Katherine C. "'The Skies and Trees of the Past': Anne Thackeray Ritchie and
    William Makepeace Thackeray." *Daughters and Fathers.* Ed. Lynda E. Boose and
    Betty S. Flowers. Baltimore: Johns Hopkins UP, 1989. 361–83.
Himmelfarb, Gertrude. *The Idea of Poverty: England in the Early Industrial Age.* New
    York: Knopf, 1984.
Hints on Early Education Addressed to Mothers: By a Mother. London: Masters, 1852.
"Hints on the Modern Governess System." *Fraser's Magazine for Town and Country*
    Nov. 1844: 571–83.
Hofland, Barbara. *Ellen the Teacher.* 1814. London: Griffith, 1879.
Holdsworth, Annie E. *The Years That the Locust Hath Eaten.* New York: Macmillan, 1895.
hooks, bell. *Black Looks: Race and Representation.* Boston: South End, 1992.
Howe, Suzanne. *Geraldine Jewsbury: Her Life and Errors.* London: Allen, 1935.
Hughes, Kathryn. *The Victorian Governess.* London: Hambledon P, 1993.
Hunt, Margaret (Mrs. Alfred Hunt), and Violet Hunt. *The Governess.* London: Chatto,
    1912.
"The 'Imperialism' of Kipling and Stevenson." *American Monthly Review of Reviews*
    19 (1899): 466–67.
Rev. of *In the Permanent Way* by Flora Annie Steel. *The Critic* 32 June 1898: 398–99.
Ireland, Alexander. Introduction. *Vestiges of the Natural History of Creation.* 12th ed.
    By Robert Chambers. London: Chambers, 1884.
Irigaray, Luce. "This Sex Which Is Not One." *New French Feminisms: An Anthology.* Ed.
    Elaine Marks and Isabelle de Courtivron. Brighton: Harvester, 1985.
Jameson, Anna. *The Relative Position of Mothers and Governesses.* 1846. London: Spot-
    tiswoode, 1862.
Jewsbury, Geraldine. "New Novels." *Athenæum* 25 Apr. 1863: 552–53.
Johnson, Claudia. *Equivocal Beings: Politics, Gender, and Sentimentality in the 1790's.*
    Chicago: U of Chicago P, 1995.
Johnson, Elizabeth A. *She Who Is: The Mystery of God in Feminist Theological Discourse.*
    1992. New York: Crossroad, 1997.
Jones, Ann Rosalind. "Writing the Body: Toward an Understanding of *L'ecriture Femi-
    nine.*" *Feminist Studies* 5 (1981): 247–63.
Kanner, Barbara, and Ivanka Kovacevic. "Blue Book into Novel: The Forgotten Industrial
    Fiction of Charlotte Elizabeth Tonna." *Nineteenth Century Fiction* 25 (1970):
    152–73.
Kaplan, Cora. Introduction. *Olive and The Half-Caste.* By Dinah Mulock Craik. Oxford:
    Oxford UP, 1996. ix–xxv.
Kavanagh, Julia. *Women of Christianity, Exemplary for Acts of Piety and Charity.* New
    York: D. Appleton, 1852.
Keating, Peter. Introduction. *The Sorrows of Satan.* 1895. Oxford: Oxford UP, 1996. ix–xx.
Keightley, Thomas. *The Fairy Mythology, Illustrative of the Romance and Superstition
    of Various Countries* 1828. New edition 1850. London: George Bell, 1878.

Kershner, R. B. "Joyce and Popular Literature: The Case of Corelli." *James Joyce and His Contemporaries.* Ed. Diana A. Ben-Merre and Maureen Murphy. New York: Greenwood, 1989. 52–58.

Kersley, Gillian. *Darling Madame: Sarah Grand and Devoted Friend.* London: Virago, 1983.

Kestner, Joseph. "Charlotte Elizabeth Tonna's *The Wrongs of Woman:* Female Industrial Protest." *Tulsa Studies in Women's Literature* 2 (1983): 193–214.

———. *Protest and Reform: The British Social Narrative by Women.* Madison: Wisconsin UP, 1985.

Kingsley, Charles. *The Saint's Tragedy. Poems.* London: J. M. Dent & Sons Ltd. and New York: Dutton, 1927. 7–134.

Kipling, Rudyard. *Kim.* 1901. Ed. Alan Sandison. Oxford: Oxford UP, 1987.

Kowalczyk, Richard L. "In Vanished Summertime: Marie Corelli and Popular Culture." *Journal of Popular Culture* 7 Spring 1974: 850–63.

Kranidis, Rita S. *Subversive Discourse: The Cultural Production of Late Victorian Feminist Novels.* New York: St. Martin's, 1995.

Krueger, Christine. *The Reader's Repentance.* Chicago: U of Chicago P, 1992.

Kucich, John. "Curious Dualities: *The Heavenly Twins* (1893) and Sarah Grand's Belated Modernist Aesthetics." *The New Nineteenth Century: Feminist Readings of Underread Victorian Fiction.* Ed. Barbara Harman and Susan Meyer. New York: Garland, 1996. 195–204.

"The Lady Novelists of Great Britain." *Gentleman's Magazine* 40 (1853): 18–25.

Langland, Elizabeth. *Nobody's Angels: Middle-Class Women and Domestic Ideology in Victorian Culture.* Ithaca: Cornell UP, 1995.

Lawrence, Arthur H. "Miss Marie Corelli." *Strand* 16 (1898): 17–26.

Lecaros, Cecilia Wadsö. *The Victorian Governess Novel.* Lund U: Lund UP, 2001.

Lenard, Mary. "'Mr. Popular Sentiment': Dickens and the Gender Politics of Sentimentalism and Social Reform Literature." *Dickens Studies Annual* 27 (1998): 45–68.

———. *Preaching Pity: Dickens, Gaskell, and Sentimentalism in Victorian Culture.* New York: Peter Lang, 1999.

Levine, Philippa. *Feminist Lives in Victorian England: Private Roles and Public Commitment.* Oxford: Blackwell, 1990.

Levy, Anita. *Other Women: The Writing of Class, Race, and Gender, 1832–1898.* Princeton: Princeton UP, 1991.

Lewes, George Henry. "The Lady Novelists." *Westminster Review* 58 (1852): 129–41.

Lewis, Sarah. "On the Social Position of Governesses." *Fraser's Magazine for Town and Country* April 1848: 411–14.

"Literature of the Month." *Victoria Magazine* May 1863: 95.

Lucas, John. "Marie Corelli." *Great Writers of the English Language: Novelists and Prose Writers.* Ed. James Vinson. New York: St. Martin's, 1979. 283.

Lyall, A. C. "The Anglo-Indian Novelist." *Edinburgh Review* 190 (1899): 415–39.

MacKay, Carol Hanbery. "Hate and Humor as Empathetic Whimsy in Anne Thackeray Ritchie." *Women's Studies: An Interdisciplinary Journal* 15 (1988): 117–33.

MacKenzie, John M. *Propaganda and Empire: The Manipulation of British Public Opinion, 1880–1960.* Manchester: Manchester UP, 1984.

Maison, Margaret. *Search Your Soul, Eustace: A Survey of the Religious Novel in the Victorian Age.* London: Stag-Sheed, 1961.

Mangum, Teresa. *Married, Middlebrow, and Militant: Sarah Grand and the New Woman Novel.* Ann Arbor: U of Michigan P, 1998.

Mansel, Henry. "Sensation Novels." *Quarterly Review* 113 Apr. 1863: 481–514.

Margaret Stourton, or a Year of Governess Life. London: Rivingtons, 1863.

Marshall, Emma. *The Governess: or, Pleading Voices.* 1876. Norwich: Jarrold, n.d.

Martineau, Harriet. "The Governess: Her Health." *Once a Week* 1 Sept. 1860: 267–72.

Masters, Brian. *Now Barabbas Was a Rotter: The Extraordinary Life of Marie Corelli.* London: Hamilton, 1978.

Maturin, Charles. *Melmoth the Wanderer.* 1820. Ed. Douglas. Oxford: Oxford UP, 1989.

Maurice, Mary. *Governess Life: Its Trials, Duties and Encouragements.* London: Parker, 1849.

McCarthy, Ellen, Acquiring Editor for Ann Arbor Paperbacks. Telephone Interview. 16 Sept. 2002.

McCaul, the Rev. Alexander. *Equality of Jew and Gentile in the New Testament Dispersion. A Sermon Preached at the Parish Church of St. Clement Danes, Strand, on Thursday Evening, May 2, 1833 ... .* 6th ed. London: London Society's House, 1878.

McClintock, Anne. *Imperial Leather: Race, Gender and Sexuality in the Colonial Contest.* New York: Routledge, 1995.

M'Crindell, Rachel. *The English Governess: A Tale of Real Life.* London: Dalton, 1844.

Mellors, Anne K. *Romanticism and Gender.* New York: Routledge, 1993.

Meyer, Michael A. *Response to Modernity: A History of the Reform Movement in Judaism.* New York: Oxford UP, 1998.

———. *The Origins of the Modern Jew: Jewish Identity and European Culture in Germany, 1749–1824.* Detroit: Wayne State UP, 1967.

Milman, Henry Hart. *The History of the Jews, From the Earliest Period Down to Modern Times.* From the newly rev. and corr. London ed. 3 vols. New York: Widdleton, 1874.

Milnes, Richard Monckton. "Unspoken Dialogue." *Cornhill Magazine* Feb. 1860: 194–97.

Mitchell, Juliet. *Women: The Longest Revolution, Essays in Feminism, Literature and Psychoanalysis.* London: Virago, 1994.

Mitchell, Sally. *Dinah Mulock Craik.* Twayne's English Authors Ser. 364. Boston: Twayne, 1983.

———. *The Fallen Angel: Chastity, Class and Women's Reading 1835–1880.* Bowling Green, OH: Bowling Green U Popular P, 1981.

M'Neile, the Rev. Hugh. "The Jews and Judaism. A Lecture ... Delivered Beforethe Young Men's Christian Association, in Exeter Hall, February 14, 1854." *Lectures Delivered Before the Young Men's Christian Association ... .* London: Nisbet, 1854. 411–46.

Moers, Ellen. *Literary Women.* New York: Doubleday, 1977.

Moore, George. *Confessions of a Young Man.* London: Heineman, 1928.

More, Hannah. *Cheap Repository Tracts.* Vols. 1–8. New York: American Tract Society, n.d.

Murphy, Mary Patricia. "Timely Interventions: Gender, Temporality, and the New Woman." Diss. U of Iowa, 1997.

Nash, Susan A. "'Wanting a Situation': Governesses and Victorian Novels." Diss. U of New Jersey, 1980.

Neusner, Jacob. *Rabbinic Judaism: Structure and System.* Minneapolis: Fortress P, 1995.

Niditch, Susan. *War in the Hebrew Bible: A Study in the Ethics of Violence.* New York: Oxford UP, 1993.

Nightingale, Florence. *Cassandra and Other Selections from Suggestions for Thought to the Searchers After Religious Truth*. 1860. Ed. Mary Poovey. London: Pickering, 1991; New York: New York UP, 1992.

Norman, E. R. *Anti-Catholicism in Victorian Britain*. New York: Barnes, 1968.

"The Novel of the Mutiny." Rev. of *On the Face of Waters* by Flora Annie Steel. *New Review* 16 (1897): 78–83.

"Novels with a Purpose." *Westminster Review* 26 (1864): 24–49.

O'Brien, Fitzjames. "What Was It?" *Australian Journal* 25 Aug 1866: 827–830.

Oliphant, Margaret. *Janet*. London: Hurst, 1891.

———. "Modern Novelists—Great and Small." *Blackwood's* 77 (May 1855): 554–68.

———. "Novels." *Blackwood's Edinburgh Magazine* Aug. 1863: 68–82.

Oliphant, Mrs., et al. *Women Novelists of Queen Victoria's Reign: A Book of Appreciations*. 1897. n.p.: Folcroft, 1969.

Oppenheim, Janet. *"Shattered Nerves": Doctors, Patients, and Depression in Victorian England*. New York: Oxford UP, 1991.

Orliac, Antoine. *Veronese*. Trans. March Chamot. Ed. André Gloeckner. London: Hyperion, 1940.

Owens, Louis. *Other Destinies: Understanding the American Indian Novel*. Norman: U of Oklahoma P, 1992.

Pankhurst, Sylvia. *A Sylvia Pankhurst Reader*. Ed. Kathryn Dodd. Manchester: Manchester UP, 1993.

Parry, Benita. *Delusions and Discoveries: Studies on India in the British Imagination, 1880–1930*. Berkeley: U of California P, 1972.

Patwardhan, Daya. *A Star of India: Flora Annie Steel, Her Works and Times*. Poona, India: Griha Prakashan, 1963.

Paz, D. G. *Popular Anti-Catholicism in Mid-Victorian England*. Stanford, CA: Stanford UP, 1992.

Pearce, Richard. *The Politics of Narration: James Joyce, William Faulkner and Virginia Woolf*. New Brunswick: Rutgers UP, 1991.

Peterson, M. Jeanne. "The Victorian Governess: Status Incongruence in Family and Society." *Suffer and Be Still: Women in the Victorian Age*. Ed. Martha Vicinus. Bloomington: Indiana UP, 1973, 3–19.

Pillsbury, Edmund P. "Federico Barocci." *Dictionary of Art*. Ed. Jane Turner. Vol. 3. London: Macmillan, 1996. 253–58.

Pool, Daniel. *What Jane Austen Ate and Charles Dickens Knew: From Fox Hunting to Whist—the Facts of Daily Life in Nineteenth-Century England*. New York: Simon & Schuster, 1993.

Poovey, Mary. *The Proper Lady and the Woman Writer: Ideology as Style in the Works of Mary Wollstonecraft, Mary Shelley, and Jane Austen*. Chicago: U of Chicago P, 1984.

———. *Uneven Developments: The Ideological Work of Gender in Mid-Victorian England*. 1988. Chicago: U of Chicago P, 1988; London: Virago, 1989.

"The Popular Novels of the Year." *Fraser's Magazine* Aug. 1863: 253–69.

Porter, Jane. *The Scottish Chiefs*. 1808. Chicago: Rand, McNally, n.d.

Prest, T. P. *Susan Hoply: or, The Trials and Vicissitudes of a Servant Girl*. London: Lloyd, 1842.

Prochaska, F. M. *Women and Philanthropy in Nineteenth-Century England*. Oxford: Clarendon, 1980.

Pykett, Lyn. *The "Improper" Feminine: The Woman's Sensation Novel and the New Woman's Writing.* London and New York: Routledge, 1992.

———. *The Sensation Novel from* The Woman in White *to* The Moonstone. Plymouth: Northcote, 1994.

Ragussis, Michael. *Figures of Conversion: "The Jewish Question" & English National Identity.* Durham, NC: Duke UP, 1995.

Ransom, Teresa. *The Mysterious Miss Marie Corelli: Queen of Victorian Bestsellers.* Phoenix Mill, UK: Sutton P, 1999.

Reardon, Bernard M. G. *Religion in the Age of Romanticism: Studies in Early Nineteenth Century Thought.* Cambridge: Cambridge UP, 1985.

———. *Religious Thought in the Victorian Age: A Survey from Coleridge to Gore.* 2nd ed. London: Longman, 1995. Rpt. of *From Coleridge to Gore.* 1971.

Richards, I. A. *Practical Criticism: A Study of Literary Judgment.* New York: Harcourt, 1929.

Richardson, Alan. *Literature, Education, and Romanticism: Reading as Social Practice 1780–1832.* Cambridge Studies in Romanticism 8. Cambridge: Cambridge UP, 1994.

Richmond, or, the Adventures of a Bow Street Runner. London: Colburn, 1827.

Rigby, Elizabeth (Lady Eastlake). Rev. of *Vanity Fair* and *Jane Eyre. Quarterly Review* 84 Dec. 1848: 153–85.

Ritchie, Anne Thackeray. *Anne Thackeray Ritchie's Journals and Letters.* Commentary and notes by Lillian F. Shankman. Ed. Abigail Burnham Bloom and John Maynard. Ohio State UP, 1995.

———. *Letters of Anne Thackeray Ritchie.* Selected and edited by her daughter Hester Ritchie. London: John Murray, 1924.

———. *The Village on the Cliff.* London: Smith, 1867.

Robbins, Bruce. *The Servant's Hand: English Fiction from Below.* 1986. Durham: Duke UP, 1993.

Ross, Ellen. *Love and Toil: Motherhood in Outcast London 1870–1918.* New York: Oxford UP, 1993.

Ross, Miss. *The Governess; or, Politics in Private Life.* London: Smith, 1836.

Rowbotham, Judith. *Good Girls Make Good Wives: Guidance for Girls in Victorian Fiction.* Oxford: Blackwell, 1989.

Rowlette, Robert. "Mark Twain, Sarah Grand, and *The Heavenly Twins.*" *Mark Twain Journal* 16.2 (1972): 17–18.

Ruether, Rosemary Radford. *Women and Redemption: A Theological History.* Minneapolis: Fortress, 1998.

Ruskin, John. *Sesame and Lilies.* 1868. Philadelphia: Henry Altemus, n.d.

Russell, Dora. *The Vicar's Governess. A Novel.* London: n.p., 1874.

S., H. *Anecdotes of Mary; or, the Good Governess.* London: Newbury, 1795.

Sadleir, Michael. *XIX Fiction, a Bibliographical Record Based on His Own Collection.* London: Constable, 1951. 2 vols.

Sassoon, Siegfried. *The Best of Friends: Further Letters to Sydney Carlyle Cockerell.* Ed. Viola Meynell. London: Rupert Hart Davis, 1956.

Saunders, Rebecca. "Gender, Colonialism, and Exile: Flora Annie Steel and Sara Jeannette Duncan in India." *Women's Writing in Exile.* Ed. Mary Lynn Broe and Angela Ingram. Chapel Hill: U of North Carolina P, 1989. 303–24.

Scott, William Stuart. *Marie Corelli: The Story of a Friendship.* London: Hutchinson, 1955.

Scult, Mel. *Millennial Expectations and Jewish Liberties.* Leiden: Brill, 1978.

Secord, James. E-mail to Lucy Sussex. 11 Oct. 1999.

———. *Victorian Sensations: The Extraordinary Publications, Reception, and Secret Authorsip of Vestiges of the Natural History of Creation.* Chicago: U of Chicago P, 2000.

Seigfried, Charlene Haddock. *Pragmatism and Feminism: Reweaving the Social Fabric.* Chicago: U of Chicago P, 1996.

Sellar, W. Y. "Religious Novels." *North British Review* 26.51 Nov. 1856: 216.

Selous, Henry Courtney. *The Young Governess: A Tale for Girls.* 1871. London: Griffin, 1872.

Senf, Carol A. Introduction. *The Heavenly Twins.* 1893. Ann Arbor: U of Michigan P, 1992. vii–xxxvii.

Sergeant, Adeline. "Mrs. Crowe. Mrs. Archer Clive. Mrs Henry Wood." *Women Novelists of Queen Victoria's Reign: A Book of Appreciations.* London: Norwood, 1977.

Sewell, Elizabeth. *Amy Herbert.* 1844. London: Longman, 1858.

———. *Principles of Education, Drawn from Nature and Revelation, and Applied to Female Education in the Upper Classes.* London: Longman, 1865.

Sharpe, Jenny. *Allegories of Empire: The Figure of Woman in the Colonial Text.* Minneapolis: U of Minnesota P, 1993.

Sheppard, Francis. *London 1808–1870: The Infernal Wen.* Berkeley: U of California P, 1971.

Sherwood, Mary Martha. *Caroline Mordaunt, or, The Governess.* 1835. London: Darton, n.d.

Showalter, Elaine. "Feminist Criticism in the Wilderness." *Critical Inquiry* Winter 1981: 179–205.

———. *A Literature of Their Own: British Women Novelists from Brontë to Lessing.* Princeton: Princeton UP, 1977; Rev. ed. London: Virago, 1982.

Shuttleworth, Sally. "Demonic Mothers: Ideologies of Bourgeois Motherhood in the Mid-Victorian Era." *Rewriting the Victorians: Theory, History, and the Politics of Gender.* Ed. Linda M. Shires. New York: Routledge, 1992.

Silverstein, Alan. *Alternatives to Assimilation: The Response of Reform Judaism to American Culture 1840–1930.* Hanover and London: Brandeis UP, 1994.

Singer, Steven. "Orthodox Judaism in Early Victorian Britain 1840–1858." Diss., Yeshiva U, 1981.

Smith, Robert Michael. "The London Jews' Society and Patterns of Jewish Conversion in England, 1801–1859." *Jewish Social Studies* 43 (1981): 275–90.

Smith, Sheila. *The Other Nation.* Oxford: Clarendon, 1980.

Stanton, Elizabeth Cady, et al. *The Woman's Bible.* 1895. Boston: Northeastern UP, 1993.

Stead, W. T. "'The Sorrows of Satan'—and of Marie Corelli." *Review of Reviews* 12 July–Dec. 1895: 453–64.

Steel, Flora Annie. *The Garden of Fidelity: Being the Autobiography of Flora Annie Steel, 1847–1929.* London: Macmillan, 1930.

———. *In the Permanent Way and Other Stories.* 1897. London: William Heinemann, 1898. 150–64.

———. *On the Face of the Waters.* New York: Macmillan, 1897.

———, and Grace Gardiner. *The Complete Indian Housekeeper and Cook: Giving the Duties of Mistress and Servants, the General Management of the House and Practical Recipes for Cooking in All Its Branches.* 2nd ed. Edinburgh: Frank Murray, 1890.

Stephen, Leslie. *Sir Leslie Stephen's Mausoleum Book.* Oxford: Clarendon, 1977.

Stocker, Margarita. *Judith, Sexual Warrior: Women and Power in Western Culture.* New Haven: Yale UP, 1998.

Stoneman, Patsy. *Brontë Transformations: The Cultural Dissemination of* Jane Eyre *and* Wuthering Heights. London: Prentice Hall/ Harvester Wheatsheaf, 1996.

Rev. of *The Story of a Modern Woman. Athenæum.* 16 June 1894: 770.

Stowe, Harriet Beecher. Introduction. *The Works of Charlotte Elizabeth.* By Charlotte Elizabeth Tonna. New York: Dodd, 1844.

———. *Uncle Tom's Cabin.* New York: Norton, 1994.

Stuart-Young, J. M. "A Note upon Marie Corelli by Another Writer of Less Repute." *Westminster Review* 167 (1906): 680–92.

Sutherland, John. *The Longman Companion to Victorian Fiction.* Harlow: Longman, 1988.

Swanson, Vern G. *The Biography and Catalogue Raisonné of Lawrence Alma Tadema.* London: Garton in Association with Scholar, 1990.

Swartz, David. *Culture and Power: The Sociology of Pierre Bourdieu.* Chicago: U of Chicago P, 1997.

Taylor, W. Cooke. *The Natural History of Society in the Barbarous and Civilized State: An Essay Towards Discovering the Origin and Course of Human Improvement.* New York: Appleton, 1841. 2 vols.

Thackeray, Anne. *The Story of Elizabeth, Two Hours, and From an Island.* The Works of Miss Thackeray. London: Smith, Elder, 1886.

Thackeray, William Makepeace. *The History of Henry Esmond.* London: Smith, 1852.

Thomas, Frances. *Christina Rossetti: A Biography.* London: Virago, 1994.

Thompson, E. P. *The Making of the English Working Class.* New York: Vintage, 1966.

———. "The Moral Economy of the English Crowd in the Eighteenth Century." *Past and Present* 50 (1971): 76–136.

Thomson, Patricia. *The Victorian Heroine: A Changing Ideal 1837–1873.* London: Oxford UP, 1956.

Tobin, Beth. *Superintending the Poor.* New Haven: Yale UP, 1993.

Tomlinson, M. Heather. "Penal Servitude 1846–1865: A System in Evolution." *Policing and Punishment in Nineteenth Century Britain.* Ed. Victor Bailey. London: Croom Helm, 1981. 126–49.

Tompkins, Jane. *Sensational Designs.* New York: Oxford UP, 1985.

Tonna, Charlotte Elizabeth. *Helen Fleetwood.* 1839–40. London: Seeley, 1848.

———. *The Perils of the Nation.* London: Seeley, 1843.

———. *Personal Recollections.* London: Seeley, 1841.

———. "Politics." *Christian Lady's Magazine.* March 1834.

———. *The System: A Novel of the West Indies.* London: Westley, 1827.

———. *The Wrongs of Woman.* New York: Dodd, 1844.

Valman, Nadia. "Muscular Jews: Young England, Gender and Jewishness in Disraeli's 'Political Trilogy.'" *Jewish History* 10 (1996): 57–88.

Warden, Florence. *The House on the Marsh.* London: William Stevens, 1883.

Warner, Marina. *From the Beast to the Blonde: On Fairy Tales and Their Tellers.* London: Vintage-Random, 1995.

Webb, Sidney and Beatrice, eds. *The Minority Report of the Poor Law Commission, Parts I & II: The Break-Up of the Poor Law; The Public Organization of the Labour Market.* 1909. Clifton, NJ: Augustus M. Kelley, 1974.

Webb-Peploe, Mrs. J. B. *Naomi or the Last Days of Jerusalem.* 1860. 17th ed. London: Routledge, n.d.

Weinberger, Philip M. "The Social and Religious Thought of Grace Aguilar (1816–1847)." Diss., New York U, 1971.

Weintraub, Stanley. "George Bernard Shaw Borrows from Sarah Grand: *The Heavenly Twins* and *You Never Can Tell.*" *Modern Drama* 14 (1971): 288–97.

Whately, Richard. *A General View of the Rise, Progress, and Corruptions of Christianity.* New York: Gowans, 1860.

Whyte, the Rev. James. "Lecture VI. Present State and Character of the Jews—Intellectual, Moral, and Religious.—What Has Been Attempted towards their Conversion by Christians." *A Course of Lectures on the Jews.* New York: Arno P, 1977. 191–259.

Wilde, Oscar. *The Complete Works of Oscar Wilde.* 1966. New York: Perennial Library Harper & Row, 1989.

Williams, Bill. *The Making of Manchester Jewry 1740–1875.* Manchester: Manchester UP, 1976.

Williams, Raymond. *The Country and the City.* New York: Oxford UP, 1973.

———. *Marxism and Literature.* Oxford: Oxford UP, 1977.

Wolff, Robert Lee. *Sensational Victorian: The Life and Fiction of Mary Elizabeth Braddon.* New York: Garland, 1979.

Wolffe, John. *The Protestant Crusade in Great Britain 1829–1860.* Oxford: Clarendon, 1991.

Wollstonecraft, Mary. *Maria, or, the Wrongs of Women.* 1798. London: Pickering & Chatto, 1991.

Wood, Ellen (Mrs. Henry). *East Lynne.* 1861. London: Dent, 1994.

Woodham-Smith, Cecil. *Florence Nightingale: 1820–1910.* London: Constable, 1950.

Rev. of *The Years That the Locust Hath Eaten. Athenæum.* 21 Dec. 1895: 867.

Woolf, Virginia. *The Essays of Virginia Woolf.* Ed. Andrew McNeillie. Vol. 3. London: Hogarth, 1988.

———. *Night and Day.* 1919. London: Hogarth, 1938.

———. *The Question of Things Happening: The Letters of Virginia Woolf.* Vol. 2. Ed. Nigel Nicolson. London: Hogarth, 1975.

———. *A Room of One's Own.* 1929. London: Hogarth, 1978.

Zatlin, Linda. *The Nineteenth-Century Anglo-Jewish Novel.* Boston: Twayne, 1981.

Index

About the Contributors

Brenda Ayres is associate professor of English at Middle Georgia College in Cochran, Georgia. She is the author of *Dissenting Women in Dickens' Novels: Subversion of Domestic Ideology* (1998), and editor of *Frances Trollope and the Novel of Social Change* (2002), *The Emperor's Old Groove: Decolonizing Disney's Magic Kingdom* (2003), and of this collection, *Silent Voices*.

Miriam Elizabeth Burstein is assistant professor of English at SUNY Brockport. Her publications include "'The Reduced Pretensions of the Historic Muse': Agnes Strickland and the Commerce in Women's History" in the *Journal of Narrative Technique*, "From Good Looks to Good Thoughts: Popular Women's History and the Invention of Modernity, c. 1830–c. 1870" in *Modern Philology*, and "Unstoried in History?: Histories of Women at the Huntington Library, c. 1650–1902" in the *Huntington Library Quarterly* (forthcoming). She is currently working on a book about historical fiction and early histories of women.

Robyn Chandler completed her Ph.D. in religious studies at the University of Canterbury, Christchurch, New Zealand. Her dissertation is entitled "Theology as Style: Dinah Mulock Craik, Margaret Oliphant, and the Development of the Modern Religious Subject." She has taught both religion and women's writing in an interdepartmental Victorian studies course.

Helen Debenham teaches eighteenth- and nineteenth-century British fiction at the University of Canterbury, Christchurch, New Zealand, and has a particular interest in women writers. She has published on various male and female Victorian writers, most recently on Rhoda Broughton's *Not Wisely But Too Well* and on Anne Thackeray Ritchie's relations with *The Cornhill Magazine*.

Mary Lenard is assistant professor of English at the University of Wisconsin-Parkside, where she teaches nineteenth-century British literature and women's literature, as well as introductory literature and writing classes. Her book *Preaching Pity: Dickens, Gaskell, and Sentimentalism in Victorian Culture* appeared as the eleventh volume in Peter Lang's Studies in Nineteenth-Century British

Literature series, and she published an article on Dickens in the 1998 issue of the journal *Dickens Studies Annual*. She has written the entry on Charlotte Elizabeth Tonna that will appear in the forthcoming *New Dictionary of National Biography*.

LeeAnne Marie Richardson is assistant professor at Georgia State University, where she teaches courses in nineteenth-century British literature and culture. Her article on fin de siècle poet Dollie Radford appears in *Victorian Poetry* (38.1). Much of her chapter on Steel was composed for her dissertation, entitled "Engendering Empire: The New Woman and the New Imperialism in *Fin-de-Siècle* Fiction."

SueAnn Schatz is assistant professor of English at Lock Haven University in Pennsylvania. Apropos to work for this collection, her dissertation was "'I would not be a woman like the rest': *Aurora Leigh* and British Women's Domestic-Professional Fiction of the 1890s," under the direction of Gail Turley Houston. Forthcoming publications include "*Aurora Leigh* as Paradigm of Domesti-Professional Fiction" in *Philological Quarterly* and entries on Mary Shelley and Charlotte Brontë in *Makers of Western Culture* (Blakeley and Powell, eds.).

Jennifer M. Stolpa is assistant professor of English and Spanish at the University of Wisconsin-Marinette. Her dissertation's title is "Revisioning Christian Ministry: Women and Ministry in *Agnes Grey, Ruth, Janet's Repentance*, and *Adam Bede*." She is also the author of "Henry Purcell and Gerard Manley Hopkins: Two Explorations of Identity" (Internet journal of the Illinois Philological Association), and co-author of "Musical Responses to Hopkins" (forthcoming in *Hopkins Quarterly*).

Lucy Sussex is senior research fellow at Melbourne University. A specialist in women's writing and early crime fiction, Sussex has published editions of Mary Fortune and Ellen Davitt. She is currently writing *Cherchez les Femmes*, the story of the first women authors of crime and detective fiction. Her novel *The Scarlet Rider*, a fictionalization of the search for Mary Fortune, was published by Forge (1996).

Cecilia Wadsö Lecaros teaches at Lund University, Sweden, and holds a post-doctorate position funded by the Bank of Sweden Tercentenary Foundation. Her current research focuses on the self-improvement ethos in Victorian fiction and conduct books. This article summarizes her book *The Victorian Governess Novel* (2001).